UNITED STATES

30°N

Oahu

Hawaii

HAWAII

15°N

North Pacific Ocean

Mexico City

Clipperton

Kiritimati

Line Islands

0° equator

COOK ISLANDS

CAN
MOA

Marquesas
Islands

Galapagos
Islands

FRENCH POLYNESIA

Tuamotu Archipelago

Society Islands

Tahiti

15°S

Rarotonga

Austral Islands

Gambier Islands

Pitcairn
Islands

Pacific Ocean

30°S

Easter

THE PACIFIC ISLANDS

Prepared for the Center for Pacific Islands Studies
University of Hawai'i at Manoa
by Manoa Mapworks, Inc.
Revised 1997.

155°W

140°W

W—E

125°W

45°S

110°W

95°W

RENEWALS 458-4574

DATE DUE

My Gun, My Brother

Pacific Islands Monograph Series 15

MY GUN, MY BROTHER

THE WORLD OF THE PAPUA NEW GUINEA COLONIAL POLICE, 1920–1960

AUGUST IBRUM K KITUAI

Center for Pacific Islands Studies

School of Hawaiian, Asian, and Pacific Studies

University of Hawai'i

UNIVERSITY OF HAWAI'I PRESS • Honolulu

03   02   01   00   99   98   5   4   3   2   1

Library of Congress Cataloging-in-Publication Data
Kituai, August Ibrum K., 1950–
   My gun, my brother : the world of the Papua New Guinea colonial
police, 1920–1960 / August Ibrum K. Kituai.
      p.   cm. — (Pacific islands monograph series ; 15)
   Includes bibliographical references and index.
   ISBN 0–8248–1747–8 (cloth : alk. paper)
   1. Police—Papua New Guinea—History—20th century.   2. Papua New
Guinea—Politics and government—To 1975.   I. Title.   II. Series:
Pacific islands monograph series ; no. 15.
HV8280.5.A2K57   1998
363.2'09953—dc21   97–38820
                                 CIP

 Maps by Manoa Mapworks, Inc.

Book design by Kenneth Miyamoto

To my parents, Ibrum and Kegeriai,
and to my Papua New Guinean informants

Editor's Note

August Kituai's *My Gun, My Brother* is the fifteenth volume in the Pacific Islands Monograph Series (PIMS), and its publication in 1998 marks the fifteenth anniversary of the series, which was launched in 1983 with Francis Hezel's *The First Taint of Civilization.*

Manuscripts that eventually become PIMS volumes come to the attention of the editorial board in a variety of ways, and in this instance we are indebted to Stewart Firth, formerly of Macquarie University and now at the University of the South Pacific. Convinced that August Kituai, a young scholar from Papua New Guinea, was producing a work of unusual merit, Firth first called our attention to *My Gun, My Brother* when it was still a doctoral dissertation in the making at the Australian National University. Firth's assessment proved correct.

Dr August Kituai is now a member of the faculty, Department of History, of the University of Papua New Guinea, and the volume at hand is a revised version of his dissertation. I am confident that readers will agree that *My Gun, My Brother* represents both an original and significant contribution to Pacific history on several fronts.

Kituai is concerned with the indigenous policemen who served under the Australian patrol officers, or kiaps, in the territories of Papua and New Guinea during the four decades between 1920 and 1960. The police were at the interface, the actual point of contact, between the colonial administration and indigenous people at the village level. Colonial rule was direct, and the police provided the raw force that brought unpacified areas under control and enforced the pax Australiana. The Australians depended on the bushcraft of the police and their familiarity with the lifestyles of their fellow New Guineans. In the last analysis, many a young kiap learned his trade under the tutelage of the senior policemen nominally under his authority. The local police were an indispensable element in the authoritarian structure of Australian colonial rule in New Guinea.

Various accounts of the indigenous police are found in the writings of kiaps and other colonial officials once on the frontier of imperial control. More often than not, the police are portrayed in praiseworthy terms, and in many instances, bonds of genuine affection and respect linked the two sets of men. However, no indigenous voices are heard in that literature, and Kituai cautions the reader that it must be viewed with skepticism. The accounts are often idealized and sanitized versions of things past, and the portraits of the policemen themselves are patronizing, reflecting the authors' deep conviction of their own racial superiority.

In his research, in addition to published accounts and archival materials, Kituai has drawn on two other major sources. First, oral histories were collected from more than two dozen retired indigenous policemen, the most well known of whom was the late Sir John Guise, a former governor-general of Papua New Guinea. Second, a smaller number of former and mainly retired patrol officers provided written responses to a questionnaire mailed by Kituai.

As a Papua New Guinean himself, Kituai was in a privileged position to interview the aged (and sometimes now deceased) policemen, and as Firth has commented in his correspondence with me, "Kituai writes of his policemen with a genuine interest in their lives."

Kituai is a patient scholar. His research extended over a span of several years, and the sheer volume of his data is impressive. Further, Kituai skillfully weaves the material from his diverse sources into a well-organized and richly detailed account. He graphically describes the violent nature of the frontier, the extent to which force and violence were accepted instruments of colonial policy, and the Janus-like quality of the police force itself. On the one hand, the service attracted some of New Guinea's finest young men. As photographs in the volume reflect, rigorous training shaped them into superb physical specimens, and by and large they had the reputation of being a well-disciplined lot. They were a local elite with a strong esprit de corps, and Kituai convincingly argues that they had much in common with policemen the world over.

On the other hand, the policemen came from cultural traditions that sanctioned the use of force in personal and intertribal affairs. Violence was sometimes sanctioned by patrol officers in the field and was a characteristic of the interface between the administration and the indigenous people of Papua New Guinea. Not infrequently, the police fell short of the ideal code of conduct of their service, and exercised authority and force, sometimes in the pursuit of their own objectives, beyond their jurisdiction. Kituai shows that Australian patrol officers regularly ordered, connived, or looked the other way at cruelty on the part of the police. Kituai suggests that much of the violence witnessed today in the behavior of the police in Papua New Guinea or the military defense force on Bougainville represents a continuity with the past, both the colonial history of the nation and the very nature of its tribal societies.

Kituai's work is highly original. His scholarship is impeccable. His history challenges accounts that paint a more benign view of the Australian administration in Papua New Guinea. *My Gun, My Brother* easily ranks among the best work produced by Pacific historians today.

Robert C Kiste

Contents

Illustrations   xiii
Preface   xv
Acknowledgments   xix

Introduction   1
1 The Role of the Patrol Officer in Papua New Guinea   19
2 Recruitment of Police   42
3 Training   85
4 Policemen at Work   110
5 The Use of Force   138
6 Police Involvement in the World Wars   164
7 Perceptions of the Police by Goilala Villagers, Papua   204
8 Perceptions of the Police by Gende Villagers, New Guinea   223
9 Officers' Perceptions of the Police   244
Conclusion   264

Appendix 1 Response of Rick J Giddings to Questionnaire   271
Appendix 2 Interview with Sir John Guise   285
Appendix 3 Interview with Petrus Tigavu   309
Appendix 4 Interview with Sasa Goreg   320
Appendix 5 Interview with "Wizakana" Tawi   335
Appendix 6 Kegeriai's Eyewitness Account of Tawi's Ordeal   354
Notes   357
Glossary of *Tok Pisin* Words   375
References   377
Index   405

Illustrations

Maps

The Pacific Islands   front endpaper
Mainland Papua New Guinea   back endpaper

1	Administrative districts and centers, 1948	33
2	Selected police recruits by district	50
3	Military activity in World War II	170
4	Gende villages	224

Figures

1	The last full report on the Papuan Constabulary	46
2	A typical annual report on the New Guinea police establishment	48
3	The enrollment form used for recruiting in Papua	76
4	Corporal Gurawa's examination paper	100

Tables

1	Backgrounds of fourteen former colonial officers	24
2	Numbers of police in Papua and New Guinea, 1890–1960	44
3	Names and length of service of selected police recruits, by district or division	51
4	Recruitment into the Royal Papuan Constabulary	177
5	Rankings for police officers	180

Preface

This study covers the forty-year period 1920–1960. It is concerned with aspects of the social and political history of members of the Royal Papuan Constabulary and the New Guinea native police forces when they were at the peak of their careers, and when Australian rule was confident and expanding. It is not a comprehensive history of the Royal Papua New Guinea Constabulary, though it covers many aspects of its history between 1890 and 1960. It is a compound of what some former policemen said in interviews about their years in the government uniform, the evidence found in the written records of the time, and the reminiscences of colonial officials as expressed in their writings and in response to a questionnaire.

Rather than providing an exhaustive chronology for the institutional development of the police, in this study I attempted to link information about events, and about policemen's relationships with government officers (or kiaps) and villagers, to wider issues in the colonial history of Papua New Guinea and, by extension, of the Pacific Islands and elsewhere.

Many colonial officials, including Sir Hubert Murray, doubted the capabilities of Papua New Guinean policemen. It was said that Papua New Guineans lacked the capacity to make the necessary changes of their own volition and therefore required the paternal guidance of European colonial agents to raise them to the highest stage they were capable of reaching. This study provides concrete evidence of eager and energetic policemen who effectively destroyed that myth and that of the lazy native, who performed better than many government officers, and whose commitment to Australian colonization of Papua New Guinea was both surprising and significant.

From their formation in the 1890s, the Royal Papuan Constabulary and the New Guinea native police force played pivotal roles in the spread of German and Australian colonial rule in Papua New Guinea.

Acting as intermediaries and occupying positions without precedent in their traditional backgrounds, the policemen became the eyes, ears, spokesmen, and punishing agents of the colonial governments at the main administrative center and on the frontier.

Policemen worked willingly for the government and acted as civilizing agents of the general *nupela pasin* of law and order, peace, and hygiene. They also assisted villagers in breaking away (some with difficulty) from a past of cannibalism, homicide, infanticide, and isolation. Some of the methods used in securing these results were dictatorial and brutal, particularly when the rifle was the symbol and reality of much colonial expansion.

This study brings out the corporate strength felt by the police—the sense of privileged brotherhood that bound them together and the contradictions between the actions and ideals of many of them. Through specific cases, it explores the extent of and the reasons for police violence. It connects the policemen to their own village background, both before and after police service, and it examines the relationships between policemen and other villagers.

In their given responsibilities—policing of minor matters, exploration, apprehension of murderers, pacification of villagers, participation in the world wars—policemen showed exceptional skills. So much of the administration's dirty work was done by the police that without their patience, allegiance, discipline, and courage colonial rule in Papua New Guinea would have been profoundly different in form and application. In their own perceptions, and in the views of the villagers, policemen were the most effective and ubiquitous of the colonial agents. They consistently crossed the divide between the colonial rulers and the villagers under their jurisdiction and informed them about the new order.

Several important aspects of the topic are not treated in this book. Because of the nature of this investigation, details of uniforms, wages, quality and quantity of guns and ammunition, the scale of rations, types of housing, and personal details on families are not covered. These can be found in various sources quoted in other contexts.

For convenience, the present name Papua New Guinea is used throughout.

In places throughout the text *Tok Pisin* and *Polis Motu* words or sentences are used where there is no good English equivalent or where there is a chance of loss of intended meaning through translation. They are also used where they refer to particular official designations. Those occurring more than once are listed in the glossary.

In general, the ranks of the men are not mentioned because of regular changes through promotions, and some demotions. The majority began as constables and a few reached the rank of sergeant major first class, then the highest rank open to Papua New Guinean policemen.

Unless otherwise indicated, quotations from twenty-six of the men are transcriptions from interviews conducted in *Tok Pisin*. As the police expressed diverse opinions, the records of interviews with three men, Sir John Guise (conducted in English), Petrus Tigavu, and Sasa Goreg appear as appendixes 2, 3, and 4, respectively. Replies to my 1987 questionnaire to former patrol officers were in English. In this book, only that part of the work that patrol officers performed as field staff is discussed. No detailed analysis is made of subsequent responsibilities in the administration. As an example of the officers' responses, Rick Giddings' transcript appears as appendix 1.

Finally, Tawi and Kegeriai spoke in Gendeka, my first language, and I did the translation. The record of their respective testimonies appears in appendixes 5 and 6.

Unless noted otherwise, the photographs of Papua New Guinean informants and others used as illustrations were taken by myself.

Acknowledgments

In the course of researching and writing the thesis on which this book is based, I received very generous help and encouragement from many people and institutions. Without them, completion would not have been possible. I am grateful to Professor Hank Nelson of the Pacific and Asian History Division, Research School of Pacific Studies at the Australian National University, for his guidance, patience, constant encouragement, and friendship. I am also indebted to the staff and students of the school who helped in various ways, in particular, Professor Donald Denoon. I would also like to thank Dorothy McIntosh, Karen Haines, Julie Gordon, and Jude Shanahan for going out of their way to help me in times of need.

My debt to my family is enormous. My parents, both of whom died before my project was completed, and the rest of my family were patient and understanding without quite knowing exactly what I was doing, and why it took me so long. I thank them for their wisdom.

My friends in Canberra have been supportive and helpful in various ways—Klaus Neumann, Bill and Jan Gammage, Helga and Jim Griffin, Donald Denoon and family, Hank Nelson and family, the Spira family, and Michael Bourke and family. To Robin and Kathleen Kituai I offer very special thanks for their continuing support and encouragement, especially Kathleen, for her kindness in typing all the transcribed interviews.

It would be remiss of me not to thank Jim Griffin and Max Quanchi for "filling in" for me in 1989 and 1992 respectively, so that I could conduct further research and writing. In that context I thank Professor Ronald Huch and the staff of the History Department of the University of Papua New Guinea, in particular Vagi Amos, Seia Drohas, and Dr Colman Renali for the use of the department's facilities.

I am also indebted to my informants. Fourteen former patrol officers and an officer of the Royal Papua New Guinea Constabulary provided me with information in response to my questionnaire and through letters. They are T G Aitchison, George Anderson, J B C Bramell, Ken Brown, Ivan Champion, H E (Lynn) Clark, Robert R Cole, Ken Connelly, Rick Giddings, Maxwell Hayes, Chris Normoyle, James Sinclair, Bill Tomasetti, G W Toogood, and Malcolm Wright. I thank them for their time and cooperation. Peter Ryan, director of Melbourne University Press, sent me a copy of his book, *Fear Drive My Feet,* and information on Sergeant Major Kari. Both sources were useful.

Of the Papua New Guinean informants—Amero Bega, Sakarias Anka, Avila, Iworo Beu, John Boino, Peter Daguna, Enau Daulei, Piaka Empere, Sebastin Goro, Sasa Goreg, Sir John Guise, Kamuna Hura, Athanasius Igarobae, Aladu Iwagu, Kambian, Kasse, Veronika Kegeriai, Mohaviea Loholo, Meraveka, Moru Moag (Wadis), Joseph Naguwean (for his father), Nandie Nanduka, Nivil Ongi, James Ori Evara, Lelesi Orovea, Nungulu Pumuye, Tate Sarepamo, Sesetta, Sono, Naguna Tamutai, Petrus Tigavu (whose testimony inspired the title of this work), Tawi, Ben Elipas ToWoworu, Rewari, Jojoga Yegova—and their families showed me warm hospitality, patience, and tolerance beyond expectations. Many "adopted" me, however temporarily, as part of their families and not as a guest. To them, and to my parents, this book is dedicated.

My graduate study in Australia was made possible by a generous scholarship awarded by the Australian National University, which also financed my first period of fieldwork in Papua New Guinea in 1985. I am most grateful for this financial support throughout most of my PhD studies. My thanks likewise go to the Research Committee of the University of Papua New Guinea for the outlay of money and field equipment for fieldwork in 1986 and 1989.

Various libraries and the Australian Archives in Canberra welcomed me and helped me to locate published and unpublished material relevant to my research. Staff at the Menzies, Chifley, and National Libraries were often generous with their time and assistance. In Papua New Guinea, the staff of the National Archives in Waigani, and the New Guinea Collection of the Sir Michael Somare Library of the University of Papua New Guinea, assisted in retrieving and photocopying sources. I am especially grateful to Joe Naguwean.

My final thanks go to the Staff Development Unit, in particular its chairman, Professor Lands Hill, and Director A Kasokason, and to the University of Papua New Guinea for seeing value in such a study as I proposed and for giving me the privilege of a long leave of absence, as well as their administrative, financial, and moral support.

Remaining shortcomings are my own.

My Gun, My Brother

Introduction

For most villagers during the period of Australian rule in Papua New Guinea, the government was a white field officer and a troop of eight or so policemen. In Papua, unless there was a risk of attack from villagers, it was government policy to restrict personnel on government patrols to one European officer, eight to ten policemen, and enough bearers to carry essentials to last the estimated period of patrol. The rationale was that "a large party requires a large transport, and transport is always a difficulty in Papua; and furthermore, a large party is more difficult of control, and there are always stragglers who get out of hand and who are apt to steal from gardens and otherwise excite the hostility of the local natives" (Murray 1925, 165–166). The New Guinean policemen confirmed this number, principally for the same reasons. The patrols explained what the "government"—this strange new force in the land—wanted, checked to see if the government's demands were met, and punished those who had failed to obey.

This book is about the police as individuals, as actors in an institution which they partly fashioned for themselves, and as agents of foreigners and foreign ideas. But it necessarily begins with an examination of the broader context in which the patrol officers and the police worked. Papua New Guinean policemen served under the direction of two categories of white public servants: district administration officials who held commissions in the field police, and commissioned (or warrant) police officers. Under a general arrangement until the 1950s, the first category did police work in the rural areas, and the second did police work in the towns. Often the white officer named as policeman in Port Moresby had no police experience and little police training (Tomasetti 1987). Horace Hides, father of Jack Hides, is a good example. He started his public service career in 1906. In 1909 he was appointed head jailer and sanitary inspector. "By virtue of his appointment Hides also received the rank of Warrant Officer in the Armed

1

Constabulary" (Sinclair 1969, 9–10). From modest numbers in the early years, the number of police grew to some twelve hundred in Papua by 1960 and almost eighteen hundred in New Guinea, whereas the number of European police officers involved remained relatively small, reaching a maximum of sixty-three in Papua and forty in New Guinea. As this book is concerned with activities on the frontier, no discussion is made of professionally trained police officers employed in towns.

The Colonial Setting

The colonial movement[1] of the nineteenth and twentieth centuries was the biggest and most ambitious task ever undertaken by European[2] peoples. Colonialism set in motion a new and powerful system: the subjugation of previously independent peoples by either force or passive acquiescence. In its wake "it overturned in a brutal manner the history of the peoples it subjugated" (Balandier 1966, 35), peoples whose past was steeped in proud and independent tradition. While some societies, such as the Tasmanian Aborigines, suffered near genocide through disease and a protracted and relentless drive for their lands, others, like the Tongans, never lost essential political power.[3]

In Papua New Guinea, village constables, *luluai*s, *tultuk*s, patrol officers, and policemen were given the responsibility for extending government control. Until about 1900, close control of village people was limited to pockets along the coast. Permanent government posts that could not be reached by boat were few. The only significant one in Papua before 1930 was Kokoda (see back endpapers). People in the interiors of the larger islands, New Britain and Bougainville, had never seen a German or Australian patrol in their areas.[4] After occupation, the colonial powers in Papua New Guinea (Great Britain, Australia, Germany), as in other parts of the Pacific region, attempted to consolidate their jurisdiction over their territories both economically and politically through the creation of colonial institutions using both foreign and local workers, in order to "impose effective European authority on indigenous peoples who had hitherto met with only a few individuals touting treaties" (Fieldhouse 1986, 221). For instance, in a review of his work in Papua, Sir Hubert Murray wrote of his native policy in 1914, "The duty of the Papuan Government—the duty, in fact, of any Government which wishes to remain true to the best traditions of Imperial administration—is not only to develop the resources of the Territory, but also to preserve the Papuan and to raise him eventually to the highest civilization of which he is capable" (Murray 1920, ix). In Papua New Guinea the process began officially in 1884, was at its most assertive from the 1920s to the 1960s, and continued until 16 September 1975. By concentrating on the period 1920 to 1960, I examine a component of Australian rule when that rule was confident and expanding.

Colonial rule in Papua New Guinea was "direct."[5] In the view of the longest-serving lieutenant-governor of Papua, Sir Hubert Murray (1908–1940), this system of administration was necessary because Papua and, by extension, New Guinea, did not have in place a structure of authority similar to that found in many parts of Africa and Asia to assist in "native administration." The traditional system as it existed in Papua New Guinea was believed to lack an acceptable and efficient organization and therefore was not conducive to expanding colonial control through the "indirect rule" method.

> Well, if we have no chiefs, no councils, no courts, no administrative machinery of any kind, nothing but a very problematical "collective unconscious"[6] and a few stray sorcerers, it may be argued that anything in the nature of indirect rule is impossible, and that we are driven to direct rule, even against our will. . . . So, in the absence of any native courts or laws of any kind, we had to establish courts and to apply laws of our own; direct rule, it must be admitted, of the most barefaced nature. (Murray 1935, 3, 11)

For a theoretical and comparative perspective on Murray's assessment of the situation in Papua New Guinea, see D A Low's *Lion Rampant,* a scholarly work on British imperialism in Africa and Asia (1973, especially chapter 1). For those countries, Low identified "three different kinds of initial imperial situation"; the first two are not relevant to this work, but the third confirms Murray's concern that in Papua New Guinea, as observed in some parts of Africa, "there were no distinctly political authorities to be either superseded or subordinated, only stateless societies, so that the imperial power was engaged in the extremely difficult task of creating a distinctly political authority for the first time" (1973, 9). The fundamental problem for a colonial government in Papua New Guinea was that it initially lacked legitimacy, that unlike Fiji, for instance, where paramount chief Cakobau, in concert with other chiefs, ceded Fiji to Britain in 1874 (Howe 1984, 276–277), the people of Papua New Guinea did not invite any foreign power to establish control in any part of the land, and they certainly did not believe such powers had the right to tell them what to do.

Very often, because of the slow extension and remoteness of the colonial authority, the people were prevented from knowing what was happening until it was too late. The majority of Papua New Guineans were not aware that foreign powers had made unilateral declarations to colonize them in 1884; they learned about it when a resident magistrate or official or police patrol party came into their area to tell them what had happened months, years, or even decades later. Under these circumstances, colonial governments in Papua New Guinea, as in "all modern imperial powers from the West, were quick to advance a legal and rational basis for their authority," which in turn provided the basis for the imposition of central government authority over dispersed populations with no previous linking political systems (Low 1973, 17; see also Wolfers 1975, 20). In Papua, for instance, Commodore James Erskine said in 1884 that he had come to "declare and proclaim the establishment of such [a] protectorate"; he was not there to negotiate or purchase. His main justification was that he was protecting Papuans and their lands from men acting without restraint. Four years later Sir William MacGregor "read a Proclamation declaring the Protected Territory to be from that time a British Possession." Again there was no pretense at negotiation (Jinks, Biskup & Nelson 1973, 39).

At the local or village level, Lieutenant-Governor Sir William Mac-Gregor introduced the village constabulary in Papua in 1892 (NRB 1892), and Dr Albert Hahl, governor of German New Guinea, instituted, initially around Rabaul in 1896, the *luluai* or *tultul* system (Biskup, Jinks & Nelson 1968, 84), which had by 1913 spread throughout both the islands and the littoral of mainland German New Guinea (Jinks, Biskup & Nelson 1973, 188).

> The system of luluais pioneered by Hahl around Blanche Bay was generally extended after 1899. It was applied around Kavieng in 1901, at Friedrich Wilhelmshafen in 1904, around Namatanai in 1905, in Bougainville in 1906, at Aitape in 1907, Manus in 1911, Morobe in 1912 and Manam in 1913. Its success, particularly in the judicial field, depended on several factors: the "election" of the luluais by the people themselves rather than their imposition from above; regular "circuits" by the kiap in addition to the court days held at district headquarters; and the use of the vernacular rather than pidgin in court proceedings. (Jinks, Biskup & Nelson 1973, 188)

Collectively these men, for it was almost always men who were appointed to these positions, represented the government in their respective villages, becoming in official terminology "village officials." Writing later of the village constables, Sir William MacGregor said it was one of the "two finest institutions I left in New Guinea," the other being the armed constabulary, or the Papuan police force.[7] In order not to belittle the government's work among village people, it was deemed imperative, reinforced by government decree, that the men appointed be men of authority in their own environment who had not only gained some knowledge of the colonial government but had also shown an inclination to obey it, even if this came at the expense of the villagers.[8] That was most certainly the case for the first *luluais* appointed by Hahl around Blanche Bay. Those appointed were leaders (warriors, in fact) in their own right. However, whether the emphasis on appointing leaders was strictly observed in other areas of German New Guinea is not clear. The Royal Commission Report on late German New Guinea in 1920 seems to suggest that the appointments to *luluais* in other areas were actually men who impressed at first contact: "It was the practice [in New Guinea] to ascertain the man of great influence in each community and appoint him luluai" (Australia 1920, 15). Unlike their counterparts in Papua, the *luluais* and *tultuls* were given certain "administrative and judicial powers."

The story in Papua was rather different. There, the early Papuan administration presumed that there were no "chiefs." They then attempted to appoint leaders, but when this was found to be wanting, the administration appointed men who they thought would follow their bidding. In other cases they sought to create a new society (see F E Williams 1928, 95–96). After extensive study of the (1914) *Taro Cult* of the Northern Division, Williams, the government anthropologist, was of the opinion that since the "cult" was popular and had wide support it would evolve into a new political system that could conceivably be promoted and used by the administration (Williams 1928). There were some "chiefs" in Papua but the early Papuan administration chose to ignore them, and at worst, attempted to destroy the foundations of the chiefly system as it then existed. An explicit example comes from the Trobriand Islands.

> In these islands a system of chieftainship obtained, and still survives, more complete and unquestioned than in any other part of the possession. A detail of ritual insists that the chief must occupy a position physically as well as morally higher than that of his subjects. When the chief walks, commoners must crouch so as to reduce their height to something less than that of their ruler. And when the chief sits in council, his seat is raised above those of his councillors as a material expression of his supremacy. [Sir William] MacGregor, entering the village of the paramount chief, found him so sitting. His duty was plain. He strode forward, grabbed him by the hair, and pulled him out of his seat, then sat there himself. *"No man in New Guinea"* he proclaimed, *"shall sit higher than I."* (Lett 1944, 60)

The system was nothing less than direct rule (Biskup, Jinks & Nelson 1968, 84–86). The *luluais* and *tultuls*, like their counterparts in Papua, generally executed orders imposed from above—the central government. That was the difference between "indirect" and "direct" rule. In indirect rule, the imperial government used structures of authority in traditional society for government and only intervened at the people's own request; in direct rule, even if a "chief" was appointed, as in East New Britain, the only power or authority he wielded was that given to him by the government—his newfound authority was not traditionally based, although the fact that he might have been a "chief" indirectly aided his work.

The appointment and subsequent responsibilities of *luluai*s and *tultul*s as government employees became an essential component of the colonial administrative machinery;[9] without their active support, the effectiveness of the administration in the villages, particularly in the remote parts of the country, would have been wanting. In other words, the irony in the success of colonial rule in Papua New Guinea, as in most other colonized countries, was that the people there were often used to sustain colonial domination. In the view of one author on colonial affairs, the appointment and effective use of local officials in the lower strata of the colonial administrative hierarchy amounted to nothing less than "a technique of control that had the advantage of distancing the foreign rulers from all but a fraction of [the] population, leaving to local men the hazards, the responsibilities and often the unpopularity of doing the foreigner's dirty work for them" (Arnold 1986, 9). Against this background it became all the more urgent that loyalty and obedience constituted important criteria for selection, as is shown in parts of the regulation guiding the appointment of a village constable in Papua:

> 1. The Administrator may appoint any good man to be a village constable,
> 2. When any man is appointed village constable he must promise the Administrator that he will be true to the government, . . .
> 7. The village constable is a servant of the Government, . . .
> 9. The village constable will listen to and obey the magistrate.
> (NRB 1892)

The *luluai*'s role in New Guinea in 1921–1922 was described in a government report: "He acts as representative of the Administration in the village, and sees that all orders and regulations are observed. He is responsible for maintaining good order, and he reports promptly to the Administration any breach of the peace or irregularity that may occur. He adjudicates in quarrels on minor matters of difference among the people" (quoted in Wolfers 1975, 68). After appointment—until death, dismissal, or retirement ended this service—the village constable and the *luluai* or *tultul*, like the policemen before and after them, came under the jurisdiction of the patrol officer.

This method by which the colonial administration asserted authority had two distinguishing features: it was paternal, and it used force to subdue warlike villagers. Both these aspects were adopted by Sir William MacGregor in his administration of Papua. "That the paternal form is the most suitable for a native population in the act of stepping out of savagery and barbarism into civilisation, I entertain no manner of doubt" (MacGregor, quoted in Joyce 1971, 120). The paternalistic nature of colonial rule in Papua New Guinea is evident in the readiness of the government to direct Papua New Guineans through the gradual extension of the mass of petty regulations—the "Native Administration Regulations" in New Guinea and the "Native Regulations" in Papua. The regulations show the zeal of Australians to civilize Papua New Guineans by law. Local men—the *luluais* and *tultuls* in New Guinea and the village constables in Papua—enforced these regulations under the supervision of the patrol officer. In 1924 there were no less than forty of these regulations in force in New Guinea (Ainsworth 1924, 30–31),[10] and fifty-three in Papua, with the first batch introduced in Papua by MacGregor in 1896 (Wolfers 1975, 178–179; Mair 1948, 65–69). A penalty, varying from a fine to imprisonment with hard labor, was imposed for any breach of the regulations.[11]

Until the majority of the regulations were repealed in 1968, they intruded into practically all aspects of a Papua New Guinean's life. It appears that colonists, on both sides of the border, wanted Papua New Guineans to be obedient and unobtrusive (Mair 1948, 66, 69). The village constables and the *luluais* or *tultuls* were told to enforce these regulations in their respective areas, but many were clearly irrelevant to village life. The Dos and Don'ts in the regulations covered a wide range of activities and inactivities. A villager (always male) was not allowed by regulation to venture beyond twenty-five miles from his place of residence (Papua); if not incapacitated in any way, he was expected to volunteer as a carrier or indentured laborer; he could not wander around the townships of Bulolo, Rabaul, Samarai, or Port Moresby without express permission from his employer; he could not carry his weapons into town; he could not continue singing and dancing beyond 9:00 PM within the limits of the town boundary; he could not settle where and as he pleased; he could not wear clothes on the upper part of his body (this applied to females too); he could not gamble; it was decided for him where the dead were to be buried; and generally the regulations covered a whole range of other prohibitions (Jinks, Biskup & Nelson 1973, 149–150).

Missionaries, teachers, and policemen were exempt from these rules. Although a few of the regulations helped reduce criminal activities, the majority were so restrictive and so impinged on ordinary behavior that one forms the impression that during the period of colonial rule in Papua New Guinea, at least until the 1960s, Papua New Guineans had been turned into robots synchronized to do the colonists' bidding, their initiative undermined by the regulations. The "regulations were but an increasingly paternalistic and interfering continuation of the old MacGregor regulations. . . . Yet, it was at village-level, through the extension of the system of village administration established by MacGregor, that the increasing dependence of many Papuan leaders upon European advice and guidance was built up" (Wolfers 1975, 33).

The rationale for the introduction of the regulations is clear. Colonists believed that they had a mission to "civilize" the subordinated and that strict observance of the regulations by Papua New Guineans would ultimately bring about the anticipated change in the society. Papua New Guineans would become civilized, good Christians, and develop habits of industry. This school of thought had its basis in the doctrine that the colonized peoples "were wards under guardianship and would one day attain their majority" (Mason 1971, 23, 84). The custodial role of the colonial *masta* over those subordinated was a disturbing feature of colonial policy. It not only took away the self-respect and dignity that subordinated peoples had enjoyed before colonialism, but also "turned ordinary [white] people overnight into potentates." In the context of Papua New Guinea, "Australians [and whites generally] enjoyed a huge leap in status merely by jumping ashore. Non entities at home became *masta* or *misis,* adopted the white men's uniform, [and] took credit for the achievements of western civilization" (Connolly and Anderson 1987, 18). The result of black and white races meeting, Sir Hubert Murray wrote,

> is likely to be deplorable in the case of both; the one tends to become a sneak and the other a bully. . . . It has been said that the first effect of the meeting of the primitive and the white man is the demoralization of both parties, and this seems to be simple enough; the primitive meets a superior being against whom his best protection is deceit, and the white, who perhaps never had a dog to order about before he left home suddenly finds himself with servants ready to do his bidding. (1929, 3)

Resistance to the Colonial Intrusion

The second feature is alarming, but adds testimony to the colonizers' belief, whatever their policies—of direct or indirect rule—in the right of the colonial *mastas* to use whatever force was deemed necessary to expedite submission. Force, in this instance, came in two forms—physical and psychological. Physical force occurred when there was a physical confrontation between villagers and policemen or patrol officers, and deaths, wounds, and the destruction of property resulted from the encounter. Psychological force was the impact of the mass of petty regulations controlling Papua New Guineans' behavior. While the regulations did not cause them any physical harm, the numerous taboos caused psychological trauma because the restrictions were without precedent and without community sanction. The constant threat of fine or imprisonment for any breach of any of the regulations was tantamount to forcing people to be good against their will. They were forced by circumstance to be fearful and vigilant. In Papua New Guineans' colonial experience, physical force was sometimes bloody, but never extensive; psychological force was ubiquitous and lasted for almost one hundred years. As Low wrote of Africa and Asia, in a colonial territory, "conquest" preceded "peace";[12] in fact, conquest was quicker in places like Papua New Guinea, which lacked distinct political authority (Low 1973, 17). But, Low continued,

> Apologists of empire have tended to under-estimate the use of force. It is perfectly true that many imperial administrators were very cautious about resorting to it. . . . Even so force was widely used. . . . Imperial powers used force more often than they have been prepared to admit. They made it their business, moreover, to gather into their own hands all the coercive powers which they could. The confiscation of weapons, and the promulgation of various Arms Acts were crucial to the maintenance of imperial authority the world over. Moreover, for the most part they were very circumspect about the way they handled their native police and native troops. . . . It may be argued that these were only minor operations. So they were. *But even if to the imperial power they were "little wars," to the colonial peoples they were "big wars," upon which all their energies were concentrated, and which they lost.* (1973, 21–23; emphasis added)

Many of the wars in Africa were conducted on a grand scale, and there is no comparable Papua New Guinean experience. There were, however, "minor operations" in Papua New Guinea. In Papua "there was little organized resistance . . . but, unfortunately, a population of the Stone Age, head-hunters for a great part and cannibals, can not be induced by fair words alone to adopt a more peaceful life" (Murray 1932, 8). This situation could also be true of New Guinea. Any number of examples could be cited for the purposes of illustration.[13] For a start, the account by Peter Munster (1981) of a "massacre" in February 1934 near Kainantu, in my view, comes nearest to Low's description of violent encounters in which all of the colonized people's "energies were concentrated, and which they lost."

This case involved a small highlands community—the Finintugu—living near the Karmamontina River. The massacre was perpetrated by the combined efforts of prospectors, patrol officers, policemen, and laborers in reprisal over the death of prospector Bernard Lawrence

McGrath. In less than seven days, between thirty-nine and seventy-two of their members, including women and children, were shot dead by rifle fire despite their warriors' desperate attempt to save them with bows and arrows (Munster 1981). On the last day, after a pitched "battle" of five hours, against the forces of John Black, Edward Taylor, and Bob Dugan (prospector), the Finintugu surrendered, having exhausted all their resources and recognized a no-win situation for them. The extent of this calamity[14] was such that "even in the restrained language of an Administration report to the League of Nations [the government] admits to there having occurred 'one of the most desperate affrays recorded in the history of New Guinea'."[15] "That the casualties included women and children is an element of 'the desperate Finintugu affray' that does not appear in Ted Taylor's Report [E Taylor 1934]. He and John Black did not go in and count the bodies after the Finintugus surrendered" (Munster 1981, 37). Munster believed that after this "battle" and the resultant death toll, no more whites died at the hands of highland warriors. The use of heavy-handed tactics—by police, patrol officers, and prospectors—in the highlands subdued the highlands people and forced them into submission (Munster 1981).

Further examples of explicit force of comparable magnitude by the police or patrol officers are discussed later in this book. The rationalization was that if the subordinated people proved difficult to control or civilize, then it was government policy to use force (see chapter 5). The degree of force, and the frequency of its demonstration, depended largely on the behavior and the attitudes of the people on whom the new system was imposed (Fieldhouse 1986, 221). Where there was peaceful reception, minimal or no force was applied. For instance, the people of Hanuabada received those who raised the Union Jack on their soil with open arms in 1884. In appreciation, and as a token of everlasting peace, Boe Vagi, their tribal "chief" was "constituted titular 'king', and was given a naval officer's uniform and a staff of office" (Murray 1912, 74–75). On the other hand, where there was bellicosity, and the people's warriors continued with their sense of outrage, then, in the words of Franz Fanon, "brute force" was used to curb the people's intransigence (1963, 11).

In West New Britain, in 1926, after the murder of four white men, twenty-three Nakanai warriors were shot dead by rifle fire and sixteen others given fifteen years imprisonment. The party of enraged whites and their disciplined New Guineans selected to avenge the death of the white men consisted of the district officer, assistant district officers, patrol officers, fifty European civilians of Rabaul sworn in as "special constables," ninety-eight police, and several hundred carriers. Included among their weapons was a machine gun, one of the rare occasions when a machine gun was taken on patrol by Australian officials. "The whole caravan was organized like a military manoeuvre." The episode is an excellent example of the way in which power was demonstrated to subjugate a whole community (McCarthy 1963, 20–26). Another example, from the Solomon Islands, summarizes the events that followed the murder of District Commissioner William Bell:

> In October 1927 William Bell, colonial government representative on Malaita, in the Solomon Islands, was murdered, while collecting taxes, and his party of native police massacred. Bell was an Australian [employed in a British colony], a towering figure in the pacification of the wildest island in the Pacific, and his murder by the Kwaio warrior leader Basiana was the climax of a confrontation between two strong men and two opposing ways of life, as Basiana and his followers, in the face of a pervasive threat to their ancestral way of life, resolved to challenge the power of Empire by killing its most forceful representative.
>
> This bloody act of defiance was the prelude to a destruction more wanton and complete than they could have foreseen. At the request of the British government, an Australian gunboat, H.M.A.S. *Adelaide*, steamed up to Malaita to lead the punitive expedition. A "breathless army" of Australian planters and volunteers was formed, which penetrated the jungles of the inland peoples to revenge itself upon the dreaded "Malaitamen." *The subsequent random slaughter of the Kwaio, the raping of their women, the destruction of their shrines and the desecration of their consecrated objects resulted in a severe dislocation of their way of life, from which the Kwaio have never recovered.* (Keesing and Corris 1980, jacket; emphasis added)

It is not difficult to see the similarity in the style and method of execution of both these punitive expeditions in two different colonial territories. Another example from Papua is "the Ansell case," which no doubt assisted MacGregor, early in his administration, in formulating his policy on how to deal with Papuan belligerence. MacGregor became convinced by this case that he had to meet force with force in order to teach the Papuans a lesson.

> On 29 October 1888 a trading schooner was attacked in Chads Bay [in the general area of the present-day Milne Bay Province], the captain, Ansell, killed, the crew disabled and the schooner stripped and burnt. MacGregor in his first months in New Guinea *(sic)* was forced to decide what policy he would adopt in such a case. He "determined to make an example of the perpetrators if possible, acting in the belief that severity would under the circumstances be mercy." (Joyce 1971, 129)

In the end, against the advice of Chief Justice F J Winter, MacGregor sanctioned the hanging of four of the Papuans heavily implicated in the captain's murder (Joyce 1971, 130, 132).

Who, then, in the event of an outbreak of hostility, would apply "brute force" in order to protect the fundamentals of colonial domination?

The Power of the Police

In most colonies, including Papua and New Guinea, one coercive apparatus of the administration stood out from the rest and was most directly involved in the application of coercion—the police force. Several theories have been advanced to explain the sorts of reactions of subordinated people to colonialism.[16] David Arnold (1986) proposed that police power in particular, and the power wielded by colonialism generally, had such a devastating effect on the people during the period of first contact that while there was some opposition, the majority were forced into submission. Certainly police power contributed overwhelmingly to the success of colonialism in Papua New Guinea. That many Papua New Guineans were forced into submission can be explained in the following way: Sustained force could not have been maintained in an environment considered to be hostile unless there was both a demonstration of power that the original inhabitants could not equal, and the physical presence of a sufficient number of men who had been known to use force in the past and had state sanction to use it in the future. Of the African experience, Low wrote, "If force was not directly used, the knowledge that it might be, and that if it was, the results could be very serious, was widespread" (1973, 22). In other words, psychological force. For a Papua New Guinean example see Hiroyuki Kurita, "Who Came First?" (1985). In this carefully researched article Kurita wrote of the various responses of the Highlanders generally and the Fasu people of Southern Highlands in particular to initial and subsequent European contact:

> In the Highlands area, patrol parties were often confronted and attacked by hostile highlanders. On the other hand, the natives Champion and Adamson met—the Fasu as well as the Kasua and Foi—showed no hostility to them: some were even willing to guide them. . . . It should be noted, however, that Champion and Adamson, the second Europeans to visit the Southern Highlands, received friendly cooperation from the highlanders, while O'Malley and Hides, the first, were repeatedly attacked. There is a high probability that those natives who had already seen or heard about Europeans and who knew their fighting power well would be afraid of later European visitors and would welcome them hospitably so

as not to be killed. The same may be true of the Fasu. I would like
to argue that the Fasu, like the Bosavi and the Foi peoples, wanted
to be on good terms with Champion and Adamson, for they already knew the Europeans' fighting power, even if they could not
understand at all who or what they were. (Kurita 1985, 59)

The colonial police force fulfilled the function of a physical presence that had been known to use force; without its inherent deterrent
effect, colonialism would have failed. "The coercive disposition of the
colonial state was so fundamental to its existence and to its attitudes
towards any manifestation of opposition and unrest, that it used force
as a panacea for every kind of economic and social ill" (Arnold 1986,
148). While this quotation is true for the Indian colonial experience, it
would not be a fallacy to state that wherever colonial police forces were
established, similar draconian measures were applied. The Germans
believed in the efficacy of force and used police for punitive expeditions in all their colonies to expedite submission or to curtail recalci-
trance.[17] Sir William MacGregor also believed in "swift justice" during
his early administration of British New Guinea (later Papua). During
the investiture declaring Dr William MacGregor the administrator of
British New Guinea in September 1888, the master of ceremonies, Captain Hort Day Bosanquet of HMS *Opal* advised him of the potential for
violence in an unconquered territory such as Papua, and of his readiness to assist with force even though such an act would have been contrary to official advice. MacGregor recalled:

> The Queen's sovereignty was thus declared over a new country
> with a superficial area exceeding 90,000 square miles, without a
> single soldier or policeman to support the new administration. . . .
>   Captain Bosanquet was a sailor, but he understood perfectly the
> position of a government that existed only in a proclamation. The
> position of the Administrator was not unlike that of a man dropped
> into deep water with his hands tied behind his back, and is worth
> recalling on account of some winged words of Captain Bosanquet,
> who frankly informed me he was specially instructed to not land
> any men for police or similar duty in the possession; *"but,"* he
> added, *"if I see you fellows beset anywhere with your back to a wall, I shall
> not look on with indifference." I shall always remember those few words
> with sincere gratitude, and treasure them as worthy of a British sailor.*
> (MacGregor quoted in Murray 1912, 24–25; emphasis added)

How MacGregor responded to this naval officer's advice is unknown.
Basically there appears to have been an early bifurcation in his views on
the administration of subordinated peoples. On the one hand, he
believed that he was on a civilizing mission to take Papuans "out of

savagery and barbarism into civilization," a task that required tact and understanding of indigenous institutions before alien administrative structures could be imposed. On the other hand, he believed, with various qualifications, that he had to first of all "meet force with force in order to show the Papuans that the power of the government was the stronger; the authority of the government had to be recognized before civilization could be introduced, and he came to believe that force was necessary for this purpose" (Joyce, 1971, 120, 129, 143).

Rationales for Meeting Force with Force

An early officer of the Papuan administration who strongly believed in the use of force was Monckton. In an incident involving the murders by the "Doriri" of Wanigela of an enemy tribe, he was asked by Captain Barton about the appropriate measures he would take, and promptly replied:

> "Demand the surrender of the men responsible for the more recent murders," I said. "I won't bother about anything that took place more than two months ago." "If you don't get them, what then?" asked Barton. "Shoot and loot," I answered laconically. "I don't think we should do anything of the sort," said Barton. "I think that we should warn the people that they must not raid the coastal tribes." "Rats!" I said. "They would regard us then as fools, and promptly come and butcher a score or two more of people living under my protection. The only way you can stop these beggars hunting their neighbours with a club, is to bang them with a club." Sir George Le Hunte and Sir Francis Barton sat silently listening to our conversation, and afterwards in our official minutes of instruction I found this embodied: "In the event of your finding the natives, and their opposing you, you will take such steps as may be necessary to bring them into submission." (Monckton 1921, 208)

Monckton had learned his lesson under MacGregor, and while Monckton was crude and egotistical, it is still possible to detect in him the influence of the tougher policies of MacGregor. And this is what happened, particularly at the beginning of his rule: "[His] administration had to subdue almost every district by force" (Wolfers 1975, 19). MacGregor instituted the Papuan Armed Constabulary in 1890 to assist him achieve his ultimate objective—to pacify the Papuans. Murray provided an illuminating contrast between his predecessor's administration of the frontier and his own:

> Anyone reading the old reports must be struck by the difference between the language then used in describing the steps taken to

extend the government influence, and the language which would now be used by an officer in detailing an encounter which he might have had with some new tribe in the far interior. Thus, for instance, it was necessary in 1890 to go to Kabadi in order to "curb the natives of that tribe," and, as a result, "the chief was taken to Port Moresby in irons," and "the district was completely subjected to authority." In 1891 "the powerful tribes of Mekeo would not submit to Government authority without a preliminary struggle." In 1893 "the subjection of Aroma may be regarded as complete. They fully and entirely admit the superiority of the government." In 1894 the people of Darava (Table Bay) were followed up by the Constabulary, "but declined a regular pitched battle," and in 1897–8 "the arrogant tribes" of the Upper Brown River "are reduced to peace." (Murray 1925, 21)

Even if the situation had improved during Murray's administration in those pacified areas, it would not be much of an exaggeration to write that as the frontier shifted into new territory, Murray, for all the praise that has been given for his insight into and understanding of the Papuans, on more than one occasion shared the conviction of his predecessor and dealt "ruthless[ly] with any abuse of authority. [For example], he was convinced that they must be coerced for their own good" (Mair 1948, 12). His system of administration of Papua was described by Lord Hailey, in the introduction to Mair's book, as a "well regulated and benevolent type of police rule" (Mair 1948, xvi).

Murray explained the need for his method in Papua:

Force being, unfortunately, necessary in order to maintain even the slightest semblance of order, an instrument had to be provided for its display, and also, if occasion demanded, for its use. So the Papuan Armed Constabulary was established. . . . We had before us only small scattered bands of savages, armed with sticks and stones; and sticks and stones, however cleverly fashioned and skillfully handled, can never be a match for modern fire-arms. But the difficulty and the pity of it was that the Papuans could not, until too late, be brought to realize the impossible odds against which they were contending. (1932, 8–9)

In the mandated territory, tough police practices persisted long after the Germans had left New Guinea. "The legacy of the German rule remained in a widespread assumption that natives could only be managed by harsh treatment, an assumption that was taken over by the inexperienced men who were given wide powers under the military administration. An influx into the territory at the time of the gold rush of 1926 of employers with equally little experience reinforced this belief" (Mair 1948, 13). Murray was certainly quick to stop excessive or wanton force; but not to stop force entirely. Jack Hides on his major patrols wrote of shooting people, and was praised by Murray.

This was the situation in which most of the early patrol officers were engaged. They were paternal and they believed in some degree of force to maintain control. They were also part of a larger body of men employed by the government to administer its policies to the men and women of the land, and they followed patterns of government set in motion by British, German, and Australian colonialism.[18] As they were members of a wider European community, it was inevitable that collectively, however well meaning individuals within the system may have been, they were influenced by the ideas, or at least shared the convictions of other members of their "tribe" regarding their special place over the people upon whom they came to impose the pax Australiana. While there were many others—missionaries, prospectors, labor recruiters, and planters—who stood ready to use force when and wherever they deemed it necessary, it was the policeman, through the paternal guidance and cognizance of the patrol officers, who consistently, and ultimately with the government's acquiescence, applied this force.

Father William Ross, the American Divine Word missionary who pioneered Catholicism in the Mount Hagen region of the Western Highlands once escorted a Sacred Heart Missionary from the coast on a tour of his parish. Father Ross told author Colin Simpson of the events that unfolded that day:

> I remember one of the fathers from Papua coming over here, and I took him out in the bush for a bit of a walkabout. Several times, when we passed natives on the track, I noticed that he held out the crucifix in his hand and I said, "what are you doing that for?" "Oh!," he said, "Over in Papua when we go out and we meet natives we show them the crucifix, and so they know who we are."
>
> "You do eh?" I said, and I pulled my .38 revolver out of the holster. "Over here we show em this!" (Simpson 1962, 162)

It is not suggested here that missionaries in the highlands, or for that matter anywhere else, made it their business to use violence needlessly. Father Ross was armed to defend himself. But in the event that a violent situation warranted the use of his revolver, he would use it without hesitation. In the majority of cases his .38 revolver would have been used against men armed with bows and arrows. Similar examples abound in most areas of Papua New Guinea during the period of first contact.

In 1934, the Fox brothers, who were prospectors, killed more than forty-five people in only twelve days in Tari, Southern Highlands (Chris Ballard, personal communication, 1992). Michael Leahy also was notorious for violence in the highlands.

> Mick Leahy is a controversial figure in that many of his early
> encounters with Highlanders resulted in violence. When he judged
> his life to be in danger he did not hesitate to shoot his attackers,
> and he made no secrets of this fact in public lectures he gave in
> Australia, Britain and the United States. . . . Complaints were made
> to the New Guinea Administration that the Leahys had gone
> beyond the bounds of legitimate defensive action in their dealings
> with primitive tribesmen, and an official enquiry was ordered from
> Rabaul in 1936. (Munster 1981, 7)

Acting on impulse was not a peculiar idiosyncrasy of Mick Leahy
alone. Joyce deliberated on those of MacGregor: "MacGregor's main
justifications for executions after murders, for patrols that used force,
or for exploratory journeys that were not immediately necessary, was
the effect of his actions for the future. He argued that the end for
which he was aiming—the introduction of civilization—justified the
means, however distasteful these means were to his own ideas" (Joyce
1971, 141).

From the various policemen's testimonies regarding the use of force,
the distinct impression is given that the police were generally not punished for their actions against villagers; rather, most of the recorded
police offenses were for failure to carry out specific orders from the
patrol officer. That is, the police were punished for delinquencies in
their relations with the government, not with villagers. Specific acts of
violence may have been unknown, but general behavior was known. In
the film *First Contact,* Danny Leahy commented after a massacre at Tari,
in the Southern Highlands, that "the government allowed you to do it"
and that many similar incidents in the highlands were not reported.

It is significant that while force was generally used by both the police
and the patrol officers at the frontier, it would be an exaggeration to
state that it was employed purposely to terrorize the population. In the
nature of the varied duties of both police and officers, a show of government strength was inevitable, especially at the frontier. The rational-
izations were that the newly contacted people understood only force,
and by demonstrating its power the government ultimately saved lives.
(By the same token, it could also be said that they might have saved
more lives by not going there in the first place.) Because the patrol
officers, who commanded the police, were an important element in the
theater of exploration and pacification, some knowledge of their backgrounds and the nature of their work is essential to this study, as well as
an assessment of their efficiency from their own perspective, from that
of the police, and from that of an outsider. They are the focus of the
first chapter.

The second and third chapters are based on reminiscences of

twenty-eight men about the process of recruitment and the subsequent six or twelve months of training at the depot. Recruitment of young men took place from most areas of Papua New Guinea. Because of their youth, most had no established positions in their villages but were by physique and attitudes ideal candidates for police work. Police training was concerned not just with the physical and mental development of the recruits and basic police methods, but inculcated the ideals of the colonial government and the part the police were to play in disseminating those new concepts and values to the villagers.

Exploration and pacification, the topics discussed in chapters 4 and 5, became an important part of the policemen's work during the forty years covered in this study. This responsibility generated great enthusiasm among the policemen because of its resemblance to experiences in their own traditional backgrounds. It also gave the police contact with villagers on a regular basis. In this context one important possibility became apparent to the policemen: the gun gave them prestige and power, which in appropriate circumstances allowed them to use the "naked power" strategy to uphold both that image and their contract with the government.

Chapter 6 is about the police in the turmoil of the Second World War, which was not only a dramatic new experience, but exposed the police to combat of a different kind. The chapter provides further evidence of the continued reliance on policemen in varying situations. Their understanding and knowledge of the environment, as well as the skills required to operate effectively within it, proved advantageous to whichever side employed them during the war. More important, perhaps, and particularly in the memories of their European officers, it served as further disproof of the myth of the indolent native.

The next three chapters dwell on perceptions. How did villagers and European officers perceive policemen and their work? Responses were mixed. Villagers such as Avila, Girua, Daulei, Nanduka, Ongi, and Tawi revealed the dark side of police activities. Tawi, in particular, like other men of the area, was imprisoned, caned, and exiled from his society and sent to distant places when few of his people had gone beyond the boundaries of their traditional trading networks. From the composite views of the officers, two opposing views become apparent: one group supported the police force only reluctantly; the second spoke of it admiringly. But all agreed that, in a situation such as that in Papua New Guinea, policemen were indispensable, and that, in the final analysis, pax Australiana in Papua New Guinea succeeded because of them.

Chapter 1
The Role of the Patrol Officer in Papua New Guinea

The patrol officer system was a powerful instrument of administration, whose establishment resulted from the British, Australian, and German colonization of Papua New Guinea. It was a system not unlike other institutions established by colonial powers in the nineteenth and twentieth centuries to administer subordinated people.

A patrol officer's responsibility in Papua New Guinea was broad and varied. A significant part, particularly in his early years of employment, involved the "exploration of new territory and [the] pacification of warring tribes" (Sinclair 1981, 7).[1] Until 1960 this task constituted the practical aspect of Australian colonial administrative policy. The responsibility for that achievement was left partly to the officer and his band of policemen. This area of responsibility, acted primarily on the frontier of ignorance and *nupela pasin* (new fashion) and among newly contacted people, is the focus of this book.

Until 1960, and beyond, patrol officers, as agents of the administration or as individuals, wielded enormous power. To many villagers, a kiap was a "multi powered boss" (Rowley 1972, 76). He "had extraordinary powers . . . he was everything. He was almost God's shadow on earth" (Nelson 1982, 35). His duties were linked closely to a policeman's responsibilities, if for no other reason than the powerful influence they had on a policeman's official duties. Once a policeman was released to his charge, after six or more months of training, it was the officer's responsibility to guide and direct that policeman's daily work. From the very beginning of a policeman's career, until the end when he was either dismissed or resigned or retired from the force, the officer was his immediate boss. To an observant villager, so close was that working relationship that, in the end, what they did separately or in conjunction was often construed, rightly or wrongly, as having been achieved through each other's connivance. "The police detachment must in many cases have been used as the instrument of an arbitrary despotism, its actions reflecting the idiosyncrasies of the 'kiap'; so that his character might mean a great deal to the natives of his district" (Rowley 1958, 211). An extreme example, the activities of George Ellis and his policemen at Angoram in the Sepik at the outbreak of World War II, is discussed in chapter 9.

Backgrounds of Some Patrol Officers

The patrol officers in Papua New Guinea were all men, and, according to official regulation, Caucasian and of British nationality. With few exceptions, and especially after 1906, they came from Australia (*PAR* 1947–1948, 9). They were referred to officially, and by villagers, by a variety of designations including "kiap," "patrol officer of the Royal Papuan Constabulary," "government agent," *"taubada," "gavamani," "*out-side man," "big-man," "big boss," "an officer of the field staff," "cadet patrol officer," and literally hundreds of other names reflecting the many languages in Papua New Guinea. While early annual reports for Papua give relevant information on the numbers of field staff, the same is not true of New Guinea annual reports, particularly in 1920. For New Guinea, only total figures are given for all the officers in the classified positions of the public service, indicating the numbers in each of three divisions. This has made it impossible to paste together any semblance of the numbers involved for each category. For instance, after the 1920s each division included officers of various occupations. The district officer, the highest-ranking official of the field staff officers, was listed in the first division. The patrol officers were in the second division, together with members of the clerical staff, surveyors, a draftsman, the superintendent of police, the postmaster, and the cadets. Both the drill instructor and warrant officer of the police came in the third division (*NGAR* 1926–1927, 8). However, some statistics are available from secondary sources for the period after 1920. In 1922 in New Guinea there was a total of 41 European members of field staff (Reed 1943, 166). In 1933 there were 76 (Mair 1948, 33), a number reduced to 73 the following year (Reed 1943, 166). According to the findings of the Amalgamation Committee Report of 1939, there was a total of 46 field staff in Papua and 100 in New Guinea (Eggleston, Murray, and Townsend 1939, 24). By 1955 there was a total for the year of 526 officers holding permanent and temporary positions in the Department of Native Affairs, and 204 officers were members of the field staff (Sinclair 1981, 186).

The diversity of the origins of the officers needs to be seen against the changing conditions and opportunities at various times. In New Guinea there was—except for brief periods of financial stringency—an expanding service. The field staff doubled in the 1920s and 1930s. The

Papuan service, smaller and more static, was less than half that of New Guinea at the outbreak of the Pacific War. The differences in the two territories reflected first that New Guinea, with its flourishing gold-fields, was largely protected against the depression of the 1930s; the New Guinea government's revenue at the end of that decade was three times that of Papua. Second, the greater number of foreigners in New Guinea and their movement into the interior placed greater demands on the New Guinea government to keep up with prospectors and recruiters. Third, there were simply more people in New Guinea, and their distri-bution through major islands meant that more staff were needed.[2]

The following discussion is based in part on information received from a questionnaire circulated in July 1987 to former officers of Papua New Guinea's colonial administration. The response to the question-naire was disappointing—of the 35 sent to ex-officials, only 14 replies were received, including one from a man who had not been a patrol officer. Jim Keogh was appointed in 1946 and first worked as a senior clerk in the Department of Health. He was transferred to various other jobs before he retired from active duty in 1967. On his own admission, he received no "structured education." The other 13 men began their careers as patrol officers in, until 1955, the Department of District Ser-vices and Native Affairs (thereafter, Native Affairs), District Administra-tion, and Division of the Administrator, respectively (Sinclair 1981, 7). Some of the respondents recorded only the barest minimum of infor-mation, making it difficult to gauge the part they played in the adminis-tration. My discussion proceeds despite these shortcomings.

Most of what has been written on the officers concerns their involve-ment in Australia's administration of Papua New Guinea, that is, their official duties. The accounts normally begin with an officer stepping off a boat, his subsequent enlistment in the relevant section or depart-ment, and the length of his engagement before his retirement from the colonial service. While this sort of information is useful, there are few accounts of the officers' early lives. Some officers wrote about them-selves, giving some autobiographical information, but the vast majority wrote virtually nothing about their work in Papua New Guinea or about their life before recruitment. Vital information is missing about their official and private lives. Although the discussion here is by no means exhaustive, it at least provides some basic biographical information, in the hope that through the accounts of these few, some insight will be gained into the experiences of the majority.

Of the thirteen men, two were born in a colonial territory.

Francis William ANDERSON, the son of a Norwegian boat captain and a mother whose ancestry began in diverse countries such as Ireland, Scotland, England, and Australia, was born on 27

August 1914 on Samarai, Milne Bay. Anderson first attended school in Samarai. When he was seven years old, his mother and six other children moved to Brisbane, while his father, Captain C O Anderson, continued as a ship's captain on the Papuan coast. While young Anderson was in Brisbane he attended the Sherwood State School until he was about twelve years old, when he transferred as a boarder to the Church of England Grammar School, East Brisbane. He continued in that school until he sat and passed the Junior Certificate examination at sixteen years of age. He had no career plans and expected to find work as a junior clerk, but the Great Depression started to hit hard, and retrenchments were heavy. Unperturbed, Anderson applied for a ship's officer cadetship, although his father opposed it strongly, pointing out to him that he would have little home life. He was not offered a cadetship, and with job opportunities scarce in Australia, returned to Papua and found employment with Steamships Trading Company. Initially, prospects in the company looked promising. He hoped eventually to become an inspector. However, after only four years he resigned, because he felt he had not been properly rewarded for his efforts, and joined a dredging company expedition to the upper Fly River as a storeman and overseer of casual laborers. The group established a base camp at Kiunga on the Fly River in the Western Division. He received a promotion to junior prospector while still in the area. Anderson was working in this capacity when he first received an offer from the government to become a patrol officer. Reluctantly, he refused, wishing to honor a four-year agreement he had made with the company. By good fortune, the company wound up its activities and closed operations after only eight months in the field. Soon after, Anderson, with little experience in colonial administration save some knowledge of the country and its people, was appointed an officer of the government. His first posting as a patrol officer was to Tufi, in the North-Eastern Division (G Anderson 1987).

Ivan F CHAMPION also had a long association with Papua. He was born in Port Moresby on 9 March 1904. His father, H W Champion, was a New Zealander who, at the age of eighteen, went to Papua in 1898 and worked for Burns Philp Company. Four years later, in 1902, his father resigned and joined the government service as a storekeeper. His mother was an Australian from Cooktown, Queensland, who had lived in Port Moresby since 1892 as the wife of Neville Chester, son of H M Chester (the man who in 1884 hoisted the Union Jack). Chester died a short while after their marriage, and she married H W Champion in 1902. The young Champion attended, with two younger brothers, the first primary school in Port Moresby in 1911. The family moved to Queensland during World War I, and Champion attended the Southport School as a boarder from 1916 to 1922. He later found a job as a bank clerk in Sydney in 1922, but office work did not suit him. After only a year, he resigned and returned to Port Moresby. For the rest of 1923 he was attached to the magisterial staff. In 1924 Champion's official duties with the Papuan administration began. His first position and posting was as a patrol officer in the Gulf Division (Champion 1987).

Significantly, the number of locally recruited Papuan field officers was a factor distinguishing the Papuan field staff from the New Guinean. Among those who had an association with Papua before joining the service and were appointed by Murray were Jack Hides, J B C Bramell, Sid and Lea Ashton, Ronald Speedie, and Ivan Champion's two brothers, Claude and Alan. It is interesting that Hides, the Champions, and the Ashtons were all from the tiny Port Moresby school for whites (1911), and another of that group, Tom Grahamslaw, entered the Papuan customs service and did some memorable wartime patrols (Hank Nelson, personal communication, 1988). These locally recruited Papuan officers were probably more likely to think that work in Papua was for all their career, not just an adventurous part of a working life, and their attitudes toward Papuans were formed from childhood and through many different relationships. It is also likely that men such as the Hides and the Champions felt a personal obligation and loyalty to Hubert Murray. This level of commitment to place and the administration was different from that in New Guinea, which was not "home" to the most dedicated officers.

The other eleven officers who answered the questionnaire were born either in Australia or in a European country. The majority were at least second-generation Australians whose ancestry began from one of three backgrounds: English, Irish, or Scottish. Their first appointments were as either cadets or patrol officers. These two positions were not their first and only occupations—rather, they were for some a second employment and, for the great majority, the beginning of a long career in Australia's administration of Papua New Guinea.

In this chapter, I emphasize the work of the kiaps as field staff officers, or the first stage of an officer's career in the colonial administrative structure. A significant number of the field staff officers ended up in senior positions and made decisions that affected their successors. Table 1 gives some indication of their backgrounds and range of responsibilities. Although the sample is small, it is an important supplement to the many written reminiscences.

Table 1 Backgrounds of fourteen former colonial officers

Name	Nationality of Grandparents or Parents	Place & Date of Birth	Education before Recruitment	Prior Employment
Aitchison, T G	Australian	Australia 1919	Melbourne University/ASOPA	?
Anderson, F W G	Norwegian fa; Irish-English-Scottish mo	Samarai 27 August 1914	Junior Certificate Examination	Steamships Trading Company; Oroville Dredging Company
Bramell, J B C	British/Australian	Australia	Sydney Boys High School; 3 months ASOPA	?
Brown, Ken	British/Australian	Australia	Dubbo High School, NSW; ASOPA no 2 diploma course	Local Government Council, RAAF
Champion, Ivan	New Zealand fa; Australian mo	Port Moresby 9 March 1904	Southport School, Queensland	Bank clerk, Sydney
Clark, H E (Lynn)	Australian	Australia 29 November 1924	Leaving Certificate; ASOPA	RAAF
Cole, R R	British/Australian	Australia 1914	Dubbo High School, NSW	Chartered accountant's office
Connolly, K E	British	?	Lawrence Military School (India); ASOPA	?
Giddings, R J	British/Scottish/Australian	Australia 1938	Victoria Matriculation Certificate	?
Keogh, Jim	British/Australian	Australia ?	No structured education	?
Normoyle, W E	Australian	Australia 1930	Rabaul Public School	?
Tomasetti, W E	Swiss-Irish-British (gp); Australian fa/mo	Australia 1920	Victoria School Certificate	Australian Imperial Force
Toogood, G W	Scottish	Scotland 1909	English Public School, Law at Cambridge	Burns Philp Company
Wright, M	Scottish/Australian	Australia	Toowoomba Grammar School to Matriculation	?

Note: Where necessary, further information is given in the text for some officers.

Age at Recruit- ment	Marital Status	First Appointment	Last Position	Length of Service	Post Retirement
22	Single	Cadet	Acting Director DS&NA	7 June 1933 to 18 January 1968	Administrator sheltered workshops; breeding livestock
22?	Single	Patrol Officer	?	1936–1949	Native Affairs Dept, Australia; Premier's Dept
23	Single	Patrol Officer	Land Titles Commissioner	1936–1967	Motor trimming
23?	?	Cadet	District Commissioner	June 1947 to July 1974	Overseas travel, hobby farming, assembling memoirs
19	Single	Patrol Officer	Senior Commissioner of Native Land Commission	24 May 1923 to 1964	Lands Commissioner 1968
21	Single	Patrol Officer	Assistant District Commissioner	1946–1965	Medically superannuated; writing
24	Single	Cadet	Police Commissioner	1938–1965	Retired
?	Single	Cadet	Industrial Registrar & Commissioner Workers Compensation	September 1948 to June 1974	Business; employment in private sector; government statistical authority
18½	Single	Cadet	Senior provincial magistrate	5 March 1956–	Still active duty
?	Married	Clerk	Land Titles Commissioner	1946–1967	Dept of Social Services; Police & Education
18	Single	?	Deputy commissioner for local government	1948–1965	Industrial relations officer & personnel manager
26	Married	Patrol Officer	Senior lecturer, Administrative College	June 1946 to November 1978	Conservation; peace movements; writing
24	Single	?	Administration	1933–1969	Consultant; Honorary Director of National Trust
20?	Single	Cadet	District Commissioner	1936–1951	Commonwealth public servant

Source: Derived from responses to questionnaire.

Only two features of table 1 require further comment—age and educational background. In the selected sample, the eldest of the field staff officers to have joined the service was Bill Tomasetti, but at twenty-six years of age he was hardly an old man. The youngest was Normoyle at eighteen. The officers were young when they first entered the colonial service in Papua New Guinea. Six had between one and four years of beginner's level work experience and, of those who became patrol officers, only Tomasetti was married at the time of recruitment. Like many other older recruits, Tomasetti was an ex-serviceman.

Eleven had finished high school or completed the Australian junior certificate examination (High School Certificate). This schooling, if relevant for employment, was designed for the Australian environment and essentially western in orientation. Aitchison attended Melbourne University. It is not clear from his statement whether he was awarded a degree. Toogood enrolled for some time for law studies at Cambridge University, but did not complete the degree. Tomasetti received a first class honors degree from Queensland University in 1967, but only after he had been in the service for twenty-one years. The curriculum of the officers' early education did not cover colonialism generally, or anything about the people subordinated because of it. By their own admission, at the time of recruitment the officers had received a broad education that did not prepare them for professional jobs in their own community, and, for the majority, told them nothing about working for a colonial government. Why then, ill-prepared as they were, did they decide to seek employment outside what was familiar? During the depression hundreds applied for jobs in Papua New Guinea, doubtless driven by economic conditions in Australia. The standards of entry therefore went up. The late John Black, with some university education but no degree, was one of those selected during that period (personal communication). From a general perspective, "The men who became kiaps went north with the same mixture of motives that prompted other Australians to leave home, but they were probably more strongly attracted to the romantic ideals of adventure and duty on the frontier" (Nelson 1982, 33).[3] For one recruit, "It was during the great depression when jobs were impossible to get that I applied for a position with the Papuan Administration. I did this mainly due to my family's affiliation with the Territory in the first place and I therefore felt part of it" (Bramell 1987).

Most patrol officers who came to Papua New Guinea with some knowledge of the area had acquired it while in uniform. The ex-servicemen of the two wars were important sources of recruits, and the men who applied in the 1950s and 1960s grew up on wartime stories of Papua New Guinea (Giddings 1987).

At the age of nineteen, after joining the Royal Australian Air Force, Lynn CLARK was posted to Merauke and Tannah Merah in Dutch New Guinea on active service. His experience there prompted him to want to become a patrol officer in Papua New Guinea. On his release from the air force he applied to the secretary, Department of External Territories in 1945 but, "as a civilian," his first application was not successful because the territories were still run by Australian military personnel. In 1946 he applied again, and was accepted in Lae as a patrol officer at the age of twenty-one and transferred to Madang for active duty (Clark 1987).

A number of kiaps applied in response to advertisements placed in local newspapers in Australia. Rick Giddings applied in Victoria in 1955, and was accepted as a cadet in 1956:

> Fortunately, towards the end of 1955 vacancies for cadet patrol officers were advertised in the Victorian newspapers and I decided to apply. The job suited my interests. It incorporated police work in an out-of-doors situation in an exciting country! I had long been interested in PNG; ever since the time my father had returned from the War with stories of enchanting islands, glorious weather, sparkling clear water, verdant jungle and pleasant people to live and work amongst. It sounded good to me! I did not worry at all about the career part of it in terms of salary, conditions, promotion etc. I was excited at the thought of working in such an exotic place, and my excitement was not misplaced. (Giddings 1987)

Each candidate had to submit satisfactory evidence of his date of birth, good character, health, and physical fitness for employment in the tropics (NGAR 1926–1927, 8[7]). The emphasis on physical fitness was partly practical: the patrol officer had to be capable of sustained hard walking in the bush and have the capacity to meet emergencies, whether environmental in the form of flooded rivers, or human—a sudden attack by an axe-swinging villager. Malcolm Wright recalled his fellow cadets in Sydney in 1938:

> Not one of us could be regarded as a "brain" or had achieved much in the academic world, but most of us were better than average in the field of sport. Dal Chambers and Greg Benham were first-grade cricketers, and good ones; Charlie Mader was a State high-jump champion and Lloyd Purehouse had won a State public school's sprint title; Pat Mollison and Ted Styants had played first-grade Australian Rules football and during the course Ted was selected for the State side; Ian Downs and John Murphy were considerably better than average boxers; Eric Mitchell had held a

> country golf title, and I had competed in State swimming cham-
> pionships In addition, Leslie Howlett, a young man of consider-
> able memory, could quote every major winner in horse racing and
> every current record in the sporting field; he told us that on a long
> patrol he had forgotten to take books, and Miller's *Sporting Guide*
> was all he had to read. (1966, 72)

The Administrators chose sportsmen for an additional reason. The ideal of the empire builder was pervasive. The young man who could excel for school, club, and state on the sports field, who could give and take and stick by the rules, was also the one to represent his nation on wild frontiers.

In New Guinea, applicants were required to be unmarried and had to agree to remain so for their first two years of service (Downs 1986, 100). Those selected to attend Sydney University "were required to enter into a bond of two thousand pounds to return to the territory of New Guinea for a period of at least two years and not marry until a period of two years had elapsed." The restriction was imposed for two basic reasons. First, there was a lack of suitable married accommodation. Second, patrol officers particularly were required to conduct regular patrols, which meant they would be absent from the station for long periods, a lifestyle considered inappropriate for a married person. However, there were exceptions.

The guidelines for selection were expedient. From the beginning, applicants should have been required to learn Motu or Tok Pisin (both later became prerequisites), the two languages most widely spoken in Papua and New Guinea, respectively; as an early prerequisite, they should also have been required to learn something of the customs and cultures of the people they were to meet for the first time. Few, if any, white Australians interacted with the customs and ways of life of other races. Even if some contact had been established with, for instance, traditional Australians—the Aborigines—it was at best a fleeting experience: sustained contact with the Aboriginal people for the great majority of white Australians was not common (Bill Gammage and Hank Nelson, personal communication, 1988). For the officers, a creditable educational background was not a criterion for selection at any stage of colonial rule in Papua New Guinea, the emphasis being more on practical experience than on high academic qualifications (Rowley 1972, 68).[4] There was some improvement during the 1920s in New Guinea, but in Papua, Murray continued to "personally select his staff, choosing them as far as possible from men who had grown up in the country, a qualification which he regarded as superior to any special training: and in appointments to the few specialist posts which the service carried he attached little importance to expert knowledge" (Mair 1948, 12).

Numerous examples testify to Mair's assertion that an association with the territories was more common for Papuan government officers.

   While standards of colonial rule advanced in other parts of the world, Murray was still bent on making "appointments of amateurs to the colonial administrative service" (Mair 1948, 13). (Some of these men—Jack Hides and Ivan Champion—spoke Motu and were excellent bushmen.) In retrospect, after thirty-two years' experience in Australia's administration, Bill Tomasetti wrote in 1987: "During the colonial period, the education required to serve as a kiap should have been at least a bachelor's degree in the relevant social sciences." In New Guinea, mindful of the officers' lack of relevant education, the government passed legislation introducing the cadetship system in 1925. During that year, six cadets were appointed to the service, and an additional five in 1927. From the beginning, "The cadets selected are all young men, of good physique and character, who have passed either the intermediate examination or the Leaving Examination [High or School Certificate] of some Australian University. Their appointments are probationary for two years, during which period they receive a systematic training by competent officials" (NGAR 1926–1927, 12).

The Australian School of Pacific Administration

From 1926 five or more cadets after a period of practical training in Papua New Guinea were selected each succeeding year and sent for further training to the University of Sydney (Nelson 1982, 40). In 1947 the Australian government established a School of Pacific Administration at Mosman, in Sydney, that was built expressly to train officers of the administration of Papua New Guinea. The school was a continuation of the cadetship system established by the commonwealth government in 1925. It developed "from a nucleus organization established by the Australian Army in 1944." For the first years of the cadetship, cadets were instructed in tropical medicine, topographical surveying, systems of keeping accounts, general clerical duties, elementary law, and introductory anthropology. Over the years a host of other courses were introduced, in keeping with changes in the administration of the territories (NGAR 1946–1947, 16; 1926–1927, 12). Further details on the school, and the people who attended it, have been provided by Nelson:

> The cadets who went to the Mandated Territory from 1926 returned to Sydney University for two terms of study after two years in the field. During the Second World War the School of Civil Affairs operated at Duntroon to train Australians for service in Papua New Guinea. But in 1947 it transferred to Mosman in Sydney where it

was renamed the Australian School of Pacific Affairs [*sic*], ASOPA.
(1982, 40–41)

In 1947 and thereafter, cadets received instruction in colonial administration, anthropology, law and order in Papua-New Guinea, practical
administration, elementary medicine, tropical agriculture, geography,
scientific method, Tok Pisin and Motu, animal husbandry and entomol-
ogy, and "the machinery of administration and administrative policy in
New Guinea." (Whether or not Tok Pisin and Motu were offered in the
early years is not clear.) The length of the course varied from three
months to two or more years. Successful candidates were appointed to
the territory's public service, where most found themselves working as
patrol officers in the Department of District Services and Native Affairs.

The responses of the officers who attended some of the Australian
School of Pacific Administration courses at Sydney University confirm
that a vacuum had been filled—it gave them a boost, a confidence that
was previously lacking in their dealings with the people. Was this course
of instruction sufficient? Giddings gained much at the school—without
it he says his work in Papua New Guinea would have been wanting. Giddings' sense of achievement after attending, the lasting utility of the
courses in the field, and the impact on his own personal advancement,
are confirmed by his testimony:

> I attended ASOPA on two occasions: during February 1956 and dur-
> ing 1959. As a result of these courses I was given a sound ground-
> ing in anthropology, government law and the history and practice
> of colonialism. We learnt much about the British colonial experi-
> ence in Africa and were grateful that we had more or less come to
> Papua New Guinea, at least we were bringing our work to fruition,
> after the British had learnt the lessons of how and how not to
> administer dependent people. The great English colonial adminis-
> trator, Lord Lugard, was held up to us as a model of what an ad-
> ministrator should be.
>
> The training we received at ASOPA was adequate enough for the
> purpose it was intended to serve. It aimed, in effect, to produce
> administrators who were attuned to the history and culture of the
> people they were working amongst and to demonstrate to us both
> the pitfalls and successes that one human group can have in gov-
> erning another. The philosophy of ASOPA was progressive in that
> the faculty saw a not-too-distant future when PNG would govern
> itself, whereas we kiaps reckoned that self-government in fifty years
> and independence in 100 years was more likely to be the case. Of
> course we sadly overestimated!
>
> I was particularly assisted in my work, and in my private interests,
> by the study of anthropology because it provided me with the tools

needed to unlock the pattern of Melanesian culture. Before doing the Certificate course in 1959, I had experienced difficulty in finding out about the Bougainville people; about their property inheritance patterns, for instance, because I did not know what questions to ask them.

I had little knowledge of the principles governing inheritance in a matrilineal society. Once I was taught those principles, it was easy for me to apply them to the people I wished to study, and to find out what I wanted to know about them, because I was able to ask them appropriate questions. It intrigued me to learn how Melanesian societies operated; particularly to learn the myths and legends which validated it. My work became my hobby after ASOPA, and I was enriched as a human being, not only as an administrator. (Giddings 1987)[5]

The sentiment is shared by the other twelve respondents to my questionnaire. The immediate benefits were significant (see Wright 1966, chapter 7). In addition, the experience created a gulf between the young men who attended the school and the "old hands" in authority, whose knowledge of administration of subordinate peoples was limited to their experience in Papua New Guinea.

The Australian administration was jejune, unproductive of ideas and suffering from the poor education and limited background of most of those at headquarters. . . . Those in authority liked things as they were: coconuts, gold and native labour. New crops, forest resources, mineral wealth other than gold and the education of the people beyond that available in mission schools, had never been properly investigated. . . . Our senior officers showed little interest in policies and planning so we looked elsewhere for guidance and inspiration. (Downs 1986, 77, 105)

Unfortunately, the Australian School of Pacific Administration came after twenty-six[6] years of Australian administration in New Guinea and forty-one years in Papua. After attending the school, the officers were considered "qualified to wield great administrative power" (Rowley 1972, 68).

By the early 1950s, then, officers who had entered the service by diverse tracks were still at work in the districts. There were men personally recruited by Murray, men with much local knowledge, a commitment to the place, to the people, and to a style of government. There were men recruited into the New Guinea service when competition owing to the depression was at its height and when short professional courses were provided in Sydney; there were those who had gone to New Guinea in the armed forces, liked the place, and stayed; and there were the young men recruited after the war and trained at the Australian School of Pacific Administration. It was a service without the strong bonds that result when people come from the same social classes, attend similar schools, and experience similar training.

Sources of Patrol Officers' Power

Most patrol officers worked in the districts in New Guinea and the divisions in Papua (map 1; "Division" in Papua was abandoned in 1951 in favor of "District").[7] As pacification progressed, the numbers and sizes of districts or divisions that came under the jurisdiction of field staff increased. In New Guinea there were eight administrative districts in 1948, namely, Madang, Sepik, Morobe, and the newly declared Central Highlands on the mainland,[8] New Britain, New Ireland, Manus, and Kieta in the islands (NGAR 1948–1949, item 19). Seven divisions existed in Papua in 1948: Western, Delta, and Gulf Divisions to the west of Port Moresby, Northern, Eastern, and South Eastern to the east, and the Central Division (PAR 1947–1948, item 77). The districts and divisions were further subdivided, with the names of the subdivisions changing from time to time. In 1952, for instance, the Sepik District was divided into four subdistricts—Angoram, Aitape, Wewak, and Maprik. In Angoram there were three patrol posts—Lumi, Yangoru, and Dreikikir. By contrast Manus, the smallest district, had just two patrol posts—Balaun and Pasusi. At various times police camps were maintained in newly administered areas (NGAR 1951–1952, 29–33).

The district officer was in control at the district headquarters, officers of various ranks on stations and substations, and a senior resident policeman at the police camp (NGAR 1930–1931, 94, item 288). The arrangement of field staff in Papua generally paralleled that in New Guinea. In each of the divisions there was a resident magistrate, an assistant resident magistrate, and a patrol officer. Like the hierarchy in the central administration in Port Moresby and Rabaul before World War II, a similar structure that was much smaller in size existed within the division organization. The size of the district officer's and resident magistrate's staff, including both white and local employees, depended on the geographical extent of the district, the degree of control, and the population of the area. In the majority of cases the district officer had an assistant, below whom in rank were the patrol officers. When the cadetship system was introduced in New Guinea, cadets stood on the bottom rung of the hierarchy within the district organization.[9] They were told that "Cadets are lower than shark's dung . . . and that is at the bottom of the ocean" (Wright 1966, 1). In a typical district the European officials consisted of a district officer, an assistant district officer, a medical officer, three or more patrol officers, and one cadet on practical train-

Administrative Districts and Centers, 1948

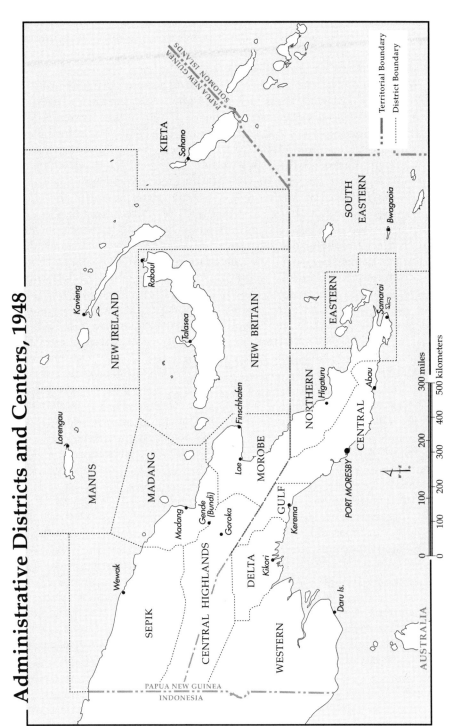

Map 1

ing—a total of seven men. In most areas, as one moved farther away from the district headquarters, the number of white officials dwindled. For instance, in the late 1930s, Ian Downs was the only patrol officer in Simbu (not yet a separate district) supervising and controlling seventeen policemen and three hundred thousand people (Donaldson 1984, 197). However, despite their lack of numbers, kiaps,[10] either together or individually, became the most powerful people in the district.

It seems incongruous that a group lowly placed on the colonial administrative ladder should have so much power. Where did their strength come from? There are three possibilities: it derived from the villagers, the policemen, or the officers themselves. First, the villagers occupied center stage. Much of this book is concerned with events on the colonial frontier where the police and patrol officer were in regular contact with the villagers. They were the essential targets of exploration and pacification and the whole process of colonization. They were inevitably active participants—either positively or negatively or both—in the colonization process. Whether the patrol officer failed or succeeded in his attempts depended on what the villagers did. From a broad perspective, even if it took longer for some, the majority of Papua New Guineans generally were convinced that the patrol officers wielded so much power that they did not have the resources to sustain open resistance and gave either passive or positive acceptance to their dominance. The immediate sanction of force could be applied to the occasional deviant by the patrol officer, or through his orders, by the policemen, but the whole society had to be convinced that the system was necessary or inevitable: power had to be demonstrated so that villagers not only became aware of its potential but also accorded, for whatever reasons, acceptance of its reality. A man might appear to be brave and courageous, but if he could not demonstrate those feats in real situations then he would only be a *man natin* (ordinary man, man of little consequence). In various ways the patrol officer and his police demonstrated their power. What the villagers did not know was that an officer's power was circumscribed, that he could not legally exceed the limits set by regulations.

Villagers reacted to the show of power in two ways. On the one hand, many villagers accepted almost without question the officers' right to make and enforce laws. The main reason, as stated in chapter 8 by Tawi and other villagers interviewed, was their fear of the officer's and the policemen's demonstration of unusual strength and force of character. Officers and police were outside any system of constraints and powers known to the villagers. Who knew what violence they might unleash? Villagers had to accept that the intruders were stronger and apparently ruthless and unpredictable. In Reed's term, this was "negative acquiescence." On the other hand, some villagers, recognizing the power of the government, allied themselves with patrol parties and requested assistance in fighting enemy tribes. This was "positive acquiescence" (Reed, 1943, 174). In either case, the crucial factor was that the villagers based their response on a belief in the strength of the newcomers. Villagers who dug pit latrines or buried their dead in graves were not persuaded by arguments about health. "The natives do not accept regulations because they believe that the white man knows what is best, for it is rare to find natives with the sympathetic confidence that such an attitude would demand. It is true that among the younger men there is a growing appreciation of the enforced peace, but the administration's motives are still suspect" (Reed 1943, 174). In acquiescing, villagers consciously or unconsciously enhanced the patrol officer's power.

As auxiliary subinspectors of the Papua New Guinea constabulary, patrol officers controlled the policemen assigned to the district as field police.[11] The details of salaries and seniority were unknown to the villagers, but they all interpreted what they saw: the police by their salutes, by the way they received orders, by the work they did, and by the way they lived on patrol and at the station were under the command of the patrol officer. It was the kiap who sat at the folding table, and had cooked food carried to him. Later, villagers might learn of weaknesses in the capacity of the patrol officer to know and control, but there can be no doubt that he was seen as a man of authority. His relationship to the police can be described using Mike Donaldson's assertion that the policemen "were essentially [the kiap's] warriors in navy blue." From the perspective of villagers, these policemen were broad-shouldered, awe-inspiring men who worked for the kiaps and performed with distinction and loyalty. Consciously or unconsciously, they acted the roles of warriors and displayed qualities of "resourcefulness, courage, political acumen, and a certain firmness of purpose, even ruthlessness" (Donaldson 1984, 200). Among the highlands people, for example, these traits were respected, if not feared. Such behavior, coupled with their .303, kept the villagers in check. The policemen therefore were vital in enhancing the officers' presumed greatness: their actions and behavior gave substance to notions of the patrol officers as powerful men. Left without the services of the policemen, the officers' power would have been much reduced, or it would have necessitated the despatch of expensive Australian policemen or soldiers as substitutes. Australians were probably not prepared to pay that political and monetary cost.

Why did the policemen assist the patrol officer? While it is possible that some policemen may have developed great love for the officers,[12] and indirectly for the government, and did everything to demonstrate that devotion, a more realistic picture is given in chapter 2 by the majority of those interviewed of why some policemen gave exemplary service. Most of the reasons these men advanced are not the same as those given by the officers (see chapter 9). If the patrol officers' claims about police performance are of doubtful validity, then they call into question whether they really understood the reasons for their policemen's dedication. The explanation for the policemen's good working relationship with the patrol officer was that their interests coalesced in an unusual marriage: it was expedient for them to maintain good relations. While the average patrol officer of the period strove to explore the country and pacify the people of Papua New Guinea so that the pax Australiana could gain a permanent place in the country, the average policeman was ignorant of broader implications and only concerned himself with what was apparent to him in his immediate surroundings, or had some relevance to him as a result of his previous village life. It was in the policemen's best interest to serve the officer in whichever ways he ordered because he controlled all forms of reward: he was in charge of recruitment and final selection for police service, recommended individuals within the service for promotions and raises in salary, and determined dismissals. Most policemen practically waited on the doorstep of their barracks to be the first to volunteer for patrols and other jobs. Amero Bega, for instance, was convinced that the patrol officers were reasonable men, that they had eyes to see and ears to hear, and would recommend rewards for policemen who showed initiative and demonstrated flair and dedication. Wherever posted, Amero was one of the many policemen who had, metaphorically speaking, one foot outside the door at all times. In summary then, the patrol officers engaged the policemen to expand colonial domination, and the policemen exploited this situation to enhance their own sociopolitical and economic position in their villages. As a result, the policemen made a great contribution to the authority and power of the patrol officers.

Three broad factors helped sustain the officers' impressive image. The average patrol officer commanded power from a personal, material, and political perspective. At the personal level, he was himself a source of power that appeared to come from within. For a persuasive explanation one needs to remind oneself of the Papua New Guineans' initial responses to the advent of white men. How the foreigners were perceived and received at the time of first contact laid the basis for early relationships. Generally most Papua New Guineans regarded Europeans as spirits or returned ancestors. Even when the villagers realized that the white men were not spirits, they still assumed that the patrol officer had access to supernatural powers. The fact that the newcomers were regarded in this way immediately set them apart from the people they visited and the web of relationships established with neighbors.

The traditional village arrangement, complex, variable, and familiar, was unable to contain the foreigners. With the newcomers, villagers had to establish new patterns to encourage mutual contact. However, it immediately became obvious that the new link began on an unequal footing, with the newcomer having an edge over the well-established socioeconomic and political organizations. In other words, the new relationships disturbed traditional foundations and demanded modifications. It is contended here that this attempt at redefining the old in order to understand the new not only induced villagers to identify the newcomers as spirits but also began a nomenclature not in keeping with tradition. For instance, an officer, like all Europeans in Papua New Guinea from the time of first contact, or as soon as Tok Pisin or Police Motu was learned, was placed in a position of nominal superiority. He, like the other Europeans, was called a *masta* in New Guinea and a *taubada* in Papua. The terms implied honor and prestige, even a reverence that was mystical. Socially it gave the officer virtually unlimited power over all Papua New Guineans, whatever their status. Often villagers overlooked a patrol officer's mistakes first because he was a European, a *masta* or a *taubada,* and therefore beyond reproach, and only secondly because he was a colonial agent representing the government in Port Moresby or Rabaul, about which they knew little. The basis of the patrol officer's first power was that he was a white man, and the people accorded him respect, born of ignorance, for that difference. Therefore, an officer's sense of self-importance was cultivated from circumstances originating in the country, and upheld for as long as he was still in Papua New Guinea, and for so long as the people were willing to reserve that special honor for him. It might be called social-cultural power.

Like the missionaries and prospectors, patrol officers controlled trade by distributing European wealth to villagers. So great was the desire to possess the new wealth that whoever controlled its flow was treated with great care, attention, and jealousy by village communities. Numerous examples show how European wealth penetrated traditional trading networks, and the ways in which villagers exploited its introduction for personal, tribal, and kinship groups. During the 1930s one item that arrived in great quantity and was highly prized by the Highlanders was shell. Myriad shells of various shapes and sizes were brought into the central highlands by missionaries, gold prospectors, and patrol officers to augment the depleting but much-coveted stock of steel axes. Some of the shells arrived from as far away as Manus and Thursday Island. Ian Hughes has calculated that between 1933 and 1942 at least a million and possibly five million shells were brought and distributed throughout the central highlands (1978, 308–318). These were used mostly to buy food (especially pigs), wages for laborers, bride-price payment for policemen's wives, and for a whole array of other mission, miner, and patrol officer expenditures requiring exchanges with the local population. The people were overwhelmed by the sheer quantity, which surpassed the scale of traditional transactions, and naturally viewed those responsible as possessing an abundance of power

In many places the patrol officers were in the vanguard of the distribution of wealth, the scale of which was previously unknown.[13] The officer was again seen as a man of unlimited capacities. Although the manufactured goods originated outside Papua New Guinea, the power resulting from them was not imported, but originated from local circumstances.

Finally, the patrol officer not only supervised and directed the policemen, but was perceived by the villagers as being a "big boss." While working as a lance corporal in Simbu in the 1930s, Amero Bega was told persistently by the Norame people that they were most impressed by his patrol officer because he was not only in charge of the police but also appeared to control the activities of other Europeans (1985). Similar impressions were gained of James Lindsay Taylor by Mokei Korua Kolta of the Western Highlands. Of the missionaries, miners, and government officials, Kolta had no hesitation in identifying who was in charge:

> The white men all looked the same with their clothes and trade goods, but we knew that Taylor had more power than the others. We wondered often why he was respected even by the other white men. Father Ross—he was quieter. He used to watch us and never captured us or put us in jail. We figured Taylor must be above the others in some way. Whatever was said, matters were always referred to the kiap. We realised he must be the boss—as in our society, he was the big man. Mick [Leahy] and Dan [Leahy] were working, but we felt he was the boss over them. (Quoted in Connolly and Anderson 1987, 261)

There are two reasons for the villagers' perception. The first is based on their own values. Donaldson argued that the patrol officer was looked on as a big-man because "the kiaps killed pigs, controlled trade, administered justice, and enjoyed the obedience of their warriors. They also exhibited the personal traits of arrogance, aggression, and authoritarianism which were the hallmarks of the greatest of bigmen. It seems to be that the kiaps not only acted but were perceived as big-men, and the police as warriors and/or big-men depending on the proximity of white authority" (1984, 200).

The second reason can be discussed with the aid of two examples. The patrol officer was part of an imposed political system that was pervasive and dominant. Placed on the frontier as an intruder, he was forced to adopt measures that would guarantee his survival. If this could not be achieved through words then the alternative was direct or indirect force. Besides playing the role of big-man, he had to be seen as ruthless. He could establish this ruthlessness in various ways. In Simbu, a few months before World War II, the Yongamugl tribe "resumed violent activity by provocative pig stealing followed by a well-planned and bloody ambush of the owners" (Downs 1986, 120–121). Downs, with the assistance of two thousand men from two aggrieved tribes, took "hostage" almost the "entire" resources of livestock, numbering five thousand screaming pigs. It shattered the Yongamugl. Downs explained:

> We had effectively destroyed all bride price agreements in marriage contracts, and driven the Yongamugl out of the circle of ceremonial festivities for which pigs were an essential part. The punishment was harsh: we only returned some of their breeding pigs. From the rest we repaid those who had been plundered, paid our helpers and established a government pig farm. . . . In quick succession we took similar action in four other troublesome locations. Each time we used different tribal groups to help us. This was the end of serious fighting in Chimbu and the statistics prove it. (Downs 1986, 120–121)[14]

Although it is true that violence in this instance was directed against pigs, it indirectly reduced the socioeconomic strength of the communities concerned and rendered them weak among their competitors. A harsher example is provided by Connolly and Anderson. They calculated on the basis of documents that for the highlands region "total casualties to gunfire directed by white prospectors and patrol officers throughout the 1930s might conceivably have amounted to a thousand men, women and children" (1987, 250). These "body counts" could easily be underestimates. People would have died later as a result of gunshot wounds, and some corpses would have been removed by relatives or fellow warriors (Donaldson 1984, 193–194).

Those highlands cases provide excellent illustrations of the various ways in which government officials, at the colonial frontier, adopted the "naked power"[15] strategy and resorted to violence either to counter violence, or to demonstrate their power. Apart from brief skirmishes it was always an unequal affair, and the patrol officers, when they commanded their police and other friendly tribes against hostile groups, knew of this advantage. But expediency demanded that force be used to demonstrate their power. It was terrifying, destructive, and led to some of the worst excesses of Australian colonialism. Either actual force, or the threat of it, helped subjugate whole communities, rendered them powerless, and strengthened the patrol officer's dominance.

Summary

This is by no means the end of the story of the patrol officers' involvement in Australia's colonial administration and the nature of their supervision of the police. In Papua New Guinea's colonial history it would be difficult to separate the nature of a policeman's work from that of his patrol officer, for their responsibilities were complementary. The officer was his superior, and the policeman, at whatever rank, was his subordinate. Both exhibited enormous power on the colonial stage, first on the frontier of ignorance and *nupela pasin,* and later through the supervision of the village officials in the enforcement of the regulations directing Papua New Guineans' behavior.

The patrol officer was part of an imposed political system. Where necessary, force was used to establish the system's dominance and legitimacy. Toward the end of his rule, Sir William MacGregor was determined to see western concepts of law and order triumph over presumed anarchy in Papua. He wrote in 1898, "We never fight with them [Papuans] at all if we can possibly avoid it until we are in a position to make it a final and decisive move. We hardly ever have to fight twice in the same district. If we do fight, I always insist upon fighting it out, and never leave it in doubt as to who is master" (quoted in Sinclair 1990, 18). There was continuity and consistency of practice on both sides of the border. After his painstaking research into the Finintugu "massacre" of 1934, Munster concluded, "news of the Finintugu affray spread far and wide through the Eastern Highlands, and people now knew, if they hadn't known before, that European guns could kill. No other white men died at their hands after Finintugu. The massacre did help to establish the supremacy of the European. Although an unfortunate basis on which to build effective administration, violence as a means of obtaining control was well understood by the Highlands people" (1981, 44). It can also be said that after pacification, colonial rule brought peace (Low 1973, 23). However, the nature of this peace should be the subject of another in-depth study.

> The communities that they [kiaps and policemen] tried to pacify and control held a variety of views about them. Generally it was a love/hate relationship. Like the beachcombers of the 1800s, the [kiap] and policemen were the interpreters of European culture to the indigenous people. Many villagers were confused about this *nupela pasin.* What did it mean? Why did they have to stop fighting their enemies and abandon their cannibalism, sorcery and head-hunting? They were told that it was because of the new law that had come into their midst. An end to these activities would ensure that: they made bigger and better gardens; wives would no longer wait anxiously for the return of their husbands from their hunting; children would, if they did not die from natural causes, live to inherit their parent's possessions; and peace would reign within their communities. (Kituai 1986, 27)

Other advantages accrued as well—health, freedom of movement, and so on, and the patrol officers played a big part in bringing them.

Many patrol officers were dedicated men. Within colonial society their responsibilities were the most taxing. They not only dealt with villagers struggling to cope with the force of change, but the extent of their operations was limited by official regulations. Despite physical difficulties and legal restrictions, on their shoulders fell the burden of practical administration. At the time of engagement many were young and inexperienced, but most matured while working among the villagers. Giddings, for instance, has fond memories of the people of North Solomons, "because I grew to maturity, to manhood, amongst them. I learnt much from them about the meaning and practice of life, about inter-personal relationships. In hindsight I realize that they served me better than I ever managed to serve them" (1987; see appendix 1).

Patrol officers became victims and beneficiaries of circumstance: the colonial system gave them opportunities they would otherwise not have had in their own countries. While some misused these opportunities, others used them well. Overall, patrol officers, with their loyal policemen, were the backbone of the administration. But some of their officers were men of myopic vision.[16]

Chapter 2

Recruitment of Police

Thousands of Papua New Guinea men served as policemen in the Papuan Armed Constabulary and the New Guinea police force from the forces' inception in the 1890s, according to the total yearly establishment figures for the period. The Papuan Armed Constabulary Ordinance of 1890 and a similar declaration in German New Guinea in 1896 made provisions for the recruitment of men between seventeen and forty years of age. However, recruiters concentrated on enlisting mostly young men. Of those I interviewed, John Guise, who was recruited at the age of thirty-two, was an unusual case. According to his testimony, his recruitment may have had something to do with his having received some education from the Anglican Mission school. The more important reason appears to be that his grandfather was an English public servant and a trader (J Ryan 1969, 138).

In Papua there was gradual slow growth[1] in the police force, from just over one hundred in 1896–97 to nearly three hundred fifty in 1920–21. An administrative decision in June 1921 to reduce the force to two hundred fifty accounts for the decline in 1921–22, and thereafter the numbers gradually grew back to about three hundred fifty on the eve of World War II (table 2). According to Halford W Thompson, "about 60 raw natives join[ed] the force as recruits" each year in the Papuan service (PAR 1914–1915, 104). If the numbers entering the police averaged sixty each year, then over the fifty-year period 1890–1940 some three thousand men are likely to have served in the Papuan police prior to the war.

In New Guinea there was rapid growth in the police force, which had increased in total strength from more than five hundred men in 1925–26 to well over a thousand on the eve of World War II (table 2). At the Rabaul depot 138 new recruits were trained in 1921–22, 127 in 1922–23, and 175 in 1923–24.[2] The average for these three years is 147. If this average remained constant over the entire period, then a total of 2,940 men served in the New Guinea police in the twenty years between 1920 and 1940. A combined total of 3,137 men served in the police in Papua and New Guinea during the period 1940–1945. Unfortunately, from this period to 1960 no useful information is given for either force that might have assisted in making proper calculations of the yearly averages. In the absence of vital information, the following discussion is an attempt to explain the anomaly.

Among the provisions guiding police recruitment and subsequent behavior while in uniform, a man could, if he met all the conditions of the force, continue to reengage as many times as he wished until he was well beyond forty years of age. Thus, the total annual figures given in table 2 represent men at various stages of seniority, from new recruits undergoing training at the headquarters to, say, a forty-one-year-old sergeant major who had recently reengaged for several years.[3] Ideally one would want to know the percentages of men in each of these categories in order to calculate new recruits, discharges, and reengagements each year. The commandants of the Papuan Constabulary established a tradition from the beginning and, in compliance with official regulation, furnished detailed information in their annual reports. For some unknown reason, the demonstrated commitment of earlier years declined in the late 1920s; the last full report is reproduced as figure 1.

From the information provided, it appears that during the year 1928–29, 64 men left the force for various reasons, and 41 attested (excluding 16 local constables), bringing the total for the start of the new year to 261 men of all ranks, a reduction of police numbers from the previous year of 23 men. As this total includes only 41 new recruits, 220 men were already in the force the previous year, including the 72 men reengaged, and the rest at various stages of their last signed terms.

Had this style of compilation continued into the 1960s, it would have facilitated precise calculations for Papua. Unfortunately, after the mid-1920s, Papua adopted the methods used in New Guinea. For instance, a typical New Guinea annual report on the police establishment included only general information, as is shown in figure 2 for the year 1926–27.

While this report has some useful information on the composition of the New Guinea police—the nature of changes to their training methods, distribution, discipline, and attainment of new skills in the 1920s—it lacks the range of specific detail of the early Papuan police reports, which give insights into recruitments, reengagements, discharges, and so on every year. Because of the absence of such detail in the later years for both territories, I have used the yearly establishment figures, where available, as the basis for calculating the totals that appear in table 2. Beyond what I have calculated here and in the table, it is not possible to know how many men enrolled during the period 1920–1960, or which districts or divisions supplied the greatest number of men each year for the forty years under investigation.

Table 2 Numbers of police in Papua and New Guinea, 1890–1960

| Year | Papuan Armed Constabulary | | | New Guinea Police Force | |
	Papuans	European officers[a]	Others[b]	New Guineans[c]	European officers[d]
1890–1891	13	3	14		
1891–1892	49	2	10		
1892–1893	45	1	10		
1893–1894	60	1	4		
1894–1895	67	2	1		
1895–1896	78	2	0		
1896–1897	108	2	1		
1897–1898	110	na	0		
1898–1899	na	na	0		
1899–1900	115	1	0		
1900–1901	130	1	0		
1901–1902	150	1	0		
1902–1903	150	2	0		
1903–1904[e]	150 (162)	1	0		
1904–1905	150	1	0		
1905–1906	160	1	0		
1906–1907	185	1	0		
1907–1908[e]	185 (188)	1	0		
1908–1909	216	1	0		
1909–1910	213	1	0		
1910–1911[e]	235 (236)	2	0		
1911–1912	221	2	0		
1912–1913	250	6[f]	0		
1913–1914	287	3	0		
1914–1915	na	2	0		
1915–1916	287	2	0		
1916–1917	295	1	0		
1917–1918	300	1	0		
1918–1919	340	1	0		
1919–1920	340	1	na		
1920–1921[e]	350 (345)	1	0		
1921–1922	250[g]	1	0	445	na
1922–1923	na	1	0	484	6
1923–1924	257	9[h]	0	506	6
1924–1925	260	1	0	506	6
1925–1926	272	1	0	506	6
1926–1927	284	1	0	611	10
1927–1928	284	1	0	588	10
1928–1929	na	na	na	535	18
1929–1930	na	na	na	643	26
1930–1931	na	na	na	575	29
1931–1932	na	na	na	497	29
1932–1933	na	na	na	633	29

Table 2—*Continued*

Year	Papuan Armed Constabulary			New Guinea Police Force	
	Papuans	*European officers[a]*	*Others[b]*	*New Guineans[c]*	*European officers[d]*
1933–1934	na	na	na	704	31
1934–1935	na	na	na	706	34
1935–1936	296[i]	na	na	748	33
1936–1937	na	na	na	841	34
1937–1938	na	na	na	883	35
1938–1939	na	na	na	934	37
1939–1940	na	na	na	1,115	37
1940–1945	1,334[j]	na	0		
1941–1945				1,803[j]	na
1946–1947	943	21	0	1,357	37
1947–1948	1,344	21	0	1,357	37
1948–1949	1,112	20	0	1,236	22
1949–1950	1,112	63[k]	0	1,544	29
1950–1951	982	63	0	1,246	29
1951–1952	1,116	19	0	1,324	30
1952–1953	1,133	24	0	1,391	28
1953–1954	1,025	21	0	1,541	30
1954–1955	1,051	25	0	1,488	38
1955–1956	1,110	27	0	1,579	37
1956–1957	1,115	28	0	1,755	38
1957–1958	1,043	30	0	1,688	44
1958–1959	1,051	37	0	1,728	42
1959–1960	1,200	35	0	1,775	40

Sources: PAR 1890–1960; NGAR 1921–1962; others as noted.

Notes: a Includes only white officers appointed as commandants of the Armed Constabulary. All government officers in charge of detachments had the rank of European officer of the Armed Constabulary.

b Includes 2 Fijian noncommissioned officers and 12 Solomon Islanders who formed the first nucleus of the Armed Constabulary in 1890. By the end of 1897 the only foreigners in the Armed Constabulary were the European officers.

c Includes noncommissioned officers and constables. The numbers for the war years do not include those who served as police for the Japanese.

d Includes European constabulary "proper" from the Australian police forces.

e Total establishment figures do not match recruitment numbers for the relevant annual reports. There appear to be errors in the arithmetic. Numbers in parentheses are author's corrections.

f This is an unusual increase because patrol officers, in addition to the commandant, were mentioned as police officers.

g In June 1921 a decision was made to reduce the number of police to 250 from a strength of 345 men (PAR 1920–1921, 64).

h Includes patrol officers as well as "proper" trained policemen from the Australian police forces.

i Australia: "Police Forces. . . ."

j Numbers for 1940–1945 and 1941–1945 represent totals enlisted.

k There was a dramatic increase in the number of European officers in these years. Variations were made in the organization of the police force, but no reasons were given for the increase.

Armed Constabulary

(Report by) T. R. Horan, Acting Head-quarters Officer.

302. The establishment of the armed constabulary is 284, and the distribution [is] as follows:—

Daru	30	Abau	12	Cape Nelson	15
Kikori	30	Samarai	26	Buna	16
Kerema	18	Bwagaoia	10	Kokoda	16
Kambisi	22	Kulumandau	3	Ioma	16
Kairuku	12	Losuia	2	Head-quarters	34
Eigo	10	Baniara	12		
				Total	284

During the year the following increases were made in detachments:—Samarai 5, Daru 6, Kikori 9, and Kambisi 7.

Re-engagements and time expired.

303. One hundred and thirteen non-commissioned officers and men became time expired, of this number 72 re-engaged for further service, varying from one to three years.

Discharges.

304.	Time expired	41
	Medically unfit	9
	Misconduct	5
	Desertion	3
	Total	58

Attestations.

305. Fifty-seven men were attested during the year, of this number 16 were local* constables.

* Recruits for the Papuan Armed Constabulary were deployed wherever they were needed. In contrast, local constables worked only in their own areas and were one category of village officials, not policemen as such. Local constables have been excluded from the calculations.

Transfers.

306. Eighty-four non-commissioned officers and men were transferred between out-stations and head-quarters during the year.

Deaths.

307. Six men died during the year from the following causes:—

Pneumonia	3
Heart failure	1
Accidentally drowned	1
Accidentally killed	1
Total	6

Health.

308. Apart from the usual colds and malaria, the health of the men has been very good.

Discipline.

309. During the year 148 offences were recorded; of these 116 were for petty breaches of discipline, and 32 for forbidden acts; these figures are much lower than many of the preceding years.

Three local constables deserted after only two weeks service; apparently they had not settled down in their new environment.

Figure 1   The last full report on the Papuan Constabulary
Source: Papua Annual Report 1927–28, 39.

Part xv – Miscellaneous
Military Clauses of Mandate

242. No military or naval bases have been established and no fortifications have been erected in the Territory.

There are no military organizations in the Territory, and the only military training received by the natives is given to the police for disciplinary and instructional purposes in connexion with the discharge of their police duties.

New Guinea Police Force.

243. The European police establishment consists of a Superintendent of Police, five permanent and three temporary warrant officers (constables), a drill instructor and a clerk.

In addition, the following are *ex officio* members of the Force:—

> The District Inspector, who is *ex officio* Senior Inspector of Police.
> All District Officers, who are *ex officio* Inspectors of Police.
> All Patrol Officers, who are *ex officio* Warrant Officers of Police.

244. The number of native police in the Territory is 611, distributed as follows:—

Depot and Rabaul	217
District of New Britain	80
District of Morobe	51
District of Madang	42
District of Aitape	50
District of Sepik	30
District of Manus	37
District of Kavieng	26
District of Namatanai	33
District of Kieta	45
Total	611

Only intelligent natives of good physique and character are admitted to the police force. They are usually selected by the District Officers, from volunteers.

The native police receive training in:—

a. Squad drill with and without arms, platoon drill, extended order drill, musketry, guard and sentry duties;
b. the duties of prison warders;
c. police work in townships — the prevention of crime and the apprehension of criminals;
d. fire brigade duties;
e. patrol work (when drafted to out-stations).

Discipline is a special feature of the training of all native police, but particularly of those employed on out-stations who may be called upon to accompany District Officers on patrols to new or disturbed areas.

Under the direction of experienced and able officers, a high standard of efficiency is reached by the native police.

Figure 2   A typical annual report on the New Guinea police establishment
Source: Australia 1927, 89.

A career in the respective police forces began only after selection and eventual recruitment by authorized officers. On the whole, recruits represented some of the best young men in the land in terms of physique and intelligence.[4] In accordance with each community's social and political organization, many were sons of chiefs,[5] and others of big-men. These sons most likely aspired to achieve or inherit positions of influence similar to those of their fathers. But their parents could not know that before their sons reached maturity they would be wearing police uniforms and, armed with a .303 Lee-Enfield, traversing paths far beyond their own lands.

In the rest of this chapter discussion is confined to the initial stage of recruitment, focusing attention on the selection process and the men's eventual recruitment into the police forces. During the period 1985 to 1989 I interviewed 28 former policemen, 1 former local constable, 2 village constables, and 5 villagers. Of the twenty-eight ex-policemen interviewed, one had served as a village constable for two years in prewar Papua, and the rest had all heard of and seen police work and practice before their own recruitment. The majority of those interviewed came from Papua: 13 former policemen, 1 former local constable, 2 former village constables, and 3 villagers. Of the total of those interviewed, 13 were recruited from the Papuan region.[6]

The testimonies of three men interviewed in 1989, one New Guinean and two Papuans, confirm those of many of the other men—that during the 1950s they worked in either territory without making any fundamental changes in their working habits.[7] Beu, of Oro Province, also said that, as a result of close kinship ties in the Waria, most of his youth was spent in the Morobe District where he observed closely German and later Australian police at work. He felt that his own police work in Papua was influenced more by New Guinean than Papuan police practice, which he saw later intermittently as a village constable.

As a group, the ex-policemen represent hundreds of others, a number of whom are still alive and others long dead, who through no fault of their own left no written records. Obviously this cannot be claimed as a statistically representative sample. One justification for this collective study, through the oral testimony of a few, is that apart from individual idiosyncrasies they, as individuals, and as a group, held similar aspirations, but endured a variety of experiences.[8] Their testimonies enrich and balance the official records, memoirs of patrol officers, and comments by observers.

Introducing the Men

The men interviewed came from a wide geographical and administrative area, representing what was from 1949 to June 1971 Papua and

Selected Police Recruits by District

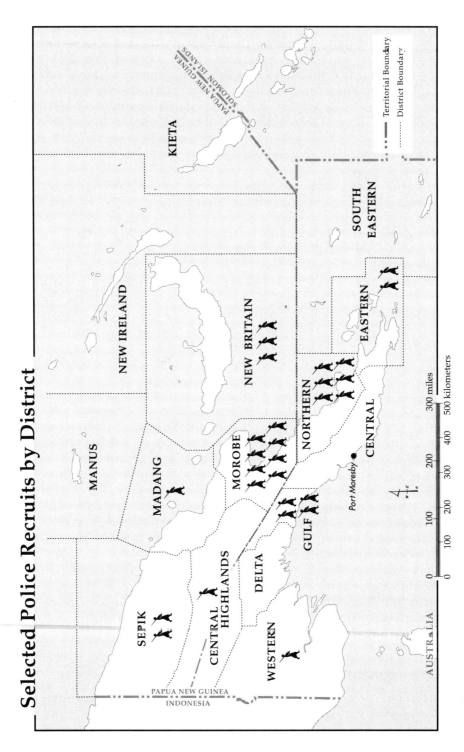

Map 2

Table 3 Names and length of service of selected police recruits, by district or division

NEW GUINEA

District	Name	Period of Service
Sepik (2)	Naguwean	1942–1971
	Kambian	1956–?
Madang (1)	Petrus Tigavu	1944–1977
Central Highlands (1)	Tate Sarepamo	1943–1968
Morobe (8)	Sakarias Anka	1934–1967
	Piaka Empere	1956–1981
	Aladu Iwagu Iaking	1931–?
	Sasa Goreg	1939–1945
	Kamuna Hura	1923–1954
	Moru Moag	1956–1964
	Sesetta	1938–1972
	Sono	1936–?
New Britain (3)	Kasse Aibuki	1934–?
	Amero Bega	1934–1941
	Ben Elipas ToWoworu	1936–1954

PAPUA

Division	Name	Period of Service
Northern (6)	Athanasius Mandembo Igarobae	1942–1967
	John Boino	1941–1950
	Sebastin Goro	1941–?
	Rewari	1942–1966
	Jojoga Yegova	1943–1974
	Beu Iworo	1940–1961
Eastern (2)	Peter Panau Daguna	1951–1978
	John Guise	1946–1954
Western (1)	Naguna Tamutai	1942–1981
Gulf (4)	Mohaviea Loholo	1947–1982
	Meraveka	1947–?
	James Ori Evara	1953–1983
	Lelesi Orovea	1952–1982

Note: Numbers in parentheses show the distribution of the policemen. See map 2.

Source: Interviews.

New Guinea.[9] Of the 13 ex-policemen recruited from various parts of Papua, 6 were recruited from the Northern Division; 2 from the North-Eastern Division; 4 from the Gulf Division, and 1 from Western Division (map 2; table 3). The local constable was recruited in the Kunimaipa area of Goilala and served only part of his term in the region before resigning from the service. The two village constables came from diverse social and cultural backgrounds in Papua—the Southern Highlands and the wild Goilala territory.

Of the 15 men of the New Guinea police force, 3 enlisted from the New Guinea Islands; 2 enrolled at Goroka, in the present-day Eastern Highlands Province; and the remaining 10 came from coastal main-land New Guinea (2 from the Sepik region, and the other 8 from the Morobe District (including 4 from the Markham Valley and 3 from Garaina). The oral evidence of these men, collected during almost four-teen months of field and archival work between 1985 and 1989 testifies to the processes involved from the beginning to the end of their careers, and forms the basis of this and subsequent chapters. Some of the men were, of course, more articulate than others and expressed opinions much more clearly. Some, in their old age, did not remember the finer details of their work, while still others talked of conquering Papua New Guinea without anyone else's support. The responses received were varied and filled with nostalgia, sentimentality, humor, and egotism. They expose the policemen's wide-ranging experiences in an occupa-tion that had no precedent in their own society. Wherever necessary other source materials are used to elaborate and clarify points. How-ever, it is not possible to check all oral evidence against written docu-ments, because often no written documents exist. Under this circum-stance, I have been forced to work with the raw evidence as presented to me by the men. I am well aware that new political developments, changing moral values, and just old age may have altered perceptions of things observed on active service. However, because the general re-sponse has been "I was hoping that one day someone would come and take an account of my career in the police force," it may be assumed that their willing cooperation has resulted in frankness. It is my firm belief that the information divulged represents the release of a long yearning to be heard and remembered.

In what follows, an attempt has been made to answer the following questions: Who were these men before recruitment? How familiar were they with government patrols and the work of the policemen? What were the recruiting procedures, and why were they recruited?

The men were recruited at various stages of their lives.

At thirteen years of age, John BOINO of Obea village, Tufi, Oro Province, was the youngest man to enlist into the Australia New

Guinea Administrative Unit's (ANGAU) police force in 1941 (photo 1). The sense of hopelessness presented by the war for those who had left their villages was the circumstance of his recruitment. On account of his age, he was not employed in any capacity in the introduced cash economy but was raised in the small administrative center and port of Buna. Boino and his elder brother left their village and the rest of their family at an early age and lived with their

Photo 1   John Boino seated in front of his Laloki home. The land was given to him by the army in appreciation of his services to both the police force and the army. (20 September 1989)

uncle, then employed as a prison warder at Buna. While there,
Boino attended a government school. When the war came he
could not go home, so he enlisted along with his elder brother
and approximately two hundred others from the region. It took
them two weeks to reach Abau for their introduction into a life
that was disciplined and unfamilar. For the duration of the war he
supervised carriers bringing supplies to the front line at Kokoda.

Before engagement, BEU worked on Sogeri's rubber plantation
for three years during the 1930s before becoming an "unofficial"
village constable in late 1937 (photo 2). This experience came
quite by accident to Beu Iworo (phonetic) of Tave village, Ioma,
Northern Division on the border between Oro and Morobe Provinces. In his youth, and for much of his adult life, Beu and his
people enjoyed trade and other friendly relations established by
their ancestors with the people of Morobe. Beu saw New Guinean
police at work in Morobe during his many trips there, and had the
benefit of observing policemen of both territories before his own
recruitment. As a consequence of Anglican missionary influence

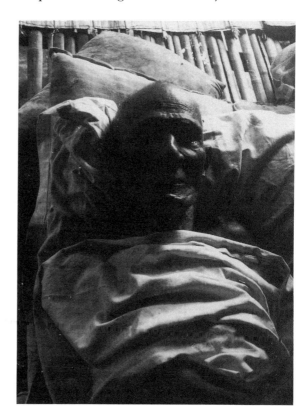

Photo 2 After a short
illness, Beu Iworo
had been bedridden
for two years and
depended on rela-
tives for all his needs.
(6 December 1989)

in the area, the people of Tave and the surrounding villages made a point of walking the long track to Ioma for Christmas celebrations each year. The lure of the Christian festive season of December 1937 was no exception. Led by Karatok, Beu's elder brother and the village constable of Tave, men, women, and children of the village braved the precipitous track[10] and walked to Ioma. During the festivities an argument raged between Karatok and the wife of Koge; Karatok, a government agent not known to control his aggressive impulses, assaulted the woman and was charged and put in prison at Ioma. Consequently Beu, second in line to the leadership of the Tave people, had succeeded his brother as the village constable by early 1938. For the next two years he made routine checks of conditions of houses and toilets, intervened in fights, and kept the village census book up to date. In addition, he occasionally accompanied constables from neighboring villages to recapture escaped prisoners or track down and arrest troublemakers. Whenever an arrest was made, the guilty person was handcuffed, brought back, and handed over to the patrol officer and the policemen of the station. In 1940, when calls were made for young men to enlist in the Papuan Infantry Battalion, Beu and his brother Karatok, residing in the village after the short term of imprisonment, enlisted at Ioma. Soon after, accompanied by other young men, they walked to Abau and continued on to Sogeri for a rushed training and eventual active duty. According to Beu, the officer in charge of the Papuan Infantry Battalion did not think it wise for two brothers to join the same military organization. Consequently Beu joined ANGAU's police force.

Eight others had experience of work in European-run enterprises as domestic servants, as carriers, in gold mines, and as general crew on ships and trawlers. Their terms of employment extended from one to sixteen years.

Of this group of eight men, John GUISE (later Sir John) was the oldest (photo 3). He was born on 29 August 1914 and was recruited into the Royal Papuan Constabulary in 1946, at the age of thirty-two. Previously, Guise had worked for the Burns Philp Company for sixteen years from 1926 to 1942 in Samarai, where he was born. At the time of his recruitment he had been educated up to grade four. Of his physique he recalled, "I was thirty-two years, I was a sportsman. I am damned sure that I had a good physique" (Guise 1985). Among others, his favorite sport was cricket. By 1946 he had married his second wife from Lalaura village in Central Province. Guise, with his normal fluency, spoke of the police as a great moral force. He believed the police forces of the era established a "noble tradition" and their work showed no blemish (Guise 1985) The record of his interview reveals him as overly protective toward the force of which he was once a proud member.

Peter Panau DAGUNA was from Bogaboga village in the Milne Bay Province (photo 4). At the time of my interview he lived in Gerehu and had been living in Port Moresby for some thirty years. Panau worked on a boat, a government trawler, in Milne Bay. After an unexpected trip to Port Moresby, he learned of vacancies in the army, made inquiries, and enlisted in the Pacific Islands Regiment in 1951. After only four years, he was lured away by memories of his father's outstanding record in the Royal Papuan Constabulary, and joined the Papuan police force in 1955 (Panau 1986). In other words, he followed a tradition established by his father in prewar Papua.

NAGUWEAN of Wantogik village, Dagua, in the East Sepik Province and Sono of Kasu, in Garaina, Morobe District, both left their homes at an early age and worked in the gold mines of Bulolo and Wau. Naguwean, a well built man, enlisted in 1942 after only two years in the mines, at the approximate age of twenty-two (photo 5). He received no formal education and first saw a European when a recruiting official went to his village in the late 1930s (J Naguwean 1985). According to his son Joseph, who volunteered information about his father and his work in the Royal Papua New Guinea Constabulary, he was a forthright man who believed that a little force was necessary to keep "belligerent communities under control." Naguwean died in 1975, four years after he retired from the New Guinea police force after serving twenty-nine years.

SONO came from Kasu village, Garaina, Morobe District. He enlisted in 1936 at the age of about eighteen, through the influence of his "cousin brother" who was already a sergeant in the New Guinea police force (photo 6). Sono spent most of his police career in the Islands areas (Talasea, West New Britain District). Though he had only fond memories of the police force, he was vague, and his recollections were not as revealing as some of the others'. Both his wives had died and he was left with four children, three sons and one daughter. Sono's first wife was from Bougainville and was the mother of his first son, who lived in Kasu. His second wife, the mother of the younger children, was from his own village, Kasu. This is just one example of the mixing of genes resulting from policemen moving about the territories (Sono 1985).

Photo 3 Sir John Guise. This photograph was given to me by Sir John after I interviewed him. (9 February 1985)

Photo 4 Peter Panau Daguna standing near his home in Gerehu, Port Moresby. (2 August 1986)

Photo 5 Naguwean, the policeman. The number indicates his placing in the New Guinea police.

Photo 6 Sono with his war decorations at Garaina subdistrict. (5 May 1985)

Talasea proved a strange place for young AMERO Bega when he was brought in from his village on Nukakau Island, off the southwest of West New Britain, to work as a kitchen hand in about 1929 (photo 7). This was his first exposure to a European settlement, and he decided quickly that he could not adjust to a clock-dominated life and returned to Nukakau. On 14 October 1934 a recruiting team came from Rabaul and, after much persuasion from both the government officer and the government appointed *luluai* and *tultul* of the village, he placed his mark on the enrollment paper. Two days later he traveled by canoe to Talasea station, and the following day boarded a ship to Rabaul with fifteen others from the Talasea subdistrict for training at the police depot (Amero 1985). During my interview he showed himself to be alert, holding vivid memories, and a very social person, inclined to exaggerate and be verbose. He was impressive in his ability to retain minute details, and his only regret was that he did not receive a pension. His fine physique had deteriorated to such an extent that he walked with a permanent stoop and with the aid of a stick. As his only sister was too old to look after him, Amero depended on communal assistance for his daily sustenance.

TIGAVU (no photo taken) of Yandera village, Gende (Bundi[11]), Madang Province, worked as a domestic servant for the newly established Catholic mission station[12] in Guiebi village in about 1936, and enlisted in the force in Goroka, after the war had passed through the area in 1944. Once married with two wives, both of whom were living apart from him and from each other, he lived with his eldest son in Madang before he died in 1986. (One of his wives was a Gende, the other a foreigner.) At the conclusion of the interview in 1985, he exposed an arrow wound and beamed, "I was in the thick of it up in the Highlands."

Jojoga YEGOVA, a burly man in his late fifties came from Buna, Oro Province (photo 8). A chief by birth, with a sharp tongue acquired through discipline, he was the epitome of the strict sergeant major. When the war came he volunteered for a carrier's job and spent the whole of 1942 assisting in the campaign in the Buna area for the Allied Forces. At the end of that year, he grew bored as a carrier and enlisted in the wartime police in 1943, at the approximate age of seventeen. After Yegova retired from the Royal Papua New Guinea Constabulary in 1974, he returned to his village and resumed the life of a subsistence farmer (Yegova 1985).

Photo 7   Amero Bega on Nukakau Island, Talasea subdistrict, West New Britain. (2 March 1985)

Photo 8   Jojoga Yegova standing at the edge of Buna village. Behind him is the *haus win* (rest house) normally used for entertaining guests. (13 December 1989)

Photo 9   Ben Elipas ToWoworu in front of his house in Konedobu. The house was built on reclaimed land. (20 February 1985)

Ben Elipas ToWoworu came from Dawaun village, Kokopo (photo 9). He was of slight build and insisted that physically he had not changed much over the years. He maintained a stance reminiscent of a man who has spent long years at hard physical labor. He appeared to be a person of fortitude and humane temperament. At the time of his enlistment in 1936, he was completing grade three in the government primary school at Malaguna. Fortunately for him, he was one of the few men selected by David Crawley to become a member of the police band started by Crawley in 1938. ToWoworu claimed himself a "citizen" of Papua on account of his living on reclaimed land in Konedobu since World War II. He died in 1987 or 1988 (ToWoworu 1985).

These ten men had regular exposure to European ways prior to their recruitment. John Guise, Beu, Panau, Naguwean, and Sono had han-

Photo 10 Meraveka, at the time of my interview, lived with his family at Nine-Mile, about fifteen minutes' drive from Port Moresby. (June 1985)

Photo 11 James Ori Evara lived at the Erima settlement with relatives from the Gulf region. (June 1985)

dled money, the last two earning as much as four shillings a month.[13] Boino, Guise, Panau, Jojoga, and ToWoworu, grew up in, or close to European permanent settlements at Samarai, Buna, and Kokopo.

The remaining eighteen men had not traveled beyond the confines of their own tribal territories, or outside the areas of their traditional trading partners for work in the cash economy when recruiting officers first came to their villages. Meraveka, Evara, Loholo, and Orovea of the Gulf Division had all been to London Missionary Society schools in the area before they volunteered for police service in 1947 and the early 1950s (photos 10, 11, 12, 13). The mission was established before they were born. Athanasius Igarobae of Ioma and Rewari of Musa, in Tufi, Northern Province, also had some contact with Christianity before their recruitment in 1942 (photos 14, 15). Rewari was posted to Samarai in 1946. In 1956 he was transferred to Lae and worked there for two years before being again transferred to work in Mt Hagen in 1958 (Rewari

Photo 12   Mohaviea Loholo was elected chairman of the village magistrate's court following his retirement from the police force in 1982. He lived at Erima settlement, close to Evara and Orovea. (Klaus Neumann, 1986)

Photo 13   At the time of the interview in 1985, Lelesi Orovea was unemployed and lived off his monthly pension money. He lived near Evara and Loholo. (June 1985)

1989). Iwagu Iaking Aladu was born in Taemi, Finschhafen, in 1911 (photo 16). He received some education as a Lutheran Mission "teacher" and taught in the school for two years before being recruited by Patrol Officer Kail (phonetic)[14] in 1931, at the age of twenty. At seventy-five he was agile and looked ten years younger (Iwagu 1986). In preparation for adult life, Anka Sakarias, Sasa Goreg, Moru Moag, and Piaka Empere from the Markham Valley, Morobe Province, were being "schooled" to become subsistence farmers when, following a request from the district office in Lae, they signed up at the Lae office (photos 17, 18, 19, 20). Anka, who was originally from Mukip village, enlisted in 1934. Much of his police career was spent in the highlands. He then lived permanently at Okiufa village, Goroka. Sasa Goreg was training at the police training depot in Rabaul in 1939 when news of the war

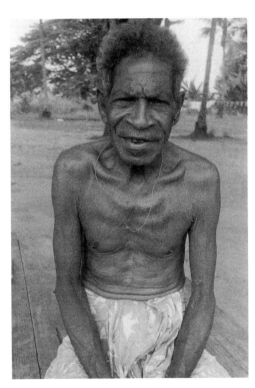

Photo 14 Not long after he retired, Athanasius Igarobae became actively involved in church activities, in particular the Christian Revival Crusade. He operated out of his village in Ioma. (10 December 1989)

Photo 15 Rewari resigned in 1966 after twenty-four years in the police force and settled at Laloki. His family lives behind Boino. (29 September 1989)

in Europe reached Rabaul. Moru Moag and Piaka Empere, who were from the same village as Sasa Goreg—Gabsongekek, Markham Valley— enlisted in the early 1950s. Empere worked mostly in the lowland areas, but also worked some of the time in Papua, principally in the Western Division. Goro of Sanananda was a formidable man who still walked

Photo 16 Iwagu Iaking Aladu in Taemi village, Finschhafen.
(Klaus Neumann, 22 November 1986)

straight "like a leech" when interviewed (photo 21). He enlisted in the
wartime police in 1941. Sesetta of Garasa, Garaina, was of slight build
and spoke with a soft voice (photo 22). He retired from the Royal
Papua New Guinea Constabulary in 1972 and returned to live in his village, Au. During the interview, he was alert and remembered his police
service with nostalgia (Sesetta 1985). Kasse of Nukakau, Talasea, enlisted on the same day as Amero, 14 September 1934 (photo 23). In his
view, the police force did nothing for him. On his return to his village
he received no pension and lived the life of a simple subsistence farmer
(Kasse 1985). When he was not working in his gardens on the mainland, he helped his son make copra to sell for a little cash in Kimbe.

When SAREPAMO of Okiufa, Goroka, was born in the early
1920s, no European had entered the Goroka Valley (photo 24).
Sarepamo was the son of a highlands big-man and, though big

Photo 17   Anka Sakarias of Mukip,
Markham Valley. (July 1985)

Photo 18   Of the interviewed policemen, only Sasa Goreg worked for the
Japanese as a policeman. (12 August
1986)

physically, had neither the reputation nor the popularity of his father. He was already about ten years old when he first saw a white man, and then only briefly. However, by the time of his recruitment into the wartime police in 1943, Goroka had a small European population and soon became the administrative center for the whole of the highlands region (Sarepamo 1985). In 1985 Sarepamo owned a coffee plantation, a village *nait klab* (disco), and was an elected village court magistrate.

Of the eighteen men, KAMUNA Hura of Wakaia, Garaina, was the oldest, having joined the police force in 1923 (photo 25; Sesiguo 1977, 244). He was the last of his generation to be inducted into his traditional initiation house which resembled, if not in style, then in reputation, the Sepik *haus tambaran*.[15] His people were still engaged in fierce tribal fighting among other Waria tribes and against the Goilala people from the other side of the Owen Stanley Range. He had heard of, but had not seen, a European

Photo 19 Moru Moag at Gabsongekeg village, Markham Valley. (11 August 1986)

Photo 20 Piaka Empere at Gabsongekeg village, Markham Valley. (11 August 1986)

before he was recruited by a sergeant major of the New Guinea police force, possibly because in his youth his people lived on "mountains" for security reasons; Europeans passed through the valley below (Sesiguo 1977, 221). He had seen policemen and carriers on a number of occasions before his enlistment. Kamuna died on 22 September 1987, aged about eighty-one.

The last two men of this category of recruits are Kambian of Parandi village, Ambunti, East Sepik; and Naguna Tamutai of Oropai village, Bamu, Western Province (photos 26 and 27). Both men had seen policemen and patrol officers at work in their respective locations on a regular basis before their own recruitment—Tamutai in 1942 and Kambian in 1956. In the case of Tamutai, the Western Division, of which Bamu is an integral part, was among the first government centers to be

Photo 21 Sebastin Goro of Sanananda village, near Yegova's house, Buna. (26 June 1985)

Photo 22   Sesetta of Au village, Garaina. (10 May 1985)

Photo 23   Kasse Aibuki of Nukakau village, Talasea subdistrict. (26 March 1985)

Photo 24 Sarepamo Tate near his
"Nait Klab," Okiufa village, Goroka.
(25 July 1985)

Photo 25 Kamuna Hura
at Bumbu settlement, Lae.
(17 May 1985)

established (*PAR* 1891, 85), providing not only the first, but also some of
the best and longest serving recruits in the armed constabulary's history. Both Kambian and Tamutai married women from the Southern
Highlands. After retirement, Kambian settled among his in-laws in
Mendi, as did Tamutai, who lived with his son Mathew, a lawyer who
had graduated from the University of Papua New Guinea.

With the exception of Guise, Tamutai, Rewari, and Tigavu,[16] the
majority of the men had fathers of some status. Most spoke of their
fathers as being "big-men," men who were fight leaders and orators,
who organized festivities, accumulated wealth, and married more than
one wife. Reed identified some of the things the men referred to when
they described their father's status:

> The "big men" in any mainland society become such not by succes-
> sion, but through qualities of leadership displayed in the various
> active spheres of tribal life. They are social rather than political
> leaders, and their prerogatives, on strictly institutional grounds,

are no greater than those of any other villager. Although they may serve at times as arbiters in intra-group quarrels, this is owing to their superior knowledge of tribal custom. If a man is physically strong, a good fighter, blows the flutes well, knows many songs, and is a tireless dancer, he gains the reputation of being a "big man." (Reed 1943, 51)

A particular example is provided by Bateson, about the Iatmul people of Sepik:

Certain men become influential in various ways: by a form of shamanism, by wealth, by magical power, by forceful character, and intrigue, by prestige in war, by mythological knowledge, and by possessing powerful relatives. This last factor introduces an element of succession, but of an unformulated kind. (Bateson 1932, 257–258)

In other words, "the qualities which make a 'big man' are achieved rather than ascribed" (Reed 1943, 51).

Photo 26 Kambian lived in Mendi, Southern Highlands, after retirement, on his monthly pension of K122.87. (18 October 1985)

Photo 27 Naguna Tamutai also lived in Mendi following his retirement. (18 October 1989)

Of the twenty-eight men, Yegova alone claimed to be the son of a "chief." His father had inherited the title from his grandfather, and now that his father was dead, he and his elder brother held the title of chief of the Sebaga Andere subclan, in Buna, Oro Province. As chief, their father settled disputes, was in charge of festivities, conducted rituals before communal fishing, and generally was the spokesman for the people (Yegova 1985).

The status of Sesetta's father appears to be an anomaly. He was held in high esteem and referred to often as a big-man, not because he was a fighter or a man with a great deal of wealth, but simply because he had the capacity to restore peace between hostile groups. In other words, he mediated among and for his people. "My father was not a fight leader but he was a peacemaker. After trouble had erupted he would try and make peace between the parties. Other men with more robust and boisterous characters took on leadership roles which were more aggressive, befitting their nature" (Sesetta 1985).

At the time of recruitment, an important feature of the men (except Guise) was their youth. As it was not the common practice in village communities to bestow positions of responsibility on young men, the majority of them were only observers and inexperienced in the ways of their people. Although their fathers held positions of authority and responsibility, they themselves were young men of no particular status. They merely aspired to achieve or inherit the status of their fathers.

Though none of the men interviewed had been prisoners at any stage of their lives, they knew of recruits who had been convicted of an offense, and had served a term or more in jail. It appears, particularly during the early period of colonial administration, that a number of the men in the ranks of the police force were ex-prisoners, who, at some earlier stage of their lives, had been convicted criminals. "Criminals," in the context used here, refers to persons found guilty of what a westerner considered a crime. To a Papua New Guinean of the time it may have been an accepted form of behavior. For instance, a murder to a Papua New Guinean living before the advent of white men, was construed to have been "sometimes a duty, sometimes a necessary part of social etiquette, sometimes a relaxation, and always a passion" (Murray 1923, 10). In an address to an attentive audience in London, Murray generalized:

> [W]e have no criminal class in Papua. For instance, most of the crimes which we call murder, and punish in our courts, are to the Papuan no crimes at all. To him the act which we regard as an offence against the law is perhaps the discharge of a sacred duty to a relative whose death he is avenging, or a matter of social eti-

quette, or an act of courtesy to oblige a friend, or perhaps it may be due to a natural and even laudable desire to prove that he is not a milk-sop, and to gain the good opinion of the women of the village; but the offence rarely amounts to anything more than a compliance with native custom, and the offender has, generally speaking, only been carrying out the traditions of his tribe or village. (Murray 1931, 572)

And more to the point:

Thus a Papuan will confess, without shame and even with complacency, to have committed a murder which seems to us revolting and treacherous in the extreme. Such a case is reported by Mr. Humphries from the North-Eastern Division. Two men, he says, came to his camp and told him that they were guilty of some rather bad murders for which they had no reason, except that two women had asked them to kill certain persons. They had themselves no object to gain, and had probably never before seen their victims; when asked why they had obeyed these women they could only answer "because." Such cases are not uncommon, and no Papuan would feel the slightest difficulty in understanding the motives of these men and in applauding their action; but a case which certainly seemed rather strange to me was one in which Romney, a mission native, and his wife Hilda, were murdered by a man called Baiburu and others. For in this case the murderers appeared as hired assassins, who had been paid to kill these unfortunates, whom they had themselves no wish to injure. Baiburu's story was that he happened to go to Komabun village, and that certain people, whom he did not know but could identify, proposed to him that he should kill Romney and Hilda as they came to their garden, which was described to him. The victims were to be speared; poisoning, he was told, was unsatisfactory. He did not, he insisted, kill Romney and Hilda "for nothing"; he had good ground for killing them inasmuch as he was paid for it. (Murray in PAR 1928–1929, 9 [item 22])

Because of this conflict, and because western laws were imposed on an unsuspecting Papua New Guinean community still engaged in tribal feuds, murders, and cannibalism, many of the ringleaders were arrested and brought to the main station for imprisonment. During or after their terms of imprisonment, many joined the respective police forces. Jack Hides, with his eye on a popular title, borrowed from Murray and called these men *Savages in Serge*.[17] At least in the Papuan service, it became a common term for the armed constabulary. Frequently, it was used as a synonym for the police force because it was believed to give

expression to the popularly held view of the time that these men were
"savages" who were "civilized" after their term in gaol; only then were
they considered suitable to wear the blue serge uniform. The transformation was seen as evidence of the effectiveness and morality of Australian policy. Since many of these men had been leaders in their own
communities and had the added advantage of being educated in the
ways of the white man, they were in a better position to transfer this
new knowledge to their people. In much of the available literature on
their activities, many were said to be influential in making known to
their people the ways of the colonial government in their capacities as
policemen, carriers, or simply as returned prisoners. Jack Hides was
one of the many colonial officers who had the greatest admiration for
these ex-prisoners. His esteem for them is revealed in a passage in
Savages in Serge: "I shall always think of them as *'Savages in Serge'*, for
many of the best have served sentences for murder. I have told
how, killing in accordance with tribal right, they had come to the jails,
and then acquired understanding; and how with pride they went from
the prison walls to don the serge *dabua* and help bring understanding
to their peoples in all the hostile corners of the land" (Hides 1938,
229–230).

Familiarity of Recruits with Government and Police Work

The responses of the men varied. However, it is obvious that the degree
of familiarity depended on the proximity of a person's home to an area
of European settlement. On the one hand, those whose villages were
closest to white settlements grew up seeing Europeans—government
officers, missionaries, traders, and naturally government patrols and
the work of the policemen—on a regular basis. The villages of these
men—John Guise, Yegova, Panau, and ToWoworu—were close to European towns—Samarai, Buna, Lae, and Kokopo. Also included in this
category would be men who were born into societies already under government control but whose villages were located some distance away,
with irregular contact, perhaps, two or three times a year. Such was the
observation of Sono of Kasu, Garaina:

> Later in my youth I learnt from my people that Garaina had been
> subjected to government control from Lae sometime before I was
> born. As for myself, I was a small boy with no clothes on when I
> first saw a European kiap. We were told that his name was Robin-
> son.[18] When he came, he took our names and wrote them in a
> [census] book. He was accompanied by some policemen and car-
> riers. After this visit, government patrols were regular, perhaps,
> three times a year. (Sono 1985)

As a child Tamutai had similar experiences with policemen and patrol officers. However, their influence in the area was small and his people were still enjoying fully their traditional lifestyle along the banks of the Bamu River:

> When I was a small boy in Oropai I saw policemen and kiaps quite regularly. They came from Daru, which was an established government centre. They would come and have a look around the village. They sometimes told my people to keep the village clean, maintain peace and listen to the village constable at all times. Even though their visits were quite regular, I was still frightened of them whenever they came. My parents, and those of the others as well, were also frightened. Often on their trips they made an assessment of the place in regards to hygiene, health, census, law and order, and so forth. If someone had been troublesome, or broken the laws of the clan or tribe or that of the government, the individual or persons concerned were arrested and brought to Daru for imprisonment ranging from four to six months. A term of five years or more was given to murderers. Daru Island had a big prison for offenders. Unlike the Southern Highlands where I conducted patrols on foot, the policemen that came to my village came on boats or canoes. (Tamutai 1989)

On the other hand, when Sarepamo and Tigavu were born, white men had not been heard of or seen in the highlands by them, their parents, and the many generations that had gone before them. This comes as no surprise. By 1930 only three white men—prospectors Michael Leahy, Mick Dwyer, and Assistant District Officer James Taylor —had passed through Goroka Valley from Kainantu.[19] If any of the communities then lived near the tracks of the first or subsequent patrols, they had an opportunity to see white men and develop some kind of relationship with them. On one such occasion Sarepamo first encountered white men and their retinue of policemen and carriers:

> I first saw white men when I was a child. I was not old enough to cover my genitals with woven *bilum*.[20] The warriors of my village advanced on the approaching party, and some even took aim with their bows and arrows. I was very frightened. I walked at a slow, unsteady pace, and at a distance. It was the first time that my people saw men like ourselves dressed in laplaps[21] and shirts [policemen and carriers]. They arrived from the direction of Kainantu. We could not understand the language they spoke so they used sign language. The strangely dressed men came and left their belongings in houses which were then near the present site of the Goroka Teacher's College.[22] Immediately after they had unloaded, the men

were directed to our graveyard thinking that the new arrivals had somehow risen from there. My people killed pigs and presented them as presents. The strangers slept there, some in our houses and others in their own houses [tents], and left the following morning. (Sarepamo 1985)

Southwest of Goroka and about sixty miles away, Tigavu, in Gende (Bundi—see map 6), had a similar experience when the first European missionaries arrived in 1932. "I do not know the exact date, but I was quite a big boy when the first missionaries came and established a station at Guiebi and Bundi. The people called the two European men *poroi krunaga*. Some spoke of them as returned dead ancestral spirits. They searched around where the missionaries slept to see if they had dropped anything of value such as beads and shells" (Tigavu 1985).

It is an interesting, if familiar, response of people in a first-contact situation in Papua New Guinea, that the Gende should refer to *poroi krunaga* to describe the people's assessment of the missionaries' coming. In Gende cosmology, there were two types of forces operating equidistantly from the center that controlled their spiritual world. They were commonly identified by the term *poroi*, which generally means spirits, but could also mean abstractions. As the Gende were an earthy people, anything that went beyond their realm of reality was collectively looked upon as spirits. In other words, the Gende did not know whether the spirits really existed, nor had they any idea of the spirits' origins, because the spirits did not play an active part in the Gende's daily human life. They believed, however, that evidence of the spirits' presence was manifested in the order or otherwise of the nature of the Gende world; there was a beginning and an end, sickness and death. Another term was added to *poroi* to distinguish between the different types of spirits: an untamed spirit was referred to as *poroi uva;* a bad one as *poroi briki;* and the most dreaded was *poroi krunaga*. It dwelt in marshes, under the buttresses of large trees, and at the mouths of large rivers, but was always some distance away from the people's daily activities. It was a parasitic spirit; for its daily sustenance it sucked on the blood of pigs and other animals and crawled out of its dwelling place at night to feed on the bodies of dead relatives. They were the most feared of spirits. On first impressions, Father Schaefer and his entourage were looked upon as *poroi krunaga,* because the people believed that the visitors were really transformed *poroi krunaga* and that it was only a matter of time before the whole village population would be eaten.[23]

How familiar were those interviewed with the work of the policemen? The general response was that they were familiar with police patrols. However, none had any prior knowledge of what the policemen actually did in the barracks or at the depot. Prior to their own enlistment, the men had only become acquainted with the end result of a policeman's training, when he was at work—out in the village and on patrols.

Procedures and Numbers

From the 1920s the onus for the recruitment of men rested with government officers for both territories. After an officer became satisfied that a village could provide potential recruits he called the people to attention and made a general announcement. On 14 October 1934, Kasse of Nukakau, Talasea, West New Britain was one of those recruited. In a vivid recollection he repeated a speech by the patrol officer: "I am not here to get you forcibly to join the New Guinea police force; the government that I represent is not going to use force to get you. I am only asking for volunteers. If anyone of you young men wish to join the force, then come to me and I will register your name in the book. If you do not feel like it, do not force yourself to come" (Kasse 1985).

Kasse recalled the names of twelve of his peers who also responded to the patrol officer's appeal and yet was surprised that the officer only registered four of the young men. Kasse did not realize that the patrol officer was restricted by regulation. By the end of the circuit, seventy-eight men from the Talasea subdistrict were assembled on the station. In some places, particularly in areas where there was a threat of depopulation, recruitment of young men for engagement outside their own environment was heavily curtailed. In others, recruiters were not allowed to go beyond the set quota. Entry into the police force was hard. For full admission to the force, the young men had to satisfy six conditions (not necessarily in order of importance). They had to:

   a. be of superior physique and intelligence;[24]
   b. be of good character;
   c. be 5 feet 4 inches[25] or more in height, with a chest measurement of 33 inches;
   d. be between seventeen and forty years of age and unmarried;
   e. be able to converse in any one or a combination of three languages: English, Tok Pisin, and Motu; and
   f. have knowledge of the work of the colonial government.[26]

   The set of conditions seems straightforward, except that one might question the intelligence of the person responsible for specifications (b) and (d). In a situation of cross-cultural judgment, where the recruiter had only a brief meeting with the recruit, then obviously only

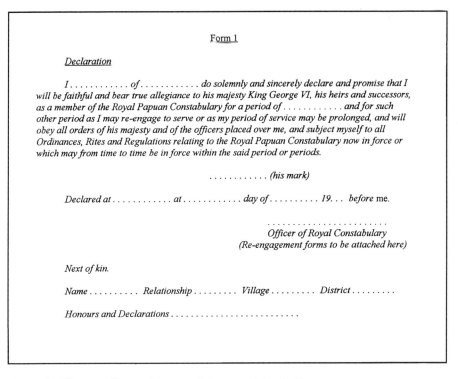

Figure 3   The enrollment form used for recruiting in Papua
Source: Royal Papuan Constabulary Ordinance no. 11 of 1939, paragraph 7(1),
Australian Archives ACT CRS A432. Item 39/947.

the wildest guess could have been made about the character of potential recruits. As it turned out, a number of men assumed to be blessed with such attributes turned out to be rogues in their subsequent service.

It was presumably also difficult to find many unmarried men between the prescribed ages of seventeen and forty, because men in many Papua New Guinean societies married before the age of twenty. The problem was recognized early in Papua, as evidenced in the annual report for 1890–1891: "It was not an easy matter to procure recruits at first. The native is in the very great majority of cases, married before he is of age to serve as a constable, and very few husbands or fathers are willing to leave their wives and children to become constables" (xix). The period before World War II saw a rigid adherence to this regulation, but it was relaxed after the war ended.

After careful scrutiny and eventual selection, the recruit was told to place his mark, or signature, on the enrollment form. The form used in Papua is reproduced as figure 3, and the New Guinea papers were similar.

From the outlying divisions and districts the men were brought together to the main administrative centers in Konedobu, Port Moresby, or Tavui, In Rabaul, for further observation and training. At the end, those considered not measuring up to the standard required were returned home and the remainder divided between the main centers and each of the outlying posts. The great majority were posted to various "outstations," the bulk of them being sent to newly opened posts and to areas where most disturbances were reported.

Papua

The Papuan police records are available in the annual reports,[27] which fortunately go back to 1890. In that year the first fourteen foreign men, two Fijians and twelve Solomon Islanders from the Fijian police force, were sent to Papua at the request of Sir William MacGregor to form the first legally constituted police force—the Papuan Armed Constabulary. The authority for the establishment of the force came through the proclamation of the Armed Constabulary Ordinance on 20 May 1890 (Papua 1890). At the end of the first year, Commandant George Wriford reported the circumstances of the men's recruitment in Fiji, transportation, and eventual engagement in Papua's new police force:

> Legislative authority to create the above force was given by an ordinance "to provide for an Armed Constabulary," which passed the Legislative Council on 20th May 1890. Your honour thereupon, with the kind co-operation of the Fijian Government . . . arranged for the enrolment in that colony of a small but well-selected body of native constables to act as a nucleus for the further organisation and development of a force in the Possession. Two Fijian non-commissioned officers were therefore enlisted, and agreed to serve here for one year; with them were engaged, under a written agreement to serve for three years, twelve picked Solomon Islanders. All receive moderate wages, and are provided with accommodation, rations, clothing, arms and ammunition. Reasonable medical comforts and attendance are also secured to them, with the cost of their conveyance both from and when returning to Fiji at the expiry of their agreement. From my perusal of the papers accompanying the latter document, and the appearance and conduct of the men, it is evident that every care and consideration were shown by the government of Fiji to meet the wishes of this government and secure satisfactory results. It was a fortunate circumstance, also, that through the kindness of Captain Castle, R.N., of H.M.S. *Rapid,* they were brought direct to Samarai and received by the Resident Magistrate of the Eastern Division on the 25th August 1890. A considerable saving was thus effected in the cost of their transport,

while the men avoided the temptations sure to be put before them
in the Australian towns. (Wriford 1891, 85)

Among the provisions of the ordinance, three are relevant here:

  a. The armed constabulary would be made up of "a Commandant
     and of such commissioned officers and non-commissioned offi-
     cers and constables" as was to be determined from time to time
     by resolution of Legislative council (Papua 1890, para 11).
  b. In the event of a shortage in quota, compulsion was to be ap-
     plied to enlist men of "sound bodily constitution" and between
     seventeen and forty years old (para 23).
  c. Enrolment in the force was for "not more than three years and
     not less than one year . . . and no person so enrolled[28] shall be
     liable to a second term of service" (para 29).

In Papua, the first nine members of the constabulary who worked
with and eventually took over from the two Fijian noncommissioned
officers and twelve Solomon Island constables were men from the Eastern and Western Divisions. "Eight aboriginal natives of the possession
have been added to the Force from Kiwai and the adjacent islands,
Parama and Yaru, and one from the Eastern Division. None have enlisted in the Central Division as yet. These men have done their work
willingly, and have improved in everything since joining, but some time
must lapse before their knowledge and self-reliance can be depended
upon."[29]

Preference was shown to men of the Western Division because they
met the requirements easily and had a reputation of not being afraid to
command people, even kinsmen, who came under their control. This
was in sharp contrast to men of other areas who were said to be reluctant
to give orders to close relatives; "they will 'run in' a man from another
district with the greatest of alacrity, but men from one's district can, as a
rule, rely on the old proverb that 'blood is thicker than water' " (PAR
1906–1907, 100, App J). Consequently, offenses of a serious nature
were seldom reported to higher authorities (Murray 1925, 59–60). More
important, the recruitment of men from the Western Division was
encouraged because many of them spoke a smattering of English from
their contact with Torres Strait. As Tom Dutton reported, "Their ability
to speak 'English' made them popular as early recruits into the police
force . . . and as boss boys on plantations and in mines" (1987, 90).

Men of the Western Division dominated the Armed Native Constabulary from 1890 until well into the early twentieth century (Dutton
1987, 93) by which time, because of their longevity and experience,
they were given positions of seniority in the force. For instance, "In
1914 Simoi of Katatai village in the Western Division of Papua was

appointed a sergeant major in the Papuan Armed Constabulary at a salary of £5 a month. At the time he probably held the most responsible position entrusted to a Papuan, and the police force continued to be an avenue—to positions of prestige" (Nelson 1974, 76).

By then, however, an increasing number of men from other divisions began to join the force and continued to do so well beyond 1960, as a consequence of the continuing expansion of government influence into new areas. Notable among the new enlistments were men from the Northern and North-Eastern Divisions: Mambare, Kumusi, and Tufi (Dutton 1987, 68), recruits who worked with the utmost dedication and loyalty, and many soon outshone the reputation of the Western Division men. Despite the great interest of most men throughout the different divisions to join the force, men of the Central Division blatantly refused to, one reason being that they had developed "a most decided objection to the life and discipline of the force" (*PAR* 1911, 57). Only a few enrolled from the Gulf Division. Resident magistrates and practically all of the colonial officials found men from that area cheeky and troublesome. European attitudes to the Gulf people were largely a matter of prejudice and stereotyping, as is common in colonial situations.[30] Consequently, their numbers in the force were low (A Inglis 1974, 20), and not many Europeans entertained the idea of employing men from the Gulf region in any other job where loyalty, obedience, and respect were demanded of a Papuan—demands that were emphasized most strongly in a policeman's life, from enrollment to retirement.

Recruitment for the old armed constabulary in Papua expanded slowly in the 1920s, but increased quickly during World War II. Table 2 shows the total establishment figures available for each year from 1890 to 1960.[31]

New Guinea

In New Guinea similar developments took place once the New Guinea police force became legally instituted in 1896. Initially the German officials preferred Malays and men from the Buka Strait area in Bougainville to other New Guineans (Hahl 1980, 20, 34). At the conclusion of their training they became "police soldiers." During the 1890s there were forty-eight of them to serve the whole colony (Firth 1982, 50). For the remainder of German rule in New Guinea, no police statistics are available in English except toward the end of the regime. In 1913 there were approximately six hundred policemen distributed disproportionately: "fifty each at Rabaul, Kavieng, Namatanai, Manus, Aitape and Morobe; one hundred and twenty at Madang, one hundred and twenty in the expeditionary troop and seven at Kokopo" (Firth 1982, 111). The Germans used their police to fight against the Australian landing force in New Guinea; more New Guineans than Germans died in defense of German New Guinea. But when the Japanese landed at Rabaul in 1942, the Australians did not immediately use the police. Their reasons had more to do with a lack of confidence in the police than in a humane desire to keep the police out of a foreign war. By 12 September 1914 there were approximately 1000 native members of the police force when the Australian Naval and Military Expeditionary Force took over the administration of Germany's former colony. Of this number, 100 men were distributed to each district. A highly trained police troop of 250 was permanently stationed in Rabaul to be deployed in emergency situations to subdue disturbances or to carry out punitive expeditions (Mackenzie 1987, 222). From then until the return of civil administration on 5 September 1921 the expeditionary force took over the administration of the territory, which was held "in military occupation in the name of His Britannic Majesty" (NGAR 1921, 5).

After the return of civil administration, Ordinance 12 of 1922, "To provide for the constitution and regulation of the New Guinea Police Force," appeared in the *Commonwealth of Australia Gazette* (New Guinea 1922, 122–126). Among other things, this ordinance provided that:

> the force would consist of "such commissioned officers, warrant officers, non-commissioned officers and constables," consistent with the specifications of that ordinance (para 3[1]);
>
> enrolment for an indigenous member would be for five years and unless anything untoward happened, would serve the full term and upon completion of a term he would either resign or sign on again "for a period of not more than three years and not less than one year" (para 22[1–2]).

The conditions for enrollment in the two forces showed legal differences. Although there was a specific age limit in the Papuan force, no such stipulation was given in the ordinance for the New Guinea force. In Papua it was legal to use compulsion to enlist men into the armed constabulary if there was a shortage; in New Guinea the men initially signed on for five years, two more than their Papuan counterparts, and could reengage for not more than three years and not less than one year x number of times. In Papua volunteers could reengage any number of times; even though a provision for compulsory enlistment existed in the ordinance, it was not exercised in practice because the yearly quotas were always met.

On the strength of this ordinance and subsequent ones, both New Guinean men and European officers enlisted in the New Guinea police force. The annual total strength for each category of recruits is given in table 2. Unfortunately, the *New Guinea Annual Reports* do not contain information on recruiting areas for the period. However, from secondary sources it can be observed that during the 1920s recruiting officers began to divert attention from the traditional recruiting grounds in coastal Bougainville, East New Britain, and the Islands to cover a much wider area. The aim was to facilitate recruitment of men from all the regions, which was supposed, theoretically, to be the generally accepted rule. In practice, however, officers showed preferences for men from certain areas. Patrol Officer Allert Nurton, for instance, considered men of Long Island (Madang District), to be more suitable and wanted to see the island preserved exclusively for police recruiters:

> Long Island people are [an] exceptionally refined type of native. He is unusually tall, of splendid physique. He is good and confident, and his intelligence abnormal to that of other Papua New Guinea natives generally.
>
> I obtained seven good police recruits all of whom were well above the present difficult police measurement standard.
>
> If I had my way, I would close the island to general recruiting, and favour it for special police recruitment. Every adult male one meets is a potential police recruit of splendid courage, natural dignity, intelligence and confidence, and of a height of up to 5 feet, 4 inches. (Nurton nd)

Despite the officers' desire to recruit young men from areas of their choice, there were youths from practically all of pacified New Guinea who not only satisfied the requirements but displayed a keenness similar to that of their Papuan counterparts. It was not unusual for a son to follow in the footsteps of his father and become a policeman, if he met the criteria set. Such was the observation of Patrol Officer J K McCarthy, in his book, *Patrol into Yesterday,* of the men in Waria in the present-day Morobe Province.[32] They were:

> highly regarded as members of the constabulary and for years a tradition had grown in the Waria villages that the best young men of each village would join the police. In many cases this became a family custom and a youth would follow his father or uncle to become a policeman. A high proportion of the N.C.O.s were Waria men and it was no uncommon thing for a recruit to say that his father, and even his grandfather, had served in the old German Constabulary. (McCarthy 1963, 116)

With this type of enthusiasm shown by the men and youths of not only Waria but generally speaking of the pacified areas of New Guinea, there was at no time a shortage of willing men ready to join the force.

Reasons for Recruiting

The government wanted recruits for a paramilitary force, but each man had his own particular reasons for deciding to join the police. Naguwean of East Sepik was representative of the views of one group of police recruits. His explanation, as given by his son Joseph, mirrored that offered in the official interpretation. He was adventurous. Unlike his peers, he left his village at an early age and worked in the gold mines of Bulolo for two years before the Second World War. When the war came he enlisted in the New Guinea Infantry Battalion. At the end of the war in 1945, he stayed on in the New Guinea police force. He learned from wartime police that policemen earned more money than mine workers. He was impressed with the power of the government and equally impressed with the power deflected to those who worked for the government. The temptation to grasp a share of that power and authority, and the perceived respect that would be forthcoming from the villagers because of it, lured Naguwean into the police force (Naguwean 1985). This view was popular among the majority of the men I interviewed. Boino, Kambian, and Yegova, for instance, believed that the colonial government put an end to internecine warfare and brought peace and "development" to the communities. As far as they knew the police were responsible for this situation, and they wished to contribute to the process. They enlisted willingly when the opportunity came (Boino 1989; Yegova 1985).

Sarepamo provided similar reasons and made an additional point. When colonial rule spread to the people of the highlands, apart from the handful of European officers, the carriers of this *nupela pasin* were men from the coastal regions. This situation caused disputes between the two camps. Generally the Highlanders despised the domination and heavy-handedness of the coastal men and longed for the day when their own people would take control of education or the police force. Sarepamo stated succinctly:

> I joined the police force because the policemen from the coast came and made a mess of the life of the people from the highlands. I wanted to stop their arrogant behaviour. When there were enough of us, we made sure the policemen from the coast did not overstep the line. We very much wanted to take revenge, not by way of doing them any physical harm, but rather to demonstrate to them that our own people were capable of looking after us. (1985)

The reasons advanced by six men (Tigavu, Sono, Sesetta, Empere, Kasse, and Amero) have their basis in traditional social and political organization. Amero was the son of Topakari, a big-man of Nukakau Island, West Kove, West New Britain. At the time of his enrollment, though about seventeen or eighteen years old, he was preparing himself to achieve the status of his father. However, he knew from personal observation and through stories told him by his elders that becoming a big-man went beyond the fantasies of a young man. It involved much toil and hardship. He had to prove to his people that he was a good fisherman, fighter, and gardener, that he possessed many fathoms of shell money, and was generous to others less fortunate than himself. Achieving these leadership qualities and accumulating the required wealth promised to take a long time. He was an impatient young man (a trait that remained with him for most of his life) and wanted to achieve the position of village headman before his peers. However, he was well aware that there was no easy alternative within the village structure. When an opportunity came for him to enlist, he walked forward willingly, even though he was not keen on becoming a policeman. Amero had an ulterior motive. He wanted to work for the government for five or more years and then return to the village, with the symbolic "power" the government had bestowed on him and, through its influence, achieve the status of a big-man, quietly and cheaply.[33]

When Kamuna Hura was a young boy, there was a celebration in which his people were asked to attend a festivity of some Goilala people. His hosts were relatives of his mother some two generations back. Kamuna, his family (consisting of parents, two sisters, three brothers) and relatives accepted the invitation, and, loaded with presents and produce from their gardens, left for their hosts' village. The following evening, Kamuna's younger sister, Sobia, accompanied some of the young girls of the village to a nearby stream to fetch water for the elders. Down by the stream, Sobia was the last to fill her container. As she seemed to take a long time to fill, the other girls grew impatient and began walking, intending to wait for her farther up the slope. When the girls were out of sight, men of an enemy tribe pounced on Sobia and killed her. News of the killing reached the village and their warriors rushed down to the stream, but the murderous men had all disappeared. Kamuna was furious, and vowed that day to take vengeance on the Goilala tribe concerned.[34] When the opportunity came for him to join the police force, he did so gladly, because he hoped to get his revenge through the police. But Kamuna's enemies' lives were spared: he was not posted to work among the Goilala people. Little did the police recruiter understand the intricate complexities of Kamuna's traditional background. Kamuna in 1920 was still very much influenced by the beliefs and aspirations of his ancestors; payback killing for unwarranted deaths was the law that he and his people understood.

From the oral testimonies two points emerge. The statements by Naguwean, Yegova, and Sarepamo imply a correlation between explanations given officially and by some of the other men. They confirm the official explanation that their enthusiasm for enlistment was a manifestation of their acceptance of colonial rule and a desire to see that rule extended. They were also attracted by the power and prestige that came with the uniform. But it is obvious from comments by the interviewees that not all the men held the same opinion. Official views do not always correlate with those of other recruits; in fact, some men's views are diametrically opposed to official interpretation. These men revealed that they were not overawed by the government and the power it seemed to wield over unsuspecting tribesmen. Nor were they immediately attracted by the uniforms, rifles, and other accoutrements of the police; their appreciation only came about once they learned of their utility in the depot. In other words, through regulation and frequent orders to respect government property, they eventually developed some kind of affinity with it. According to their testimony, represented by Amero, the men's enthusiasm was not so much their demonstration of an acceptance of the new order as much as their realization that colonial rule had acted as a catalyst for change in the social, political, and economic organization of the old village ways. As they aspired to achieving positions of prestige within that changing society, they wanted to be in the vanguard of that process. In short then, Amero, and those he represented, joined the police force so that its influence could be used as a springboard from which to gain a speedy entry to positions of status and authority in village politics.

Revenge, the other important motive, is interesting both sociologically and historically. Its sociological relevance lies in the organization of Kamuna's society, where payback killing was an accepted way of life among the Wakaia people of the middle Waria. Their tribal enemies also understood its implications; for every person they killed in Kamuna's village, they expected Kamuna's people to retaliate. Historically it is known, and the men themselves admitted, that men and women were shot dead and wounded by the policemen. How many of those killings were carried out as part of their normal police duties, and how many were related to revenge?

Summary

The police came from a wide geographic area and were recruited in very different circumstances. They were adventurous men, prepared to leave what was familar to them and embark on something they knew little about. Even though before recruitment they had no definite knowledge about the exact nature of police work, they had all seen policemen in their villages. In that respect they were not like men going to unknown plantations and mining jobs. The policemen were, to them, all men of prestige and authority. If the new recruits themselves were not warriors and men of authority in their villages, their fathers probably were. Consequently, for a good number of them, one of the main reasons for joining was to inherit positions of prestige and authority when they grew older. The recruits went into the police expecting to command; such an expectation was likely to attract a certain type of recruit and to influence their behavior when they went into the field.

Chapter 3
Training

The history of police training in Papua New Guinea falls into five phases. Some of these are not particularly distinctive, but are demarcated for the convenience of discussion and to indicate the beginnings of changes that may have continued over time. During the first phase, no legislation allowed for a police force in either possession, a situation that ended in Papua in 1890 and in New Guinea in 1896. The second phase, which lasted until 1910, saw the establishment of police forces and was characterized by haphazard training and punitive expeditions. In the third phase, from 1910 to 1940, the police forces were consolidated and a coordinated and systematic training program was inaugurated. The disruption and trauma of World War II characterized the fourth phase, from 1940 to 1946. The fifth phase, which began after the war and continued into the 1960s, was marked by changes in structure and organization to accommodate changing conditions.

During the first phase, company and colonial officials, planters, prospectors, entrepreneurs, and others of indeterminate occupation had to protect themselves with whatever private means they had at their disposal or rely on the occasional visit of an armed naval vessel. Because it was illegal to have a police force in Papua during this period, civilian men were sworn in as "special constables" to help with the security of the protectorate. For example, Sir William MacGregor appointed miners and traders as special constables in 1888 in the Ansell case (Nelson 1978, 130). In New Guinea in 1888, the New Guinea Company took over the responsibility for the formation of a "peace keeping" force for the maintenance of law and order wherever the Germans had established jurisdiction. Until then individuals were responsible for their own security, assisted by "occasional punitive expeditions" by visiting ships. This arrangement was unsatisfactory, and the New Guinea Company recommended the formation of the New Guinea police force in 1887. "It was found that the bombardment of native villages from German warships was inadequate largely because it did not always follow immediately on the heels of the crime" (quoted in Hayes 1967, 4). However, very few Papuans and New Guineans were included in the early forces, which were composed mainly of foreigners: Australians, British, Germans, Malays, and South Sea Islanders (Dutton 1987, 62–63; Sinclair 1972, 918). No direct information is available on the nature of training or instruction, if any, the men received for the jobs entrusted to them.

In Papua the annual reports for the period between 1890 and 1910 indicate that the training of new recruits was at best haphazard and at worst nonexistent. Dutton quoted from several of them:

> Recruits were taken to Port Moresby for an initial training programme before being distributed around the various Government stations. . . . It is not clear how much training the first recruits received in Port Moresby, but it could not have been very much as MacGregor had different sections on patrol and the Commandant took five recruits to the Western Division in December 1890 where four Solomon Islanders and four locals were left by MacGregor. Four of the Kiwai men (from Kadava) were sent to the Western Division in March 1891. However, by 1900, Barton, the Commandant, was requesting an assistant because "for the next year or two there will be an average of at least 30 recruits at Headquarters." A. W. A. Law was appointed in January 1902 as Headquarters Officer with duties to train recruits and to act as clerk and accountant of the force. (Dutton 1985, 251n41)

Dutton's last sentence suggests that things began to improve for the armed constabulary from 1900. Whether parallel developments took place in the German police force prior to 1900 is not known. However, up to 1900 and for the next ten years, according to Hayes, the German annual reports "make frequent note of punitive expeditions," implying a paramilitary type of training.[1] Hayes summarized the reports:

> The natives of the Admiralty Islands had to be chastised for the murder of a European trader; the deserted villages of Kauron and Mot, where a police party had been attacked a few months before with the loss of life of two police and ten villagers were visited by a stronger party and the villages burned to the ground. Since then peace had not been disturbed on the Rai Coast; in the [hinterland of the] Herzog Mountains [Markham Valley] an expedition was sent to investigate the murder of a white Bird of Paradise hunter [in January 1911]. After several hours of fighting during which forty natives were killed, the villages were seized and burnt. The conditions at Potsdamhafen [an area on the mainland opposite Manam Island] now assume a peaceful aspect. (Hayes 1967, 5)

In my assessment, the third phase, from 1911 to 1940 was the most significant. It not only marked the beginning of a coordinated and systematic police training program, but also set a pattern that continued to be influential after the war. In the 1920s and 1930s the police established what they considered were normal procedures, and outsiders made important judgments about them (Hides 1935, 1936, 1938; Lett 1935, 1944; and J K McCarthy 1963).

The fourth phase, 1940 to 1946, spanned the dramatic era of World War II. Because of the exigencies of the situation, policemen of both forces underwent short but intensive military training in Port Moresby under the auspices of the Australia New Guinea Administrative Unit before being deployed wherever they were most needed. The nature of the training received has no parallel in the pre- or postwar forces of either territory.

The fifth phase began after the war, gaining momentum in the 1960s. For example, "As part of the re-organization of the Police Branch [of Papua] a clerical division has been created to cope with expanding administrative requirements and the nucleus of a modus operandi section established" (PAR 1957–1958, 32). The structure and organization of the force were revamped to accommodate inevitable changes within it, marking the beginning of a process that has continued to the present time. Two important developments occurred during this period. First, the forces were amalgamated in 1952 and subsequently renamed the Royal Papua and New Guinea Constabulary with the consent of Queen Elizabeth II (Hayes 1967, 7). This was the culmination of a process begun at the start of the war, when Papuan and New Guinean men trained together in the same training depot under the same officers to work in the same unit after they had "graduated." Changes in the police force reflected the changes occurring generally in the colony as a consequence of the war. For instance, the two territories ended a tradition of separate political and economic development to form a unified system. Consequently the members of the Royal Papua and New Guinea Constabulary could now work in *either* territory. During and after the union of the forces, there was no official rush to dismantle police practice and behavior of either force, in statute books, or by patrol officers; if anything, the transition passed without much official action or harangue, suggesting that police work in Papua and New Guinea was fundamentally similar before and after the war.[2]

Second, "on the 23rd June 1961, a separate Police Department was formed and it is intended at a later stage to establish the Police Force as a statutory authority outside the Public Service" (PAR 1960–1961, 46).

During this phase two other momentous events reflected the great achievements of the forces. First, in 1950,

A Police Contingent, including the Police Band, visited Australia and was honoured by being appointed to lead the Anzac Day March held in Sydney on April 25, 1950 to commemorate the landing by Australian and New Zealand troops at Gallipoli during World War I. The Contingent also paraded in the main capital cities including Canberra and received commendation for its parade ground efficiency and the demeanour, bearing and the carriage of its members. (NGAR 1949–50, 13)

Second, in June 1953,

a Special Contingent of Royal Papuan (sic) and New Guinea Constabulary, comprising three European officers and twenty-five indigenous personnel, fifteen of whom were from New Guinea, represented the Territory of Papua and New Guinea at the ceremony of the Coronation of Her Majesty Queen Elizabeth the Second in London. The Contingent travelled to London by sea and returned by air. The tour occupied approximately three months and during that time the indigenous members of the contingent had the opportunity to see many different countries and the way of life of the people of those countries. For these men, who had not been outside their own country, the tour had considerable educational value. (NGAR 1952–53, 19)

While the postwar period marks an exciting phase in the development of the constabulary, and of the country as a whole, the period after the 1960s is outside the scope of this discussion. However, except for the war years, the physical component of the training was much the same as it had been during the 1920s and 1930s, consisting of, among other activities, physical culture, foot drill, and rifle training (PAR 1959–60, 38).

There were three main training centers for new recruits, in various parts of Port Moresby, Rabaul, and, in the 1950s, Goroka. The training received at these centers represented just the beginning of a long training process that continued with on-the-job training conducted by patrol officers in the various districts or divisions.

Until 1960 the process followed by most of the recruits was similar. Confirmed recruits were brought in from their villages to the main government station in their respective district or division. The officer-in-charge checked their names against his own record, after which, if he was satisfied that correct procedures had been followed, he made arrangements for them to be brought to the main administrative centers for training. In Papua for the first five years, the main training depot of the armed constabulary was situated in Granville West, as it was officially called, near Ela Beach, within what is now Port Moresby. It was then moved to Granville East, Konedobu, "where there was a three-acre site available" (PAR 1894–95, 27; 1895–96, 75; see also Dutton 1985 251n41). From 1890, Samarai maintained a separate detachment, whose members were engaged independently from the main force in Port Moresby (PAR 1897–98, xxv). During and after World War II, the main depot was shifted from Ela Beach and Konedobu to Bisiatabu, Sogeri, and then to Kila Police Barracks (near Vabukori) (Dutton, pers comm 1987). These places were used for both police and military training (Yegova 1985). In New Guinea in the 1920s, both the main administrative center and the police training depot were situated in Rabaul; the police depot was at Tavui. In January 1929 this depot was closed and the responsibility for the training of recruits was left to newly trained noncommissioned officers in the districts, the official explanation being that the facilities would then become available for a school of instruction for New Guinean noncommissioned officers of police (NGAR 1928–29, 96). This explanation appears to be spurious, considering that in January 1929 indentured laborers and the Rabaul town police combined for a short-lived demonstration that has since become known as the most significant early industrial action in New Guinea (NGAR 1928–29, 96). Without dwelling on this "strike," it is possible that the transfer of training facilities to the districts was an overreaction, on the part of the small European population of a few hundred people, to avert another imagined uprising by the town police. The experiment proved unsuccessful, however; training in the districts was abandoned and transferred back to Rabaul in 1932–1933 (NGAR 1932–33, 113). Besides Rabaul, the only other police training depot in New Guinea was established in Kefamo, Goroka, during 1950–1951. It was "an ancillary Training Depot," built principally to train raw highland recruits and to provide refresher courses to the policemen in the central highlands detachment (NGAR 1950–51, 13).

Physical Training

There were two types of police training—physical and intellectual. Of the five phases just described, in phases two and four, or the periods from 1890 to 1910 and 1940 to 1945, as well as twenty years of the third phase, 1911 to 1930, training was almost entirely physical.[3] A number of factors contributed to this. Physical exertion is an integral part of training in any police organization and was not unusual in the respective Papua and New Guinea forces. The war years, 1940 to 1945, demanded that Papua New Guinean policemen provide material support to the campaign, but they were not expected to be deployed in areas where particular skills, such as the ability to handle machine guns, were required. However, they were required to be physically fit to walk the long

Kokoda Trail and similar distances many times over, supervising carriers, assisting the wounded, carrying messages, and generally performing tasks that their superiors viewed askance. The one, two, or three months of intense physical training the recruits endured was geared toward meeting that end. The main responsibility of the policemen for much of the period under study was the exploration and pacification of communities not yet under government control. Policemen were trained physically so that they could withstand the hardships that would confront them when sent out as the eyes, ears, and mouthpieces of the colonial governments into the remote and hostile parts of the country. Also, prior to the war, the policemen, like the majority of their countrymen, had not been exposed to the skills they would gain later as drivers, carpenters, tradesmen, motor mechanics, ship hands, and the like, so training in special skills did not become an integral part of police training. Even if a policeman had shown particular talent to advance above others, he would have had great difficulty in overcoming the prejudice of the time had he tried to venture beyond accepted roles for Papuans and New Guineans. A combination of these factors resulted in the recruits being given mostly physical training during the early phases of the respective forces' history. However, both physical and intellectual training were combined, at least within the Papuan force, during the last ten years of the third phase, 1930 to 1940, and continued into the fifth phase, 1946 to 1960 and beyond, in order to meet the changing needs and aspirations of the force and of individuals in it.

The nature of the physical training, and instruction in the use of the rifle and tactics for small-group fighting, clearly indicated the paramilitary nature of the forces. For the armed constabulary, wherever possible, this was the style of training from the beginning: "The constabulary are now fairly trained in manual, firing and the bayonet exercise, and understand something of skirmishing" (*PAR* 1890–1891, 86). The method was formalized in 1911, with the introduction of what came to be known as the "Infantry Training 1911" manual into the armed constabulary's training syllabus. Most important, the training was methodical, which was a change from the casual approach of previous years. It was so successful that it was retained for most of the prewar period and adopted for the combined force after the war. The police recruits followed almost exactly the routine of army recruits:

> The training as laid down in the Syllabus in "Infantry Training 1911," for the instruction of recruits is being strictly adhered to. Six hours per week are being devoted to physical training. The tables for infantry recruits set forth in the Army Manual of Physical Training are closely followed, and all exercises which can be done without apparatus, or with improved apparatus, are performed dur-

ing the course, so that a harmonious development of the body is assured. Great care is taken with these exercises in order to obtain the best results, and the physical fitness and development shown at the end of the course amply repays the attention to small details. The remaining twenty hours per week are allotted to different portions of the drill book, as provided for in the syllabus. This allows for four parades a day. More time than this, on parade, is not desirable, as recruits would lose interest and become weary. If their progress warrants it, musketry training is commenced towards the end of the third month. All recruits have fired a recruits' course— with due regard to economy in ammunition—and the majority of them would, with practice, become first-class shots. (*par* 1912–13, 62; 1926–27, 56)

The changed diet and regular exercise changed the physique of the recruits, adding to the esteem of the police and increasing their differences from newly contacted villagers.

In New Guinea the physical training of policemen during the prewar period, particularly after the establishment of civil government in 1921, appears to have been similar to that in Papua. "The native police receive training in:—Squad drill with and without arms, platoon drill, extended order drill, musketry, guard and sentry duties."[4]

What was the purpose of all this physical activity, and how successful was it? Murray provided the rationale:

> In training a body of men like the Armed Constabulary the most important thing is to inculcate such ideas as loyalty to the Government, pride in their uniform, and, eventually, a tradition of service; and I think I may say that we have succeeded in doing this. A Constable will stand up against any odds, for the police tradition does not allow him to run away; and he will go to certain death rather than disgrace his uniform. For instance I remember the case of a Constable who was under orders to report at a Government station on a certain day, and who could just arrive in time if he could get round a point where the sea was breaking heavily. It was a rough night, and he was warned that no one but a very strong swimmer could get past the point. He was a bush native and could not swim at all; but he wore the police uniform and must obey orders. So he braved the passage, and was drowned. (Murray 1932, 9)

Physical exercises for recruits began on the morning of the first day. When the first bell rang at 6:00 AM they were wakened by the shouts of the noncommissioned officers on duty and immediately introduced to the rituals of the training depot. Between 6:00 and 7:00 AM they had their first physical drill, after which they washed; for many, that meant a quick jump into a river or the sea. They then returned to the barracks and made their beds while they waited patiently for breakfast, which consisted of biscuits, pancakes, and black tea. For about an hour after breakfast they returned to the barracks and cleaned up the area. A little after 10:00 AM they marched down to the parade ground for squad drill. However, every morning before the physical component of the training they were made to stand to attention and sing a song. During the 1930s, on weekdays, the Papuan recruits sang "Garuwa's Marching Song":

> Left, right, left, marching is a pleasure,
> Head up straight, minding tune and measure,
> Shoulders back, and chest throw *(sic)* open wide,
> Fingers close, and hands by your sides.
>
> Left, right, left, hold your foot quite ready,
> Heels down fours, keep your shoulders steady,
> Point toes out, and mind your knees don't bend,
> Round the room with careful steps you wend.
>
> Left, right, left, moving feet together,
> Eyes in front, striving to do better,
> No bent backs to spoil in straight line,
> But just like a soldier stepping all in time.[5]

Similarly, in Rabaul, between 1930 and 1940 a tune, but not the words, resembling a verse and a chorus from, "Marching through Georgia"[6] was sung to the incessant yelps of the commanding noncommissioned officers. Only the words were changed to suit the local flavor:

> We in the morning
> We get up and march off to drill,
> We eat too much biscuits,
> Often, all day long.
> We try hard, through the days, year long.
>
> Hurrah, hurrah, we are New Guinean police.
> Hurrah hurrah, we are in the depot,
> We try hard we go all the way
> We try hard through the days,
> Year long.[7]

After the songs, both the new recruits and those in the advanced stages of training were made to perform daily activities consisting mostly of manual labor and physical exercise. Fatigue duties ceased between 4:30 and 5:30 PM, and recruits marched back to the barracks to wait for their evening meal. Those in Rabaul could walk around China-town for about two hours after the evening meal while waiting for the first bell to ring at 8:45 PM. They would then walk back to the barracks and prepare for sleep at 9:00 PM. Those in Papua had similar experiences.

> At 6.00 a.m. they are roused from their beds by the non-commissioned native officer in charge, generally a sergeant. At 6:30 they fall in for parade, and are drilled for half-an-hour, and the attention and painstaking manner in which they endeavour to excel in their rifle exercises and marching is highly creditable. At 7.30 they attend to the airing of their blankets and cleaning the barracks. At 8.00 o'clock they fall in again and are dismissed for breakfast. At 9.00 o'clock they give attention to the cleaning of the parade ground and reserve surrounding the barracks, or are engaged in all police duties required. At 12 (noon) they again fall in, and are counted by the sergeant and dismissed for dinner. At 2.00 p.m, they again resume work until 4 p.m., when they are at liberty until 6.00 p.m., when they fall in for tea. From that out *(sic)* no man can leave the precincts of the barracks without the permission of the European officer in charge, and then only to 9.00 p.m., when they fall in, are counted, and dismissed to bed. Surprise visits are paid at night at irregular intervals to the barracks, and the men counted as a check against leaving the barracks after the stipulated hour. Of course, this system applies only when the men are in the barracks, but when on patrol the European officer in charge uses his own discretion as to discipline. (O'Malley 1908, 84)

There was no fundamental change in the routine in 1927:

> The police at Head-quarters are being trained in accordance with the Manual of Infantry Training 1914.[8] The instructional staff consists of Sergeant-Major Simoi and Corporal Mamadeni. . . . The training and discipline is very strict, and together with good food and regular hours it is most gratifying to see what can be done with the Papuan native. The daily routine is as follows:—
>
>> 6 a.m.—Reveille.
>> 6.30 to 7.15 a.m.—physical exercises and swimming.
>> 7.15 to 8 a.m.—Breakfast.
>> 8 a.m.—inspection of police, guard and orderlies to Port Moresby.
>> 8.15 to 9 a.m.—Cleaning barracks.
>> 9.15 to 10.15 a.m.—squad drill.
>> 10.30 to 11.30 a.m.—Tent pitching or rowing.
>> 11.45 to 1 p.m.—Musketry instruction, aiming or fatigues.

1 to 2 p.m.—Dinner.

2 to 4 p.m.—Instruction on care of arms, cleanliness of kit, tent pitching, or fatigues, &c.

4.30 to 6 p.m.—Company drill on barracks square.

6.15 p.m.—Town guard to Port Moresby.

9 p.m.—Roll call.

9.15 p.m.—Lights out, finish of the day. (*PAR* 1926–27, 56)

It can be seen from the routine that any diversion from the daily physical exercises was work related; that patrol work was still of paramount consideration is illustrated by training in rowing, swimming, and tent pitching.

The recruits were expected to acquire habits of industry and regularity—different from what was considered to have been the leisurely lifestyle of singing and dancing they had known in their villages. Their training called not only for hard physical labor but also for mental conditioning. They had to learn to be punctual and to obey orders. They were disciplined into accepting the cult of obedience.

The ordinary recruit who has signed on for three years goes through a fairly complete course of training at Port Moresby; he bathes in the sea every morning, goes through a course of physical culture, learns the infantry drill, and is taught to shoot, to row a boat, to pitch a tent, and to keep himself and his clothing neat and clean. It is already gratifying to see that the constabulary has already established a tradition and a very strong esprit de corps. (Murray 1931, 578)

In official accounts, what featured most prominently in their training was the development of the physique of the recruits rather than their intellectual capacities. It even appears that this was practiced so widely and proved so rewarding that the need to develop the intellectual abilities of the recruits was neglected. Photographs 28 to 33, particularly the three depicting physical exercises, demonstrate the high level of achievement in this area of training for the Papuans during the 1920s. Physically, the men appear to be in excellent condition, as they should when this particular aspect of training was performed approximately three times a day, five days a week. The capacity of the police recruits at the end of their training to look impressive, and to move efficiently and precisely to commands, was always taken to be a demonstration that they were now disciplined:

The Armed Constabulary of Papua are a hardy and vigorous body of men, muscular and well set up, and they cut a picturesque figure as they swing along the road in their uniform of navy blue and red; and they have this rather remarkable fact to their credit that

Photos 28, 29, 30 The Papuan Armed Constabulary at physical drill, 1926.
Note the various physical exercises and the condition of the men after six
months' training at headquarters. (L Logan, in *PAR*, 1925–26, 104)

Photos 31, 32, 33 The Papuan Armed Constabulary headquarters detachment receives marching orders (31), and is ready for route march (32, 33). The landscape at the back of the photos gives the impression that they were taken in Konedobu. (L Hogan, *PAR*, 1925–1926, 105)

they, a mere handful of "savages in serge," with no assistance from outside, have kept order among an absolutely lawless population in a Territory nearly as large as England. (Murray 1931, 571)

For many recruits of both forces, physical training was hard and long. It lasted from six months to a year, and if a man could not hit the target or the bull's-eye with a rifle, then he had to painstakingly start his shooting training all over again. Regardless of hardships, the noncommissioned officers who trained them showed no mercy. Guise recalled, "but if you disobeyed any Sergeant Major, you know what you got, a full-pack on your shoulders and you were made to run for about fifteen to sixteen miles" (Guise 1985). In Rabaul, Amero also vividly recalled his noncommissioned officers using a stick to beat them around the legs if they showed any signs of fatigue or clumsiness (Amero 1985). It is also likely that the tough image of the successful policeman—the noncommissioned officers—had some influence on the way the recruits themselves thought they should behave.[9]

The origin of this military style of police training can in part be traced back to the Royal Irish Constabulary. During the early nineteenth century, Ireland went through a turbulent period. To assist in minimizing the increasing acts of aggression against the British, the Irish Peace Preservation Act was passed in 1814 under the guidance of the Irish Secretary, Sir Robert Peel. This Act authorised the organization of a constabulary "in any area which was proclaimed to be in a state of disturbance" (Jeffries 1952, 30–31). Its position was consolidated with the passage of a similar Act in 1822, which provided for "the establishment of a permanent uniformed and armed constabulary force under four Inspector-Generals, one for each of the Irish provinces" (Jeffries 1952, 31). Whether or not the establishment of the Irish Constabulary solved the problems of Ireland is open to debate; what is important here is that it proved significant for the spread of colonial rule. Sir Charles Jeffries, the author of *The Colonial Police,* stated succinctly:

[F]rom the point of view of the colonies there was much attraction in an arrangement which provided what we should now call a "para-military" organization or gendarmerie, armed, and trained to operate as an agent of the central government in a country where the population was predominantly rural, communications were poor, social conditions were largely primitive, and the recourse to violence by members of the public who were "agin the government" was not infrequent. It was natural that such a force, rather than one organized on the lines of the purely civilian and localised forces of Great Britain, should have been taken as a model for adaptation to colonial conditions. (Jeffries 1952, 31)

This feature of training was shared by the armed constabulary and the New Guinea police force—with each other and with the police forces of other former British, German, or Australian colonies.

Intellectual Training

The second type of training was intellectual,[10] and should be understood in a very broad sense. It is used here to contrast what was largely an attempt to develop the physique of recruits with the attempt to train them to use their intellectual capacities. It would be an exaggeration to claim the colonial governments of either territory made any serious attempt to educate Papua New Guineans to any great level for much of the period under study. However, Papua New Guineans who took advantage of the few opportunities to obtain special skills provided by the governments and missions immediately before the war were recruited into the police. During the 1930s young men in Rabaul learned simple arithmetic, simple English,[11] to tell the time of day by observing changes in the daily routine, and, for those selected for the police band, to read music. During 1933–1934, recruits with particular technical skills were accepted for the first time:

> Following an amendment to the Police Force Regulations providing for the enrolment of native members of the Force as motor drivers and tradesmen, made during the year 1932–33, two constable-carpenters and one constable-plumber were enrolled. These tradesmen now carry out all minor repairs to police and prison buildings in Rabaul. Police motor vehicles are driven by native constabulary personnel.
>
> A constable-clerk, educated as a boy and as a youth at the Administration school at Malaguna, was also enrolled in the Force. He is now employed as a typist and a clerk at Police Head-Quarters, Rabaul, and had proved to be most useful and efficient. (NGAR 1933–34, 102)

Just before World War II, the total number of technically educated policemen recruited into the New Guinea force included

> one sergeant-clerk-typist; five constable-clerk-typists; one armourer-sergeant; one constable-armourer; one lance corporal-carpenter; one constable-carpenter; one lance corporal-plumber; one constable-plumber; six constable drivers (motor vehicle); and thirty-one constable-bandsmen. All these specialists are members of the Native Constabulary Branch of the Force and are trained police. (NGAR 1938–39, 127)

In Port Moresby the Papuan recruits did not receive any more than the most basic book learning, "and this is very important they have lessons in English, in counting, in telling the time, and so on. All orders are given in English; and a policemen must know some English before he can be sent to work on an outstation. Every afternoon they have lessons in English, and they have two night classes as well each week"[12]

After the war the length and variety of training of men before they joined the police expanded greatly. In 1947–48, a Special Branch Section was created in both Papua and New Guinea within the police organization where policemen, it appears for the first time, were taught other skills to meet new police needs (PAR 1947–48, 30; NGAR 1947–48, 9). For instance, a new training syllabus introduced during 1956–57 "produced good results. The course covers a period of six months' depot training followed by six months' in-service training. The syllabus caters for instruction in first aid, report writing, elementary law, physical culture, hygiene, foot drill, rifle training, police functions, and traffic control" (PAR 1957–58, 33). The Special Branch included wireless telegraph operators, armorers, and bandsmen as well as those with traditional skills.

Until 1960 no further changes were introduced to either the training syllabus or the range of technical skills in the Special Branch. During 1959–60, except that the length of training had increased to twelve months, the set of instructions remained the same as in 1948 (PAR 1959–60, 38).

Of the three Papuans interviewed in 1985,[13] only Guise could converse fluently in English. It is possible that he learned English at an Anglican school in Milne Bay, rather than at the police training depot, and through his associations with people outside the police force before he joined it. Guise was also "mixed race" and presumably had the benefit of exposure to English from an early age. Yegova spoke *Tok Pisin* fluently; and both Goro and Yegova knew Motu, but neither of these men could speak or write in English. Boino complained that the level of English instruction he received during and after the war was only elementary. Some idea of the education level reached after the completion of the six months training at the depot in Papua is revealed by Corporal Garuwa's examination paper (figure 4). Two lance-corporals vied for promotion to the rank of corporal in the Papuan Armed Constabulary in 1932. As both men had given meritorious service to the force, an examination was conducted to decide the one most eligible for the promotion. Corporal Garuwa made only one mistake and was promoted.

Views of Former Policemen

The experiences of the men recruited and trained varied. Some had to travel for miles over rivers, mountains, and seas; others simply walked to the depot in a matter of hours. Sarepamo, a burly Highlander,

Corporal Gurawa's
Examination Paper.

~

How many days are there in a
      year ?
How many months are there in a
year ?
How many Sundays are there in a
year ?
How many ounces are there in a lb. ?
What is 28 lb. ?
How man lb. make 1 cwt. ?
How many cwt. make 1 ton ?
Give the name of the money you
know ?
How many inches make one foot ?
How many feet make one yard ?
Write in figures 1 to 50 ?
Give the names of the Gentlemen
you know on the Council.
Give the names of all the out-stations
you know.
Do these three sums:—
    (1) 26)8197682(
    (2) 7532431 × 7649
    (3) 23652198
        43721752
        33694513
        ————
        ————

Lance-Corporal Gurawa answered all
these questions correctly except that
some of the Gentlemen on the Council
had their names spelt wrongly and one
was left out.
Lance-Corporal Gurawa is now a
Corporal.
        ————

Figure 4   Corporal Gurawa's examination
    paper *Source: The Papuan Villager* 4
    (10): 75 (October 1932).

walked only a few miles to Kefamo for his initial training in 1943.[14] Sarepamo had no prior knowledge of police training, and what little his kinsmen told him only confused him. Before he left his village he was told by some elderly men, who were themselves none the wiser, that he would be doing nothing more than playing some game that was to be introduced into Goroka and the highlands region generally. At the depot he observed the first day's events with keen interest. On his arrival his name was checked against a list. When the officer was satisfied that Sarepamo was the potential recruit, he was ordered to take off his meager clothing, issued with khaki laplaps, two blankets, and other paraphernalia, and shown to his sleeping quarters, a typical thatched highlands roundhouse built on the ground. There were four houses on the premises. That evening after a scanty meal consisting of "European food," corned beef and rice, he returned to his quarters, stretched out on his bamboo woven bed, and slept soundly until the early hours of the morning, when the raucous cries of the duty noncommissioned officer woke him in fright from a deep slumber (Sarepamo 1985).

The three men from Garaina—Kamuna, Sono,[15] and Sesetta—followed a similar routine even though they were recruited at different times. They walked to Lae and traveled on ships (the *Bulolo* and the *Macdhui*) to Rabaul. On the way each ship stopped at Kavieng, and the recruits had an opportunity to see some of the early German-built establishments there. As it was against regulation for new recruits to roam freely about Rabaul, noncommissioned officers from the Tavui depot awaited their arrival at Simpson Harbour and despatched them immediately to the barracks. Of the three recruits, Sesetta was the most apprehensive; for weeks he would neither talk to the other men nor wander through the grounds of the barracks after official activities ended. However, at the end of two months he discovered, to his disbelief, that some of the men he had refused to talk to earlier were from his own area. Two of them were already veterans of the New Guinea police force, Kamuna having joined in 1923, Sono in 1936, and Sesetta himself in 1938.

From the New Guinea Islands, Amero, Kasse, and ToWoworu were recruited and trained before the war. Amero and Kasse enlisted together in 1934 on their island of Nukakau, Talasea, in West New Britain District. Accompanied by twelve others from the Talasea subdistrict, they traveled by canoe to Talasea and boarded a ship the following day for Rabaul. ToWoworu's experience was slightly different from the rest of the New Guinea recruits in that he had received some elementary western education from the Malaguna government primary school before his recruitment in 1936. Those recruited with him from the school also formed the first police band in New Guinea in 1938. This is a particular aspect of his long service in the force that he remembers well and from which he received much personal satisfaction. In many respects, he was one of the pioneers of what is today the Royal Papua New Guinea Constabulary Band. At the depot, young men in his group were trained separately from those recruited for the police proper. While others performed fatigues, he received instruction in music.

With the exception of Guise, who was recruited after the war, in 1946, seven men—Boino, Goro, Naguwean, Rewari, Sarepamo, Tigavu, and Yegova—like thousands of others, were recruited specifically to help in the war campaign. Goro of Sanananda, Northern Division, and Boino, a resident of Buna but originally from Tufi, walked with "hundreds" of others to Port Moresby in 1941. Rewari's group, recruited in 1943, walked to Abau before being transferred to Sogeri. However, in 1943 Yegova of Buna was flown to Port Moresby on an army plane, which was a thrilling new experience for him. What he saw there amazed him:

> When I arrived in Port Moresby I saw very few village people. They had all been removed to some other place. Port Moresby was teeming with soldiers, both black and white men. At the training depot there were literally hundreds upon hundreds of Europeans and Papua New Guineans: men from Bougainville, Manus, Madang, Morobe, Sepik, Gulf, Northern and Western districts. I was overwhelmed by it all. Communication with the others was difficult at first, but it was not an insurmountable problem and we overcame it in the end, when we could speak either Motu, *Tok Pisin* or English. As I remember it now not many Papua New Guineans could converse in English. At the depot we queued for registration. We were then issued with blankets, mosquito nets, two laplaps[16] each and a bed cover. I was then brought to the barracks used only by the men from the Northern Division. (Yegova 1985)

Generally, three types of answers were volunteered by the men to the question: "You spent six or more months at the training depot. What kind of experience did you have, and did you enjoy your stay there?" Of the 27 respondents, 17 had no reservations, 8 were more reserved in their praise, and 2 found their training oppressive.

For the first and largest group—Amero, Anka, Beu, Boino, Empere, Evara, Guise, Goro, Igarobae, Iwagu, Kambian, Meraveka, Moru, Naguwean, Tamutai, Tigavu, and ToWoworu—being at the depot was a new and challenging experience, which they enjoyed. Amero, Naguwean, and Tigavu, for instance, had a real fascination for the rifle when they were first issued one after about a month of rudimentary training. They were given practical demonstrations on its use: how to clean it, how to use it at drill and at the shooting range. They were told that when they completed their training they would be working mainly in the bush, among mostly unpacified people. Most of the time they would not be certain how these people would receive them. Hence, they should be prepared at all times. Being prepared meant being able to defend themselves when they were attacked by men from those aggressive communities. Obviously, in those circumstances the rifle might save them. It was necessary for all new recruits to learn to use it correctly and with some degree of proficiency. To these three men the gun, with the magical power it seemed to wield and the prestige associated with it, was adequate compensation for the banal and tiring daily activities of the depot and the traumas of separation from family, friends, and home.

ToWoworu's jubilation at being selected as a pioneer in the New Guinea police band never waned until he retired from the force in 1954. He realized that his selection promised him a long career with the colonial government. In his own estimation, only the fortunate were given this opportunity, and he considered himself one of a privileged minority. For Guise, his twelve months' training, and the subsequent nine years he served in the force, were some of the best years of his life because "it showed me the spirit of comradeship which no other organization other than the police force has taught me."

> We had a teacher there who taught us about law and order and the various laws of the country which we as policemen had to uphold. We were told about what the colonial government was trying to achieve in the country and what our role as policemen would be in the process. We were lectured on how we would treat the people; that we were their friends and were to provide protection for those in trouble and in need of our assistance. As for the police force itself, we were given to understand that we were the mainstay of any government whether it was colonial or otherwise. The police force was the most important body because it carried out law and order on behalf of the government. These and many other things were told to us on both the parade ground and when any other opportunity availed itself. (Guise 1985)

Interestingly, Guise was adamant about the virtues of his police training, whereas the accounts of the other twenty-seven men were less positive. They conceded that a fair amount of lecturing was heard, but most of the training concentrated on how to get physically fit, how to do manual work, and the need to respect their officers. To the best of their knowledge, no worthwhile lectures were given on any subject. When most of them completed their training, they had only a vague idea of what the government was trying to achieve and what their role was to be. Possibly those kinds of things were not taught at the time these men were trained. Some of them were trained either before or during World War II. Guise, on the other hand, was trained in 1946, at the beginning of a period of rapid changes in Papua New Guinea. Records in the annual reports for both administrative centers for the period before World War II did not always summarize what constituted proper training for the police force, but they frequently provided statistics on recruitment and distribution after training. Also, many of the men spoke at best only a smattering of English, and they could have grasped only the bare minimum of what an officer said or someone else interpreted to them.[17]

The second group—Kamuna, Mohaviea, Orovea, Panau, Rewari, Sare-pamo, Sesetta, and Sono[18]—who were more reserved in their praise, said that had they been given the opportunity during the first few weeks of training, they would have left without any sense of guilt. Later, however, even if they as individuals felt no compulsion to remain, as a group they somehow felt morally obliged to stay and serve the government. They were bonded into a group that assumed the obligations of individual members. They began to rationalize their reasons for remaining. If they had not desired to be recruited, they could have wriggled out. It was their own fault that they were recruited in the first place. Their own traditional etiquette obliged them to serve the government and see their period of "contract" through. In addition, Sesetta felt that if he returned home his family and friends would be disappointed, and it would be evidence of his inability to cope in the new world introduced by the Europeans.

> I could not allow myself to be lazy with the prospect of being sent home and thereafter bring shame upon myself. My parents and relatives would look upon me with disdain. I therefore trained very hard, and soon turned out to be a model trainee even though it was all hard work and the two shillings that I received was little compensation for my efforts at this new and strange activity. (Sesetta 1985)

The third type of response was the antithesis of the first. Of the two men—Yegova and Kasse—the one who gave the least angry assessment was Yegova. His outrage was limited to the period of training; beyond that he held nothing but nostalgic memories of the foundations he believed he helped build for the present Royal Papua New Guinea Constabulary. He gave several reasons for his vexations during the six months of training: The regulations were repressive. He felt he had been robbed of the freedom he enjoyed in his own village. Life was restricted to the confines of the training depot. The compensations he received in the form of rations and cash were small consolation for the traumas he experienced leaving his home and family for this alien lifestyle:

> Frankly, I hated it. It was just like being a prisoner. You had to be in bed by about 9:00 PM. If you failed to get up of a morning the duty NCOs would pour cold water over your head. And if by any chance you were found to be sitting by the river instead of being in it, you were physically picked up and thrown in it. On many occasions, some of the recruits were punched, caned, and, if the offense was serious enough, tied to a pole and left in the sun until the Sergeant was satisfied that they had been adequately punished. The English and Arithmetic we were taught then is nothing compared

to what they teach now. We were not given any books to read; most of the time we did not understand what our instructors were saying, most of all, if they spoke in English. If I had been taught anything worthwhile I would have remembered it. (Yegova 1985)

Yegova joined the police in 1943, during World War II, when the style of training was tougher, more urgent, than that provided in peacetime. Yet there is a consensus among the recruits that a certain amount of force was applied during training to reinforce discipline among the men.

Kasse offered the extreme opinion that neither the police training nor his subsequent employment as a member of the New Guinea police prepared him for anything except a return to subsistence. He thought there were too many restrictions, and the men had been robbed of their freedom. Generally life in the barracks was hard for him. In his view, it would have been far better if he had not allowed himself to be recruited.

The men discovered early that conditions at the barracks, whether before, during, or after the war, were different from those of their villages. Not only was the place devoid of women, children, and the aged, but the rules and regulations were hard and repressive. Under those circumstances they learned to make quick adjustments or suffered the humiliation of being forced to do so by the noncommissioned officers and their white supervisors.

Achievements and Failures

Men from one culture were being taken to serve as the enforcers of notions of right behavior from another culture, and they were to impose these rules on yet other cultures. As Sir Hubert Murray observed,

There is sometimes a tendency, in dealing with natives, to forget their limitations—to expect too much from them, in fact, to expect considerably more than one could possibly get from a white man, and, in that case, disappointment is inevitable. If you take a man who is running wild in the bush, with nothing on him but a piece of string and a streak of paint, you cannot, simply by putting him in a serge jumper and sulu, give him the steadiness and discipline of a trained soldier; but if you put him in the police barracks for a few months, under a good sergeant, and a white officer in whom he has confidence,[19] you will find that you have got much nearer to it than you could have imagined possible. (Murray 1931, 573)

Murray was sympathetic to the difficulties faced by the trained police but he had in part accepted a prejudice of his time. He wrote as though the police were just "running wild" before recruitment, living without rules of right and wrong, and in their training these "civilized" codes were given to them. In fact, of course, most police grew up learning strict rules—which may have allowed, even demanded, brutality[20]—but they were certainly not living in some primitive community where an absence of clothes and laws went together.

Physical training made both positive and negative contributions to the overall development of the young men. An immediate and obvious achievement was the marked improvement in their physique. The rigors of physical training, together with better food, developed a splendid bodily poise for the men. Better food had the greatest impact on the younger men, but all recruits responded to the new diet. It was noticeable in the shine and clarity of their skins and in the bulk of their upper body muscles. Even plantation laborers, who were often less well fed and not so carefully selected, responded physically to the higher protein and better balanced diet. The emphasis on discipline gave the young men an air of self-confidence and a readiness to prove themselves in the field. Their physical development, coupled with their uniforms and rifle, made them formidable, so much so that in the beginning they became the subject of conversations among many of the villagers (Naguwean 1985). To that extent physical training for the policemen had the desired effect.

Second, from this training grew a bonding, a feeling of oneness among the men. For many, the new experiences were traumatic. It was not as if they were simply brought to a neighboring village, where similarities of custom and tradition would have left them at ease. Instead, the healthiest and most agile men were, in a manner of speaking, "snatched" (Lacey 1979) out of their villages and a known way of life and placed in the middle of a colonial environment to live a life of rigid and strict discipline. They were forced by this circumstance to work together, and soon a new identity, an esprit de corps, bonded them together as "brothers-in-arms." In Papua, the feeling of brotherhood among the recruits emerged early in Port Moresby:

> The service enlarges the views of the young men who compose the force. The force being drawn from all parts of the Possession, there is a great diversity of type and character, and although youths from one or neighbouring districts are apt to keep together, it is not unusual amongst older members of the force to see strong intimacies established between lads that have come from districts widely apart. Although, as might naturally be expected from a number of youths, there is plenty of chaff and a certain amount of rough play amongst them, quarrels and fights are practically unknown. One fight, which started between two of a small detach-

ment at work on the government jetty at Port Moresby, was promptly put a stop to by the native corporal in charge, who arrested the
two angry youths and took them forthwith before the Commandant. To the satisfaction of the rest of the members of the force,
who freely expressed their opinion that the conduct of their two
comrades was disgraceful, they were both put in the lockup for a
short period. (*PAR* 1894–95, xix)

Third, the acquisition of a common language during training was important. It was not only administratively expedient, but also saved much
confusion and misunderstanding. Recruits from New Guinea were
taught English, but not very effectively, and they "picked up" *Tok Pisin*
from their contact with other *Tok Pisin* speakers. Papuans were taught
English, but almost equally ineffectively (Dutton 1985, 250n35). The
languages most widely spoken among the policemen after only a short
period were *Tok Pisin* in New Guinea and Police Motu in Papua. The
benefits of a common language were realized early in Papua:

> [T]he constabulary has done a great amount of good as a teaching
> institution. It is the most effective means in operation for the dis-
> tribution of a common tongue over a wide area of country. The
> languages of the constabulary are principally English and Motuan.
> The latter tongue is more easily acquired than the former, and it
> has been carried by retired constables to numerous places where it
> had never before been heard of. (*PAR* 1893–94, xxx)

The six or more months of training did achieve something of lasting
consequence for the recruits. They learned about discipline and how to
respond instantly to the commands of authority. Further, they were
made aware of the ethics of industriousness. The new languages acquired ensured they maintained effective communication with those
with whom they came into contact, as well as increasing their knowledge
and understanding of the customs and traditions of their colleagues.
Finally, the esprit de corps that developed between them, in the barracks and outside, fostered new and binding relationships that cut across
narrow tribal affiliations and sowed the seeds for future nationalist
struggles and industrial organizations in Papua New Guinea.

For the moment, two shortcomings are noted. The first is indirect
and can only be understood in the context of the overall change that
was brought to Papua New Guinean communities by the impact of the
west. One of the most notable effects was the movement of people away
from their villages and their subsequent involvement in the cash economy introduced by the Europeans. Seen in that light, the establishment
of the police institution and its recruitment of young men away from
their heritage followed a pattern set with the coming of colonialism.

This process is often referred to as alienation. Though the introduction
of the police force was not wholly responsible for the disruption of many
traditional societies, it nevertheless contributed to their general disinte-
gration.

Second, the Papua New Guinean policemen of the period did not
receive professional training in the same way as a teacher, lawyer, or
economist. There were no hard theories to be learned, for instance, in
social anthropology, to assist them in their work, and no mind-stretch-
ing examinations to be sat. A policeman's training from the 1890s to
the 1960s was brief and intellectually slight, both from the traditional
perspective and in comparison to the training given today. The training
they received might be compared favorably to the excellence achieved
by an athlete, but only in the context of the daily physical exertions
they underwent in order to develop a balanced physique. Apart from
that, their important achievement was as part of a small mobile army
unit—foot patrolling, keeping guard, using the rifle, and maintaining
law and order. In this they were quite effective. But the training they
received did not prepare them to deal effectively and intelligently with
the problems of the villagers. They were taught to use their brawn
more than their brains, and indoctrinated to be extremely loyal to their
officers and the colonial government. If, however, during their service
they performed diligently and achieved things in a manner in keeping
with those who received professional training, then credit must go to
the noncommissioned officers and officers who continued their training in the field—and to their own initiative, innate abilities, and understanding of local conditions.

Summary

If a distinction has to be made on the level of the intellectual training
the respective forces received before the war, it is clear from the information given that the New Guinea force included more technically
skilled New Guineans, but most had received their "education" outside
the force and were recruited and trained as policemen to meet needs
within it. In Papua, in contrast, limited elementary education was provided to the men while in the force, but did not advance to any great
level. In both forces intellectual training in prewar Papua New Guinea
was subordinate to physical training. After the war a Special Branch was
created in each force to accommodate the increase in the number of
men with special skills, but a close look at their qualifications reveals
that the majority were still clerks, carpenters, motor mechanics, and
drivers who were regarded as the "artisans of the Force[s] and perform
all the skilled work required within the Force[s]" (*PAR* 1947–48, 30; *NGAR*
1948–49, 15). To 1960 then, or within the forty years of this study, the

respective police organizations failed to provide adequate intellectual training to the Royal Papua New Guinea Constabulary, although the men excelled in physical fitness. That was the result their instructors aimed for, and they succeeded, mainly because for much of the period under study, exploration and pacification were still of paramount consideration. Fit, steady, disciplined policemen, led by officers who were also conscious of the need for fitness and bushmanship, became the undisputed champions of the colonial governments to the villagers.

The methods and techniques used in training the policemen to achieve excellent results were based on the introduction to the "Infantry Training 1911" manual, which was historically linked to British armies and the Royal Irish Constabulary. It proved attractive initially to the Papuan force, and later to the combined force. The police in the field demonstrated the effectiveness of their training. They had the ability to subdue acts of aggression against the colonial governments quickly and decisively with the use of arms. In the policemen's testimonies, the rifle was what they used in troubled times and to demonstrate their authority over villagers.

Chapter 4
Policemen at Work

> Without the Constabulary, all native administration would cease. Every Magistrate of a Division or district has a detachment of this force to carry on his work. The police are his eyes, his ears and his hands. He depends upon them almost solely for everything he knows of the natives of his Division. They accompany him on all his patrols and act as his interpreters on all occasions. Whatever has been done to pacify the various tribes— apart from the Mission influence on the coast—has been done by this force. For twenty-five years *(sic)* they have fought and marched and explored under their white officers, and they have proved themselves so brave and steadfast, that a couple of armed policemen are sufficient to put hundreds of natives to flight.
>
> G H Nicholls, "Armed Native Constabulary"

By 1913, when Headquarters Officer Nicholls of the armed constabulary was writing, the police had established a tradition of excellent work that spanned twenty-three years. The message in Nicholls' calculated assessment is clear. The responsibilities of the armed constabulary were many and varied; their contribution in all facets of native administration was without equal. Without their involvement, native administration in Papua at best would have suffered public ignominy because little had been achieved, and at worst would have "ceased." More than thirty years later their New Guinean counterparts continued to receive equal praise for their participation in the processes of native administration. In response to my 1987 questionnaire, Rick Giddings observed:

> I thought the performance of the native Constabulary up to 1960 to be very good. They carried out the tasks allotted to them with perseverance, loyalty and, in many instances, great courage—be that courage in the face of warring tribesmen or when confronted by raging rivers which they had to cross on their mail-runs. As to

the contribution the native Constabulary made to the overall colonial administration of PNG, I would ask—could we have done without them? I wonder! If we could have then it would have cost us a lot more in money and manpower to do what we were able to do with their assistance. They were a cheap (no patrol allowance for policemen and no overtime in those days) and effective means of bringing government to the people—of interpreting one to the other.

Yes. In all they showed the same determination and zeal in extending the authority of government as I did. They certainly had a harder job doing it. The long carrier line on patrol mainly carried bits and pieces of patrol equipment to make my stay in the bush more comfortable and, therefore, more endurable. On the other hand, a policeman would set out for a week's excursion in the bush with nothing more than a haversack over one shoulder and an unloaded rifle slung over the other! (Giddings 1987, 15–16)

The kind of work the policemen did depended on where they were posted after training. During the period under study there were two principal areas of employment—the "bush," and the "station." Activity was centered in the bush, and involved going on patrol, making contact with communities, opening up new territory, undertaking punitive expeditions. It generally included all business that took place away from pacified, controlled, and "civilized" areas—in short, towns and other well-established places. Posting to bush or station was not a permanent arrangement. Men engaged in the bush could be recalled to the station at any time, and vice versa. The station included all those areas where policemen were employed principally to guard property and personnel, and to provide assistance to those officers and men extending government influence in the bush as well as those retained at the training depot to train new intakes. Station policemen were engaged in the main administrative centers such as Rabaul, Lae, Madang, Port Moresby, and Samarai, as well as the subdistricts.

Station Work

Policemen selected for the station were divided into two main groups—the town guard, and the headquarters detachment—while a third, smaller group consisted of noncommissioned officers and recruits at the training depot. The principal responsibilities of a town guard involved the maintenance of law and order and the enforcement of those petty regulations which the colonial administrations thought essential—for the convenience of the white community or for the improvement of the black:

The town guard consists of one European officer and twelve native police. During the year, on actions brought by the town guard, 291 convictions were recorded for gambling, absence from quarters, assault, &c., within the township. The guard patrols the different sections of the town day and night, and takes all native offenders first to the officer in charge of the police station. Their work brings them frequently before the Court for Native Affairs in Port Moresby, and consequently they soon obtain knowledge of the regulations which they are required to enforce. Some of the more intelligent men shape very well in these prosecutions, occasionally even conducting their own cases. Besides dealing with offences committed in and about Port Moresby, the town guard do valuable work tracing wanted men, relatives of deceased natives, &c., and as these inquiries are constantly being called for the town guard are ever busy. I think it may be said that they do valuable work in that they do it well. (*PAR* 1926–27, 56)

In contrast, the policemen based at headquarters were often auxiliary policemen providing service wherever it was required. In Port Moresby, for instance,

The Headquarters is the place from which the impossible is expected, and during the year under review has been kept very busy supplying reliefs to the sixteen out-stations in order to keep their detachments up to their authorized strengths, besides supplying escorts to travelling medical officers, anthropologists, orderlies to different offices in Port Moresby, carriers for overland mails, men for special patrols, escorts to prisoners transferred from one station to another, besides detailing men to act as warders to prisoners when in hospital and detailing additional men to the European constable when required for special duty. A number of trained men, including those of the town guard and orderlies, are kept at Headquarters in order to cope with any emergency that may arise. [All in all] the life of the police at Headquarters is very strenuous. They are on duty from 6.30 a.m. till 6 p.m., and never know when they will be called upon for duty during the night; but still they are a very happy lot and the *esprit de corps* amongst them is something to be proud of. (*PAR* 1926–27, 56)

Work on the station encompassed various responsibilities for the policemen. A constable could be assigned to instruct new recruits, provide security as the "town guard" to people within the "town" boundary, carry mail and messages to officers in the bush, perform skilled jobs such as carpentry and plumbing, play in the police band, join the elite squad to be deployed in emergency situations, and perform an array of other tasks requiring police attention on the station, including the training of police as prison warders (*NGAR* 1926–27, 89). Generally, after the completion of training, the officers selected those to be sent to the district or division headquarters or posted to the "plantation."[1] All the men interviewed agreed, without hesitation, that because they were members of a disciplined force they had no say whatsoever in where they were sent. But the majority said that the officers' choice of their eventual destination depended on their performance during training. Only a select few were retained at the training depot. Because these men had performed exceptionally well during training, they were kept to train new recruits at the depot along with older policemen who, because of their long experience on the outstations, were brought in to "educate" the younger men. Most of the older men had not only risen through the ranks but had worked long enough within the "system" to know what was involved. It was felt that their presence on the station would be a source of inspiration to the young recruits.

For much of the time the headquarters detachments were based in the main administrative centers such as Port Moresby, Rabaul, Madang, Morobe, Sepik, or Samarai. Each detachment consisted of two or more sergeants, corporals, and lance corporals, and between twenty and thirty constables.[2] While a variety of tasks were performed on the station, generally the lower the rank, the more menial the responsibilities. The annual reports for both territories are not consistent and do not provide details of police duties for all years. However, where information is provided, the details of engagements are quite specific. For example, for the two months of August and September the constabulary were engaged in:

> the cleaning and mending of the road from Port Moresby to the top of the Astrolabe Range. . . . All things considered, they did the work very well. They also procured a number of piles for buildings, from a point on a coast some 20 miles west of the port. At the outstations the men are employed at different kinds of labour; sometimes as the crews of small vessels and boats, sometimes at agricultural work, road making, house building etc. (*PAR* 1901–02, 24)

The policemen in both forces were, in effect, a captive labor force for the government; they were the builders of colonial rule in reality and metaphorically. According to Governor Hahl, he took great pains for some years to train a group of twenty-four New Guineans for police work for about two hours in the morning, only for them to be called away by the New Guinea Company to work on its plantation (Hahl 1980, 11). In police and army jargon the menial jobs were referred to as "fatigue duties," a synonym for simple, often repetitive and dirty manual, often unskilled, labor. Fatigues included cooking, washing uniforms, cutting grass around stations, building houses, making gardens to supplement their diet, and carrying mail from the headquarters to or within one or more divisions and districts. Often the distribution of mail from one destination to another involved arduous walks:

> They were used during the year as overland mail carriers, and in this respect did really valuable work. From Port Moresby alone there are three distinct mail services. These mails are fortnightly, and leave for Kokoda, in the Northern Division, connecting with another mail therefrom to Ioma. This service the fleet-footed constabulary carry out in nine days on an average. Many times it has been done in less, and the record so far has been six days, a remarkable walking feat. Another mail leaves for Yule Island, tapping all the points of settlement en route, and this is carried out in three days. The third service is to Rigo, which is done in two days. These services are carried out splendidly by the men, and during the year not a single mishap occurred to the mail. (O'Malley 1908, 85)

On the longer treks mailmen were equipped with light trade goods such as tobacco to enable them to obtain food from the villagers along the way, and to avoid delaying them unnecessarily from completing the task at hand.

Except from about the last ten years before the war until about fourteen years after it, an increasing number of young men from both forces found themselves posted to the expanding administrative centers because they had acquired special skills before their recruitment to the police force. After the completion of their police training, it made sense to keep these men at headquarters, where their additional skills could be better used. To accommodate this change within the New Guinea police force, certain amendments were made to the police regulations under the Police Ordinances of 1930 and 1931, which read in part, "for the organization, administration, control and management of the Police Force" (NGAR 1930–31, 32). Some of the more common skills included carpentry, plumbing, typing, bookkeeping, and motor-vehicle driving. There are no similar records for the Papuan police during the 1930s. Indications are that some changes occurred, but the extent is not clear. For instance, in 1914–15, "Two armed constables have for the last five months been receiving instruction in carpentering in the Public Works Department, and should be useful men on out-stations" (PAR 1914–15, 105). By the 1950s the Papuan force certainly had men with skills similar to those of their New Guinean counterparts. James Ori Evara of Gulf, for instance, worked as a clerk at Kila police barracks after the completion of his training in 1953. Prior to his recruitment he had received some education in English at a London Missionary Society school in his home district. Except for a brief period in the detective section, he spent most of his police career as an accounts clerk in the police barracks at Kila (Evara 1986). Likewise, Panau of Milne Bay began as a police driver in 1955 and continued in that role until he retired in 1978. He went on patrols occasionally, but rarely beyond the bounds of Central District (Panau 1986). With the enrollment of these "educated" men the police forces became self-reliant in specific technical skills. The carpenters, for instance, were able to carry out minor repairs to buildings that previously had re-quired the services of experts from outside the forces (NGAR 1933–34, 321). It was not unusual for noncommissioned officers to be in charge of a number of jobs on the station. Guise, as the regimental sergeant major of police in Port Moresby, was in charge of all the Papua New Guinean policemen stationed there (members of both the New Guinea police and the Papuan Constabulary), in addition to supervising all the civilian local office staff. His favorite job

> was going through the court papers which dealt with courts of native matters, courts of native affairs and the court of petty ses-sions, returns of which were coming in from the districts. It was my duty to go through these court returns and try and locate any mis-carriage of justice. In one instance, I managed to pick out a couple where a magistrate had exceeded his powers in jailing a policeman under section 14 of the then Police Act. I then pointed out the dis-crepancy to the European Officer. An appeal was then made to the supreme court and the matter was quashed. (Guise 1985)

The performance of the policemen under him received high praise from senior officers. However, the Port Moresby detachment, and gen-erally members of both forces, did not have the essential background to work in the detection of criminals. Indeed, in Sir Hubert Murray's considered view, the majority of the Papuan force, at least in 1908, were "almost absolutely useless as regards the detection of crime—in fact, they are hardly ever employed in this way" (PAR 1908–09, 23–24; see also Murray 1912, 241–242). Despite the extra training given, no major im-provements were evident within the force in 1934. Up to that time only two men in the Papuan force were thought by Europeans to have skills as detectives: Sergeant Major Simoi of Daru who died on 28 February 1934 after giving distinguished service, and Sergeant Major Bagita Aro-mau of Fergusson Island (PAR 1934, 6; A Inglis 1982, 22, 49–51). The majority, their officers said, failed to grasp what detective work was all about, having had no previous experience in this field. In the case of a murder, for instance, the police were not brought in until after the murderers had been identified, usually by villagers, and an officer requested the assistance of someone to arrest the culprits rather than to conduct an investigation (Beaver 1920, 35). However, the policemen were of the view that because of their better command of languages and better knowledge of local gossip they were better able to know who the guilty people were before their officers did. The officers' notion of the Papua New Guinean policeman having no skills in detection conformed to a stereotype of the loyal, tough, but unimaginative black policeman. Despite such presumed shortcomings, both the headquarters detachments and those posted to other main stations often performed their given responsibilities with diligence and dedication. There was no better qualified person to sing their praises than Guise, with his knowledge of the internal organization of the force and an intimate understanding of its daily operations:

> I will say this much, I think that the Papuan and New Guinean Constabulary, when I was a policeman, upheld law and order. They had discipline, very, very strong discipline that ran right through the ranks. And the way they diligently carried out their duties towards the protection of life and property and the way they carried out the patrols every day and every night with honour and dignity was something that I would now look back and say, "I wish it were done all over again." This real dedication to work contained the criminal element, it contained it very well. (Guise 1985)

Whether at training or out on patrol, the policemen's daily activities were regulated with military precision. For instance, on an average police station the bugle sounded between 5:30 and 6:30 AM, when the police, except for those who had been on night duty, had to be out of bed and ready for work. Breakfast consisted of black tea and navy biscuits, and sometimes "flour" pancakes. After roll call and a short parade, they marched off to their respective assignments, including supervising prisoners at work, escorting the sick to the hospital or the medical orderly, buying food from the nearby villagers, pursuing escaped prisoners, watching over station hands cutting grass, cleaning roads, and attending to any other job that required their attention that day. They rested between 11:00 AM and noon, had their first big meal for the day, and soon after returned to their duties until 5:00 PM, when the bugle was blown again for the end of afternoon work. The men in Port Moresby assembled at the parade ground for a short inspection before they marched up to Government House and lowered the flag. After the ceremony they returned and gave the group's final salute to the administrator as the titular police commandant, then returned either to the single barracks or, after the war, to the married quarters. Dinner was served between 6:00 and 6:30 PM. By regulation no one was allowed to leave the precincts of the barracks without permission from the European officer in charge. From dinner until 9:00 PM those not on night duty were "free" to do what they felt like (within reason, and in accordance with the station's regulations), but only within the confines of the barracks area. Those in Rabaul were allowed to stroll around Chinatown until the first bugle at 8:45 PM. They then hurried to be back before check-in time. At 9:00 PM the lights were out in the police quarters and the jail. The occupants were then supposed, legally, to be in bed; in reality many men whispered to each other and stayed awake for "hours" after the lights out call. Night duty policemen continued to patrol the perimeter of the station at irregular intervals to ensure that silence was maintained and for general security (Townsend 1968, 53–54). This outline of an average policeman's work, sometimes for seven days a week if he was not out on patrol, was supported by the men interviewed. Their accounts were quite vague when it came to recollecting the times for different activities. Guise gave a detailed account of the daily routine of the men under his supervision in Port Moresby (1985).

Patrol Work: The Official View

Working in the bush constituted the single most important part of a policeman's work outside the station during the period under study. Bush work, like station work, encompassed a wide range of responsibilities. It involved physically walking over long distances through hostile and intimidating terrain; exploring new territory; bringing *"nupela lo bilong gavman"* (the new laws of the government) to unsuspecting tribespeople and instructing them, through appointed officials, on how best these should be observed; conducting punitive expeditions and arresting suspected troublemakers wherever required, and much more. By the 1950s, the urgency of the work became apparent when Sir Paul Hasluck, the minister for external territories, complained that vast areas of the colony were still virgin territory and set in motion a series of directives to his subordinates on how best to solve this problem. Despite Hasluck's resolute intentions, the problem persisted beyond 1960. But it needed to be solved, and quickly, because it was the only way the central government could present and enforce its views on most villagers (Hasluck 1976, 78-79). Consequently, the majority of the policemen, at one stage or another in their police career, had a stint at bush or patrol work.

Officially patrol work was divided into two types—"administrative" and "penetrating." The first was quite easy to manage after the initial traumas were overcome. Its purpose was basically to monitor progress made in a pacified area and to introduce various mechanisms for tax collection, census taking, inspection of indentured labor recruiting, inquiring into land disputes, and checking on any other matters requiring attention, such as roads, bridges, and the general cleanliness of the villages (*NGAR* 1931–32, 88). The second type of patrol is less easy to

define. Known in official circles as "penetrating patrols" and sometimes
referred to in colonial literature as "peaceful penetration" (Chinnery
1920, 440–452), these patrols were "for the purpose of extending the
influence of the administration into new areas, or consolidating the
influences gained in areas previously visited but not yet under control"
(*NGAR* 1931–32, 88).

A declaration in the first Australian New Guinea annual report
serves as an introduction:

> On the native police falls the work of bringing new territory under
> government control, the suppression of cannibalism and inter-
> tribal warfare, and the enforcement of law and order among tribes
> already under government influence. All patrolling in the territory
> is carried out by the police.[3]

The effectiveness of administrative arrangements at the district or division level rested on the efforts of both European officials and Papua
New Guinean policemen, who walked into many villages, assembled
villagers, and told them, through interpreters, what they were trying
to achieve. In the main this involved the dissemination of regulations
regarding the type of law and order the government wanted the people
to observe. Furthermore, it was left to the patrols to interpret two
dichotomous legal "systems" to the people: the British or Australian
one and the Papua New Guinean *"lo bilong tumbuna"* (traditional laws,
or laws passed down from the earliest ancestors). In practice, few or
none of the traditional laws were used to reach a settlement of any
kind. By and large the people were left to solve their own problems
with the aid of their own social control mechanisms. However, if disagreements between individuals or village groups could not be solved
by traditional means, and there were prospects that they were going to
disturb the peace the colonial government was attempting to establish,
then the policemen, as the government's watchdog, were sent in to
quell any disturbance. Then introduced European laws were used to
resolve the dispute.

From the colonial government's perspective certain indigenous
practices were "repugnant to [a European's] ethical code." J A Todd's
study of "Native Offences and European Law in South-West New Britain"
(1935) identified the main offense as homicide (which, of course, was
not confined to New Britain). Offenses that occurred with some frequency included "the immolation of widows, warfare, head-hunting,
cannibalism and infanticide as well as murder and manslaughter." Also
included in his classification were sorcery, rape, incest, sodomy, and
other "unnatural" sexual acts (Todd 1935, 444). The elimination of
those "abhorrent" practices required both extensive exploration and
intensive pacification. For orderly development during the early 1930s,

district officers and their staff were ordered to prepare maps of the districts that fell under their jurisdiction, distinguishing the degree of government influence by means of a fivefold classification:

1 Area under control—an area into which an unarmed police constable could go to make an arrest and be sure to get the support of the people.
2 Area under partial control—a police constable could go to make an arrest but the assistance of the villagers would not be relied upon.
3 Area under government influence—where a government party would not be resisted in effecting an arrest, and where the lives and property of the government officers and staff were safe.
4 Area penetrated by patrols—where government patrols had been but contact with the people had not yet been established.
5 Unknown area. (Townsend 1933, 424)

At the end of this exercise district personnel had a fair idea of the degree of influence in each section of the district under their control. Only then was the senior member of the field staff in a position to delegate responsibilities to officers to conduct regular bush patrols. It was hoped that constant attention from government patrols would ultimately advance the lesser-known communities to the level of those in the first category.

To hasten the process of "contact patrols" an effective method evolved by patrol officers involved the establishment of "police camps," which in Papua "were to be the furthermost outposts, bringing the Government to the wild men of the Papuan mountains" (Sinclair 1969, 24). When it was known that a certain area was marked out for penetration, a patrol officer with two noncommissioned officers and about ten or twelve police constables, a medical officer, and carriers walked to the area and established a police camp in a central location or on a site thought to be a buffer zone (photo 34). This was important because if any of the nearby communities got the slightest impression that favoritism was being shown to one group, the others would not cooperate. The first few days were spent near the camp, assessing the reponses of the people and distributing gifts. When no major incident was reported, the officer and his men began to patrol the surrounding areas. The people were told, through interpreters, of the purpose of the visit, and villagers were ordered to build rest houses for future patrols. After a few days of observation and more patrols, the party either moved on to another area or returned to the subdistrict for rest and replenishment of supplies before the next patrol (Reed 1943, 168–169). The process in Papua was described, perhaps idealized, by Murray:

Photo 34 Ian Downs' camp, north of Wabag, 1938. (Courtesy of Bill Gammage)

There is a policy known to the French as *la tâche d'huile* —the policy
of the oil stain, the theory . . . being that the civilising influence of
the government will percolate from certain fixed centres right
through the surrounding country. And we have acted upon this in
Papua. After establishing stations in places which we considered

suitable, we proceeded . . . to connect these stations by a series of cross patrols from one another; and the result was that, on the analogy of the oil stain, the influence of the government extended throughout the intervening country. (Murray 1944, x)

Although I have no information on whether officers in the New Guinea administration were aware of the French policy, this method of pacification was practiced extensively in New Guinea. It may have been learned through contact with Papuan officials, or, and more likely, it evolved independently of Papuan and French influence because of similarities of conditions on the frontiers of both territories.

Patrol Work: The Policemen's Views

From the men's oral evidence, three strong elements of their work in the bush emerge. First, the policemen had an eye for detail and a demonstrated knowledge of bushcraft that contributed to the success of many difficult patrols. Second, they revealed a fundamental insight into the nature of their work in the bush. They came to see themselves, as did many village communities, as "social workers," as interpreters of the *nupela pasin,* and as agents of the central government. Third is the important question of violence: why did they think it was necessary to use force? This is the subject of the next chapter.

Patrol Routines

It is obvious from official statements as well as those given by the men that no responsibility pleased a policeman more than to be selected for patrol duties. Sir Hubert Murray, who may have exaggerated, wrote in 1908, "As regards this part of their duty, they are almost too keen; they weep bitterly when a patrol goes out and they are left behind" (*PAR* 1908, 23–24). However, none of the men interviewed said he wept because of being left behind. They certainly felt disappointed but they always looked to the bright side and strove harder in the hope of getting selected the next time. From all accounts there was stiff competition among the policemen to impress their white officers. They said it required punctuality, commitment, obedience, and sheer hard work.

Most policemen, except for those enrolled during the late 1950s, agreed wholeheartedly that they enjoyed patrol work more than they did the more banal duties of the station. It was interesting, full of mysteries, and fraught with dangers. They never quite knew what was waiting for them beyond the limestone country between the headwaters of the Kikori and the Strickland Rivers, within the makeshift hamlets of the unpredictable Binandere, at the top of the precipitous ridges of the

Photo 35 Police detachment at Gogme patrol post, Simbu, 1935. (Courtesy of Bill
Gammage)

Nakanai Mountains, at the foothills of the great Sepik River, or beyond
the towering mountains of the highlands. For many, their zeal and determination to explore the country for its own sake played as important a
role as extending government influence through the length and breadth
of the land. In this work a policeman could shine and show his natural
ability, a task he could perform with courage, diligence, and unquestioning loyalty. The most extravagant praise, particularly from the patrol
officers, was heaped upon the policemen for their dedication and noble
achievements. With his bulging rucksack hung heavily on the middle

left side of his body, left arm firmly gripping his .303 Lee-Enfield carbine, hair neatly cut, fine physique, and police uniform hanging tightly against his body, the policeman looked formidable to the inhabitants of many village communities, still clad in their meager traditional costumes.

While in the bush on patrol, a policeman was one step away from the trappings of the colonial establishment. If outwardly he still felt bound by his responsibilities to the government, he nonetheless experienced a temporary psychological release that allowed him to live close to his traditional lifestyle (photo 35). In an office with all its government forms, the village-recruited policeman was usually in an alien and disturbing environment; in the bush he was comfortable, "at home," and able to reverse, or at least modify, the relationship between himself and the white officer. The officer came to him to ask basic questions concerning what ought to be done about imminent attacks, crossing a flooded river, getting food from villagers, setting up camp for the night, arresting murderers, and so forth. Was the policemen's advice of any importance? Rick Giddings was emphatic that on patrol a policeman's advice was essential and could only be ignored at the officer's own risk:

> I soon learnt that on all occasions kiaps should listen very carefully to what their senior policemen and NCOs had to tell them. It was wise to weigh what they said very carefully before rejecting it. Indeed, the rule was "reject their advice at your own risk." If a policeman said that river was too wild (in flood) to cross then you did NOT cross it. It was as simple as that. If he said it was time to make camp it was time to make camp. If he said that a particular situation was so tense that to press the point was to risk a showdown and wisdom insisted that we should withdraw and try a different approach on another day, that was invariably the best course of action to follow. I was always very insistent on that point with my juniors—"Listen to the advice your NCO or *'namba wan polis'* [senior ranking constable not having NCO rank] has to give you, and disregard it at your own risk." (Giddings 1987; see Appendix 1)

Giddings wrote of his experiences with his policemen in the Trust Territory of New Guinea after the 1950s. He may have been unaware that officers of the armed constabulary of an earlier age had already given lavish praises to the Papuan policemen. Like him, they too found the services of the police in the bush indispensable. W M Strong, officer in charge of the armed constabulary, North-East Division, wrote of the nature of their involvement in 1913:

> The principal police work of the Division is the accompanying of the European officers on patrol, and an officer has to rely on his police for information as to tracks, fordable rivers, &c.; and away

from the coast he is lucky if he can talk to any natives except through the medium of a constable. (*PAR* 1911, 61)

A common element in the officers' experiences through time and space is the nature of the responsibilities of the policemen they described—ability to detect fordable rivers, to find suitable tracks, knowledge of various languages, capacity to assess hostile situations, and so on.

Much of the detail of patrol work did not change over fifty years. Elaborate preparations had to be made to assemble food supplies and equipment, recruit carriers, and arrange logistical support before a patrol was considered ready to depart. An average patrol lasted about a month. The following description of a typical month-long patrol is composed from statements made by three of the men who worked in different geographical locations at different times: Anka in the Eastern Highlands during the early 1930s, Empere in the lowlands of the Western Division from the early 1950s, and Sono in Talasea in the island district of West New Britain in the early 1930s.

> Say, for instance, one was the senior policeman of the station and the kiap wanted us to conduct a patrol which he thought would take a month. He called the senior policeman by his rank and name and told him this, and the day the patrol was to begin. He also informed him of the area where we were to carry out the patrol. That was all he did. Many kiaps were only young men who hardly had any experience in the field. Many of the senior policemen actually initiated these kiaps into how to conduct and behave themselves during patrols.[4] In that respect it was left to the senior policeman on the station to attend to the finer details. He decided on the quantity of rations we would require, the materials for trade with the people, and the number of carriers and policemen that would be needed. From knowledge acquired through past experience, for a month's supply he assembled 10 bags of rice, 2 cartons of tinned meat, 1 carton of fish, 1 dozen bush knives and 2 dozen little knives. He also listed the kinds of things that the people of the area liked to trade with us. During our time the most common were salt, paints, beads, knives, axes, shells and pieces of red cloth. For the camps we put together lamps, kerosene, matches, tobacco, etc. He then selected the doctor boy and the interpreter and appointed his own assistant. If there was no corporal, he appointed the most senior constable as the corporal to assist him on the patrol. Having decided on what to carry he sent two to three policemen to recruit nearby villagers as carriers. If there were not enough men to carry for us he asked the kiap to release some of the prisoners to do the work. Prisoners often carried for us because they preferred patrol work to the drudgery of the station's fatigue duties.

The policemen returned in the afternoon with whatever carriers they could enlist. The carriers were fed, received instructions and shown to their sleeping quarters. The senior policemen then called the police in for duty and issued them with 5–10 rounds of cartridges. When everything was packed and ready, he reported this fact to the kiap.

The following morning the senior noncommissioned officer distributed the cargo among the carriers. He then arranged the men in the order they would walk. And then, after bidding farewell to the rest of the policemen, labourers, and prisoners left on the station, the retinue set off at a brisk pace. At the head of the patrol was a constable. He was our scout and sometimes our interpreter. The kiap walked behind him. He only carried his rifle, compass and pistol. He often wore boots with nails, khaki shorts and shirt and a big hat that provided plenty of shade for his face. The senior policeman walked directly behind the kiap. Then followed the carriers and in between them the constables. About three constables and a corporal walked at the tail end. That was because a lot of the time warriors attacked us from the rear. For this reason we doubled our security there. On a normal day we walked from about 6:00 AM to 4:00 PM. The routes we followed ran through jungles, rivers, plains etc. The kiap used a compass which we sometimes called "clock" because it looked like one.

At about 4:00 PM we stopped and set up camp and the flag, sometimes in the middle of the jungle, for about an hour before it was taken down again. Here it was the policemen's responsibility to put up tents for the kiap, carriers, and themselves. They chopped posts, collected ropes, firewood, dug a latrine for the kiap and generally attended to most of the things that would be needed that night. After everyone had been fed they moved into their tents and settled in for the night. Some of the policemen were appointed for sentry duties. They worked in shifts. Inside the tents the rest of the policemen told stories and sang a few songs. The stories ranged from serious conversations to dirty jokes. It really depended on the story teller. Some policemen were religious and did not join in. But they pretended to sleep and listened intently. There were some songs that we all knew and these we sang vociferously but occasionally one had the urge to begin a traditional song and this was sung by those who knew it while the rest hummed along quietly. But even in the jungle the government's laws pursued us and we "slept" when the lights were turned out. We followed a similar routine for about a month until we returned to the station for rest, collected our monthly pay and the married men were reunited with their families. Most of the patrol work was done on foot, an established tradition from when the police forces were first engaged in this type of work. We did not have the luxury of using police patrol cars, much less helicopters, to rush us to trouble spots. Certainly this part of our work was hard and taxing but we carried it out with discipline, loyalty, and forbearance. And we thoroughly enjoyed it. (Anka 1986; Empere 1986; Sono 1985)

The correlation in these separately recorded accounts reinforces the basic premise of this study that not only was patrolling an important preoccupation of many policemen, but the type of work they performed in the bush was fundamentally similar in both Papua and New Guinea. Rewari, having worked in both territories, testified that the style and method of patrol work was the same in Samarai and Mt Hagen, though he noticed some differences in the attitudes and the response of the people to a patrol party. In Mt Hagen men were more aggressive, but the instructions he received from his officers in the bush in the respective areas were the same: *"Ol man bighet na ol sutim yu, yu tu ken sutim ol"* (If the people do not accept your advice and shoot you, you too can shoot them; Rewari 1989).

Further, Ivan Champion was a stickler for details. If Papua's operational methods in the bush were different from those of New Guinea, he would at least have advised his policemen and carriers of the differences before they crossed the boundary into New Guinea. His book *Across New Guinea* (1966) makes no mention of such an instruction.

The composite account complements the officers' assessments of the policemen's performance in the bush, particularly with young and inexperienced patrol officers whom policemen introduced to the rigors of bushcraft. Where differences in police work existed, they were due not so much to differences in colonial policies but to such factors as the geographical isolation, the degree of government influence, and the diversity of societies. In some places, for instance, the reception of a patrolling party was cordial, while in others it steamed with hostility. Among still other groups it was difficult to determine what the people really wanted. For a time they might show all manner of friendliness, which temporarily established good relations between them and the government, but at a sudden yell from their leader the patrol would be attacked as if the officer and police were complete strangers who had just trespassed on their territory. Moru Moag, who was recruited in 1953, continued the story:

After a three-year stint with the fire brigade in Moresby I was transferred to Kerema in the middle of the 1950s. Using Kerema as our base camp we patrolled regularly into the Kukukuku, Menyamya and Kaintiba areas. At first, I found the people there to be timid, very reserved, and curious about our coming into their territory.

But after the first phase they seemed to become accustomed to our presence. Though the real reason is not readily apparent, it is most likely that one of the main attractions was the generous distribution of gifts. In particular they developed an intense desire for salt. In order to get at it the men threw their spears into the bush lest we prevent them from coming near. However, by a curious treachery they undermined our generosity and friendly gestures and attacked us at every turn, cunningly enough, after the end of every trading session. This was strange behaviour and one I did not see again during my postings in Garaina or anywhere else in Morobe District. (Moag 1986)

Apart from human and environmental problems, the police had to contend with difficulties caused by their own errors. Food shortages were frequent, particularly in areas where there were acute shortages in the gardens of the communities they visited. For instance, an expedition conducted in 1933 by Patrol Officer Allert Nurton and ten policemen to provide protection for a party prospecting for precious metals had to be abandoned due to a lack, among other things, of food for the policemen and carriers. In his submission to Edward Taylor, the district officer of Salamaua, Nurton wrote:

The partial failure of the expedition was due, in my opinion, to:

(c) lack of consideration for the carriers, causing them to weaken through insufficient and unsustaining food and rough, thoughtless treatment. . . .

(d) further, we were unable to purchase sufficient foods for the large number of our natives from the small village we visited; often the carriers and police boys received but one small meal of "kaukau" in the 24 hours of labour in rough cold country in high altitudes.

(e) the final decision to abandon the expedition was forced upon the party when it entered apparently uninhabited country for two days with no adequate reserve of food for the natives. (Nurton 1934)

After experiencing these hardships, it was a relief to return "home" to the station in whatever condition they were in:

I wonder if the reader knows what I mean? Can he picture a little band of men, their frames no more than skeletons, the bones of their faces showing out and dull eyes sunk deep in the sockets; and can he picture them dragging their frames over limestone rocks, exerting those frames again and again with no promise of food, with nostrils filled with mucus that strength is not there to clear away? I never want to see such tortured and pitiable humans again. (Hides 1936, 166)

Jack Hides, described by many of his colleagues as one of the best patrol officers in the Papuan service,[5] wrote this after a gruelling patrol into the limestone country at the headwaters of the Kikori and Strickland Rivers in late 1935. In his introduction to Hides' book (1935, xv), Murray eulogized this patrol as "the most difficult and the most dangerous patrol ever carried out in the whole island of New Guinea."[6] Hides' account of the state of his men and the country they traversed is nightmarish. Yet from the accounts given by the men, only a week or two of convalescence on the station reinvigorated them, and they were ready to pick up their rucksacks and trudge on again.

"Social Work"

> When the axe came into the forest,
> The trees said:
> The handle is one of us.
>
> Turkish proverb quoted in George Danns,
> *Dominance and Power in Guyana*

The Papua New Guinean policemen did not receive professional training in meeting and controlling peoples on the frontier. Four factors support this conclusion: The men considered that their being Papua New Guinean contributed to their success; they established lasting friendships wherever they were posted; they believed they were on a civilizing mission; and they were committed to upholding the integrity of the police force.

First, most of the men were convinced that the success of their work was because they were Papua New Guineans. Despite the diversity in customs and traditions, an element of similarity cut across wide-ranging differences. The recognition of this commonality between villagers and policemen hastened their understanding of each other's behavior. The people could see that the person hidden behind the splendid uniform was like themselves. When they realized that the uniform could be taken off and worn again, it dawned on them that it was no different from their own daily change of the leaves and tree bark that formed their clothing. The people quickly came to the conclusion that the European officer whom the policemen accompanied must have been responsible for the differences in their attire. In this regard the total stranger was the patrol officer, not his band of policemen. Other small things the policemen did enhanced understanding between themselves and their hosts. Invariably after the initial curiosities were over, the policemen were the first to sit down among the people and share betelnuts, tobacco, and food. Through their actions the people came to see and accept that the policeman was "one of them." The people's recognition of their unspoken close links with the policemen helped to destroy fear and suspicion, thereby accelerating the process of pacification.

Second, and a corollary of the first factor, was the establishment of lasting friendships between the policemen and some people wherever they were posted. The ultimate proof of this friendship lies in the number of marriages that took place between policemen and women in whose areas they served. Of the twenty-eight policemen interviewed, eleven—Amero, Anka, Guise, Moru, Kambian, Panau, Sarepamo, Sono, Tamutai, Tigavu, and ToWoworu—married women outside their traditional areas. Of the eleven, seven brought their wives back to their villages when their service in the police force ended. Three men—Anka, Kambian, and Tamutai—settled permanently on the land of their in-laws, one in Goroka and two in the Southern Highlands. They wished to record that had it not been for the pleading of their in-laws they would have returned to their respective homes. But they had no regrets for having succumbed.

> I am now living in Agautoka village, and have done so for many years. During this long period I have not got into any strife with anyone over land, custom or anything else for that matter. When I got married to one of their daughters, they accepted me into their midst as one of them, and I reciprocated and accepted them as my own people. I worked in the highlands for almost the entire period of my police career, and I came to understand many of their ways. So I was not exactly a novice. Though I am from Markham, I do not think there is anything fundamentally different from the ways of my adopted home to those of my own people. Besides we are now one people and my marriage to my wife confirms the new identity that was fostered through the work of the early policemen. (Anka 1986)

Marriage, then, became symbolic; it was a bridge built across fear and suspicion. It confirmed the close relationship the policemen established among the people and demonstrated the people's trust, confidence, and acceptance of their presence among them.

Third, the policemen were convinced, as were their European officers, that they were on a "civilising" mission. They firmly believed that they had been given a head start, and now it was their turn to tell the others of the new order. If they themselves could not instruct the people, due to difficulties in learning a new language, they captured some small boys, brought them back to the station, and inculcated in them the intentions of the government. When these captives became fluent in the language of the police and acquired general knowledge about the government, they were either sent back to their homes or engaged as interpreters for patrols. In the eyes of the police, the bulk of the Papua New Guineans not yet contacted and brought under the government's control were "bush-kanaka"—people who did not wear European clothes and continued to engage in traditional practices, particularly tribal fighting, head-hunting, cannibalism, and sorcery— people who were not like them (Naguwean 1985). The police were even able to find words in the local vernacular to describe the people's condition. An uncivilized Papuan was known as *kunika*, the Motu equivalent of "bush kanaka." The Papuan police, who used the term to describe Papuan people who had not been brought under government control, viewed such people as wild, uncompromising, and belligerent toward patrol parties (Yegova 1985). In Talasea the police used *kaulong* to denote the people of each administrative area least influenced by the government and foreign customs (Niall 1933).

   To the police, many of the villagers were confused about the *nupela pasin*. What did it all mean? Why did they have to stop fighting their enemies and abandon their cannibalism, sorcery, and head-hunting? Faced with such questions the policemen told them that it was because of the new law and order that had come into their midst. An end to these activities would ensure they made bigger and better gardens, wives would no longer wait anxiously for their husbands to return from hunting, their children would live to inherit their parents' possessions, and peace would reign in their communities. If anyone committed an offense against them, they were not to deal with the matter themselves but instead to report it to the patrol officer, or the resident policeman, who would deal with the offender on their behalf. The policemen's effectiveness in translating this *nupela pasin* resulted from their living on out-stations for long periods, unlike the European officials who were transferred quite regularly. They were in a position to do more for the people on a permanent basis than the itinerant patrol officer. Many therefore ended up not only maintaining law and order but also indirectly performing the duties of "social workers." They instructed the people about hygiene, escorted the sick to the hospital, assisted people in growing cash crops, settled their disputes, and instructed them in myriad other small things. But most important, they firmly believed they were invaluable servants of the government. Through their efforts the people learned much more about the government and how its presence would affect their lives, as an Australian field officer recognized in 1932:

> Previously these natives were very timid, and very shy, and seemed afraid of the police. Now the greatest confidence is shown everywhere especially amongst the women and small children. The constables in charge are good steady reliable types of natives, who

seem to have a great interest in their work, and take pride in demonstrating the improvements they have effected. The constables
spend most of their time in patrolling the villages, and do not sit
down on the base camp for long periods. Their work is amongst
the natives, and there they spend their time. The constable being
so much amongst the natives is able to get a thorough insight into
all the aspects of their life, and so forms a liaison between the
natives and the administration. (Niall 1933)

The sentiments expressed by the policemen do not always reflect
what sometimes happened in reality. Some policemen developed into
benign dictators, controlling goods and services to the local population. Mike Donaldson wrote about how Constables Gunua and Kum-
bagan used their positions as policemen to receive free gifts of food
and sexual favors from the local women in the area of Kainantu. If the
men and women failed to respond to their requests they were punished
(1984, 200–201).

The fourth factor was the depth of the policemen's commitment to
their job. Most of them, regardless of the length of service they gave to
the government, showed no complacency about one important aspect
of their work. Almost in unison they claimed that whatever they may
have thought of the government or the police force, they, individually
or as a group, did not knowingly engage in activities that placed the
integrity of the office they held in jeopardy. This strongly stated sentiment illustrates the integrity and dedication that the men who then
served as policemen believed they brought to their tasks. It was demonstrated best in their work as investigators of cases before they were
heard by the Australian patrol officer. This component of their work
was generally performed by senior policemen. The men admitted that,
lacking adequate education, they did not fully understand the labyrinth of legal processes they were to uphold; but through their work,
they learned a very important aspect of it—to show no partiality to
friend or foe. On many occasions policemen were offered bribes in the
form of women, pigs, and other material things in exchange for leni-
ency in their reports to the patrol officer, but a steadfast policeman,
they said, did not give in to blackmail and extortion. This statement is
important in the perception the police brought to their work. (However, Donaldson's investigation of police behavior in Kainantu [1984]
gave another version of what the police were actually doing, not what
they knew about the ideals of police work, and in chapters 7 and 8
other evidence is given of policemen who misbehaved and breached
government regulations regarding their relations with villagers.)

An anecdote illustrates how Guise's loyalty to the government and
the office he held was tested one day, when his son, with some of his

Papuan friends, went for a swim at Ela Beach and was told to leave the area immediately because it was the preserve of the white residents. Reduced to tears, Guise's son went to his father and asked for help in his capacity as sergeant of police in Port Moresby. Guise's laconic reply:

> I am a policeman working to uphold the law within the system that operates and rules our lives at this time. I took an oath of allegiance. I cannot break that law for you or anyone else. The stipulation of one of the regulations states specifically that a native is not allowed to swim in the sea at Ela Beach. I am sorry but I cannot help you in my official capacity as a Sergeant Major of police. (Guise 1985)[7]

This stance demonstrates the conflict of interest between Guise's official devotion to his work and his fatherly instinct to help his son in distress. This was the type of predicament many policemen had to face. Guise was more able to express the ideal of the impartial policeman than others of his generation, but the other police were equally aware of the ideal and were quick to claim it governed their behavior. For many, the desire not to jeopardize the integrity of the official position they held far outweighed other considerations. At least, that was one way they remembered and talked of police work. Violation of police ideals, then, was not a result of ignorance.

"Gan Em i Givim Mipela Stron": The Gun Gave Us Strength

One experienced policeman, a burly Eastern Highlander, told me, "Under the circumstances in which we worked, the gun proved useful, it became our most important security. Without it the colonial government would have crumbled, and the policemen would have been virtually useless" (Sarepamo 1985). The value of the gun became abundantly clear to the policemen before and after they joined the police forces. They were recruited to work for an alien power whose standing army (metaphorically) consisted of a few aging administrators and equally few field staff officers, some of whom were inexperienced in dealing with people of other races. The policemen could see that numerically their employers were clearly in the minority. Surrounding them were a horde of people with alien customs and traditions. In the main, the people were suspicious of the intruders, regarding many of them as enemies who should be fought, as they had fought other strangers in the past, in order for a warrior to establish his position in his society.[8] The policemen knew, from their knowledge of their own societies, that the village warrior was a fierce fighter who would struggle to the end to protect the honor of his tribe, family, and territory. That being the case, the policemen had to be prepared to confront the village warrior with equal force, or with a more lethal weapon, in case the villager decided to attack.

When a new recruit was introduced to the power and effectiveness of the rifle as a weapon during training, he was determined to become proficient at its use. He could see that the .303 carbine rifle[9] was more than a match for spears, clubs, bows, and arrows. And every day during training the recruits were encouraged to strive to be the best marksmen, even if they were not always successful at first:

Marksmanship

With practice and instruction the Papuan policeman can be trained to be a fairly good shot, more especially as he naturally has a very keen sight. The progress made in this line during the past year has been good, but to get the force up to proper state of efficiency constant target practice is essential. Unfortunately the duties of the European officers in charge of the police are so multitudinous that attention to this particular branch of the policeman's training cannot receive the attention it is deserving of; but nevertheless the officers are so exceptionally keen on making marksmen of their men that no opportunity of giving them target practice is lost. Considerable difficulty is always experienced with the native policeman in drilling him into a knowledge of "sighting," his natural impulse being to point his rifle at the target and blaze away, without ever a thought to "sighting." In this way he seldom gets near the target, and then the lesson on the value of "sights" begins to sink home, and he is readily eager to grasp all the points he can, with consequently better results. They are usually taught to fire from four postures—lying down, sitting, on one knee, and standing. The latter is undoubtedly the favourite posture, and the results are always better. They are exceptionally keen on shooting, and are as eager to put up good scores as any European soldiers. At Port Moresby a new rifle range has been built, with disappearing targets in place of the old fixed iron target, and the results are bound to prove much more satisfactory. I have not the slightest doubt that, with plenty of practice and instruction, the Papuan policeman can be made a good shot. (*PAR* 1908, 85)

Needless to say, training was a serious business in Papua, from the perspective of both the trainer and the trained. Only then were they to be considered valuable employees of the government. The colonial governments introduced this weapon, knowing it to be lethal, and knowing that the people did not possess an equivalent weapon, and demanded that the policemen be proficient at its use so that they could go among the people and demonstrate the might of the colonial government. It was hoped that the demonstration of the government's power would frighten people into submission. But, if the people did not submit and instead retaliated against the intrusion, then the rifle-carrying police force patrolled the bush to ensure their compliance.

The gun served many useful purposes for the policemen. It gave them prestige, honor, and power over the village communities. It gave them confidence and a source of power that seemed to radiate from the rifle. It raised their status above that of their peers in the village. It gave them the strength, courage, and determination to *"Suvim het igo insait long ples bilong ol kanaka. Ol kanaka save pret long mipela polisman igat gun. Ol i suruk tru"* (Force our way into the people's villages. The people were afraid of us policemen with guns. They were really and truly scared). On their own admission, without the rifle and the impressive image it gave them, many of the policemen would not have been brave enough to work for the government, particularly on patrols. In the end, the rifle became one of their most valued possessions: they cleaned it every day, slept with it, and never let it out of their sight (Sarepamo 1985). It became their inseparable "companion." Tigavu of Gende (Bundi) said eloquently:

> When the gun was issued to me I was told that it symbolically represented my *big brother* back in the village. If I took good care of it and did not let it out of my sight, I would be saved and would be able to return home to see those people whom I loved. When I was armed with the rifle I felt big and strong. People jumped at my command. They got scared of me, not because I threatened them with it but because they had seen how dangerous it could be when used. Naturally, they held its owner in awe. So much so that in the areas that I worked, people held me in such high esteem that my reputation and popularity as a policeman grew quickly. In the end I had the same reputation as some of my traditional fight leaders back home. (Tigavu 1985)

Esprit de Corps

> The worst thing about being a policeman is that you must always know that you are serving the public who will always say "help me, help me," but will not turn around to say "thank you" to you. If they saw you winking at a girl they will very quickly criticise you and make it blow out of all proportions, to make you look like the ugly policeman. That's the hard part of a policeman's life. When you join the police you must always remember that you are serving a public who are mostly ungrateful. They will never reward you for the good that you are doing, but judge you on the little faults that you may make. (Guise 1985)

Despite their diverse backgrounds, the ease with which the police worked together as "brothers" was extraordinary. In fact, virtually all of the men said, apart from petty quarrels between individual policemen, they worked together as a group as if they were from the same mother. In one important but parochial view, it might seem that colonialism had succeeded with the Papua New Guinean policemen. They were apparently submissive and were excessively supportive of, and loyal to, the colonial government and its agents. However, from a broad perspective, the bond that developed between the men was not a novelty that sprang out of the experience of the Papua New Guinean policemen only. It was common in police forces all over the world. The common denominator appears to be the work, and, insofar as the policemen are concerned, undeniably in response to the reaction of the people toward their performance as policemen. As Guise stated, the public is "mostly ungrateful" for the duties policemen perform on its behalf. The nature of their activities—arresting people for criminal behavior, invading people's privacy, mistreatment of prisoners, and, in the case of early Papua New Guinea, taking innocent villagers' lives— often made them feared and unpopular among the public. In order to protect themselves from society's anger, they grouped together to form a united body that would be able to withstand the pressures of outsiders. As an American researcher on police responsibilities stated,

> Loyalty is one of the core values of the police culture. As one patrolman expressed the matter, "I'm for the guys in blue! Anybody criticizes a fellow copper that's like criticizing someone in my family; we have to stick together." The police culture demands of a patrolman unstinting loyalty to his fellow officers, and he receives, in return, protection and honor: a place to assuage real and imagined wrongs inflicted by a (presumably) hostile public; safety from aggressive administrators and supervisors; and the emotional support required to perform a difficult task. The most important question asked by patrolmen about a rookie is whether or not he displays the loyalty demanded by the police culture. (M Brown 1984, 82–83)

For the Papua New Guinean policemen this feeling of oneness developed during training and matured during their work in the field. Whether on the station or in the bush on patrols, a policeman was loyal to his comrades and to his officer. The officers, in turn, reciprocated. For them, this entailed overlooking a policeman's minor faults and, at times, even failing to report more serious offenses:

> The average officer, impressed by the obvious loyalty which safeguarded him, on patrol, inspecting labour and dispensing judge-

ments and punishments for labour offences, adjudicating in disputes and collecting tax, would fail to look further, at least until he had gained experience; and comparatively few seem to have remained district officers long enough to have done so. (Rowley 1958, 210–211)

The policemen protected each other during working situations as well as during times of distress. If one of their members was up on a charge they would corroborate their evidence so that their colleague would be acquitted or given a reduced charge. In answer to a question on what would happen to a policeman found guilty of misconduct, Guise said the man concerned would sometimes receive a jail sentence "but as policemen we stuck together. We gave the same evidence when we went to court to defend each other" (1985). In the bush they protected each other from hostile villagers. On a more personal level, many contributed to each other's bride-price payments and established friendships that went beyond the bounds of their responsibilities as policemen. Some invited their friends to marry local women and settle permanently in their villages. A few did. Sarepamo asked his long-time friend Anka of Mukip, Markham, to settle in Goroka, and he did after marrying a woman from Agautoka village, Okiufa. Apart from occasional visits to Mukip, Anka continued to live among his in-laws from then on.

The development of esprit de corps within the police organization proved an essential part of the police culture in Papua New Guinea, as elsewhere. It helped the police work together as a team in their endeavor to protect life and property. It gave them strength, confidence, and the support an individual needed to perform a task with authority. Without such support the policeman's job could become a lonely one.

Summary

After training, Papua New Guinean policemen were introduced to a radically new occupation—principally that of maintaining law and order among their own people. The laws that they had to enforce were foreign, and their understanding of the new rules and regulations was inadequate because they were not taught enough to interpret them to the villagers in a professional manner. What they lacked in formal western education they picked up from their own informal knowledge about how Papua New Guineans conducted their lives in different situations. They excelled in their given responsibilities because of their ability to coalesce different viewpoints in a balanced way.

Patrol officers were responsible for translating many of the colonial government's directives to the policemen. Through their influence a policeman acquired paternalistic views about other Papua New Guineans. The police were confirmed in these attitudes because of their devotion to their job, their loyalty to their officers, their obedience to the colonial government, and their own vanity about their new status.

In the course of their work, the police sometimes found it necessary to use their rifles. Two cases of the resulting violence are examined in the next chapter.

Chapter 5
The Use of Force

In chapter 1 some possible rationales are offered for the establishment of a police force in the colonial context, and why it was necessary for the police, as an instrument of the colonial regime, to use force. Before examining the degree of force that a Papua New Guinean policeman was legally allowed to use during the course of his work, some general factors must be considered.

Ideally everyone wants to live in peace without fear for themselves, their relatives, or their property. In most countries therefore a large section of the community endorses the organization of a police force by the state, and its presence may act as a deterrent against criminal activities. When there is a breakdown in law and order the responsibility for restoring security falls heavily on the police organization. To counteract criminal activity within society, the police are given authority through legislation to equip themselves with whatever means are considered necessary and consistent with the preservation of basic human rights to prevent disruptive situations from getting out of hand. In other words, the police are given legal authority to use force:

> The significance of this fact extends beyond the narrow responsibility for enforcement of the criminal laws: coercion defines both the role of the police and lies behind or is instrumental in the accomplishment of most police functions. It is the use of coercion that unites the otherwise disparate activities of the police; it is present in both the act of enforcing the law and in that of peace-keeping (M Brown 1984, 4)

Coercion then becomes part and parcel of police work. To what extent police coercion is used depends on the nature of the crime and the country in which police are employed. In some countries the use of coercion by police is normal. In a country where the maintenance of order is paramount, the state sanctions the use of force through its own coercive apparatus. Force was used in Papua New Guinea. From the standpoint of the interviewed policemen the basic instrument of coercion was the gun. Under what circumstances were Papua New Guinean policemen allowed to use it?

The Official Position

Sir Hubert Murray on 1 October 1909 issued a set of official instructions on how officers of the Papuan Armed Constabulary and their contingent of policemen should conduct themselves in the execution of their duties. His official directive was specific and condemned the use of unnecessary force. However, he conceded that some force could be used under special circumstances:

1 Officers in command of Armed Constabulary are reminded that they can never, under any circumstances, be justified in firing upon natives by way of punishment. Without attempting an exhaustive statement of the law of homicide it may be taken that there are three, and, so far as officers of the Constabulary are concerned, only three, cases in which life may lawfully be taken:
    (i) In self-defence, including the defence of police, carriers and others.
    (ii) For the purpose of preventing the escape of a person who has been arrested, or whom it is sought to arrest, upon reasonable suspicion of having committed certain offences (including murder and manslaughter).
    (iii) In overcoming a forcible resistance to the execution of process or to an arrest.
2 The sections referred to do not justify the taking of life except in cases of necessity—that is where there is no other way of protecting the life of the person attacked, or of preventing the escape, or of overcoming the forcible resistance. The section should be studied carefully.
3 It should be borne in mind that these sections lay down the conditions under which life may, in extreme instances, be taken without incurring criminal liability; they should not be taken for guides as a matter of general practice, but should rather be regarded as danger signals marking the extreme limits of legality. Further, officers should never forget that it is the settled policy of the Government not to resort to force except in cases of necessity when all other means have failed, and that it by no means follows because an officer may have a good defence on a charge of manslaughter that his conduct will, therefore, escape censure.

4 Questions of the capture of fugitive offenders and of overcoming resistance to arrest arise less frequently than that of self-defence, and officers may take it that they will not be justified in opening fire, by way of self-defence, unless they have been actually attacked—that is, unless arrows have been discharged or spears thrown. Even then they will not be justified unless their own lives or the lives of others are actually endangered. Threats of attacks can rarely amount to a sufficient justification. (Murray 1909)

Patrol officers and cadets[1] of the New Guinea Service were issued with a similar set of standing instructions in 1925 (New Guinea 1925). It contained precise information on virtually everything that patrol officers needed to know about the administration of their districts. For instance, in the event that a tribal war raged in a "controlled" area, or murders had been committed as a consequence of it, the regulations allowed for a patrol party to proceed to the area and remain there until the situation was brought under control. The instructions for the administration of justice were specific and included five guiding principles:

Instance: 1. A police party is approaching a village to arrest one or several members of a tribe reasonably suspected of having committed inter-tribal murders. The tribe throw spears or hold spears in such a manner as to make the police, who are endeavouring to make the arrest, reasonably consider that the tribe or members of the tribe intend to throw them. The police open fire.

Lawful Action: 1. The police are justified in firing for such time as is consistent with the law as is set out in section 254 Q.C.C. viz., "it is lawful for a person who is engaged in making any arrest to use such force as may be reasonably necessary to over-come any force used in resisting such arrest."

Instance: 2. A police party is approaching a village to arrest one or several members of a tribe reasonably suspected of having committed inter-tribal murders. When the police approach the warriors of the tribe stand up fully armed but remain passive.

Lawful Action: 2. The police have no lawful justification for firing. They must endeavour to effect the arrests. They are only justified in firing if armed resistance is offered them.

Instance: 3. A police party is approaching a village to arrest one or several members of a tribe, reasonably suspected of having committed inter-tribal murders. On the approach of the police, all members of the tribe take to flight.

Lawful Action: 3. The police can fire only on the persons whom they reasonably suspect to be the murderers, and then only after such persons have been called upon to surrender, vide section 256 Q.C.C., viz., "When a police officer is proceeding lawfully to arrest . . . a person . . . and the person sought to be arrested takes to flight in order to avoid arrest, it is lawful for the police officer . . . to use such force as may be reasonably necessary to prevent the escape of the person sought to be arrested, but this section does not authorize the use of force which is intended or is likely to cause death, except in a case where the person sought to be arrested is reasonably suspected of having committed an offence punishable with death.

Instance: 4. A police party, in an endeavour to apprehend natives reasonably suspected of having committed inter-tribal murders, find they cannot arrest them by pursuit. They capture other members of the tribe and hold them hostages.

Lawful Action: 4. The taking and holding of hostages is illegal, vide section 355 Q.C.C., viz., "any person who unlawfully holds . . . another . . . against his will . . . is guilty of a misdemeanour."

Instance: 5. A police party, desiring to put down inter-tribal murders between two tribes, who have taken to flight, by methods of intimidation, burn houses.

Lawful Action: 5. The burning of houses is illegal, vide section 461 Q.C.C., viz., "any who wilfully and unlawfully sets fire to any . . . building . . . is guilty of a crime." (New Guinea 1925)

In Papua life could lawfully be taken in three awkward situations—in self-defense, in attempting to prevent the escape of an arrested person thought to have committed a serious crime (or "whom it is sought to arrest"), and in overcoming resistance to arrest. The rule book stressed the need for restraint, that the taking of life must be the last resort when all other means had been exhausted. In New Guinea, firing with intent to kill was lawful in only one instance out of four, when the crime for which the person being arrested was punishable by death. Under any other circumstances, force causing death, or the use of other types of punitive measures, would be deemed unjustified action for which the guiding principles provided penalties.

There were no fundamental differences in the principles guiding officers in the administration of justice for both territories; they were basically similar insofar as both conceded that life could be taken only in the same limited circumstances. However, the cardinal principles set out for the New Guinea officers were more general than those detailed for their Papuan counterparts. If Murray's guiding principles were not accepted as government policy in New Guinea, Acting Crown Law Officer E B Bignold could say that the spirit of "the principles enunciated apply with equal force to officers of the Provisional Administration [New Guinea] wherever they may be. . . . [T]he principles are constant whilst the circumstances to which they apply may be infinite in their variety" (Bignold 1947b). Also, in New Guinea a life could be taken if a patrol party reasonably considered that the tribesmen they wanted to arrest threw spears (distance not specified), or had positioned themselves in such a way that a spear could be hurled with no great effort. But, as stipulated in the third instance, cowardly acts could not be tolerated.

Officially, officers from both territories were instructed to use force only under special circumstances.

The Situation on the Frontier

To probe the circumstances of each individual's use of coercion—both officers and men—from the 1920s to the 1960s would be time-consuming and possibly futile. However, it can be stated generally that many Papua New Guinean men and women were shot dead, or suffered other forms of atrocities (hanging, flogging, whipping, imprisonment, and the like) at the hands of private persons as well as colonial officers, during the whole period of colonial rule. Essentially, this was caused by the colonial government's determination to establish its authority over the tribespeople. They were imbued with the determination to spread the pax Britannica, pax Australiana, or pax Germanica and to impose their conception of law; that a few lives were lost was, in their view, a reasonable cost for the general advancement they eventually hoped to bring to the villagers. Details of these tragic events, of fights between police or patrol officers and villagers, and the resultant deaths, occur in some but not all patrol and annual reports for this and earlier periods. To augment discussion, selections from the reports are quoted here.

> [In 1906, a] large amount of patrolling has been done, both by the headquarters detachment, under the Commandant, and by the several divisional detachments. On only six occasions has there been hostile collision between native tribes and the police, and in

these affrays fifteen natives are reported to have lost their lives. The Assistant Resident Magistrate of the Eastern Division, in endeavouring to arrest two murderers of a village near the coast, met with the most determined resistance. The natives, in the first instance, advanced to the attack in war paint and plumes, and when driven back they took refuge in their stockaded village, on the peak of a steep hill of bare granite. From this vantage point they slung stones with such precision and in such quantities that the Government party were unable to rush the stockade. . . . Finally the village was taken by a flanking movement, the natives losing three men. (*PAR* 1906, 16)

More than twenty years later, in another region of Papua, at least thirty-two village warriors from the Strickland and Purari area died from gunshots during the patrol of Jack Hides and James O'Malley in 1934 and 1935.[2] In New Guinea during the early 1930s, Jim Taylor investigated the activities of prospector Michael Leahy and found that six villagers had been killed. Taylor's letter to the district officer of Salamaua before he proceeded on that patrol is worthy of note:

I have not had the opportunity of investigating Leahy's brushes with the natives, but it would appear that, at one place, six were killed and at another, one wounded. Leahy is not a man to shoot unnecessarily, and if prospectors are given free access to remote parts, then the right to shoot when necessary must go with it. (Taylor 1933)

Taylor's view contradicts that of Peter Munster, who believed that the Leahy brothers' activities were considered by the administration to be unacceptable in their treatment of New Guineans: "When Brother Eugene and Father Morschheuser were killed in the Chimbu not long after, it is significant that the Leahys, ever eager to demonstrate the white man's strength, were expressly forbidden by government officers to become involved" (Munster 1981, 33).

Another example comes from West New Britain, where A W Winston (1922) reported four men shot dead during a "punitive expedition." An observant officer wrote about patrol reports:

A "Patrol Report" is supposed to be an "official verbatim account of the actual day-to-day events on patrol." But in most instances they are masterpieces of understatement.[3]

Such comments as, "The natives were hostile and after a brief encounter they disappeared into the bush . . ." would only conjure up in my mind an ambush, arrows loosed from black palm bows, inpenetrable jungle green, a few fleeting shadows, shots fired and perhaps general panic among the police and carriers.

Another comment, "stayed in this village for three days until two old women appeared and said they would bring the men," read between the lines, meant that the patrol systematically set about plundering the garden, chopping down plantations and "cooking" [burning] a few houses, to force the natives to the conference table. (Kerr 1973, 54)

Two additional examples, one each from New Guinea and Papua are from the highlands region, which by the 1960s was the remaining major frontier of contact. They clearly demonstrate the rhetoric of official directives and their application in patrol situations.

The Central Highlands Case

On 21 July 1947 five innocent men from the Kouno area of the Central Highlands District of New Guinea were shot dead by a company of eleven policemen. My account of the circumstances of the presence of the patrol party at Dika, the shooting of the warriors, an investigation by the Department of District Services and Native Affairs into the causes, and the resultant exoneration of those concerned is compiled from available primary documents (see McDonald 1947).

In early July 1947 the assistant district officer for Simbu, John Amery Costelloe, received a complaint from Geru, leader of a subclan of the tribe of Karap in the general area of Kouno in the Simbu subdistrict, that two women from the village, while tending their gardens, had been chopped to pieces by men of their enemy tribe—the Dika. During a previous encounter ten lives had been lost, five men from each side. As a result of these deaths, the Dika committed a cowardly act, according to Geru, by taking the lives of the two women (Symons 1947b). All previous attempts to settle the matter peacefully, and to get the Dika to compensate the aggrieved families, had failed. Instead, according to Geru, whenever compensation demands were raised the Dika became more aggressive and challenged the Karap warriors to a duel to settle the score. It had been a drawn-out affair, and Geru, wishing to avoid another bloody confrontation, sought the protection of Costelloe. Consequently a patrol party consisting of Costelloe, Patrol Officer Craig Andrew John Symons, and eleven policemen gathered at Kerowagi and set off for Karap village on 11 July 1947, intending to arrange a peace settlement between the two warring factions.

After receiving an urgent telegram on the night of 12 July 1947 at Dimbin, Costelloe departed for Port Moresby the following morning. He left Symons in charge, with a strong warning that he could proceed slowly as far as Karap village, but to go no further until he returned.[4] Symons was warned in no uncertain terms of the "extreme danger to be

expected" beyond that point and advised that if he had to have an audience with the tribal leader of the hostile group he could only do so if
Mek, the leader, came to Karap (Costelloe 1947b). At some stage after
reaching the Kouno area, and before his departure, Costelloe issued
fifty-five rounds of .303 ammunition to eleven policemen.[5] On 17 July
1947 Symons and his entourage finally arrived at Karap village and for
the next three days he tried in vain, through the assistance of messengers, to persuade Mek of Dika to come to Karap. Mek continued to
maintain his defiant stance and refused to come to Symons. He sent
back Symons' messengers with loads of insult and the occasional present.
Mek's arrogance, and his persistent refusal to obey orders from a government officer, irked Symons in no small measure. On 21 July, against
the strong advice of his superior officer and with a suggestion of bravado, Symons walked to Dika, accompanied by his party of policemen
and villagers from the aggrieved tribe. In the ensuing confrontation,
five men were shot and killed.

Costelloe returned from Port Moresby on 23 July. When Symons told
him of the tragedy on 27 July, he was understandably shocked and soon
after wrote to James Taylor,

> I am sorry to advise that young Symons mucked things [up] in
> Kouno and became involved in a totally unwarranted shooting
> affray, killing five men. . . . I instructed him to proceed as far as
> Karap, there to remain until I got back.
>
> For some reason or other [Symons] *disobeyed* my orders. The
> usual insulting messages were brought to him and I guess that he
> took them to mean a reflection on his own courage—anyway he
> went looking for trouble. As he approached the hostile people,
> they laid down their arms and shields and fled. He had told the
> police to open fire if that happened and they immediately did so,
> shooting five men in the backs and killing them. *Most unfortunate
> and unjustified.* There was no attack at all and the fact of them lay-
> ing down their arms indicated their desire to parley. He then *per-
> mitted his party to lay waste some banana patches*—totally unjustified.
> (Costelloe 1947a; emphasis in original)

Although Costelloe was an experienced officer, Symons was new to
Papua New Guinea and the Central Highlands, having only recently
arrived from Sydney. After completing a program of instruction at
the Australian School of Pacific Administration on 17 February 1947,
he had been posted to Chimbu District "for duty and further training." By 11 July 1947 he had been in the country for a little less than
five months. In sum, Symons was young, inexperienced, and incom-
petent with *Tok Pisin,* "which is so essential when giving instructions
to the police," it being the lingua franca of most New Guinean police-

men (McDonald 1947). Despite his obvious shortcomings, the New Guinea Administration in their wisdom, or (with the benefit of hindsight) lack of it, posted a new and inexperienced young man to an area inhabited by a spirited and robust people even veterans of the region found difficulty in handling (see, eg, Downs 1986, particularly 108–127).

Taylor's reply to Costelloe, in a letter forwarded two days later from Goroka, was prompt.

> Please advise a/Patrol Officer Symons:—
> 1. To submit a confidential report to you (pass to me).
> 2. That I shall not order an inquest; that if I were to do so and that the evidence produced indicated that natives were shot when his or the lives of his police were not in real and imminent danger and that he gave the order to fire, the coroner would have no alternative but to commit him and such police who fired, for trial upon a charge of unlawful killing. . . .
> 5. Not to discuss the subject with anyone except yourself or write about it to his friends or other members of the service. Publicity may cause legal action with possible disastrous results to himself.
> 6. Not to worry. His error is one of youth and I shall protect him, but he is to obey lawful orders implicitly. (Taylor 1947a)

Advised by Costelloe, and with the incident fresh in his memory, Symons wrote down the facts as they had occurred at Dika. His report, written on 7 September, was forwarded to Costelloe at Chimbu, as suggested in Taylor's letter of 13 August, and was then delivered to Taylor in Goroka. Parts of Symons letter read:

> On July 11th I reported to the A.D.O. Mr Costelloe at Kerowagi. We were to proceed to the Kouno area to investigate the report of "boss boy" Geru, that a group of natives had come down from Dika to Karap and decapitated two women, who were working in the gardens.
>
> When I arrived at Karap on July 17th the two "boss boys" who had gone ahead to contact the headman Mek at Dika, reported that he refused to come down to Karap and make payment to the husbands of the two women who were killed. On the following day I again sent a party of natives, from the area, to try and get Mek to come to the station. The natives reported that Mek refused to come in and that he hurled abuse at them (for working for me as "go-betweens"), and at me, daring me to come to his place. I decided to send another party the following day, consisting solely of natives from Magin, who were particularly friendly with the natives of Dika. They too were unsuccessful.

During the afternoon of the third day of my stay at Karap a native from Wanku (the next village to Dika) was sent in by Mek with a bunch of bananas which he presented to me, and told me that it was food for myself and police to take us back to Kundiawa, that Mek didn't want us remaining at Karap. I sent the bananas back and advised Mek to come in to me the following day.

He didn't arrive, so I decided, although Mr. Costelloe had told me if I struck any trouble, to remain at Karap and await his return, that I would go to Dika and see if the line would talk it over with me there.

As we approached the houses of Mek's line at Dika seven of the police were in front, I was a little way behind with the "boss boys" and the natives and four police brought up the rear. When the police came to the crest of the hill they called back to me that Mek and about 30 natives were just a little way ahead and that they had made a heap of their spears and shields and were standing a little way behind them, and that it looked as though they wished to talk it over. Those police who could make themselves understood called out to Mek to stop there leaving the spears etc. on the ground and we would come to him. Geru and the other natives with me would put their spears down in a heap the same way and we would talk it over.

We walked along the crest towards them. We were quite close to where they stood when suddenly Mek rushed down the side of the hill. I called out to him to stop but he kept running, not calling out to his line, who were thoroughly disorganised and were rushing in all directions.

I thought there was the danger that this was just a trick to get the police chasing the escaping natives so that in the resulting confusion the whole party could be ambushed. *I shouted to the police not to follow the natives into the thick bush at the sides of the track but to shoot. They were following orders when they started shooting and five natives were killed* [emphasis added]. I ordered the natives with me not to join in and they obeyed orders but one of the natives with Geru rushed ahead and set fire to one of the houses before I could stop him. I forbade them to do any further damage. We returned to Karap. (Symons 1947a)

In short, the thrust of Symons' written admission was that, although the men had not contravened any official regulation, he had ordered his policemen to shoot the fleeing men, under what turned out to be a false impression[6] that their actions were a "trick" to ambush his party. The indiscriminate shooting killed five men, namely: Denimp, Du, Kum, Manimp, and Waim (McDonald 1947).

Meanwhile, on his own initiative, Mek walked to Kundiawa to complain to Acting District Officer Costelloe (McDonald 1947).

Strange as it might seem, after this correspondence the tragic fate of the five Dika men would have rested, if Taylor's letter to Costelloe of 13 August 1947 is any indication, had it not been for an unsubstantiated report of a Subinspector Bernard's inquiry[7] into the deaths at Kouno that triggered an official inquiry. The probing of Australian newspapers[8] the following year into the secrecy surrounding the whole affair also helped publicize the tragedy to an international audience. How the Australian newspapers came by their story, or who commissioned the little-known, short-lived Bernard Inquiry is unknown. But Taylor's attempted cover-up failed, and he learned that Bernard was conducting an inquiry:

> I am informed, though I am not certain of the accuracy of the information, that Sub Inspector Bernard, R.P.C., is now in the Kouno area, Chimbu Sub-district, . . . that he is there making inquiries into the subject of this memorandum with a view to submitting a full report to the Superintendent of Police. If the inquiry is in fact proceeding, it is being conducted without any advice to me from the Superintendent of Police, or to the Assistant District Officer, Chimbu Sub-district or myself from the Inspector. (Taylor 1947b)

That the inquiry avoided Taylor as a point of reference is no real surprise, but he seems to have acted swiftly to get a head start on Bernard's inquiry and to further discourage what in his view might involve unnecessary and protracted court proceedings. He wrote to his most senior officer—the director of the Department of District Services and Native Affairs, Mr J H Jones—and enclosed the correspondence between himself, Costelloe, and Symons regarding the deaths at Dika: "I am forwarding you a confidential file in respect of an incident that occurred at Dika in the Kouno area of the Chimbu Sub-district on the 21st July last" (Taylor 1947b). His letter ended with a strong plea not to reveal the contents of Symons' report to anyone who might be disposed to use it against Symons in the future:

> I draw your attention to the fact that Mr. Symons' report is a confidential one, perhaps induced by my memorandum to the Assistant District Officer, Chimbu, of 13th August 1947 (attached), and I submit that its contents should not be allowed to become known to any persons who might be concerned in a prosecution of that officer and who might use it in evidence should such a prosecution eventuate.

Fortunately the enclosed correspondence between Taylor and his two subordinates was not swept under the carpet by the acting director of the Department of District Services and Native Affairs. Instead, Jones circulated the three documents among the relevant authorities—Administrator J K Murray, the government secretary, Acting Crown Law Officer Bignold, and, through the advice of the administrator, Minister for External Territories E J (Eddie) Ward, in Canberra. These authorities therefore saw the documents and on prima facie evidence agreed that both Taylor and Symons could not be let off lightly. Their initial reactions agreed with the gravity of the situation that five lives had been lost, and that from the available evidence someone ought to be held responsible. In a letter dated 28 October 1947, Bignold wrote to the then administrator, Colonel J K Murray, advising him of the urgent need to bring a charge of unlawful killing against the government officers and men involved in the death of five men so that "a court may determine whether there was any justification or excuse" (1947a). On receipt of Taylor's earnest plea, the acting director of the Department of District Services and Native Affairs sent a memorandum to the acting government secretary:

> It will be noted that the District Officer's letter to Mr. Costelloe is dated the 13th August 1947 whereas the report to this Department is dated the 10th October 1947. From this, and the general trend of the correspondence, it would appear that Mr. Taylor's original intention was not to report the case to this Headquarters, but deal with it as an administrative matter, taking the responsibility for such action upon his own shoulders. *Maybe Mr. Bernard's enquiry caused the District Officer to change his mind* [emphasis added].
>
> If it had been an ambush affair, or a clash in uncontrolled territory against armed warriors, I would be inclined to support Mr. Taylor, but the reports make it quite clear that there was no ambush, the natives shot were unarmed and in face of the fact that Mek voluntarily reported to the Assistant District Officer at the Government station Chimbu shortly after, no doubt to complain, it cannot be claimed that the area is uncontrolled.
>
> I can understand the District Officer's impulse to shield Mr. Symons, but I am afraid there is little we can do, for on the facts as reported I just cannot support Mr. Taylor by recommending that action be taken along the lines he suggests; but would ask that the papers be seen by the Administrator before being referred to the Crown Law Officer in case His Honour may be prepared to accept the responsibility of confirming the action taken by Mr. Taylor as coroner, and directing that no further action be taken. (Jones 1947)

On receiving the director's memorandum, the government secretary sent a full report to Administrator J K Murray. Parts of his covering letter read:

It is with a full appreciation of the gravity of the matter disclosed by the correspondence that I send these papers to you, for in my view they reveal an affair which, on the one hand, is shocking, and, on the other hand discloses an attitiude by the District Officer which I cannot comprehend.

There is as you will no doubt observe a suggestion of abuse of office, which has its genesis in the personal views of Mr. Taylor as to how matters in his District should be dealt with. That they have exposed him to a possible charge of being an accessory after the fact to what appears to be at this stage an unlawful killing is set out in the memorandum by the Crown Law Officer while the killing of the five men in such circumstances is just tragic.[9]

In a letter to the administrator, Colonel Murray, dated 8 November 1947, Crown Law Officer Bignold expressed concern about the way in which the administrator was handling reports of the shooting of five men at Dika. His opening remarks read, "I have read with care your rough drafts . . . and, with respect, they seem to me to constitute an unsound approach to a problem going to the very root of our Administration" (Bignold 1947b). The administrator summarized the available documents on 8 November 1947 and sent them to the minister for External Territories, Mr E J (Eddie) Ward, in Canberra, for his immediate attention. His covering memorandum began:

> On October 29 I was informed for the first time of a very serious happening in the Highlands in which five native people were killed. I am attaching copies of a series of papers relating to the incident.

Two paragraphs at the end read:

> I sincerely regret that I must recommend to you that you approve of both officers being suspended. Pending the result of the police enquiry, and any action taken upon it, the pay of these officers should continue.
>
> Although three and a half months have elapsed since the incident occurred, nevertheless I think there is a degree of urgency in regard to the matter, and I should be pleased if you would let me have your decisions at your earliest convenience. (J K Murray 1947a)

The minister's response is not among the documents at my disposal, but it is evident that he concurred with the administrator's recommendation. Both Symons and Taylor were suspended from active duty pending the outcome of the official police inquiry headed by the newly appointed police inspector, J H McDonald (J K Murray 1947a). Ordinarily

McDonald was an assistant director of the Department of District Services and Native Affairs, but for the purposes of the investigation he "was gazetted an Inspector of Police at the discretion of His Honour the Administrator" (J S Grimshaw 1947). While an exact date for the inquiry is not available, McDonald was on the plane to Lae on 11 November, en route to Chimbu (J K Murray 1947a). He submitted his completed report to Mr J S Grimshaw, superintendent of the Royal Papuan Constabulary, in Port Moresby on 11 December 1947, and subsequently circulated it through his office to the appropriate authorities in Port Moresby and the minister for External Territories in Canberra.

On the basis of this investigation, and the support it received from the various authorities, Symons and his policemen were exonerated from any charge (McDonald 1947). This position represented a dramatic reversal of the earlier decision that someone be held responsible for the deaths. The raw evidence could have left little doubt in their minds as to who was responsible, but with elapsed time, further reflection, and additional information the guilty verdict was overruled.

What Changed Their Minds?

This question necessitates a review of the various viewpoints arising from the inquiry; namely, those of Inspector McDonald, Superintendent Grimshaw, Administrator Murray, and Minister Ward.

As his terms of reference for his report, McDonald interviewed Acting District Officer Costelloe, Assistant Patrol Officer Symons, four policemen (including Sergeant Bus of Manus, Constable Numibi of Henganofi, Eastern Highlands, Constable Waim of Chimbu, and Constable Gande of Western Highlands), and, with the aid of interpreters, three villagers, two of whom were from Dika, one being Mek, the Dika leader. Claiming agonizing muscle pains, McDonald did not visit Dika, the scene of the murders, "but viewed it from some distance off." In his report to the director of District Services and Native Affairs he made known his position:

> I have given this matter a great deal of thought and consideration and I desire to suggest that this Department take all possible steps to prevent this unfortunate young man being brought before the Court. If he is to face a charge of unlawful killing, I have no doubt that there would be no conviction, but as people are so prone to talk of such cases, he would probably carry this stigma for many years in people's minds, especially those who do not know the facts, and probably ruin the life of a very promising man, who was endeavouring to please his superiors.
>
> The law says that all cases where the loss of life is involved are to

be decided by the court, but conditions in the uncontrolled areas are such that our present staff of young Patrol Officers are in danger of these warlike tribes every time they enter these areas.

It is my hope that this case and others of a similar nature, which are bound to follow, be kept an Administrative one, and prevent it becoming a legal action.

If officers are to face charges of unlawful killing or other court action, young men of the type that this Administration desires to employ would not be forthcoming and parents would dissuade their sons from doing so. (see McDonald 1947)

First, one would have thought that McDonald's responsibility was to conduct an impartial inquiry, but the statement here reads as if his mind had already been made up well beforehand. His suggestion, of course, was that Symons should be exonerated and that if any disciplinary action was deemed necessary it should be left to the Department of District Services and Native Affairs to take the appropriate action. In his view any contrary action would not only tarnish the work of the administration but also prevent further recruitment of young men from Australia. On the whole, it was a superficial report lacking both insight and sensitivity.

Second, on receiving the report, the superintendent of police forwarded it to the government secretary and explained his position:

After a careful perusal of Mr. McDonald's report and a careful study of all the circumstances of the incident, I am of the opinion that there is insufficient evidence to support any criminal charge which may be brought against Mr. C.A.J. Symons, Patrol Officer. The evidence shows that Mr. Symons was guilty of disobeying the instructions of a superior when he disregarded Mr. Costelloe's instructions to remain at Karap and not proceed beyond that point. It would appear that Symons was guilty of negligence in not making his instructions with regard to the use of firearms by the police clear and definite and, from the evidence of the Constables, too much latitude was given to the individual with regard to the use of firearms. From the evidence it is quite obvious that Symons was too far away from the Police and the scene of the shooting to exercise effective control. (J S Grimshaw 1947)

This is certainly the impression one gets from reading the report of the inquiry after four months had elapsed. The last sentence reads as if Grimshaw had forgotten what Symons wrote in his initial report—that the policemen, himself, and the rest of the men in the party were already quite close to Mek when he fled down the slopes; in fact, Symons had been so close that he even called out to Mek to stop: "We walked along the crest towards them. We were quite close to where they stood when suddenly Mek rushed down the side of the hill. I called out to him to stop but he kept running" (Symons 1947a).

There may have been another time when he called out, this time to his policemen. In the preceding paragraph of his 7 September letter he said that when his policemen had reached the crest of the hill they called back to him and described what they could see; he reported what he had heard his men say, and repeated their words to his senior officer, J A Costelloe, days, perhaps a week, later. The message was that the policemen had sighted Mek and his men, about thirty in all, that they had made a heap of their weapons and were standing behind them as if wishing to parley. The point is that if Symons was able to hear what his policemen had shouted to him while on the move to Dika village, it is also possible that the policemen could hear anything he shouted to them. They would have had an added advantage in receiving his message in that they were then stationary, having already reached Mek and his men, while Symons, in the meantime, would have come closer. His orders could not have been misinterpreted. The possibility that Symons did order his men to shoot cannot be ruled out completely. Grimshaw's conclusion contradicts not only this possibility, but also Symons' initial testimony.

One further factor must be mentioned. A good number of the policemen I interviewed indicated that there were times, in the absence of their patrol officers, when they abused the authority vested in them, but they never did this when their officer was a member of the patrol party. Three of the four policemen—Sergeant Bus, Constable Numibi, and Constable Waim—told McDonald during the inquiry that, as far as they could remember, Symons had advised them, on the night before their trip to Dika, to do one of two things: either to make friends with the Dika men if they stood still and accepted Symons' appeasement speech on behalf of Karap villagers, or to start shooting if the Dika did anything else—ran away, hurled spears, or attacked them in some other way (McDonald 1947). If the policemen reacted to the situation on the basis of the previous night's orders, then the killing of the five men was nothing less than premeditated murder. Considering that a war of nerves had raged between Symons and Mek for three long days, with Mek seeming to have the upper hand, it is not beyond imagination that an inexperienced officer would want to teach recalcitrants a lesson.

Returning to the subject of changed viewpoints, on 24 December 1947 Administrator J K Murray wrote to the minister for External Territories and aired similar opinions to those of McDonald and Grimshaw. Two significant parts of his letter read:

It is my advice that the suspension of Messrs. Taylor and Symons be
lifted, and that they should be returned to their duties in their respective posts. For this advice I accept the fullest possible responsibility.

I consider that Mr. Taylor should be severely reprimanded in
connection with his confidential memorandum to the Assistant
District Officer and which I quoted at the bottom of page 2 of my
letter of November 8; and that Mr. Symons should be reprimanded
for disobeying an order given by the Assistant District Officer, Mr.
Costelloe. (J K Murray 1947b)

As advised, the minister gave the final official nod and approved the
administrator's recommendations on 2 January 1948:

1. That Mr. Symons should be reprimanded for disobeying an
   order given by the Assistant District Officer, Mr. Costelloe;
2. That Mr. Taylor be reprimanded in connection with his memorandum to the Assistant District Officer dated 13 August 1947;
3. That in accordance with the Administrator's advice the suspension of Messrs. Taylor and Symons be lifted immediately and
   that they be returned to their duties in their respective posts.
   (E J Ward 1948)

Soon after, both officers' suspensions were lifted and they were rein-
stated to their former posts.

McDonald's Inquiry and Symons' Testimony

McDonald's inquiry was the basis on which all subsequent decisions
were made. During this inquiry Symons substantially altered the earlier
testimony of the incident he had given to Costelloe. In September he
wrote that he had ordered his policemen to shoot the men if they fled.
However, during the recorded interview with McDonald he altered his
earlier account and stated that he *did not* order his policemen to shoot
the fleeing tribesmen, nor did he know who ordered them to do so, or
who fired the first shot:

I had just come within sight of Mek when suddenly he rushed into
the bush by the side of a small clearing. The natives with him
instantly followed. Some going into the bush on the right and
some on the left. There was much confusion and a great deal of
noise. Some Police in the forward party opened fire. I was not the
one who gave the order to fire. I thought Sergt. Bus had done so;
but he later told me that he kept calling out to the Police, as I was
doing, not to follow natives into the dense bush. I do not know if
anyone called out "fire" nor do I know who was the first to fire.
(Symons 1947b)

The discrepancy is obvious. Yet none of the authorities seriously questioned why his later account was fundamentally changed from the original written version. Symons himself did not provide an explanation during the inquiry because McDonald, it appears from the content of the document, conveniently failed to ask him. The administrator took it upon himself to ask the question, Symons denied any involvement, and the administrator accepted his denial:

> I have read through the statements taken by Mr. McDonald from various witnesses and it does not appear from the statements that an order was given by Mr. Symons to fire. In order to clear this matter for myself, I saw Mr. Symons in my office and he denies that he gave an order to fire or that he was in a position to give that order. I accept his denial because it agrees with the evidence as adduced by Mr. McDonald. (J K Murray 1947b)

This prompts the question of why Symons failed to tell the truth in September instead of the elaborate fabrication? When *did* he tell the truth? The administrator also failed to ask this crucial question.

Another factor in this case points to the original statement in September being most probably the correct one. Symons initially discussed the matter with his senior officer, Costelloe, soon after his return from Port Moresby, when the incident was still fresh in his memory. Costelloe was an experienced officer with an intimate understanding of the highlands circumstance. He would have advised a fellow officer on the proper course of action to take in such matters. Costelloe's letter to Taylor on 11 August 1947 was basically a repetition of what Symons himself wrote to Taylor in September. It is possible that Costelloe did not hold the same views as Taylor on what officers should or should not do on the frontier. Taylor's view was:

> There has been some suggestion that I hold a theory of administration that is in some way unique, or at any rate different from that held by many of my colleagues. . . . You know my views in these frontier matters. I have given them to Administrators in the past. They, in my opinion, are not police or legal ones or should not be so regarded. . . . that in new areas members of the field staff, who are usually young men, are in peril from warriors and the legal machine . . . and that such unfortunate occurrences as that which the correspondence discloses are ones which should not come within the ambit of normal police inquiry without the express consent of the Administration. The aim should be, in my opinion, to keep such a matter an administrative one and prevent it from becoming the subject of legal investigation, which, once begun, must inevitably proceed and probably lead to the ruin of the life of a young officer. (Taylor 1947b; 1947c)

There is every reason to believe that in the interim period between the shooting and the inquiry, Symons and his cohorts had the benefit of advice, principally from Taylor, on how "proper" reports should be written and how they should conduct themselves in difficult situations such as the one he experienced.[10]

The second conclusion reached reflected the feeling of senior colonial officials, in particular McDonald and Taylor, that in the work of exploration and pacification the violent clash of two cultures was inevitable, particularly in "uncontrolled areas," but the work must continue regardless of the shortage of staff or the intolerance of the people. Taylor, as his correspondence shows, remained adamant from the beginning that his junior officer had committed an error that should be judged within the department, and which, under the circumstances of his work on the frontier of government influence, did not warrant an inquiry. However, in the opinion of Acting Crown Law Officer Bignold, the Kouno tragedy should have gone beyond the McDonald inquiry:

> The results of Mr. J. H. McDonald's enquiry have been carefully examined by me and it is clear, unfortunately, that the account now given by Mr. Symons differs in very material respects from that originally given by him when less time had elapsed since the shooting which resulted in the death of the five natives.
>
> It is believed by me that the unchallenged fact that the five natives who lost their lives were shot in the back is a vital factor in considering what should be done. I feel no doubt that the proper course is to charge this officer with manslaughter and further, in my view, there can be no legal justification for departing from this course on the information available.
>
> In regard to Mr. Taylor, whilst I believe him to be an accessory, I incline to the view that it would be preferable not to charge him as such but to charge him with attempting to defeat the course of justice. This is a charge which in no way depends upon the prosecution or the result of the prosecution of Mr. Symons.
>
> If these two officers were not [to] be charged it would seem to be a failure to administer the criminal law in force in that part of the Territory of New Guinea designated the Central Highlands. (Bignold 1947c)

In his final submission to the minister for External Territories on 24 December 1947 the administrator chose to overlook the acting crown law officer's advice, preferring instead opinions from outside the legal fraternity. In Symons' case he wrote:

> I do not agree with the opinion of the Crown Law officer that Symons should be charged with manslaughter in view of the fact

that it is the opinion of experienced officers that there would be
no conviction. I do not consider that a desire to find out details
concerning an affray in which five natives were killed in July last
would warrant placing a man on a charge of manslaughter if the
charge is not likely to be sustained. Such a procedure might serve
as a precedent whereby officers connected with fatalities resulting
from measures taken to protect the safety of patrols will automati-
cally be charged with homicide. Such a procedure might well be
calculated to seriously interfere with the morale of the Directorate
of District Services and Native Affairs. (J K Murray 1947b)

And on Taylor:

I find myself in a some what different position with regard to Mr.
Taylor. The Crown Law Officer, you will note from his minute,
copies of which are attached, recommends that Mr. Taylor should
be charged with attempting to defeat the course of justice. I think
it might be much better described as an attempt to prevent the
functioning of law in relation to an incident occurring in an
uncontrolled area. I do not consider that Mr. Taylor is a type who
would really attempt, or even consider attempting to defeat the
course of justice. The matter is, of course, and in part, one of
terms and definitions. I do, however, consider that Mr. Taylor was
guilty of a grave administrative error. (J K Murray 1947b)

Before writing his report to the minister, the administrator appears
to have read thoroughly a letter from Taylor (1947c) from his home in
Waverley, New South Wales, in defense of his reinstatement.

After the second round of consideration, the matter of the fate of
the five Dika men was closed. It was by no means the first and last of
the cases where officers and men were exonerated from seeming injus-
tices meted out to villagers, as examples given elsewhere in this book
illustrate.

The Southern Highlands Example

I will now quote verbatim from a 1955–56 patrol report from the Southern Highlands. The incident involved the fatal shooting of a warrior by
a patrol officer in the Southern Highlands—one of Papua's last frontiers. Several shootings had occurred in the area at different times, and
by different officers and policemen.

A patrol was made into Mai, a distance of five hours' walk from
Mendi station, to investigate reports of unrest in the area. Two men had
been murdered at a place called Ibi, as a result of which tribal fighting
broke out, setting the aggrieved tribe and their allies against the com-

bined warriors of two opposing groups. The patrol established a camp
and monitored the situation for two weeks. During this time the patrol
was attacked, and a man from the initial aggressors died from a fatal
gunshot wound. The following is an extract from the patrol diary of a
patrol conducted on 21 October 1955.

Report on the Death of Nema

Left camp at 0530 hours in an endeavour to contact the people. At
0755 hours we were confronted by a group of about thirty armed
men. They were a typical fighting unit armed with bows and arrows
and fighting shields. The two men suspected of the murders that
have given rise to the outbreak of fighting were recognized as
being members of the party. They were pointed out to me by the
Tutama headman, Woria, who was accompanying the patrol. The
names of these men are Busu and Nema of Moranda. I called out
to these two men who were about 50 yards away from us to surrender to me for questioning. They replied they would not do so and
if I attempted to take them they would attack us. I again insisted to
the group that I was not here for fighting but only desired to halt
the fighting and to question these two men. Some of the party
started to move above us and general shouting broke out—they
burst into their war cries at the same time. They were receiving
instructions from another party located in the limestone cliffs
immediately above us. We ourselves moved to a higher position to
prevent being placed in a lower and untenable position. I again
called out that we were not to be attacked and if they persisted in
the riotous manner I would put them in gaol. They did persist and
it looked likely that fighting would break out. Akuru [policeman]
pointed out that we were in range of rolling rocks if the top group
decided to push any onto us. We moved a short distance, about a
100 yards to be out of range. Immediately after my warning went
unheeded I fired a warning shot over their heads to let them be
under no false apprehension that we were unarmed.

Shortly after this we entered the bush to go down to the river
and as we were making our way along the track, corporal Akuru,
who was about 10 feet ahead of me, doubled back and said we
were being attacked. I heard the bow strings snapping and I saw
one arrow fly above him. I immediately dived behind a tree and
cocked my rifle. Within seconds a second volley of arrows flew over
our heads and natives were heard moving on our flank attempting
to surround us. I told the police to cock their rifles but not to fire
as yet. Out of the corner of my eye I saw a native with a drawn bow
and arrow. The arrow was pointed at Village Constable Kara and
myself. I swung and fired a snap shot at his arm and he dived back

into the bush. This man had been standing about 15–20 feet to my right. At the time I did not know that the native had been hit. After this shot the attackers dropped to the ground and quietness fell. I ordered my party to remain on the ground and not to fire without orders. We waited so for about 5 minutes then edged our way slowly forward. We could hear movement around us but could see nothing. After waiting a short time we scouted and V. C. Kara quickly called us over and showed us Nema, the man we had been trying to contact. He was dead and had died from a gunshot wound which had gone through his left upper arm, through and shattering his shield and hence through his body emerging above the right thigh. We retreated as soon as I considered it safe and carried the body with us. At 0815 hours we came onto a garden site and could hear the natives still following us through the bush. I called on them again to come out into the open and talk with us but no reply was received. The body was heavy and hampering our retreat so we left it in the garden for his kinsmen to collect.

In the actual ambush I do not know for sure how many men were in the aggressor party but both Akuru and myself are of the opinion that about 10–12 men were in front of us and an unknown number were pressing in on each flank. The entire attack from the moment of the first arrow to the end of the skirmish took approximately thirty seconds.

At this time when we were returning we could hear the people on the hill top shouting out to their friends that I had been killed. At the time of the attack I could not extricate my group without danger to my men and we had to remain still and quiet. At no time did I show any aggression and repeatedly insisted to the people that I was interested only in stopping the fight and interviewing the alleged murderers.

The only shots fired were both fired by myself and one of those was a warning shot and the second was fired out of dire necessity when our lives were in immediate danger. If I had not fired, I or V. C. Kara would have been wounded or killed. Nema would hardly have missed at such short range.

The patrol retreated as soon as was practicable so as to avoid further conflict and possible bloodshed. (Claridge 1956)

The response from District Commissioner Robert Cole, dated 10 November 1955, was short and to the point and is quoted verbatim:

1. This report records another of the unpardonable incidents which have occurred in the District since its establishment.
2. My only explanation for such incidents is the infrequency of consistent patrolling by experienced officers and this is occa-

sioned by the shortage of such officers to carry out this important work. In such an area as the Southern Highlands it is essential to consolidate our influence in areas contacted before moving to uncontacted areas.

The Mai area, in which this incident occurred is only five
hours walk from Mendi station, it has been frequently visited by
passing patrols and they should fully appreciate the prohibitions on fighting.

3. Mr Claridge was instructed to investigate and stop native unrest
   in the area. The fighting was caused by the Andesamai/Moranda
   natives killing two of the Kambemai/Ibi natives because they
   suspected them of killing by sorcery, two of their own groups.
   Retaliation, under these circumstances was considered justified
   and general fighting broke out after calling in neighbouring
   groups to assist. Intervention by the patrol was unwelcomed
   and the Andesmai/Moranda group finally attacked.

4. The evidence shows that there was a deliberate attempt made
   by the attackers to kill the patrol leader and no doubt they were
   urged and persisted in their endeavours by the apparent belief
   that firearms made a loud noise only and are not capable of
   serious danger. This is an accepted belief amongst natives in
   the District because very few fatalities have resulted from the
   rifle.

5. As soon as an experienced officer is available he will be sent to
   the area to consolidate. (Cole 1955)

I have quoted these items verbatim to provide an example of the
nature of reports patrol officers submitted to headquarters, and the
type of response that was sometimes received from their superiors. In
this case, a man was killed within thirty seconds of an alleged attack,
and before an arrow was let fly by a man standing fifteen to twenty feet
away. Did this death, as well as those in Kouno, occur within the framework of the cardinal principles of 1909 and 1925?

In this case, it seems that officially the patrol officer concerned
earned himself a reprimand, but under the circumstances—staff shortage, inexperienced officers, infrequency of government patrols, villagers' reluctance to observe prohibitions on fighting, the belligerence
of the inhabitants, the bravado displayed toward the gun, and the officer executing official instructions— no further action was taken against
him. As in the Kouno case, he was exonerated. Even if in the Southern
Highlands case the officer seemed to have been operating within the
rules, the point can still be made that, just as in the Kouno case, inexperience at frontier work contributed significantly to violent death.

It seems that, in any public inquiry or other sort of official investigation involving death during the period of contact, the judgments

passed often reflected field officer opinion that the onus of responsibility ought to be placed on a tribal leader, warriors of a tribe, or the aggressive villagers who generally brought about the occasional violence of officers and their policemen. But how many investigating officers actually walked the precipitous and winding tracks of the Southern Highlands, the Simbu District, or the mountainous terrain of Goilala to see the site in the bush and listen to villagers where the incidents occurred? Were the implicated villagers sufficiently instructed in the labyrinth of the western legal processes to defend themselves, or provide correct answers to appointed "solicitors" defending them? Patrol officers had two years at the Australian School of Pacific Administration and more time in the field to learn their responsibilities. Besides, officers in New Guinea were protected by the law and the administration in cases where they might have acted irresponsibly. The 1925 *District Standing Instructions* stated:

> (b) . . . District Officers are reminded that they are protected by Queensland Criminal Code should they be forced to take as officers of police certain lines of action. . . . (c) Every effort must be made to cope with the situation without opening fire, but District Officers may rest assured that if they are forced to use extreme measures, they will, provided their action is within the law, receive the support of the Administration. (New Guinea 1925)

The policemen had, in most cases, twelve months of intensive training at the depot, and more time to adjust to a new lifestyle through practical experience while engaged on active duty. What protection was there for a villager in similar situations?

Nearly all the police interviewed shared the official view that a little force was necessary to keep belligerent individuals and groups under control. Like their officers they were convinced that the people they dealt with were "primitives" who would only respond to stringent measures. Most admitted to having used some form of force against carriers, laborers on stations, prisoners, and the communities they visited from time to time. Of the twenty-eight men, eleven—Amero, Anka, Kamuna, Kasse, Piaka, Rewari, Sarepamo, Sesetta, Sono, Tigavu, and Yegova—admitted to having shot and killed one or more people. Most of these deaths seem to have taken place in the highlands (including Papua's Southern Highlands), and prior to the 1960s. Obviously this was because during the period under study much of the highlands area was still considered an "uncontrolled area." Most of the coastal regions were already under full or partial control. For instance, Amero Bega alone, during his four years in the highlands in Kainantu, Eastern Highlands, and Simbu area claimed to have shot dead fourteen people, including one woman shot through the vagina in the Bena Bena area of Eastern Highlands, during an early morning raid.[11]

The course of action the policemen took depended on the instructions they received from the patrol officer as relayed to them by the senior noncommissioned officer. In the policemen's experience there were two kinds of officers. Some were older men with many years of experience. They were conversant with official regulations and ensured rigid observance. If a policeman was found to have exceeded his legal powers, he was either punished in the field or a recommendation was sent to the administrative center for his demotion or dismissal. Any policeman who worked under this kind of officer was careful not to go beyond the bounds of his given responsibility. At the other extreme were inexperienced officers who demonstrated a clear lack of understanding of the general government policies and the nature of their own duties.

These officers depended on the expertise of the policemen to guide them through their early years in the field. In appreciation of their assistance and loyalty, the officers tended to overlook the errors of their policemen, a policy that in many instances, encouraged the policemen to use their own discretion and act independently of patrol officers' observation and guidance. If, for instance, a policeman had killed someone, or committed other acts of violence, without the officer's knowledge, and the offended persons brought a complaint before him, the officer would often deny or excuse the allegations against his policeman. In almost all cases, the reason the officers advanced for the untoward behavior of their men was that they had acted in self-defense. Almost invariably the villagers accepted the patrol officer's explanations. The *District Standing Instructions* stated:

> (b)   When dealing with the natives under his guardianship and
>   control it can readily be seen that his title of "Kiap" carries
>   with it an immense amount of prestige in the native eye and
>   that in most instances his suggestions and advice to such
>   natives will be blindly obeyed. (New Guinea 1925, 1)

Villagers rarely questioned the patrol officer or challenged his decisions. For example, Yegova Jojoga shot dead Koito, a man from Goilala, in Tapini:

> The kiap and sergeant rushed to the scene. The kiap saw what had
> happened and said "Maski" [Forget it; it doesn't matter] as the
> people were generally belligerent and the incident would probably
> force them to quieten down. However, when the people gathered
> he rebuked me, in order to have an impact, for my action. He then
> assured the people that he would send a report of my misconduct
> to Port Moresby. The people present did not raise any objections.
> Up till now I do not know whether he actually sent the report but,

as far as I know, nothing further was said of the matter in later years. In my observation, Mr Chester [his patrol officer] was a compassionate man who showed a lot of sympathy to his policemen. In a case like mine, he would blame the people for having initiated the attack. He could not tolerate the people's insolence and pigheadedness, and was of the opinion that if one of them was shot dead it was his own fault. (Yegova 1985)

This might also suggest the sense of camaraderie and esprit de corps that existed among the patrol officers and policemen.

Summary

In the tragic bloody shooting incidents described in Simbu and the Southern Highlands, six warriors died from violence committed by police and officers. Their deaths were not isolated cases. Many other Papua New Guineans had died in similar circumstances, in the highlands as well as the coastal regions, from 1884. The detailed accounts of these two unsavory episodes in the highlands allow those not involved, first, to become aware of the extent of police and officer violence on the frontier, and second, to understand the peculiarities and ambivalence of official laws and directives to officers working on the edge of government control.

The context in which these tragic events took place can be explained in two ways. First, the official position was that government patrols were dealing with people accustomed to killing each other, and therefore violence was almost impossible to avoid. In any case, a little violence that speeded up the imposition of government peace would in the long run save many villagers who would otherwise have died in intertribal violence or of diseases. Second, policemen, as individuals or as members of a new alien institution, had an explanation for their actions and their attitude to their work. Despite all the hardships, traumatic experiences, humiliations of a master-servant relationship, disparity in wages, and more, they said, they held their heads high and performed with unquestioning loyalty and obedience. They said they were proud and possessive of wearing the government's uniform. As far as these men were concerned, some fanatical force seemed to radiate from the uniforms, driving them to perform sometimes beyond normal behavior to achieve the results expected of them by the government. The uniforms were, of course, symbols of the colonial regime in Papua New Guinea. Wearing them, policemen, by their deeds and attitudes, perpetrated more acts of colonialism than the colonialists, if not in intent then perhaps through ignorance or blind loyalty.

Chapter 6
Police Involvement in the World Wars

Tribal wars in Papua New Guinea did not extend beyond broad geographical and linguistic boundaries. Alliances tended to join together particular clans rather than unite all peoples within a particular culture group. However, refugees from wars have been known to migrate to more distant places, into the territories of people who were not related to them by culture or language but who had established some link, perhaps through trade. For instance, Marie Reay found at Minj that after a major war, members of the defeated tribe sometimes made their way to Simbu and the Jimi Valley (1982, 630). Two tribes in Gende are composed mostly of refugees from Gembogl, North Simbu. The ancestors of these people fled from their enemies long before pacification.[1] Most Gende do not speak or understand the Simbu language, and the differences between the two cultures are greater than the similarities, although they traded in salt, bird of paradise plumes, pottery, and pigs. Despite its prevalence among most societies of Papua New Guinea, warfare in precontact times was generally confined to groups who lived in the same geographical and cultural areas.

Much of the warfare in Papua New Guinea was characterized by a very delicate balance of clan alliances. Leaders had to cultivate their alliances carefully through gift exchanges, marriages, and assisting others in times of violence. If one clan were to change alliances, the prospects of victory or defeat for others changed quickly. At times a clan might be pretending to help one group while secretly helping another. These complex and shifting alliances were vulnerable to slight changes in power balances—either from within or from outside. The police knew that with just slight interference they could completely change the current political and fighting power of competing clans. Because the patrol officers were less likely to appreciate the delicate local balance of power, the police could exert greater influence.

Participants in traditional warfare in Papua New Guinea were well

164

tutored in its complexities. If Kamuna's oral evidence (1955) is any proof, and enthnographers' accounts are accepted, in most societies every male child was initiated into the techniques and methods of warfare well before he reached adulthood. During his formative years he learned through his father and other men of his clan or tribe of the general organization and execution of war. He was told of the risks involved and the reparations his tribe had to make for any breach of the laws that guided the conduct of their warriors, or, conversely, that of the tribe's enemies. Before contact, warfare had evolved from the particular environment (the people's social and political organization, geography, religious beliefs, and so on) and had become a part of the people's culture. The men who joined the police were part of this culture, not just products of the Australian administrative system. Where a patrol officer might see just two hostile groups, his police were more likely to assume that here were complex and subtle alliances and enmities, and to understand the forces that pressed the clans to fight.

Of the twenty-eight men interviewed, twenty had fathers whose ascent to positions of authority and prestige in their villages had largely been achieved as leaders in tribal warfare. However, the advent of colonialism in Papua New Guinea had forcibly ended that aspect of their leadership role. Of the remaining eight men, apart from Guise, the grandfathers of Boino, Goro, Moru, Panau, Rewari, and ToWoworu had been great warriors in their youth,[2] but their fathers were born after pacification. Only three men—Kamuna of Garaina, Sarepamo of Goroka, and Tigavu of Gende—had actually participated in tribal warfare before pacification and their subsequent recruitment into the police force. Kamuna is from a coastal inland region, Tigavu from the highlands fringe, and Sarepamo from the east of what was Central Highlands region. From a brief biographical narrative in which Arenao Sesiguo wrote of Kamuna's initiation, it is evident that Kamuna was thoroughly prepared for a life as a warrior. Kamuna said:

> I, Kamuna Hura . . . am of the Kerua clan, and my emblem is the cassowary and barauva [a special type of bird]. The elders put us into the men's house . . . for the initiation ceremony. I lived in the men's house undergoing various rituals and there they gave me ritual herbs and roots to eat [to be brave in warfare] because it was the period of frequent tribal warfare. It was my uncle, Sasana, who brought the roots of a certain bush vine and while hiding behind the wall of the men's house he told me to eat the ritual herb. This I did and from then on I became short-tempered, fierce and aggressive in warfare. (Sesiguo 1977, 221)

The rest of the men gained knowledge of warfare through stories told them by their fathers and grandfathers. Later, as policemen and

during their days of exploration and pacification, many observed warfare among other people. Moreover, according to their oral testimonies, twenty-two men came from areas whose traditions were steeped in
some form of warfare. It can be assumed then that the behavior and
attitudes of Papua New Guinea police at times of violence, or the threat
of violence, were influenced by their own traditions.

World War I

In contrast to the localized, but sometimes ferocious and lethal tribal
wars, two world wars came to Papua New Guinea. During World War I,
Papua New Guinea almost escaped the violence. A semblance of military combat between an Australian force and German soldiers at Bitapaka, New Britain, lasted only one day: it began in the early morning of
11 September 1914 and ended at 7:00 PM the same day. Except for a
few New Guineans in Rabaul and other centers of government and mission influence, the majority of Papua New Guineans did not know that
a war had come and passed.[3] Significantly, New Guinean police did most
of the fighting and dying for the Germans. Among those who fought,
30 died from rifle fire, 10 were wounded, and 56 were taken prisoner
(Mackenzie 1987, 73–74; Burnell 1915).

Germany's New Guinea possessions, then known as the "old protectorate," included the northeast portion of the mainland, the Bismarck
Archipelago, and Bougainville. They came under Australian military rule
in September 1914 and remained subject to the Australian Naval and
Military Expeditionary Force (ANMEF) until civil administration was
restored on 9 May 1921. Papua remained an Australian territory, while
what was formerly German New Guinea became in 1921 a mandated
territory under the League of Nations. Australia was given responsibility to continue to administer both territories, this time under civilian
government.

World War I did not provide a catalyst for change for Papua New
Guineans. The fact that New Guinea became a mandated territory did
not for the most part improve conditions or alter the attitudes of the
Europeans to the indigenous population. In an ironical twist, while
German nationals during the war had been considered Australia's enemies, the terms of capitulation agreed to by the Australian military administration on 17 September 1914 stipulated in part that the New
Guinean members of the former German Armed Native Constabulary
were still to be employed "for the protection of the white population
against natives." The "white population" included the Australians, as
well as civilian Germans who were allowed temporarily to retain their
coconut plantations and positions in the administration (Rowley 1958,
4). The major change was that one colonial government was replaced

by another. Most other aspects of colonial life were maintained—labor regulations, the methods of recruiting laborers, poor working and living conditions on plantations, hanging of New Guinean men for murders, the tax levy on villagers, the absence of good educational facilities for the children, and the broad German administrative structure and practice for the government of the indigenous people. Hubert Murray, lieutenant-governor of Papua, wrote that the "Australian administration of German New Guinea is not very encouraging—the same old flogging seems to go on, with the same old imprisonment in dark rooms without trial, and all the paraphernalia of the old German regime" (quoted in Griffin, Nelson, and Firth 1979, 48). The open flogging of recalcitrant laborers may have stopped, but generally the situation was unchanged when, twenty-one years later, World War II struck Papua New Guinea.[4]

Insofar as the Australians who took over from the German officials were men of little experience in field administration, the power of older policemen most likely increased, particularly in the bush. Moreover, some of the Australian army personnel and patrol officers seem to have been more inclined to violence than Murray's men in Papua. Michael Piggott wrote that the Australian military personnel in Rabaul in 1914 looked askance at the New Guinean policemen. On the whole they regarded the local population with disdain, and any opposition was met with: "The procedure was obvious: if black, shoot first and ask questions later. . . . New Guineans died in considerable numbers" (Piggott 1984, 52–53; Mackenzie 1987, 311). Violence against New Guineans in some outpost areas continued to play a prominent part among commissioned officers of the Australian New Guinea Administrative Unit (ANGAU) during World War II, but attempts were made to conceal information. From a document issued in the early 1940s, it is clear that the censorship of reports of a "contentious nature" was an officially accepted practice. For example, a directive issued to district personnel from the ANGAU headquarters in Ramu in March 1943 gave detailed instructions:

> From the Administration aspect officers will not record matters of a contentious nature in patrol reports, matters which are likely to embarrass ANGAU Administration at HQ NGF [New Guinea Force]. It is not legal to burn houses, take hostages, destroy property, shoot pigs, etc., as a form of punishment for delinquent natives, however richly the man on the spot may consider such treatment is deserved and salutary.
>
> Officers will also desist from the practice of oblique advertising by direct or veiled reference to the incompetence, blundering or even illegal action of other officers in reports. If criticism is necessary of a colleague or predecessor, or attention should be drawn to

the misconduct or illegal action of other personnel it will be in
[*sic*] form of a confidential memo to the DO [District Officer] in
the first instance. (ANGAU 1943)

The officers at ANGAU headquarters knew of violence in the districts
and, indirectly, sanctioned it.

World War II

Unlike the tribal wars or the first white men's war that the policemen
had heard of or seen, the Second World War first broke from the clouds.
It was on a scale—of technology, numerical strength, and devastation—
never before imagined. The evacuation in 1942 contradicted advice to
villagers given in May 1941 by the *Papuan Villager,* that the war could not
spread to Papua and that it was not their war. It told literate Papuans:

> The war is a long, long way from here, and we do not expect it will
> ever come to Papua. The war is against Europeans not Papuans.
> The native Papuans should not be alarmed by this talk about
> A.R.P. [Air Raid Precaution]. If an enemy ever came here in an
> aeroplane he is not likely to want to hurt the native villages. He is
> at war with the Europeans, and he would want to smash the things
> that belong to Europeans, such as big stores, in Port Moresby.
> (*Papuan Villager* 13 [May 1941]: 33–34)

The destruction caused to towns and nearby villages in Rabaul,
Madang, Port Moresby, Lae, and Salamaua was worse than the most
extensive bush fires in the Markham Valley, the worst floods on the Fly
and Sepik Rivers, and the biggest eruption of the Matupit and Vulcan
volcanoes. Except for a few government-employed Hanuabadans, Tolai,
and Butibam villagers, the war caught most Papua New Guineans by
surprise. It was externally conceived, directed, and executed: strategies
for this war were not planned in Papua New Guinea men's houses. The
opportunity for the men to choose whether or not to fight an enemy
was not present. They had nothing to do with its beginnings, they only
happened to be living when and where it happened. In Papua New
Guinea, it lasted for nearly four years (Roe 1971, 138).

Hanuabadans not employed by the government were evacuated to
several villages along the coast after the first Japanese bombings in Port
Moresby in 1942. The villagers grieved at the prospect of being away
from their land: "Villagers were sad to leave their homes and their trea-
sured possessions and gardens. Many people cried at leaving but they
were so scared of the War and of further bombing raids that they were
glad to go to a safe place" (Robinson 1981, 102). When the war eventually ended, the town of Lae lay in ruins, with only a few buildings left

standing. It was a nerve-racking experience for the people of some villages: the war not only "ravaged local villages and made refugees" of them but, worse, it forced them "to lead a miserable, nomadic existence for four years in order to keep away from the savage bombing and shooting which tore up their homeland as the fighting see-sawed between the Japanese and the Allies" (Willis 1974, 129). Mair estimated that a total of 61,000 Papua New Guineans were evacuated from their homes and settlement sites in order "to make room for camps, airstrips, etc. In the case of those who were allowed to return, the whole work of planting and building had to begin afresh" (Mair 1948, 202).

From 1942 World War II engulfed much of Papua New Guinea (map 3). The first Japanese bombs fell on Rabaul on 4 January 1942, and the occupation of Rabaul on 23 January was the pivot on which the whole Japanese movement swung.[5] With Rabaul secured as the headquarters of the Pacific campaign, Japanese forces wasted no time in occupying, in logical fashion, other areas of Papua New Guinea on both the mainland and the islands. The Japanese landed in Kavieng (23 January), Bougainville (March), Lae and Salamaua (8 March), Buna and Gona (21 July), and the Japanese army was bent on marching from Buna to Port Moresby until stopped at Imita Ridge on 17 September 1942. After this the Japanese fortunes changed, and the remainder of the story of the Pacific theater of World War II between the Japanese and the Allied Forces is about the Allied counteroffensives that gradually recaptured Japanese-occupied areas until the Japanese capitulation on 15 August 1945.[6] The Allied strategy had been to island-hop north, bypassing heavy concentrations of troops, so that at the time of surrender there were still some one hundred fifty thousand Japanese troops and their captive or volunteer civilian laborers in Papua New Guinea.

As during World War I in New Guinea, the civilian government ended abruptly (PAR 1945–46, 1). Papua and New Guinea initially came under the umbrellas of two makeshift military governments: the New Guinea Administrative Unit and the Papuan Administrative Unit. However, after only a few weeks these were combined into the Australian New Guinea Administrative Unit (ANGAU), with headquarters at Port Moresby. Brigadier B M Morris, commander of the Eighth Military District, was promoted to the rank of major-general and given responsibility for the overall administration. The military organization, staffed mainly by prewar colonial officials, remained the administering authority for the duration of World War II in Papua New Guinea.[7] To achieve maximum efficiency, ANGAU's operations were divided into two main sections: Production and District Services (Oram 1976, 64, 69). The Production Service took over the running and maintenance of plantations and "other production units, such as sawmills, which supplied much needed raw materials" (Dutton 1985, 108–109). Through the

Military Activity in World War II

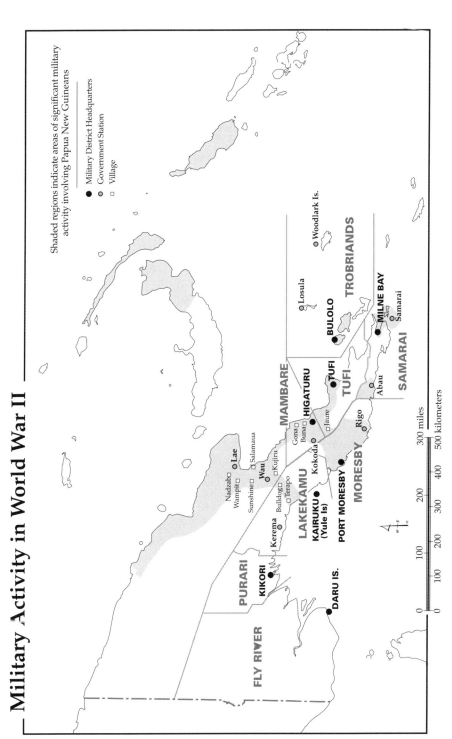

Shaded regions indicate areas of significant military activity involving Papua New Guineans

● Military District Headquarters
◉ Government Station
□ Village

Map 3

District Service, ANGAU was responsible for the smooth running of the support for the Allied war effort and for what had been the peacetime field administration (Robinson 1981, 12). As was frequently the case in colonial situations, but perhaps more so during the war, Papua New Guinean men were required to do the work to implement, under European supervision, the policies of the military government. The circumstances of this hostile situation created an environment for villagers, in groups or as individuals, to be involved voluntarily or through coercion in various tasks. In proposals put to ANGAU in 1942 by F E Williams, the Papuan government's anthropologist, Papua New Guineans could be engaged as menial laborers, plantation workers, carriers, in guerrilla fighting, in intelligence work, and could assist in general cooperation.[8]

The total population of Papua at the time of the war was estimated to be about 750,000 and New Guinea 1 million people (Williams 1942, 1). It is almost certainly an understatement. No information is available on how many of these were children, aged, physically handicapped, and women. Together they would have made up a sizable proportion of the total population. A good proportion of the adult male population in the pacified and easily accessible areas became employees of either the Japanese or the Allied Forces. The actual number of men and women engaged by the Japanese for their help in the war—or even a rough estimate of it—is not available.

Working for the Allied Forces

Written evidence of the part the Papua New Guinean policemen played in the campaign is scattered, and some confusion exists in the oral evidence, particularly from men recruited during the war years. These men were not at all certain whether they had engaged as policemen or as soldiers, because they undertook responsibilities that fell within the normal boundaries of both those occupations. In some situations a Papua New Guinean was simultaneously a policeman and a soldier. Of the twenty-eight men interviewed, eleven were serving as policemen before the war and continued in that capacity during and after it; nine were attested as either policemen or soldiers during the war and continued or reenrolled as policemen when it ended. Of the remaining eight men, one first worked as a carrier on the Kokoda Trail for a year in 1942, but rather than return to his village he joined the police force. Another worked as a guide for Bena Force until early 1944, when he was recruited at Goroka. The remaining six men joined the force after World War II, Guise in 1946, Mohaviea Loholo in 1947, and the rest during the 1950s. Of the twenty-eight men, only one worked as a Japanese policeman in Rabaul; the rest worked for the Allied Forces.[9]

By December 1942, 16,050 able-bodied males were under contract as

laborers to the Allied Forces, the majority of them Papuans. Early in
the war, Papuans featured prominently as contracted laborers because
much of the potential recruiting ground in the Mandated Territory of
New Guinea was under Japanese control. Highlands men were not recruited, except very occasionally, on account of the malaria risk. As areas
in New Guinea were recaptured, young men from these regions began
to boost the numbers of the New Guineans in the various occupations.
By the end of the war their numbers had swelled to such an extent that
they were the majority in at least the laboring jobs (Dutton 1985, 113).
In March 1943 the total number of contracted laborers rose to 18,446.
Six months later it had jumped to 30,000. At its peak in July 1943 the
total number of men between the ages of fourteen and forty years
under contract as laborers, stood at 40,000 (Peter Ryan 1968, 540).

Important as they were to the Allied cause, laboring jobs did not
appeal to most Papua New Guineans. Various Papua New Guinean fighting units won extravagant praise from officers and admirers for feats of
gallantry. Between 1942 and 1945, more Papua New Guineans served in
Australian military or paramilitary units than had served as police in the
period 1920 to 1942. Throughout the four years, 8,000 or more Papua
New Guinean men served in defense of Papua New Guinea: 3,582 in
the Pacific Island Regiment, 878 in the "M" Special Unit, 3,137 as police,
and 955 as medical orderlies.[10] Suitable Papua New Guinean men joined
and fought in several units of the Australian army.[11] The first was formed
as a fighting unit in Papua in June 1940[12] and officially became known
as the Papuan Infantry Battalion (PIB). It later expanded to include two
other battalions of the Pacific Island Regiment, whose members were
used for active engagement in various parts of Papua as well as New
Guinea (Barrett 1968, 493–494). Originally, it consisted of Papuan men,
many of whom were ex-policemen, and Australian officers, but later
New Guinean men joined, the first group being escaped laborers from
the Rabaul area brought by the Japanese to Buna (Dutton 1985, 115).
By March 1945 all three battalions were in active service throughout
the New Guinea campaign. The combined Papuan Infantry Battalion
and New Guinea Infantry Battalion (NGIB) formed the Pacific Island
Regiment (PIR). At the peak of the war an estimated total of 55,000, or
more than fifty percent of available adult males, were employed. A
minority, but still a significant group, served as policemen (Long 1963,
82–83). Thousands of others assisted in various other capacities but
have not been officially recorded; some of them were "employed as
guerillas and locally recruited carriers."

Formation and Recruitment

With the end of civil administration in 1942, the Royal Papuan Constabulary and the New Guinea police force were disbanded (AWM 1939–
1945b). At the time, the strength of the New Guinea force consisted of

29 European officers and 1,127 New Guineans of all ranks. The members of the Royal Papuan Constabulary numbered 350 (AWM 1939–1945b). Two reasons lay behind the contrast in police numbers before disbandment. The first reflected the size and rate of increase of police strength in the respective forces in the 1930s. Papua had a small force, with a slow rate of increase, almost to the point of stagnation; from 1934 "there [was] no recruitment of European Officers," and it seems as if the recruitment of noncommissioned officers of the constabulary had been halted (Australia: Police Forces . . .). New Guinea had a larger force, which was expanding at a steady pace. On 30 June 1933 the New Guinea force had a total of 663 policemen of all ranks (633 New Guineans, a superintendent, and 29 European policemen, the majority of whom were professionally trained), whereas Papua had a total of 250 men (215 Papuans and 35 European officers, many of whom were not professional policemen). In December 1934 the Papuan police strength remained unchanged at 250, while the New Guinean strength had increased by 72, bringing the total to 735 men of all ranks (Australia: Police Forces . . .). Given this trend for the 1930s, it is not surprising that at the time of disbandment Papua had fewer policemen than New Guinea. In contrast to Papua, by the 1930s New Guinea had flourishing goldfields, its government had more money to spend on the expansion of facilities, there were many more foreigners, and because of a larger newly discovered population in the highlands it needed more staff. Police strength was increased to maintain law and order in some of the new areas. For instance, in 1934–35 "the Police Force Regulations were amended to provide for the creation of a new Police District in the gold-fields area of the Morobe District" (NGAR 1934–45, 96). Further, in 1940 "the Police Force Regulations were amended to provide an increase in the establishment of the native Constabulary," resulting in an end-of-year total of 1,115 men of all ranks (NGAR 1939–40, 129).

The second reason is specific and applied principally to Papua.

> I have watched the Papuan since 1912. I have studied the characteristics of the Papuans and the reactions of these people to the new life that civilization has brought and is bringing to them. I have found the Papuan native as soon as he is brought under the influence of the government to be a man of peace, friendly towards Europeans and easily controlled. The truth of this may be seen in the fact that the mere handful of policemen tend law and order throughout the country except in those small areas in the west where government influence has not yet spread. *This means that in Papua there was no need even for a large police force. We had about 350 on a peace time strength and these men fulfilled all the requirements of the territory.* (Humphries 1945; emphasis added)

The Papuan administration believed Papuans were benign; the New Guinea officials took a less optimistic view.

At the time the police forces were disbanded it is not clear for many men whether they returned home immediately, joined the Papuan and New Guinean battalions, or remained on the stations for other reasons. The accounts of some of the men interviewed reveal that their officers' advice to them conflicted with the official proclamation in April 1942 that they were no longer to serve as policemen. Three New Guinea examples are sufficient.[13] At the Talasea police depot, Sono and the rest of the policemen were told by their white officers:

> "All of you policemen must not return to your villages or families. You must not be afraid. You must all join us and help us fight the Japanese. The Japanese are very bad people, they are cannibals." When we heard our officers pleading for our help, all the men present made a solemn undertaking in front of the officers: *"Mipela bai stap wantaim yupela ol masta na halivim yupela long faitim ol Japan"* [We will stand by you, *masta,* and help you fight the Japanese]. I remained a policeman throughout and did not join either the PIB or NGIB. But I was issued with hand grenades and a rifle. (Sono 1985)

Early in 1942, Sesetta of Garaina was a policeman in Manus. At the outbreak of the war D H Vertigan (the officer in charge) buried some money in the ground. He told Sesetta that he had to leave Manus for the mainland, but before he did so he needed to appoint someone whom he trusted to remain on the island and keep an eye out for the buried treasure and other property of the government. Sesetta was appointed: "You are a policeman of the government so I will leave you in charge of the station and the money. If the two of us were to leave Manus together and get bombed as a result who is going to tell the people where I have hidden the money?" (Sesetta 1985). Sesetta remained on Palawan Island. Some time later he was arrested and jailed by Japanese soldiers. He was caned every day because he would not reveal the whereabouts of the hidden money or his patrol officer. After about three months he was rescued by the Americans.

The third example is from Sasa Goreg of Gabsongekeg village, Markham Valley. Sasa was retained at the police depot as an instructor at the end of his police training at Tavui, Rabaul, in 1939. Only hours before the Japanese forces took over Rabaul on 23 January 1942, Police Master Alex Sinclair and the founder of the first police band, David Crawley, issued bullets to the policemen and ordered them to prepare for a retreat to the Baining Mountains. Sasa recalled the hardships and anguish of the long march to Toma, and then through the dangerous mountains to Talasea:

At Rabaul we started at six in the evening. It was difficult for some of the policemen, especially those who were married and had children. The distance was long. We walked and walked. Sometime around twelve o'clock, the two officers asked us to sit down and rest. I do not remember the exact numbers but there were definitely hundreds of policemen. We all sat down and ate biscuits and tinned food. The Japanese planes were still flying around in the dark sky above. It was hard. We were forbidden to light fires. Supplies were carried by the new recruits. These consisted of rice, tinned meat, biscuits, etc. We arrived at Toma in the middle of the night. There were more people than food supplies so we were put on rations. For instance, the first evening four men had to share one tin of biscuits. The next morning was Friday.[14] From the Toma area we could clearly see that the Japanese warships had berthed in the harbour during either the night or the early hours of the morning and we knew immediately that the small resistance there had been overcome by the sheer force of the military might of the Japanese army. Our officers then called us together and told us to dig a hole in the ground. It was a deep hole. It looked like a trench. In it we buried our rifles, uniforms, and any other material that belonged to the government. When everything was placed in the hole it was covered over with corrugated iron and timber, after which we spread soil. The Police Master then said: "You must not follow us but make your own way down to the coast of Talasea." They then appointed a sergeant from Talasea who was familar with the surrounding areas to guide us and later to assist us travel through the Siassi Islands and to Finschhafen, on the mainland. From there we had to walk home the best way we could. The officers, like some of the other whites serving in New Britain, were evacuated by boats to either Finschhafen or Lae. We, on the other hand, were to find our own way home, even though some of us had to cross over not only steep and precipitous mountains, but also a group of islands and a vast ocean. (Goreg 1986; see appendix 4)

Rather than risk his life, Sasa Goreg walked down to Talasea and stayed with some friendly locals until the Japanese found him and forced him to work for them as a policeman.

Officially, three factors influenced the issuance of the disbandment order. First, some senior officers in the New Guinea Administration did not trust New Guineans. The general opinion was that they could only be used as "batmen, servants, cooks, mess waiters, runners, sanitation crews" (Griffin, Nelson and Firth 1979, 72). Second, the Australians did not think the police would be of much use in modern warfare. At least this was the view expressed by Murray in Papua. The "Papuan native is a splendid soldier. He is courageous, and he is skilled in the use of some weapons. But I am afraid that the noise of a bombardment would devastate him" (quoted in Griffin, Nelson, and Firth 1979, 72). Some experienced officers in New Guinea made similar statements, but there were exceptions. Not everyone favored disbandment. For instance, some officers such as John Black and J K McCarthy kept their police. McCarthy, at Talasea, was angry that a force as well trained and disciplined as the police would be stripped of its arms and disbanded. He regarded the whole incident as "a gross error of judgement—it was utter stupidity" (McCarthy 1963, 196). Third, the Australians wished to protect New Guineans from violence that was not of their making. The motives indicating a lack of confidence in New Guineans were probably stronger than the humanitarian ones. By contrast, the Germans had used the police to do most of the fighting in 1914, and in Papua the Papuan Infantry Battalion was already formed and trained. In early 1942 the decision seemed to be that Papuans would fight the Japanese but New Guineans would not. The official viewpoints against the use of police as combatants are summarized by Sinclair:

> Firstly, the Army (2/22nd Battalion) did not ask for police support. Secondly, there was the example of 1914, when many of the armed police under German control deserted their posts and supported the invading Australians. Thirdly, Administration officers were instructed to escape capture, and if this was impossible, to surrender peacefully. The idea that armed police, however loyal, should have been allowed to fight for departing Australians was not to be contemplated. The general instruction for police in all parts of the Territory to give up their arms was issued to protect them from Japanese persecution and to protect village people from attacks by rogue police. (J Sinclair 1990, 124)

Whatever happened to the disbanded men, the existence of the state of emergency soon made it abundantly clear that a police force of sufficient numbers was necessary for effective administration and the conduct of the war in the territories. Consequently, through the authority of Administrative Order Number 4, a police force was reconstituted by ANGAU and called the Royal Papuan Constabulary. In theory at least it was a completely new force insofar as the authority for its formation did not arise from any of the former Papuan Constabulary Ordinances, "although it served to replace and to perform the functions of the Royal Papuan Constabulary which during or about February 1942 ceased to exist."[15] For reasons of expediency, eligible New Guinean men were allowed to serve in the reconstituted force. The official explanation was that:

The inclusion of the Territory of New Guinea in the sphere of operations of the Royal Papuan Constabulary was an expediency arising out of the war situation which existed in 1942–43. In order to assist in native resettlement, to provide better administration and control immediately and to provide against the confusion that will arise if the establishment of a police force for the Territory of New Guinea area is left until civil administration returns to Papua it is recommended that the police force now be established for the Territory of New Guinea and that such force be organized on the line of the New Guinea Force. (AWM 1939–1945b)

In reality, the former Royal Papuan Constabulary and the New Guinea police forces were amalgamated into one unit, which became the Royal Papuan Constabulary, under the direct control of the District Services branch of ANGAU.

Precise recruitment details are not available, but the pattern of recruitment for both the army and the constabulary was similar: "The policy in the past has been to obtain recruits for the PIB and the RPC

Table 4 Recruitment into the Royal Papuan Constabulary

Name	Subdistrict	Year recruited	Served in 1946	Served after 1946
*Amero, Bega	Talasea	1934	Yes	No
Anka, Sakarias	Markham	1936	Yes	Yes
Beu, Iworo	Ioma	1940	Yes	Yes
Boino, John	Tufi	1941	Yes	Yes
*Sasa Goreg	Markham	1939	Yes	No
Goro, Sebastin	Buna	1941	Yes	Yes
Igarobae, Athanasius	Ioma	1942	Yes	Yes
Iwagu, Aladu	Finschhafen	1931	Yes	Yes
Kamuna, Hura	Garaina	1923	Yes	Yes
Kasse Aibuki	Talasea	1934	Yes	Yes
Meraveka	Gulf	1939	Yes	Yes
Naguwean	Sepik	1942	Yes	Yes
Rewari	Musa	1942	Yes	Yes
Sarepamo, Tate	Goroka	1943	Yes	Yes
Sesetta	Garaina	1936	Yes	Yes
Sono	Garaina	1936	Yes	Yes
Tamutai, Naguna	Western	1942	Yes	Yes
Tigavu, Petrus	Madang	1944	Yes	Yes
ToWoworu, Ben Elipas	Rabaul	1936	Yes	Yes
Yegova, Jojoga	Buna	1943	Yes	Yes

Source: Interviews.
*Both Amero and Sasa resigned from the force, Sasa after working as a policeman for the Japanese during World War II.

entirely on a voluntary basis. It has been found that coerced natives with either units are well nigh valueless."[16]

From the interviews, examples have been selected to illustrate the experiences of those who served in the police before, during, and after the war, as well as those who were recruited into the Royal Papuan Constabulary because of the war but continued as policemen when it was over (table 4). Some police who stayed with an officer and were cut off by the Japanese seem to have been transferred from police to army with no additional training, as was the officer.

Among those interviewed, thirteen of the men had served a good number of years in one or the other of the police forces before they reenrolled in the new Royal Papuan Constabulary. Although the sample is too small to give firm indications, it is possible that at least for the early months of the war most of the prewar policemen in areas clearly controlled by the Allies reenlisted. Reenrollment had its attractions. Many of these men had already been trained, and by the time of the war they had had six or more years of experience as policemen. For instance, by 1942 Kamuna would have had nineteen years' service in the New Guinea police force. While some training would have been necessary for all recruits, it would have been expedient to give first preference to those who had prior knowledge of the work involved because in an emergency, it was obviously preferable not to spend too much time training people. It is likely that experienced policemen would have been preferred, at least for the first few months.[17]

From 1942 until the end of 1945 many Papua New Guinean men were recruited into the newly constituted police force to meet the exigencies of the war. In December 1943 a total of 2,064 men were in the Royal Papuan Constabulary, the majority of them Papuan.[18] By the end of 1944 the police numbers had increased to 2,553,[19] of whom 1,175 are presumed to have been Papuans. A month after the end of hostilities, in September 1945, a total of 3,137 Papua New Guinean men were in the Royal Papuan Constabulary (Griffin, Nelson, and Firth 1979, 98; AWM 1945), compared to a total of less than 1,400 men of all ranks in the two territories in 1941.

Training

The site for the training of the new constabulary was Bisiatabu, the old Papuan Armed Constabulary depot near Port Moresby. It was later shifted to Sogeri. Both the police and members of the Papuan Infantry Battalion appear to have gone through the same sort of training. For the new recruits (former policemen, with no change in their ranks were sent into the field after only short briefings) training was intense and short. It ranged from three to six months, with only a few whose training was extended to twelve months. In 1941, the Crown Law Officer recommended to Leonard Murray, the Papuan Administrator, that: "Officers, warrant officers and members of the police who volunteer under the provisions of these regulations shall receive such honorary rank as the Governor-General may determine but the relative seniority enjoyed in the police shall so far as is practicable be preserved" (CLO 1939–1945). Yegova was recruited into the Royal Papuan Constabulary in 1943. He remembered well the training routine:

> When I first arrived there in 1943 I joined a queue for registration. My name was written into a book. I was then issued with blankets, mosquito nets, laplaps (2) and something for the "bed." For the first three to four weeks we worked with our hands. Then we were issued with rifles. We were told that even though we would be working in the bush as policemen our training would be military in nature. We were instructed in mock battles, climbed over mounds, fences, crossed streams, swung from ropes, crawled through artificial holes, fixed bayonets, and conducted practice target shooting. I found it to be very exhausting because all these things were done at a running speed. Target shooting was done last. If a recruit was proficient he graduated and was sent away to work with the carriers, or in various other capacities. Otherwise one remained on the depot until he could prove his proficiency. Other aspects of life at the depot were much the same as those of peace times. While there I became acutely aware of three things. Firstly, Hanuabadan villagers had been evacuated. Secondly, at the training depot, there were literally hundreds upon hundreds of European soldiers and Papua New Guineans, men from Bougainville, Gulf, Manus, Madang, Morobe, Popondetta, Milne Bay, and Tolai. I was not frightened, but was overwhelmed. Many of us initially used sign language to communicate with one another until we could master Police Motu or New Guinea *Tok Pisin*. At this time also recruits were housed according to their districts. There were twenty-four thatch-roofed houses. For instance, all the young men from Sepik lived in one house. In each of these houses the men did their own cooking, each week two men cooked for the rest of their colleagues. Much to my disappointment, at the end of my training I worked as a guard in Port Moresby. (Yegova 1985)

If the basic training was the same for the two forces, they had separate training grounds. The Papuan Infantry Battalion sometimes trained at the site of the present Murray Barracks (Sinclair 1990, 132). There was one main difference in the training received by the recruits of the Papuan Infantry Battalion and the Royal Papuan Constabulary: "Native soldiers are taught to use their weapons offensively and

Table 5 Rankings for police officers

Prewar (post 1930)	1942–1946	Postwar
Superintendent	Lieutenant Colonel	Superintendent
Inspector	Major	Inspector
Officer-in-charge, training depot	Captain	Officer-in-charge, training depot
Warrant Officer Class 1	Lieutenant	Warrant Officer Class 1
Warrant Officer Class 2	Class 1 or 2	Warrant Officer Class 1 or 2

Source: AWM 1939–1945b.

shoot to kill. The police, on the other hand, use their weapons as a last resort in defense. [In theory, at least,] they do not shoot to kill" (AWM 1944).

Officers commanding these men were selected from the Australian Military Forces. However, if appointments were made from among the prewar civil field staff officers, then appropriate military rankings were given (table 5).

However, their functions remained the same as before the war:

> Apart from the allotment of military rank to the European personnel . . . the force to be established should in the interest of ordered administration and conformity with pre-war and post-war practice be organized on the lines of the civil force. That is, the CO should function as superintendent of police. Officers in charge of police districts as inspectors and other personnel as European constabulary. The superintendent of police to be responsible for the general administration of the force and the control of the HQ and training depot. Inspector of police to be responsible for the policing of various areas declared to be police districts (ie townships and adjacent areas). DO to be responsible for control of policing of each district and in this duty to be assisted by European members of the force. (AWM 1939–1945b)

The Nature of Wartime Work

Some members of the Royal Papuan Constabulary continued to perform their traditional roles, while others took on new responsibilities that overlapped with soldiering duties. For the period of the war, the nature of police involvement fell into three broad categories: law and order, propaganda, and paramilitary responsibilities. The first had been a continuing responsibility of the police since the forces of the two territories were first formed in the 1890s. The other two arose out of the war and ceased when it ended.

LAW AND ORDER

The fact of the war did not alter the need for a mobile police force to maintain law and order among both civilian and military personnel, as was formally recognized by ANGAU, the administering authority. The Papua New Guinea Administration Order (no 4, para 5) of ANGAU stipulated, "The function of the police force is the effective policing of the Territories of Papua and New Guinea. In conformity with the provision made in respect of the Royal Papuan Constabulary, the police force functions to maintain law and order among the civil population" (AWM 1939–1945b). This declaration was reinforced with the establishment of police districts in various parts of the country, with headquarters in Port Moresby, Lae, and later Rabaul. In the outer districts, a sufficient number of policemen were stationed with their officers to enforce ANGAU's administrative directives regarding the maintenance of law and order among the villagers (AWM 1939–1945b). The police worked as the right-hand men of ANGAU to reassure villagers that law and order had not collapsed as a consequence of the war; rather it was being maintained as firmly as before, if not more so. This objective was achieved through regular police patrols to villages, assistance given in the relocation of villagers away from danger areas, and by walking with and talking to groups of labor recruits and accompanying carrier lines as guards and *bossbois* (overseers). More important, the physical presence of the policemen in the villages restored the confidence of the people. When given assurances that the police were performing similar tasks to those performed before the war, many villagers shrugged off their doubts.

Briefly, in order not to increase confusion among the villagers, ANGAU emphasized the maintenance of law and order; if stability was achieved, then members of the Royal Papuan Constabulary, being in the vanguard, were mainly responsible.

But recalcitrants remained. Those who chose to resist the authority of the constabulary and ANGAU, and whose activities were construed not to be in the best interest of public peace, were arrested and brought to jail, if imprisonment was considered the wisest course of action. The police then took on another role in the continuing need for maintaining law and order: they looked after prisons and prisoners. Their authority came from the Papua New Guinea Administration Order Number 4, which empowered ANGAU "to establish and maintain prisons, jails and locks" (AWM 1939–1945b). In Papua the old prison at Koki was relocated to Bisiatabu in 1942 and rebuilt "on land held under lease by the Seventh Day Adventist Mission" (AWM 1939–1945b). In Japanese-held Rabaul, for a while at least, the jail and other sleeping quarters for the army were in long tunnels constructed into the sides of hills. To protect people from the American bombers, numerous tunnels were

dug between Rabaul and Kokopo. Sasa Goreg of the Markham Valley,
who was the senior noncommissioned officer supervising New Guinean
policemen and prisoners in Rabaul, had vivid recollections:

> I worked as a policeman for the Japanese during the war. My main
> task was to supervise Japanese prisoners, in particular New Guinean
> prisoners. For the whole of 1944 we lived in holes dug into the side
> of the mountains in Rabaul. The holes were fenced off by cor-
> rugated iron. Inside were two doors. In the event that one got
> destroyed during the [Allied] bombing raids, the other was used
> as an escape route. The beds were like bunks in a dormitory or a
> ship—one man slept on top and another underneath. Most of the
> amenities were there, including electricity, toilets and showers,
> both hot and cold. Prisoners were kept in another section. (Goreg
> 1986)

Unlike the New Guinea policemen, who looked after prisons and
prisoners from the formation of the force, in Papua prison warders were
chosen from the civilian population to work at the Koki jail (A Inglis
1982, 61–62). However, under ANGAU this responsibility was transferred
to the Royal Papuan Constabulary (AWM 1939–1945b). There was nothing exciting about prison supervision. Little had changed from prewar
practice. The policemen and their charges followed a regular and boring routine.

PROPAGANDA

The second major area of the constabulary's responsibility involved
propaganda. Papua New Guinean policemen themselves did not produce the information, but they became effective agents for its dissemination. The technique was used widely by both the Allied Forces and
the Japanese army. Although each side tried to discredit the other, propaganda was ultimately directed at the villagers. It is not known whether
the various overtures proved either amusing or flattering to the villagers.
Whatever the reactions, the rationale for encouraging its repeated application among villagers and laborers was quite simple. Both sides realized early the great contribution villagers would make to the overall
outcome of the war. They believed the cooperation of Papua New
Guineans as laborers, guides to fighting units, and assistants to downed
airmen was essential. They were prepared to go to any lengths to
spread information and disinformation about their own strengths and
their enemy's weaknesses.
    The production and distribution of propaganda was achieved
through advanced technology. For instance, G W L Townsend, a former
patrol officer and a lieutenant-colonel during the war, said his unit
dropped 23 million leaflets of Allied propaganda to both the Japanese

and New Guineans in 1945.[20] Authentic interpretations of these strange messages in terms intelligible to the villagers were largely carried out by the policemen working for the Allied Forces and the Japanese army. Although some ANGAU and Japanese officers were able to contribute because of their understanding of villagers, they were few and far between. Even if there had been more men like W R Humphries and F E Williams, their range of achievements would not, on the whole, have equaled those of the police. Having been uprooted only recently from the village in most cases, the police were in a superior position to work as mediators. "It should be remembered that service in the RPC is attractive to natives mainly because it is constantly associated with native life—the sights and sounds of the village, the dances and all the rest of it. All these things are available to the RPC" (Humphries 1945). The methods of disseminating the propaganda material were wide ranging. Some appeared in poorly produced *Tok Pisin* (see Townsend 1968, 262), Police Motu, and various dialects on leaflets and gramophone recordings, but the most popular means was the traditional method, word of mouth.

Of the propaganda lines the Japanese exploited, two were used more frequently than others. The first played on the sentiment of the people concerning ancestor worship. The Japanese claimed that the spirits of the Papua New Guinean dead were already in Japan, which was the home of the ancestors. If the villagers did not treat the Japanese well, then they would have no option but to ensure that the ancestors were given "a bad time" when they returned home (P A Ryan 1939–1945). The second set of approaches has been referred to as "masterpieces of restraint and tact." During the Japanese occupation of Madang, the people of Amele and the surrounding areas were told regularly:

> We Japanese have been sorry for you natives of New Guinea for a long time. We have thought about you a great deal and now have come to help you. Before, the Americans [Australians] in this country made laws and restrictions which were wrong. We have come to remedy the injustices that are inflicted on you and to make life good for you. We are your brothers. Your skins and ours are the same. Will you help us with our cargo and show us roads and tracks? Will all your headmen help us pray to God to help us in our work?" (Monk 1944)

In the early stages of the war the Japanese army had numerical strength, and there was little the Allied Forces could do to offset this imbalance. The villagers became impressed with the seeming invincibility of the Japanese and did not hesitate to make this impression known to the Allied Forces whenever opportunities arose. While working be-

hind enemy lines on the outskirts of Lae, Peter Ryan was scarcely sur-
priscd when villagers reminded him of this difference. He observed:

> Circumstances had made shrewd politicians of these natives, for
> they were caught between two opposing forces and were deter-
> mined to side with the ultimate winners. They sometimes argued
> with me that the Japanese were so numerous that they must win.
> "Look," they would say, "you know for yourself there are now more
> Japanese in Lae alone than there were white men in the whole of
> New Guinea before. The Japanese must be stronger." (Peter Ryan
> 1985, 95)

The Allied Forces went one step further and brought Papua New
Guinean representatives to Australia to impress them with new developments in weaponry, ammunition, and the factories where these were
mass produced, including visits to army camps, cities such as Brisbane,
Sydney, and Melbourne, airfields, bridges, large shopping centers, and
any other places where "the cumulative effect of seeing so many army
establishments and so many airfields and so many groups of aeroplanes
will be to give the impression that Australia is one vast armed camp.
And it will not be difficult to convince them that the allied arms must,
in the long run, prevail" (Visit of . . . Native Police . . . 1942). To test this
theory, in the middle of 1942 seven members of the Royal Papuan Constabulary were brought to Australia. They included one sergeant from
New Guinea, and the rest, constables in rank, came from Papua: Baubau of Mambare District, Northeast Division; Debbedowa of Rigo, East
Central Division; Kerri of Abigai-urama village, Delta Division; Kivivia
of Opa village, Gulf Division; Nanai of Babaguina village, Delta Division, and Nanai of Tubuseria village, Central Division. While in Australia the men assisted in producing gramophone recordings in *Tok Pisin*,
Police Motu, and "lesser dialects" to be distributed in most accessible
areas as well as Port Moresby. On their return the policemen were
attached to several Z field parties and were to have become "direct vehicles of active propaganda in the districts where it is most needed" (Visit
of . . . Native Police . . . 1942).

The Allies' line of propaganda was simple, but vehemently anti-Japa-
nese, accusing them of all manner of atrocities, not the least being that
the Japanese were greedy and wanted the rich and fertile farm lands of
Australia as well as to wrest control of the territories of Papua and New
Guinea. Every effort should therefore be made, the Australians said, to
stop these "wicked deceitful people" from achieving their ambitions.
They should "be wiped out [because] they are wicked people and deserve no mercy or forgiveness" (Visit of . . . Native Police . . . 1942).

The net result of the efforts of the policemen and their officers to
win support from the villagers will never be known. Some information

is given here of the numbers involved in the war. Was the villagers' involvement the result of the Allied and Japanese propaganda? It is almost certainly a fallacy to state that villagers were gullible or ignorant of what was happening. If anything, they made rational and mature decisions based on their observation and participation during almost sixty years of colonial rule. In this respect, Osmar White's sardonic assertion of the villagers' behavior toward working for the Allied Forces (and, needless to state, the Japanese), might hold some credibility if, by subtle implication, it connotes an independent and calculated choice:

> While it is true that some natives did show the qualities for which they were praised, it is equally true that the majority did their work only because the white men in command bullied them into doing it. Few if any were serving voluntarily and most would have deserted if possible. At this stage they knew of no reason and felt no desire to fight on the side of the Australians against the Japanese [and vice-versa] but the habit of obeying white men, inculcated by about sixty years of colonization, was hard to break. In some cases, of course, loyalty was a factor, but it was usually a matter of personal attachment between master and servant, not a spontaneous expression of gratitude by the brown race for benevolent leadership and protection from whites. (White 1965, 129)

PARAMILITARY

For the police, performing paramilitary duties was not new; it was as old as their history. The more important question is, why were they, easily the best trained and with the longest experience, not used as a military force, to form the first Papua New Guinean battalion? I first examine the debate that led to denying the police the opportunity to engage officially as a military force, and then discuss how they performed as a paramilitary force.

Several arguments against using the police as a military force were put forward in the debate. The first was simply that the villagers who had grown familiar with the police and their work would have difficulty accepting their new role. It would cause confusion and trepidation among them (AWM 1939–1945c). Yet Papua New Guineans were recruited not to fight in Europe, Africa, or Asia, but to help in the campaign in Papua New Guinea among their own people. Might it not have made more sense to use the police, with whose work the villagers were already familiar, for military purposes rather than to employ young recruits who not only had no prior knowledge of their new responsibilities but who also proved a real menace to the villagers? Numerous examples can be found of the way members of the New Guinea Infantry Battalion and the Papua Infantry Battalion terrorized villagers by raping women, pillaging their properties, and generally becoming a nuisance to them.[21] Only the police force had more than sixty years of experience.

The second argument ran along similar lines, except that it claimed the policemen themselves, having enjoyed sixty or more years of proud tradition, "would not understand such action" (AWM 1939–1945c). The argument is contradicted by the men interviewed. According to their testimonies, policemen were keen to join the army as a legally instituted body, but were disappointed when they were selected to look after the *bik lain*.[22] The extent of that disappointment was revealed to McCarthy when he spoke to a group of policemen fleeing from the Japanese on their way to Talasea:

> Among these refugees were native police, in khaki uniforms but without rifles. These were bitter, sullen men. Some I first spoke to evaded my questions. But I learned the reason for their bitterness when I met up with a policeman I had known for years. "The Australian government!" he almost spat. "Why didn't they let the police fight the Japanese? Why did they take our rifles from us just before the Japanese landed? They buried our rifles and now we are running like frightened women. We would have fought with the soldiers. (J K McCarthy 1963, 196)

Third, the covenant of the League of Nations of 1921 prohibited the formation of military forces and the buildup of military fortifications in mandated territories. Although this applied to New Guinea only, Papua was affected indirectly. In Papua the prohibition did not feature in discussions leading up to the war, but there can be little doubt of its influence, because until the war there was no standing army big enough to deter external attack. (The Papuan Infantry Battalion was formed by Leonard Logan of the Royal Papuan Constabulary in 1940. Likewise, the Northern Territory of Australia had few defenses in 1939. The problems were not specific to Papua and New Guinea.) Whereas the Australians abided by the conditions of the mandate, the Japanese were not constrained by them and built up bases in Micronesia. Even so, many Australians feared the Japanese were their likely enemies. The Australians were honorable, but not sensible.

Finally, there is evidence to suggest that some of the delay was caused by bureaucratic bungling. The delay in reaching a firm decision stemmed from the confusion and indecision on the part of those in authority about whether the police could be used as a military force in an emergency. In Papua in the 1930s, colonial officials discussed how to use members of the armed constabulary effectively in the event of another war touching Papua New Guinea. According to Judge Gore, early discussions took place in 1934, when the possibility of a threat from Japan was recognized after Lieutenant-Governor Murray had been there on a trip (Gore 1966, 122–123) In 1938 a blue book containing recommendations for "defence schemes" permitted the use of armed constabulary for defense purposes in Papua.[23] The Commonwealth Government of Australia rejected outright plans for the inclusion of the police, indicating that no provisions existed in the territory's regulations for the police to be used in that way. Officials in New Guinea did not make similar requests, perhaps because after the Rabaul "Strike" of January 1929 some senior administration officials did not trust the police. But the Papuan administration insisted, and submitted a redraft of an ordinance that emphasized the urgent need to provide for the use of the police in the territory's defense scheme. Parts of a letter written by Administrator Ramsay McNicoll to the secretary of the Prime Minister's Department in Canberra illustrate the legislative and bureaucratic complexities:

> With reference to previous correspondence regarding the Defence Scheme for the Territory, I desire to invite your attention to the present position of the Native Constabulary which has in former discussions always been regarded as a potential unit in the scheme.
>
> I am not aware as to the decision that was arrived at concerning the enactment of this Ordinance if necessity arose, but it would appear that, as the draft amendment to the Defence Act included in the same "Z" Scheme has not been adopted, it was not considered desirable to make provision for a New Guinea Field Force as contemplated in the proposed amendment.
>
> There are at present approximately 1,000 natives trained, or partially trained, to use rifles enrolled in the Native Constabulary and the general idea in building up this force and arranging its training was to ensure that it would be readily available for transfer to military duties if an occasion demanded.
>
> The matter is now referred for consideration as to whether it is proposed to introduce legislation to permit of the use of the Police Force as a defence unit. In the event of a decision being taken that the larger scheme which contemplated the format of a New Guinea Field Force is not to be proceeded with, there would appear to be no objection to the approval of the draft New Guinea (Local Defence) Native Forces Ordinance provided that references therein to the New Guinea Field Force were deleted. (McNicoll nd)

The debate was drawn out. The views of Director of Native Affairs Robert Melrose on the capacities, or lack of them, of Papua New Guineans did not help:

> With reference to our conversation regarding the possibility of the
> native for the use as troops, I am afraid no great use could be
> made of him.
>   Another aspect is the psychological one. Beneath the surface
> there is something of racial antagonism in this country—a con-
> tempt for the "nigger" on the one hand and distrust of black for
> white on the other. A native is not capable of distinguishing
> between the nationalities of the white races. With him they are just
> white men—in which definition he includes the Chinese and Japa-
> nese. (Melrose 1941)

Not until 1939, with war in the offing, was permission granted. Codi-
fied in the force's 1939 ordinance, and reinforced in two sections, it
stated that the Royal Papuan Constabulary:

1 shall act as a military Force when called upon by the Lieutenant-
   Governor to discharge military duties [para 33];
2 shall when the Lieutenant-Governor shall have declared that a
   state of war exists between the Commonwealth of Australia and
   any other country be subject to . . . military law [para 34]. (Papua
   1939, 7)

Paragraph 33 was specific in its intent. Should it be taken to mean
that the ordinance authorized the Papuan constabulary as a force to be
used as another Papuan battalion, or should it be viewed as a recommendation for only selected members to be deployed to other battalions,
not as policemen but as fully trained soldiers? Clearly it was the first
option. Despite the unambiguous provision in the ordinance, no steps
were taken in 1939–1941 to form a battalion of Papuan policemen. The
colonial administration seems to have been trapped in red tape. The
decision to disband the Royal Papuan Constabulary and the New Guinea
police forces in 1942, for instance, was a manifestation of this confusion and indecision, because the officials did not have a plan to use
police in an emergency such as that of 1942. With the transfer of civil
administration to ANGAU in 1942, any further opportunity for fruitful
debate on the use of the police as a military force passed, at least in an
official capacity. And with that transfer the League of Nations prohibitions were no longer binding. The Australian army took the opportunity and continued to form battalions of Papua New Guinean soldiers.
Many individual former policemen were recruited, but the police as a
unit were not deployed as a fighting force. Much to their chagrin, the
policemen were relegated to performing their traditional role, as well
as assisting the military "in an operational capacity" (AWM 1939–1945b).
   What did the phrase "in an operational capacity" mean? One interpretation was given to Sakarias Anka in Goroka. In 1943 he was told by

an ANGAU official, "Your job is not to fight in the war. You are not a soldier. Your main task is to protect carriers and help transport supplies to the fighting men, rescue personnel from danger areas and look after prisoners" (Anka 1986). Officially, then, the policemen were told to perform civil duties; they were to be guards, interpreters, warders, overseers of laborers and carriers, guides, and to carry out a multitude of other auxiliary tasks that would help the military get on with fighting. In all these responsibilities they performed splendidly. In another context this meant "combining both the military and civil role in a war emergency. Their war duties would be in accordance with a prepared plan" (AWM 1935–1945c). Between 1942 and 1945 members of the Royal Papuan Constabulary performed these dual roles: they combined their civil or administrative duties as police with their responsibilities as paramilitary troops. The situation arose not through the use of clandestine methods but as a natural outcome of the particular circumstances that existed in the country and led to the stepping up of police responsibilities. This situation confused some of the men interviewed, who were convinced they had "fought" in the war as "soldiers," whereas in fact they may have taken on military responsibilities as policemen. Certainly some men who were nominally police saw more military action than nearly all enlisted army men.

Working for the Japanese

New Guinean policemen employed by the Japanese army performed a variety of tasks. In many instances, it appears that the Japanese trusted the wisdom and experience of the New Guinea police. During Allied Forces court proceedings in Rabaul in January 1946, to hear villagers' allegations of police and Japanese brutality, three New Guinean men, who had worked as policemen for the Japanese, were asked about their work. They replied, individually, that besides the supervision of prisoners, their other duties ranged from making arrests to interpreting interrogations of villagers. Their testimonies reveal that the policemen under the command of Japanese officers meted out cruel punishment to the prisoners. On one occasion drinks and other foodstuffs were found missing from the Japanese food store. After a search, police and Japanese officers found the goods hidden in a house. Eleven men from the village were arrested and brought to Bitapaka, Kokopo, for punishment and imprisonment. On interrogation, the villagers denied that more villagers had been involved in the theft, but this was construed to be a lie. They were "thrashed" with canes. The interrogation continued in an aggressive manner. The men persisted with their denial. The beatings and the interrogations continued for the whole day. Pamoi, a New Guinean policemen from Aitape, told the adjudicators of his own involvement and observations, as well as those of the other policemen:

> When the questioning was over, the two Japanese instructed us police boys to tie the hands of all the natives and suspend them by their hands from a beam so that their toes barely touched the ground. The Japanese then asked them again about the natives they were supposed to be hiding in the village. They made denial again and the Japanese ordered us police boys to thrash them. They were beaten with canes, sticks and pieces of wood by us. These beatings and questionings were continued all the morning. They were not beaten in the afternoon but they were not cut down until about 4:00 PM. Then they were put back into the jail. They were without food or water all day. They were all cut and bleeding from the beatings. Next day they were sent to work on the normal duties of prisoners in the jail. (AWM 1946)

Masep, another New Guinean policeman from Kavieng, worked for the Japanese during the war and was made to give evidence at the inquiry. His testimony revealed that the Japanese were suspicious of everyone in Rabaul, particularly Europeans or Chinese. The New Guinean police assisted the Japanese military police to search for, arrest, and imprison them if they were found to be engaged in dubious activities. One day during a routine patrol, Masep, in the company of five Japanese and two other New Guinean policemen, went to search the residence of Chin Him, captain of the *Kwongchow*. They found in a box three electric light bulbs and a Union Jack. Chin Him was then asked how the articles came to be in his possession, how he intended using them, why he had gone from Rabaul to Mioko. To the last question, he answered that he had moved to Mioko to avoid the bombing. The Japanese accused him of lying and took him by schooner to the residence of another Chinese man about a quarter of a mile away. The two Chinese men were then both "questioned as to what had become of the money and valuables belonging to a Chinese at Rabaul. They denied any knowledge. They were then sat upon and pressed about the head and body." They were flogged repeatedly. The party spent the night at Mioko.

Early the next morning both Chinese men had their hands tied behind their backs while the other's house was searched again. Despite finding little of any significance, the Japanese persisted with their questions regarding the valuables. When the Chinese continued to deny knowledge of the valuables, they were made to kneel and in that position, "struck on the head with a stick . . . and then jabbed on the head, face and chest with a stick." The torture continued for about two and a half hours. In the end, the second Chinese was left in his home, but

Chin Him was forced to accompany the party to the police station at Rakunda. There, another Chinese man was questioned regarding some subscriptions allegedly sent to the Chinese government. Both Chinese men denied knowledge. They were both tortured and beaten for four or five days. During the course of these interrogations and tortures, a third Chinese man "who had previously been arrested for having a piece of lead wire in his possession, died."[24]

Most New Guineas who served the Japanese as police had no choice but to participate in brutality. Some of them may have hoped for favors from the Japanese by being enthusiastic bashers, but more frequently they attempted to soften or divert the savagery of the Japanese. For instance, on the Gazelle, Paliau Maloat diverted the Japanese from being tougher (see Schwartz 1962, 244). "Paliau told himself that if he did not give the Japanese immediate obedience, they would cut his throat." Obviously, he didn't think he had much choice. There is also some evidence of New Guineans diverting the Japanese from their own clans to their traditional enemies.

Perceptions of Police Wartime Performance

How did the police perform in their given responsibilities during the war? Answers to this question may be found by examining how officers and others perceived the policemen at work. From a general perspective, much praise was given to the Papua New Guineans for their involvement during the war. It ranged from the sentimental, overdramatized, and much publicized "fuzzy-wuzzy angel" image of the carriers at the beginning of the war to Major General Kingsley Norris's realistic appraisal after it ended, that "they are not gods—they are not angels— they are men, and splendid men."[25] Although policemen assisted in most areas of military activity, they made their biggest contributions in bushcraft, as guides, reconnoitering, and gathering intelligence. In a pamphlet of instructions, every new Allied soldier was told of the resourcefulness of the Papua New Guineans in bushcraft, for which they must have their unequivocal cooperation:

> The natives are [a] most important source of intelligence. It is quite impossible for any patrol or even a single man to move through the jungle without the native soon becoming aware of their presence. (Visit of Native Police 1942)
>
> At any rate he plays a good game on his home ground. He shows up better than you do in the tropical forest or the sago swamp. In New Guinea bushcraft, in hardihood, in mobility, he leaves you standing. (AGS 1943)
>
> The New Guinea natives had long since proved that they made

splendid troops for bush warfare. They quickly mastered their
weapons, being instructed by sight and touch rather than
words. . . . They could move in the bush with such stealth and
alertness that the risk of being outwitted by Japanese was slight.
(Long 1963, 83)

Examples of the policemen's performance as bush guides are too
numerous to discuss in detail. Literally hundreds of policemen were
engaged in this capacity, and undeniably the exploits of individuals
were significant. Behind most new offensives a policeman was always
employed to lead the way as guide, scout, intelligence gatherer, or simply as part of the entourage to fight the Japanese. In some areas the
police were used in larger numbers than others. For instance, in 1942
and 1943, of a total of 65 officers and 1,102 men who made up the
Bena Force, 1 officer and 243 men, or, "one third, of the operational
troops in Bena Force, in the New Guinea Highlands, were NCOs and
constables of the RPNGC."[26] However, for the police as a group, the
words of Sir John Guise suffice: "The exploits and war services of these
men during the Pacific campaign have been second to none" (Guise
1953). Still, cases of extraordinary achievements by individuals warrant
mention. Some, such as Paliau of Manus, Pita Simogun of the Sepik,
Tommy Kabu of the Gulf, and Yali of the Rai Coast, have already
received much publicity. They are seen as national heroes for their
activities during the war and for their attempts to bring about social
change in their respective communities after it.[27]

Little is known of the others who achieved a great deal. To remedy
this situation, I now present three case studies. Two, Kari of Manus and
Katue of Delta Division, are not readily known beyond the people of
their home provinces and the pages of two books (Peter Ryan 1985;
Johnston 1943). The other, Yauwiga of Wewak, is well known in the history of Papua New Guinea but is being mentioned again to strike a geographical balance. Kari served as a policeman before, during, and after
the war. Katue and Yauwiga served as policemen before the war and
then Katue was recruited into the Papuan Infantry Battalion and Yauwiga into the New Guinea Infantry Battalion. They rejoined the Royal
Papuan Constabulary and the New Guinea police force respectively
after their military service ended.

Kari of Manus

Details of Sergeant Major Kari's youth are unknown, except what Peter
Ryan has written about him in *Fear Drive My Feet* (1985), and the article,
"Debt of Friendship Must Be Honored" (1986). In 1986 Kari was
already an old man, but still much respected in his home province of
Manus for his exploits as a policeman. When Ryan first met Kari, he was
serving under officers of the New Guinea Volunteer Rifles, a resistance

group composed of former gold-miners, planters, and government officials who had retreated into the interior of Lae and Salamaua when the
Japanese landed on the mainland in March 1942 (P Ryan 1985, x). The
Volunteer Rifles' main responsibility in the area was to harass the
enemy. The aim was that the Japanese would "know that Australian
troops were spread from one end of New Guinea to the other, [and
would help] to cause uncertainty in his mind and force him to dissipate
strength which he might have conserved to meet the gathering storm
around Lae" (Dexter 1961, 263). Ryan was a member of a single com-
mando unit of the Fifth Independent Company of the Australian
defense forces assisting the New Guinea Volunteer Rifles. The two units
were combined to form Kanga Force, with its headquarters at Wau.
Much of Ryan's responsibility involved extensive travel behind enemy
lines between Wau, Salamaua, and Lae and on the Huon Peninsula.
Kari was the first constable, then a lance-corporal, appointed to assist
Ryan. Ryan described Kari as a handsome man, full of confidence,
and with a better understanding of the situation than most of his
colleagues. Ryan's first impressions of Kari augured well for future relationships.

> Lance-Corporal Kari was standing at attention outside. He was as
> black as coal, six feet tall, and so broad that he filled the whole
> entrance. He wore only a pair of spotless khaki shorts, immacu-
> lately starched and pressed. On his bare right arm was buckled a
> cloth band, with the single stripe indicating his rank. His skin was
> smooth, glossy, and hairless, and you could see the magnificent
> muscles that rippled underneath it. His expression was rather
> stern, and his face was strikingly handsome, whether judged by
> European or by native standards. He was about twenty years old,
> and it was hard to imagine a more superb specimen of young man-
> hood. (P Ryan 1985, 18)

Kari's tasks were varied. He recruited and paid carriers, trained
other policemen, carried messages from one camp to another, and
guided European officers in the labyrinth of Lae's jungle, close to Japanese positions and villages under Japanese influence. His most note-
worthy achievements involved gathering intelligence. After the war
Ryan wrote this fitting eulogy:

> Sergeant-Major Kari's story alone is the stuff of epics. Isolated
> sometimes for months deep in enemy territory, he patrolled for
> intelligence that was gold to the planners in Port Moresby and
> Australia. Cool under fire and himself a deadly shot, he and his
> kind were at the apex of a great pyramid of support—the toil of all
> his black comrades, the local genius which alone enabled the Aus-
> tralians to survive and then to advance. (P Ryan 1986)

Katue of Delta Division

Katue was another who achieved outstanding results. Not much is known of his early life. He came from Iokea village in the Delta Division, and first enrolled in the Papuan Armed Constabulary in the early 1930s. His performance as an armed constable was exemplary. He showed unfeigned courage, bravery, and commitment—traits that remained with him. When on duty, Katue showed initiative and took risks. On one bush patrol in 1936, between the Bamu and Purari Rivers, his adventurous instincts almost ended in tragedy. There are many fast-flowing rivers in the area; the Hegigo was the hardest to cross at the best of times, but even more so during periods of heavy rain. After many futile attempts, Katue decided to make one last attempt at crossing. He was so determined that no amount of persuasion from Patrol Officer Ivan Champion would stop him; he was already "in a high state of excitement" (Champion 1936b). Katue first decided to swim the roaring torrent without the aid of a rope, but when Champion objected a strong belt was fastened around his waist before he dived:

> And then I heard him hit the water for I could not see him where I stood. I had the line in my hand. He was swept along near the bank but as he came opposite me an eddy caught him, and swimming strongly, he was carried swiftly across. We were ready to acclaim his success; another stroke and he would reach the bank, and then he was borne swiftly out into midstream and carried down. There was a tremendous jerk on the line as it took his full weight, and he came high out of the water and then he went down and below to rise again, and the line went limp. (Champion 1936a, 47)

The current was too strong and swept Katue downstream but, by a mysterious dash of good fortune, he survived the punishment of the torrent and was found lying exhausted, but in good spirit, some miles down the river. Champion concluded, "Only a very strong and cool-headed man could have accomplished such a feat. He was vomiting blood and his back appeared to have been injured by the belt" (Champion 1936a, 47). Such deeds won him a "wide reputation for valour as a police boy" (Johnston 1943, 166).

The near-tragedy did not prevent him from taking further bold risks. In June 1940, at about thirty-five years of age, Katue was one of the few Papuan policemen to join the newly formed Papuan Infantry Battalion, whose exploits are well recorded.[28] Katue's "saga of adventure against the Japanese began after they landed at Gona mission" in July 1942. During a two-month patrol in the bush inside Japanese occupied areas, with fourteen other men (members of his "private army"), he killed 26 Japanese soldiers; and in seventeen days he killed another 9, making 35 in ten and a half weeks. For this feat, he received no particular assistance from the Allied Army, only the .303 and ammunition. Katue and members of his entourage lived off fruits and whatever food they could get from the villagers. George Johnston, the author of *New Guinea Diary*, was present when Katue proudly walked into an Australian army camp with the news of his first lot of killing:

> Today, squat, broad-shouldered, well-muscled, fierce-eyed sergeant Katue, coal-black warrior of the all-native Papuan Infantry Battalion—a force which has done magnificent work on jungle patrols since the Japanese landing 10 weeks ago—walked into an Australian post with a scared-looking Japanese prisoner. Katue created a profound impression. Apparently he intended to, because stitched to his standard khaki tunic was a mass of stripes, badges and regimental insignia which Katue had taken from 26 Japanese soldiers and marines, all of whom he had killed during a spectacular two months patrol. . . . When I spoke to him to-day he grinned widely, showing an expanse of broken teeth, blackened by betel nut, and in pidgin English carefully explained the rank and fate of each former owner of each piece of enemy insignia. Several of his victims were privates, with no badges to take, although Katue made it clear that he had tried to concentrate on the top men, and he shrugged his shoulders lugubriously as he explained why he didn't have more stripes on his already resplendent uniform. . . . So just to keep the record straight Katue brought back a cloth cap, bearing the anchor insignia of the Japanese marines, which one of his victims had been wearing. (Johnston 1943, 165)

That style of journalism, with its praise of bravery and naive simplicity, helped establish a stereotype of the Papuan soldier and a sense of debt among the Australian public. The stereotype was a direct extension of the one applied to the "savages in serge"; Katue had contributed to it as both policeman and soldier.

Yauwiga of Wewak

In 1982 the film *Angels of War* was first shown in Papua New Guinea (Pike, Nelson, and Daws 1982). From a general perspective, it was about the Papua New Guineans' involvement during the war as villagers, carriers, laborers, policemen, and soldiers. Both the narrators and the participants gave indications of the people's achievements and failures, sorrows and jubilations. In many ways, it was an educational film, an attempt to teach the new generation of Papua New Guineans about the contributions many of their fathers and grandfathers had made in the war. The most revealing parts of the film portrayed participants telling their own stories. In a moving narration, former Sergeant-Major Yauwiga, then about eighty years old, spoke of his injuries, his medals, his blue eye, his artificial arm, and the number of men he had killed, a total, by the end of the war, of fifty-six Japanese soldiers (Nelson nd, 2).

Little is known of Yauwiga's childhood, the number of children in his family, the positions of his parents, or basic information on the social and political organization of his people of Poroboi and Kusaun villages of Wewak (see A Griffin 1980, 7). He enrolled in the New Guinea police force at Aitape on 9 November 1930, at the approximate age of twenty-eight. Physically he was a big man, heavily built, and standing at 5 feet 8½ inches, more than three and a half inches over the prescribed minimum height for recruits. He served in various parts of New Guinea: the Sepik, Madang, Morobe, New Britain, and Kieta. His performance as a policeman was exemplary. He rose rapidly through the ranks, becoming lance-corporal on 9 November 1935, corporal on 9 September 1937, and sergeant on 9 October 1941 (Griffin 1980, 7–8). A government officer described Yauwiga in 1941 as: "a most conscientious, hard working, keen and willing NCO. Intelligent . . . and a fair disciplinarian. Should make an excellent Sergeant and a good Sergeant-Major later" (quoted in A Griffin 1980, 8).

Yauwiga's involvement in the war began in New Britain. While he was still in Rabaul the Japanese bombed the airfield on 4 January 1942, killing fifteen New Guineans "gathered at a singsing and others were wounded" (Nelson nd, 2). In Bougainville, where he was shipped soon after, and where he spent almost the next three years, "his strong personality and leadership was demonstrated" (A Griffin 1980, 8). Coastwatching became the central focus of his work in Bougainville. Working as an assistant to W (Jack) Read, an assistant district officer given the rank of a naval lieutenant during the war,[29] he aided in collecting vital information from behind enemy lines in the far north of Bougainville on the movements of Japanese troops, warplanes, and ships in and around Bougainville, Rabaul, and Kavieng.[30] Although Yauwiga participated in many daring episodes, in the company of either Read or the police or both, and against the enemy as well as the local population sympathetic to Japanese presence, two events are salutary. A pro-Japanese village near Buka passage handed over some people sympathetic to the Allied Forces. In the interest of security and to warn villagers against future betrayal, Read decided that the village should be bombed at night. At great risk to themselves, Yauwiga, with three Papua New Guinean constables and Tamti, Read's clerk, "lit fires on its outskirts when the bomber was heard" to ensure that the correct village was bombed. There was only one casualty, and this proved a sufficient deterrent (Feldt 1946, 268). On another occasion in June 1945, Yauwiga, with two other policemen, held off a determined attack by eighty Japanese soldiers led by a pro-Japanese local man, giving sufficient time for his party to escape with important equipment. The Japanese attacked with machine guns, grenades, and rifle fire, but "Yauwiga stood firm, shouted contempt for the Japanese and induced his two companions to remain with him and fight for fifteen minutes until their ammunition was exhausted" (A Griffin 1980, 9; see also Feldt 1946, 279–280). Yauwiga subsequently spread a fabricated rumor that Congong, the local assistant, had deliberately led the Japanese into an ambush. When the Japanese heard of the alleged treachery, they executed Congong and seven other "of their own most loyal agents" (Nelson nd). Yauwiga then persuaded the villagers that the Japanese were cruel and inhuman, and managed to induce many of them to withdraw their support for the enemy and help his party. For his valuable assistance in the Bougainville campaign, Yauwiga was awarded the Distinguished Conduct Medal (photo 36). Years later, Read, his superior officer for almost a decade, commented, "You can't say too much about that bloke. We couldn't have survived without Yauwiga" (J Griffin 1988).

Apart from coastwatching, Yauwiga also excelled in guerrilla warfare, having twice received intensive training near Brisbane. For a time, he

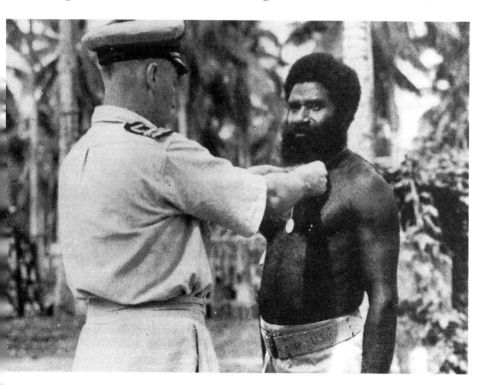

Photo 36   Yauwiga receives a medal for gallantry in World War II, 1943. (Hank Nelson)

Photo 37 Yauwiga explains a point in his village in 1980. (Hank Nelson)

worked with the United States Marine Corps in Bougainville in October 1943 and with the Allied Intelligence Bureau in Manus and Milne Bay in 1944.

By a cruel twist, on 4 June 1945 a smoke grenade used to guide planes dropping supplies accidentally exploded in Yauwiga's face. He

was blinded and almost lost his left arm. At the American military hos
pital at Torokina his arm was amputated, and he was then brought to
Holland Park Military hospital in Brisbane for further specialist medical treatment. While a patient of this hospital (and with the generous
permission of the widow), Yauwiga's right eye was fitted with the cornea
of the eye of one Sergeant Thomas Henry Roberts by Dr Peter English.
"Yauwiga's new eye was blue and he joked in later years that he was the
only blue-eyed New Guinean" (A Griffin 1980, 7). He was also fitted
with an artificial hand, but for some reason this was not a success. In
1946 he returned to Bougainville "for rural discharge" and returned
home to work soon after (photo 37).

Unlike the average Papua New Guinean of the time, Yauwiga had
experience in uniformed service. He had risen rapidly through the ranks
and traveled widely throughout Papua New Guinea and parts of Australia. For his contribution to the war he was decorated several times and
gained a position as warrant officer in a field force of the Allied Intelligence Bureau, "M Special," a unit of the Australian army. On his return
to his village in Kusaun he tried to bring about social change in his community by putting into practice some of the things he had learned and
observed. One of his lasting contributions was his attempt to encourage
technical education. Like other national heroes, Anton of Moseng,
Paliau of Manus, Tommy Kabu of Gulf, Sumasuma of New Ireland, and
Yali of Madang, Yauwiga tried to improve the lot of his society by introducing practical education. Two Pacific Island missionaries, Usaia of
Fiji and Eroni of Tonga, had told him that to be successful in life one
needed education. Although Yauwiga had no formal education himself, he later taught at the school. He also helped start a cooperative
society and further diversified his interests into cattle and a sawmill. He
remained at Kusaun after his repatriation. He died in Wewak hospital
on 18 September 1992 after a long illness. He was given a military funeral, having served in both the army and the police force. Among the
dignitaries who attended were then Prime Minister Michael Somare
and Minister for Defence Epel Tito. Yauwiga deserves to be remembered
for both his wartime bravery and his attempts to bring material benefits
to his people. A man without any formal education, Yauwiga responded
to the opportunities opened to him in the police, and there he first
demonstrated his ability to lead.

Awards

According to the men interviewed, rewards given did not match the
sacrifice, hardships, privations, and constant dangers faced in this bitter
war. Sesetta and ToWoworu were beaten cruelly for withholding information on the whereabouts of their officers. Naguwean did not think

he had fought to save Papua New Guinea, then only clusters of tribal peoples. He had fought, he believed, to save Australia from the clutches of the Japanese. He was driven to frustration and despair, going without food and comfort. Toward the end of the war his courage and determination to survive almost left him. His pecuniary reward was a pittance, not even enough to buy a bag of rice for his family. Sarepamo, a burly Highlander, said he was not paid for the duration of the campaign, getting only promises of large compensation at the end. When the end came he received no reward; the officers were either too drunk or caught up in some other form of celebration to pay him any notice. He received only a quick dismissal. Tigavu was told to pack his possessions and walk to Kundiawa for his new police posting. Most of the men had similar stories to tell, of how they had braved a hostile enemy and a hostile environment, but did not receive the recognition they deserved. Here lies the paradox of this war: at its beginning they were told it was not the Papua New Guineans' war, but by its end Papua New Guineans had not only played an active part but had contributed more than most individuals to its successful end.

Perhaps Sarepamo and others are mistaken: they may have received the ten shillings a month that was the police constable's pay throughout the war. But they consistently assert that they were underpaid. Clearly, the rewards did not match their expectations. In the whole campaign, of a total of 3,137 policemen they lost 28 men. Members of both the Papuan Infantry Regiment and the Royal Papuan Constabulary were awarded decorations. Of these, 4 police received the Distinguished Conduct Medal; 2 the George Medal; 15 the Military Medal; 8 the British Empire Medal; 297 the Long Service Medal; and 28 the Papua New Guinea Police Valour Badge. One was awarded the American Bronze Star (Long 1963, 83). Of the two men who received the George Medal, Sergeant Iwagu was decorated for his efforts during a landing near the Song River, in Finschhafen. The landing was met with heavy enemy fire. When the craft in which the company commander was being conveyed failed to reach the shore, the occupants jumped into twelve feet of water and attempted to swim ashore. The commander was wounded. At risk to himself, Sergeant Iwagu came to his aid, brought him ashore, and stayed with him until stretcher bearers arrived. Unfortunately the officer died soon after. Iwagu, in this and later incidents, "displayed outstanding courage and devotion to duty."[31] There could be no more typical display of military bravery—a landing under fire, and Iwagu risked his life to save a wounded man. But Iwagu was a policeman, and his decoration was a civil award.[29]

Two other policemen received British Empire Medals. Corporal Arwesor was arrested by the Japanese on 7 June 1943 when he accompanied Warrant Officer Lumb's party across the Markham River to arrest deserters who had escaped from the labor lines. He was tied to a tree and with a rope around his neck threatened with death unless he revealed "information concerning the number of machine guns and Allied troops in the Wau, Bulolo and Sunshine areas." Arwesor remained silent throughout the intense interrogation. At night, using his own resourcefulness, he escaped, and after five days returned with valuable information.[33] In the company of a fellow policeman, Kominiwan, Corporal Merire spent a month gathering intelligence in the Bogadjim-Madang area, which was a stronghold of the Japanese. The information he brought back was used to carry out bombing raids. He was presented with the medal for his courage, determination, and resourcefulness.[34] Six policemen received the Papua New Guinea Police Valour Badge; in alphabetical order they were, with their numbers, Constables Angel (4012), Belua (3238), Donis (3003), Lance-Corporal Nemo (5194), Suani (2086), and Walingingi (2553).[35] All took great risks to save lives, gather intelligence, recruit laborers, transport supplies, organize ambushes, and engage in other activities equally deserving not only of medals but of material benefits. Many of the men believe that their officers promised them such rewards, and they are still waiting for those promises to be honored.

The Japanese army also awarded decorations to outstanding New Guinean policemen. Sasa Goreg, as the most senior noncommissioned officer, was awarded the most prestigious Japanese medal, which remained with him until the war ended. Then, on his way to the Markham district, he says, and there is no reason not to believe him, he threw it into the Bismarck Sea because he did not have anything else to show his people that he had helped the Japanese as their *nambawan* (first class) policeman during the war (Goreg 1986).

Summary

Although policemen assisted in most areas of both military and police activity, they made their biggest and most notable contributions in bushcraft as guides, reconnoitering, and doing intelligence work. The reasons are clear. The majority of the policemen, like their counterparts in the various battalions, were trained in the use of small arms only. Many used them to good effect, as was demonstrated by Katue, Kari, and Yauwiga. However, they were not trained to handle complex machinery, operate heavy guns, or drive amphibious vehicles. Like the majority of the Papua New Guinean soldiers, most policemen were employed where they already had skills, and that was in the bush. They proved indispensable. Although such tasks were nothing new, they took on new meanings. The police combined traditional fighting and hunting skills with modern forms of warfare. If, as paramilitary police, the Royal

Papuan Constabulary's achievement was in bushcraft, then it is proper
to conclude that its technique came from the men's own traditional
backgrounds. Two of them explained how they survived the war:

> My formula for surviving the war years as a policeman was simply
> that I used traditional skills and beliefs. For instance, if a snake,
> not known to be from a certain area crossed our path, I would
> direct others and myself to follow a new route because I believed
> that not far from that spot disaster would befall us if we continued
> on that road. I also took the same precautions if I heard the cries
> of certain birds, but I followed my instincts most of all. (ToWoworu
> 1985)
>
> So we arrived by plane to Port Moresby from Bena Bena and
> slept at the police station at Kaugere. On the following morning
> we gathered at the airport together with Australian and American
> soldiers to fall in at the assembly line. Then each man with his load
> walked across the ranges to Kokoda.
>
> There early in the morning as the sun rose I took a certain leaf
> and turning my face away from the sun I wrapped its rays in the
> leaf, while I asked one of my companions to dig a hole. Then I
> dropped the leaf over my shoulder into the hole and we buried
> it. . . . The Japanese were only a few yards away but they could not
> see us. Their guards were looking up in the air while we crawled
> like snakes on the ground, dragging our guns with us. As we crawled
> towards the Japanese guards I told my comrades to take aim, and I
> fired my first shot. The others joined in almost simultaneously and
> the whole village shook with the thundering explosion of gunshots
> which left many Japanese dead. (Sesiguo 1977, 231–232)

Obviously, this was a nostalgic view of an old man for an age that has
passed. The act of magic was accompanied by incantation. He folded
the leaf, believing that the light from the sun was trapped inside it, and
wrapped it firmly. Before pacification, this method had been used
extensively by Kamuna's people during tribal warfare. It was believed
that the performance of such a magical act before a fight would make
the warriors invisible to their enemies and provide them with easy
victims. The practice may have worked when two men confronted each
other with bows and arrows; at least one had a chance to avoid the
visible arrows if he had the fleetness of foot and agility, but it would
have been difficult to apply the technique to an enemy hidden behind
shrubs and firing bullets from great distances. However, many Papua
New Guineans unable to explain the complexities of the war found
consolation in resorting to traditional practices. Kamuna, ToWoworu,
and many other Papua New Guinean policemen believed that the
wisdom of traditional warfare techniques was demonstrated in their

successes in the war. Men who quickly adapted to the demands of modern warfare (they quickly learned to exploit the smoke grenade and the submachine gun) took into battle the spiritual weapons of their fathers. This was something they shared with some of the Australians and Japanese.

Chapter 7

Perceptions of the Police by Goilala Villagers, Papua

Much has been written about the reactions, or lack of them, of Papua New Guineans when they saw white men and other Papua New Guineans for the first time. Ample literature describes the relationships experienced once the traumas of the first contact were overcome and colonialism became established. The material on first contact has echoed with a familiar ring. None has failed to mention the novelty of the meeting. The photographs taken by Michael Leahy and exploited effectively in the film *First Contact* capture better than any words the astonishment and nervous vulnerability of people suddenly confronted by absolute aliens. Few of the published accounts have failed to discuss the changes brought about in the social and economic organization of the people as a result of this intrusion. But the flow of information has been one-sided, not so much because a great deal of the available literature was written by outsiders, as because scholars have perpetuated the tradition of writing about the country and the people in the context of western influence. What has happened in Papua New Guinea is explained in terms of the impact and the response to European intervention. However, in almost every contact patrol since 1884, the most numerous meetings, and the meetings where there was most likely to be effective communication, were those between Papua New Guineans. Many of the villagers' perceptions are stored in villagers' memories waiting to be collected as oral testimonies. Unfortunately, therefore, it is difficult, at this stage, to piece together the part that Papua New Guineans played in both the wider processes of colonization and upon each other, and from the point of view of a traditional influence that might have helped provide the stimulus for change within communities. Compared to western material and conceptual and religious influences, the record of Papua New Guineans' own social and cultural impact on other Papua New Guinean societies during the colonial period is small. However, given the diversity of Papua New Guinean societies, one would expect that internal forces contributed significantly to the overall accul-turation process. The blending of the old with the new enabled many people to come to terms with the rapid changes brought about by the impact of the west. In the context of the overall discussion the most prominent and ubiquitous of the new agents of change were the police-men. The interactions and relations established between the police and Papua New Guineans, and the role played by police in the relation-ships between Papua New Guineans and colonial officers and between villagers and villagers, is the theme now pursued.

This chapter and the next deal with villagers' perceptions of police and administrative activity on the frontier of contact. In this chapter are two short case studies from Goilala in Papua, while chapter 8 pre-sents the experience of one man under Australian colonial rule on the fringe of the New Guinea Highlands. The villagers interviewed for these chapters have described events that happened in their youth; in all cases, at the time of interview many years had already passed, open-ing up the possibility of distortions and misreporting. However, wher-ever possible the villagers' oral testimonies are supplemented with both primary and secondary evidence. In chapter 9, I discuss colonial offi-cers' perceptions of policemen and how they viewed their performance.

The Goilala Area

During the period of this study the Goilala area (see back endpaper) was one of two remaining frontiers in Papua, the other being the South-ern Highlands, which by 1954 "was still a frontier district, 85% uncon-trolled and containing a considerable area of only partly explored coun-try" (Sinclair 1981, 111). Much of the rest, in particular the coastal regions, was already pacified. The people of the region lived within the bounds of an area covering

> about four hundred square miles of the Wharton Range to the north of Port Moresby in the Central District of Papua. To the South, in the lowlands, are the coastal tribes of Mekeo and Roro; to the east are the Koiari, and to the north, beyond the almost un-inhabited forests of the Giumu Valley, are the lands of the Oro-kaiva. The mountains to the west are inhabited by the Kukukuku, whose reputation as bloodthirsty and intractable exceeds even that of the Goilala. (Hallpike 1977, 1–2)

Tapini, only "eighty air miles from Port Moresby," is the administra-tive center of the subdistrict, and was initially the location of the second police camp established in 1938 (Hallpike 1977, 2, 4). The first govern-ment patrol went into the area in 1911, but it was not until the late 1940s and 1950s that "comparative peace was finally imposed" (Hallpike

1977, 4, 14). Before pacification the Goilala were a force to be reckoned with by patrol officers, policemen, and their traditional enemies,
some of whom lived as far away as the Northern Division. In 1917, for
instance, a raiding party of Goilala warriors had crossed the Owen Stanley Range and descended into the Northern Division, where they came
into contact with a detachment of police from the government station
at Ioma and, after sustaining "a few casualties," returned across the
range to Goilala (H Murray 1925, 118).

"The entire administrative history of the region is one of resistance
to the law" (Sinclair 1981, 153). They were ferocious in warfare, cunning and, at the beginning at least, seemed to have little respect for the
government. So stubborn was their resistance to pacification that Hallpike estimated that in just one area of Goilala, the Aibala Valley,
between seventy-five and one hundred Goilala were killed in their
clashes with the police and their enemies, who were receiving police
assistance, between 1917 and 1938 (Hallpike 1977, 9). The Goilala
were recognized as tough, determined fighters and perhaps the administration sent police and officers there who were thought most capable
of dealing with them. Expectation and selection would then make violence more likely.

In 1989 while reading through patrol reports for the Goilala region I
came across two paragraphs in a report for 1955–1956:

> While the patrol was in the Upper Kunimaipa Valley an old woman
> disappeared from a village in the Lower Kunimaipa Census Group.
> The patrol did not learn of the woman's disappearance until it had
> returned to Tapini.
>
> It is worthy of note that the woman's disappearance was the fifth
> in recent years from this one village. None of the previous disap-
> pearances had been solved. We believe that we have the man re-
> sponsible for the most recent disappearance; he confessed to hav-
> ing killed her and thrown her in the river. He was seen carrying
> the body, and had described his motive to another native. The
> body has not been recovered. (F D Anderson 1956)[1]

I would have passed over this report had it not been for the name of
the person who compiled it—Acting Assistant District Officer Frederic
David Anderson. He had become the subject of an official inquiry in
July 1957 for alleged misconduct of his policemen in the area early in
1956. The subject of the initial inquiry was the manner in which a man
had been charged, convicted, and imprisoned by the Supreme Court
for that missing woman.

In his account of "the extraordinary Anderson case," following official records, Sinclair described the circumstances of the conviction of
the Goilala man and the subsequent charging of one of Anderson's

policemen for his involvement in his conviction, but did not incriminate Anderson in any way (1981, 153–157).

The Official Version of the Case

Siwoi, a man from Goilala, was accused of the murder of the missing woman. Initially he denied any involvement. According to John Huon, a European medical assistant in the area, Siwoi confessed later under torture by Anderson's policemen. How Huon came to possess that knowledge is not known, but it is obvious that he had questioned the legality of the method used to extract Siwoi's confession. Most likely Huon had fallen out with Anderson, but the causes of any ill feeling are unknown. Without the apparent antagonism, perhaps the tale of the incident would not have surfaced, and no one beyond those involved would have known anything about it. But Anderson did not forget, and it is obvious that he had looked at ways of taking his revenge. In Huon's view the opportunity came when Huon burned a "derelict" Goilala house. In January 1957, Anderson laid an arson charge against Huon, and in February Huon was committed for trial in the Supreme Court. Huon could only state that he had been "framed." On the basis of this claim, Secretary for Law Wally Watkins appointed Public Solicitor Peter Lalor to defend him. Huon told Lalor everything—the missing woman, the charging, torture, and conviction, the eventual imprisonment of Siwoi, and his own subsequent falling-out with Anderson. Huon believed strongly that Anderson had a vendetta against him as a result of the "quarrel" between them and that had led to the arson charge being laid against him for his burning, in compliance with public health regulations, of a derelict house that the Goilala owner would probably have burned himself.

Huon had made serious allegations. Lalor immediately informed Watkins of them. At Watkins' request, Chief Crown Prosecutor Peter J Quinlivan flew to Tapini in May and investigated the allegations. His findings proved that there had been many instances "of abuse of power: the chaining of suspects to the station flagpole, assault, arson [and the] destruction of property" and that these malpractices extended back to the late 1940s, to the days of another patrol officer, E R (Roy) Edwards (Sinclair 1981, 154).[2] So alarming was Quinlivan's report that a second investigation was conducted in Goilala to "inquire whether there has in the recent administration of the Goilala Sub-District been any abuse of authority or office by any Administration officer or servant or other malpractice which would tend to reflect discredit on the Administration of the Territory or affect adversely the administration of justice" (quoted in Sinclair 1981, 155). Most of the allegations were proved valid. Then the administrator, Brigadier Donald Cleland, passed the result of the latest investigation to the late Sir Paul Hasluck, minister for External Territories. Shocked by the Anderson case, and reacting to advice in the report of the possibility that Goilala administrative methods were being practiced elsewhere in Papua New Guinea, Hasluck authorized another inquiry

> under Section 10 of the Public Service Ordinance 1949–1956 into the management and working of the Department [of Native Affairs] with a view to determining a number of questions arising out of the Anderson case, in particular the general efficiency of the Department, the effectiveness of the supervision of the field staff and the extent to which the practices employed at Tapini might be followed in other parts of the Territory. (Sinclair 1981, 155)

The result of this investigation was not made public (Sinclair 1981, 155).

Anderson and his most senior noncommissioned officer, Corporal Ataimbo, were suspended from active duty during the second inquiry. Ataimbo was subsequently charged with assault and jailed for eighteen months. Siwoi was pardoned and paid compensation of £200. No charge was laid against Anderson, at least for this case (Sinclair 1981, 155), but he was charged and convicted in another case, which I discuss later.

The Torture of Siwoi and Matai

Between September and November 1989 I interviewed two men, one at Two Mile Hill in Port Moresby, and the other at the Tapini station. Both were relatives of Matai, the man tortured with Siwoi (a fact not mentioned by Sinclair). Neither knew I had interviewed the other. The man interviewed in Port Moresby was present at the scene of the torture and saw everything. My Tapini informant was in Matai's village. According to the patrol report quoted earlier, the village was in the Upper Kunimaipa Valley, and my informant, at the Lower Kunimaipa, was told about what had happened soon after.

Because the two accounts of the torture of Siwoi and Matai are similar, I shall allow my Tapini informant, Girau Ogaia, to tell the story of Siwoi's ordeal as he narrated it to me in 1989 (photo 38). Girau was a "brother" to Matai. Like Matai, Girau is from Robdono, a little village in the Upper Kunimaipa. Matai was married to a woman from Ilopo in the Lower Kunimaipa. My Port Moresby informant, Enau Daulei, will assist in explaining the situation in the Goilala area as observed by him as a village constable.

One day Matai visited his in-laws at Ilopo and accompanied by Siwoi, one of his brothers-in-law, went to Bariza to make lime.[3] There was an

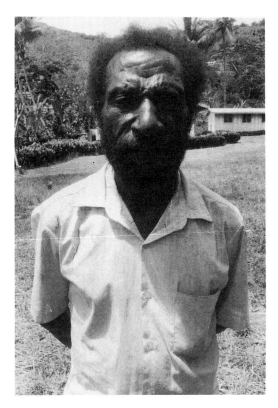

Photo 38   Ogaia Girau on the grounds of the
hospital where he worked as a medical orderly
in Tapini. (11 November 1989)

old woman at Bariza who everyone knew was *longlong* (mentally disturbed) and habitually lived a nomadic lifestyle. She moved about
frequently and slept anywhere, even in the bushes under the buttresses
of trees for days on end, until her relatives found her again and
brought her back to the village. It was nothing short of coincidence
that when the two men went to Bariza the old woman was also there.
Girau continued:

> As I was not there in person, I do not know what really happened,
> but somehow the woman went missing that day and could not be
> found in her usual places. In fact she was never found again.
>
> From the accounts I have heard so far, no one seemed to know
> exactly whether the old woman died from natural causes, or those
> two in-laws were responsible for her disappearance. No one knew
> for certain. (Ogaia 1989)

But, as it turned out, relatives of the missing woman, Muin and Maudzai (phonetic), walked to Tapini and told Patrol Officer Anderson and his policemen that the two in-laws had killed the old woman and thrown her into a river. (They assumed she had been killed and thrown into the river because there was no evidence on land to suggest any wrongdoing.) The policemen from Tapini then came and arrested Siwoi and Matai.[4] They were interrogated about the missing old woman. They strongly denied any involvement in her disappearance. The policemen persisted with their questioning and told them to admit that they had murdered the woman. However, the men stood their ground and refused to be forced into admitting any wrongdoing. After this the police lost their patience. If they could not get information as they desired, they would force it out of them:

> The police cut two strong posts, dug two deep holes, and stood the posts upright one next to the other. They then fastened both the two men's hands and feet and with strong ropes tied them onto the respective posts. While the two men struggled to free themselves, the policemen collected dried pandanus leaves, lots of them, placed them close around both men and when a heap had been made, lit them. The pandanus leaves were dry, and soon there was a huge flame. The heat got to the men as the centre heap caught on fire. Siwoi knew the heat would intensify as soon as the heap closest to them caught fire. It was then that Siwoi looked across and spoke to Matai in our language, "If we do not say anything, we will die from this terrible heat. I want you to tell a lie and accuse me, and tell the police that I actually killed the old woman so that we can be released from this heat." Matai had little alternative; he agreed reluctantly. Matai then accused Siwoi of the murder, and said he had actually seen him do it in the bush. It was only after this that the police released the ropes on their wrists and feet and, while [they were] prostrate, threw cold water on them soon after to cool them off, and then walked them to Tapini. (Ogaia 1989)

It is important to recognize that Siwoi considered the alternative of a jail term in either Tapini or Port Moresby. He preferred that to being burned. The use of fire to extract information from suspected criminals was not frequent in the area, but only when difficult situations arose; Hallpike noted that in the Goilala bush difficult situations were encountered often (1977, 4–16). According to Pumuye Nungulu, a village constable in Ialibu (photo 39), fire was also used in that area to punish people for serious crimes such as rape and murder. In Ialibu the intention was not to burn people alive, but to deter repetition. Pumuye said it was an effective method because recurrences of the same or similar offenses were reduced. The fires did scorch the skin,

Photo 39 Nungulu Pumuye was a village constable at
the time of the incident. However, he was not directly
involved, as the woman was his brother's daughter. (19
October 1989)

however. According to Pumuye these events always took place in the
bush, or at the scene of the incident. Those incarcerated were tied onto
poles with their backs exposed to the fire, or laid on top of raised plat-
forms. As in Goilala, the punishment was performed only on rare occasions. Pumuye saw only one man laid on a platform and burned in all
the time he was village constable. He described the details of one punishment he witnessed:

A man once captured would then be brought to the scene of the
incident. There a strong tree was chopped down, sharpened at
one end, and the man's arms and legs were then tied onto it with

strong ropes. A hole was dug, and the post stood upright. A fire was then built near it, but not directly underneath the man's feet. The man was usually tied about two or three feet above the ground, and the fire was built between two and three feet away from the centre of the post. The whole idea was for the smoke and the heat from the fire to reach the man, but not to actually burn the man alive.

Normally the man would be fastened with his face to the pole so that his back was exposed to the fire. The idea was that when the flame was big enough its heat would scorch the area of the buttocks and back and the rest of his exposed back area.

The fire was made at that distance so that the man would not be burnt alive but merely scorched, but there were enthusiasts whose actions did more damage than anticipated.[5]

After preliminary hearings at Tapini by Anderson, Siwoi was brought down to a jail in Port Moresby. There, Girau was told, further court proceedings were undertaken, but only after Siwoi had been in prison for some time. At this court case, Siwoi announced that he had never killed anyone, let alone murdered the old woman. He said then that he had only concocted the lie because not to have made this admission would only have meant either death or permanent injury to some parts of the bodies of both himself and Matai. Siwoi protested that the woman was *longlong* and had gone missing somewhere as usual. It was possible she had been washed away by the fast-flowing river in the area, fallen over a cliff, or come to some other misfortune unknown to all at Bariza. Siwoi said he had no motive to kill the woman; she was old, frail, and the concern of the majority of the people who knew her.

In the meantime, Matai had walked to Port Moresby for the court case and corroborated Siwoi's testimony. He told of how they had been fearful of police atrocities, and of how both had agreed to tell a deliberate lie[6] to avoid police torture. Having heard the testimonies, the presiding court official[7] was satisfied, on the basis of the information provided by the two men, that Siwoi was innocent and acquitted him of any crime. He was flown back to Tapini a free man.[8] According to Sinclair, Siwoi was "pardoned." It is curious that a man, having endured much humiliation, should be forgiven for having committed no wrong. The appropriate action would have been an apology from people who ought to have been well versed in the system of justice they were trying to enforce on ignorant villagers—the policemen, Anderson, and the court that initially passed judgment on the basis of Anderson's prima facie evidence.[9]

I interviewed my second informant on Two Mile Hill, Port Moresby, on 10 September 1989. I had met him by accident in Konedobu. It was

a Friday, a government payday, and following advice from police headquarters, I caught a bus and rode down to Konedobu to try to interview
any ex-policeman who might come in to collect his pension money. I
did not have much luck—the few who came did not oblige. As I walked
down the steps to catch another bus to return to the university, I saw a
man escorted out of the office and walking with the aid of a walking
stick. His back was bent slightly forward, and what really caught my eye
were the clothes he wore—a Papuan village constable's uniform! On
inquiry he admitted, in broken *Tok Pisin,* to the clothes being genuine,
that they had been issued to him between 1949 and 1956 when he had
been a village constable in Goilala! He had a complete set—hat, shirt,
and sulu. I asked if I could interview him about his work as a village
constable. He agreed and gave me directions to the *boi haus*[10] he shared
with his adopted son, who interpreted for me. At the time I did not
know that he had been at the scene of the torture of Siwoi and Matai,
or that he was also a "brother" to Matai.

Enau Daulei of Robdono (phonetic) village, Guari, upper Kunimaipa, Goilala subdistrict, was appointed a village constable by Patrol
Officer Roy Edwards in 1949. At the time of recruitment a small beard
had appeared on his chin; he was probably a teenager. He had two
main responsibilities—working as a government representative in his village at Robdono, and tracking escaped prisoners (photo 40). The second responsibility took him out of Robdono, and he traveled extensively throughout the Guari patrol post area and occasionally in the
Tapini subdistrict. During these patrols he became familiar with police
practice and behavior in the Goilala bush and on the Tapini station.
Whenever an ordinary criminal was captured, he would normally be
handcuffed, caned, punched about the face, and sometimes fastened
onto posts with strong ropes and hung in the village square to serve
as an example to others.[11] The intention was twofold—to scare troublemakers from committing the same or similar offenses and to encourage
acceptance of the government's introduced law and order. No fires
were lit to entice confession from those who were punished under this
category of offenses. However, whenever murderers were captured,
they were brought to their respective villages, their hands and feet were
tied to posts with strong ropes, and big fires were then built all around
them. Often the heat was so intense that the exposed parts of the skin
peeled off, mostly from the legs, face, and sides, just like roast pigs. No
deaths were recorded from this ordeal, but the experience left both
mental and physical scars on individuals who endured it. Often after
the fire was in full blaze,

> the police would stand around and wait for the fire to take effect.
> In the meantime the tied man[12] urinated, *pekpek,* and begged to be

freed. The relatives were scared of the policemen and did not attempt to assist their son/husband/father in distress. After the fire raged into full blaze and the heat became intense the police would take a stick and move it about the exposed parts of the skin. If it peeled off the man was released and, while prostrate, cold water was poured over him and the fire extinguished. However, if the skin did not peel off, they either waited for the fire to take effect or added more firewood or pandanus leaves in order to hurry the process. At the end of this ordeal the arrested men were walked to Tapini.

Photo 40 Enau Daulei beside the *boi haus* he shared with his adopted son and family at Two Mile Hill, Port Moresby. He is wearing a complete set of village constable's uniform that was issued to him in Tapini in 1949 or 1950. It has been cared for well. (10 September 1989)

Photo 41 Avila with his favorite morning chew, a betelnut. He walked to Tapini for the interview, and the photo was taken the morning after, when he was all set for the return trip home. (23 November 1989)

The policemen and the village constables heard the pleas of those persecuted but they never did anything. To them it was a lesson that had to be completed in order for it to be effective and understood by all.

The policemen who performed these punishments were from Kairuku, Gulf, Daru, and the Northern Division. (Daulei 1989)

After his recruitment, Enau witnessed men being punished by this method on four occasions before that of Siwoi and Matai, and heard about others through his contacts. Enau showed little emotion during the ordeals of the previous four men, but cried openly on this occasion, as Matai, his "brother," was tortured before his eyes. He felt like a coward, as did all the other men in the crowd, not being able to assist him in distress. (The police told the people not to interfere, and he was afraid of what they might do to him.)

The Punishment of Avila and Koupa

In September 1956 Assistant District Officer Anderson was responsible for inflicting physical punishments on Avila and Koupa at the Tapini station for refusing to admit they had tried to murder Koupa's wife, despite both men's plea that her shooting was an accident. Exactly a year after this incident, and most probably as a result of the inquiry into the incident just described, Anderson appeared in the Supreme Court and faced five charges: for assault, for handcuffing the accused to the station's flagpole, and for unlawfully confining Avila in the Tapini jail for five months between September 1956 and January 1957. At the time, Anderson believed strongly that both men had told lies, that they had in fact planned on killing Koupa's wife. His persistence in this belief reflected his unquestioning acceptance of the general assumption of the time that the Goilala were a violent people. During the court case, Anderson was convicted of four charges and pleaded guilty to the fifth. He was sentenced to a total of forty-five months in jail, to be served concurrently (Sinclair 1981, 155–157).

Avila had been recruited as a local constable and had worked as a policeman only in his own region (photo 41). I interviewed him on 23 November 1989 at the Tapini station. (Kemigara, a community leader at the station, helped with the interview.) Avila told me the following story. Koupa was his natural elder brother. They had the same parents. He accidentally shot Koupa's wife, Ivairime, in the stomach while hunting in thick bush. This was how it happened:

One fine day Avila, Koupa, and Ivairime left Zania, their village, and walked down to Tapini station to see relatives employed there. On their return they followed a small track so that they could hunt for a cassowary spotted in the area recently. Avila had a shotgun. He had learned how to use a gun while he was in the police force. When they had walked a fair distance from the Tapini station they decided to leave the track and look for the cassowary in the nearby bushes. Koupa's wife left the two men there and walked off in the opposite direction to look for fiber to make a string bag. Avila walked ahead of Koupa. The area was covered with thick bush, and visibility was poor. After they had walked some distance from the track, Avila saw a slight movement about thirty to forty yards away. But because of the very dense undergrowth, he could not see clearly what it was. He stopped walking to get a better view. He was certain that what he had seen was some part of a cassowary because a black object was moving about. He could see only the black middle section. He could not see what was above or below. The movement seemed to indicate that the cassowary was eating something off the branches. Avila continued:

> It was precisely with the hope of finding the cassowary that we had decided to leave the main track. I was elated. Without saying anything to my brother, who was right on my heels, I took aim and fired. The bullet hit the target, and there was a loud human cry of one in agony. It was a distinct woman's voice, "You have shot me, I have been hit." I could not believe it. We rushed over to the scene, and there was my brother's wife lying in a pool of blood, moaning with pain. What could I do? (Avila 1989)

They both cried to see Ivairime in obvious pain, but it was an accident. No malice was intended. Koupa was there and saw the shooting and, though obviously upset, agreed that it was not done on purpose. Avila had been on good terms with his brother and his wife. They had all gone down to Tapini together for a bit of a rest from the drudgery of gardening at Motowa in Zania. To both men it was a case of mistaken identity:

> What I and Koupa did not know was that Koupa's wife had changed into some old clothes from the ones she had on before she left in the opposite direction. The old clothes were black in colour. This fact was not known to either of us because we did not meet again until after the shooting. Ivairime had worked fast and collected the vines and had cut across to meet us farther up the track. Discovering that we had not passed the area she hung around and waited for us, meanwhile collecting more vines from the bushes. Because of the thick undergrowth and poor visibility, I mistook her movements for a cassowary and shot her.
>
> Also, because of the distance involved we did not think she would have passed us from another direction. All the while we ex-

pected her to catch up with us from the direction we had come. Besides, collecting vines for weaving string bags is time-consuming and we did not know she could finish so quickly. She did not call us when she had difficulty locating us, and we did not know she had changed into her old clothes.

So all these factors—distance, knowledge of a cassowary in the area, the change of clothes, the difficulties of vine collecting, poor visibility, and the absence of noise—contributed to the shooting.

I also knew that there would not be anyone else in the vicinity except the three of us. The area lies between Tapini station and our village. People do not normally hunt in the area. It is too far away from the village. We would not have gone into the area if we did not know that a cassowary was at large. (Avila 1989)

Ivairime bled profusely but was alive. She was carried back to the Tapini station for medical treatment. On the way Avila and Koupa made a pact that, as blood brothers, they would face the consequences of Avila's action together, whether it was a jail term or revenge attempts from Ivairime's relatives. Once at the Tapini station they brought her to the subdistrict office to explain the accidental shooting to the district officer, who had just returned to the station from "a tiring patrol" (Sinclair 1981, 155) and looked as if he were in a foul mood.

His name was Anderson. He was there when we carried Ivairime's body to the station. We told him that it had been an accident. After seeing the state of her stomach, Anderson was visibly angry. He did not believe what we told him. He punched us about the face. He then forced us out of the District Office and grabbed us both firmly by the arms and dragged us down to the station's flagpole and fastened our legs and arms onto it with handcuffs and left us standing in that manner for a whole day. We were also caned. He did not accept that it was an accidental shooting. He said "It was an evil thing you have done, you should be prepared to go to gaol." He was not even prepared to release us at the close of day, despite the fact that we had withstood heavy rain that day.

We were finally released by [Corporal] Ataimbo because he felt sorry for me because I worked with him as a policeman in Goilala before I resigned in disgust at the manner in which Goilala people were treated by policemen from other parts of Papua. (Avila 1989)

After they were released, policemen led them to the local jail. In the morning a police officer arrived from Port Moresby, and after a brief talk with Anderson, allowed Koupa to care for his wife, still in hospital. Avila was kept in jail for five months. Later, both men were flown to Port Moresby for the court case. They were kept there for three months,

at the end of which their case was heard by Chief Justice Mann. Finding
no convincing evidence against them, he released them, and they
returned home free men.

Police Methods and the Pacification of Goilala

The accounts of the two events in Goilala reveal two things—the extent
of the torture suffered by the men, in particular Siwoi and Matai, but
not mentioned officially, and the limitations of written documents when
dealing with people of other cultures whose viewpoints have not been
gauged. There is another dimension to the tale of the pacification of
Goilala. The use of heavy-handed tactics by policemen and their officers
did not end in 1938, as these atrocities occurred in the mid-1950s. Nor
was the practice limited to Hallpike's area of research; it appears to
have occurred quite regularly and in most parts of Goilala, both before
and after World War II. However, in the context of the revelations of
both the written record and oral testimony from the Goilala area during the period, the account of the torture of the four men was not
unusual. The question was one of degree—to what lengths were policemen prepared to go to expedite the pacification of Goilala?

Only a participant in the process of the pacification of the area
could answer that question. I have decided to use Jojoga Yegova's testimony as the last example for the Goilala segment, because it seems to
answer the central question. Yegova worked as a policeman in the Goilala area from the mid-1940s to the early 1950s. I interviewed him twice,
once in 1985 and again in 1989. The case discussed came from the 1989
interview. Yegova was posted to Goilala in 1946 and worked under
Patrol Officer K I Chester and others for eight years before being transferred to Mendi, in the Southern Highlands, in 1955. During the 1985
interview he said he had shot dead Koito, a Goilala man, as a result of
poor visibility, an action that earned him a firm reprimand from his
officer (see chapter 4). In 1989 he revealed the near massacre of a
tribe. I would never have heard this story had it not been for the
prompting of Wellington Jojoga Opeba, son of Jojoga Yegova. Until he
resigned to contest the 1992 national elections, Opeba was a lecturer in
the History Department at the University of Papua New Guinea. When
I returned to Port Moresby after interviewing Yegova in Buna in 1985, I
recounted to Opeba what his father had told me about his work in Goilala. He agreed to most things—including the report of a murder of a
young Goilala woman by Chester, in revenge for the death of Constable
Hareho of Gulf—because he had listened to his father's reminiscences
often enough, but he claimed his father had omitted important testimony. He then proceeded to tell me about a massacre by policemen in
the Goilala area, and that the deed had been committed in revenge for
the attempted murder of Yegova by some Goilala villagers.

I had an opportunity to return to Buna in 1989 and while there interviewed Yegova a second time. I did not tell him of the information passed to me by his son, nor did I ask him directly about the alleged massacre. I simply replayed the cassette of the 1985 interview and asked if he had omitted anything. He listened intently, and before the tape started to replay his reminiscences of his work in the Southern Highlands, he remarked that he had somehow skipped over the story of how he received two permanent scars, one on his left leg and the other on his thigh. Then he told me the story of the massacre.[13]

Yegova's Night of Fear

Sometime after the murder of Constable Hareho, the officer in charge of Mondo police post wanted to close it down and transfer equipment from it to the main station at Tapini. His intention was relayed to Tapini through a messenger. Yegova, as the noncommissioned officer, and six other policemen were sent to Mondo to assist in the transfer. The seven men slept on the way and arrived at Mondo the following day. In the morning of the next day, each of the policemen was sent to one of seven villages to engage volunteers to carry station equipment to Tapini. Yegova was sent to Korna, a village close to Ravavai. Men of this village had killed Constable Hareho, resulting in the shooting of one of their women before the rest fled into the mountains. Yegova arrived at Korna in the afternoon, and by the time he had selected volunteers the sun had set, turning the towering Goilala mountains into a picturesque dark blue. In another division, he could have returned to Mondo station in darkness, but the Goilala area had difficult terrain, and walking to any destination was a real effort at the best of times. He therefore decided to spend the night at Korna village.

After inquiring, he was shown to a *boi haus*,[14] which was on stilts, and as he prepared himself for the night a young man came in, purportedly to keep him company. However, the young man's behavior in the house warned Yegova that he had probably come to "spy" on him, because he waited until he had finalized his sleeping arrangements before slipping out, promising to return with some homegrown tobacco. The young man never returned. Normally, the Goilala men sang evening songs in the men's house before they slept, but that evening it was frighteningly quiet. Yegova suspected they were planning to attack him. Before long his suspicions proved correct. He heard movements outside, and when he peeped down he could see men in an excited mood converging on the *boi haus* from various directions. Yegova had been in the Goilala area long enough to know that Goilala people normally worked themselves into a high state of excitement before an attack. He grabbed his rifle, pushed his axe firmly into his belt, and squeezed himself out the small door. For security reasons Korna village was built inside a stockade, and the *boi haus* stood next to it, but as it was built on stilts it was possible for tall people to jump over the protective fence. Compared to the Goilala people, Yegova was a big, tall man. The men gathered below the *boi haus* cried, "He is out!" and attempted to grab his feet and legs:

> But I leaped high into the air with all the strength I could muster and landed outside the stockade amongst some *pitpit*.[15] The *pitpit* had prickly leaves and they cut into me. That meant nothing to me. I was more conscious of the imminent threat. It sounded as if all the men had rushed out of the stockade shouting all manner of abuse that echoed back with monotonous frequency from across the mountains. I got up and ran—it was already pitch dark—and the first group of men out of the stockade gave chase. Farther down the track, I fell amongst some boulders and received a bad bruise. The scar is still there on my left leg. I did not stop to nurse it, but got up and kept on running until I came to a certain spot and stepped into the nearby bushes. It turned out to be pigs' tracks. I moved on into the thicket and fell straight into a hole— a pig trap. Fortunately it was an old one and the spears staked at the bottom had rotted except for one, which pierced me on my thigh. The scar is still there and I always show it to my children when I reminisce about my police work in the Goilala. While there I heard my pursuers shout and run down the side of the hill. I loaded my rifle, placed its muzzle at the entrance, shifted dry grass and placed it across the top and waited. I thought to myself, if they find me I will shoot one or two of their men first before they end my life.
>
> The men searched and searched but I could not be found. When I was quite certain that they had stopped looking for me, I crept out of the hole and followed an abandoned track, without the aid of a torch, using both my hands and feet, and struggled through the undergrowth. From where I was on the hill, I could distinctly hear the river below cascading over broken rocks. I was no longer afraid of anything, and thought only of the distance I would have to cover to escape death. (Yegova 1989)

After examining every possible escape route, his pursuers gave up the search. They presumed Yegova had been killed, or washed away by the river below. During the night messengers were sent to relay the news that Yegova had been killed. The news of his disappearance reached far and wide. Messengers brought the news to Mondo and Tapini and, before morning, reinforcements of ten policemen, with Patrol Officer Chester and laborers from the Tapini station, arrived. Yegova met them along the way and explained what had happened.

The Goilala Massacre

The search party was furious. They marched on to Korna. The villagers had fled. They searched the area but found no one. They followed a track, which led them to a cave.

> The cave had only one opening. There was no other means of escape. The men surrounded the area and built a fire to smoke the people out. Two kids apparently saw what was happening at the entrance and tried to escape. They were grabbed by the legs and bashed against a stone, and their brains splattered in all directions. Anyone else who tried to escape was killed just like one would kill flying foxes escaping from a cave. I could see from where I stood that anyone who ran out was grabbed and battered to death. I counted six deaths. Among the labourers who accompanied the policemen were other Goilala who were traditional enemies. They used the opportunity to even some old scores. As there was so much smoke, I could not see properly, but I know that that smoke forced out more and more people and those who resisted arrest were killed instantly either by the policemen or other Goilala. I think that on the whole about two hundred men and women were arrested and between thirty and forty killed. We arrested two hundred of them and tied their hands together with big, strong ropes and brought them to Tapini for a gaol term of six months. Unlike today there was no court. You must remember also that at the time the Goilala was an unpacified area and what we did had to be done.
>
> After it kiap Chester said, "The Government is in Port Moresby. We have been sent here to pacify these people. Those in Port Moresby are eating and living well. We do not eat well. Yet we try very hard to pacify the Goilala and are undergoing many hardships. It is only because of their own hostility towards one of our policemen that we have done this. We had to do this to prove our strength."
>
> This story I have just told you, I am not narrating to you because I heard about it; I was involved in it myself. (Yegova 1989)

Yegova said Patrol Officer Chester was there, but he did not see him shoot anyone. According to his observation, Chester made no attempt to stop either the policemen shooting or the other Goilala from taking their revenge. Yegova did not disclose whether he personally shot anyone. There is no record of this alleged "massacre" by policemen and laborers in Goilala during the latter part of the 1940s in the patrol reports. The oral testimony cannot be verified. However, it is true that Chester worked as a patrol officer in the area at the time, and that Con-

stable Hareho was murdered somewhere near Ravavai[16] village in 1948
(Chester 1949). The tone of part of Chester's report after the arrest of
some of the men implicated in the murder of Constable Hareho suggests that something more than a jail term would be an appropriate
punishment:

> It is certain that the whole population of the sub-district is awaiting
> the outcome of this [punishment]. To date they have witnessed
> nothing more spectacular, than the arrest of several men . . . . The
> accused are all young men, and if found guilty, should never be
> able to return to their village, and boast that they have killed a
> policeman. For the future protection of members of the RPC, and
> village constables, and other Administration personnel, an exam-
> ple should be made of these killers, and sentences of between five
> and four years, do not have that effect. (Chester 1949)

Even if Yegova's account is an exaggerated version, there is enough
evidence in both patrol reports and oral testimony to suggest that atrocities of various gradations occurred in Goilala during the whole period
of pacification. How many actually died from police and officer activity
is not known, but it can be said that for the Goilala region from the
time of first contact in 1911 until the 1950s when "comparative peace
was finally imposed" the one hundred deaths Hallpike estimated for
the Aibala Valley were by no means the only deaths in the Goilala
region (Hallpike 1977, 14).

Chapter 8

Perceptions of the Police by Gende Villagers, New Guinea

I interviewed Tawi at Orobomarai village (Gende, Bundi) in 1985 on the last leg of my highlands field trip. Because this was more than fifty years after first contact, it is again important to keep in perspective the dangers of misreporting. However, Tawi is regarded as the custodian of his clan's traditions because of his ability to remember and narrate stories of his clan's past. Present during the entire interview session were one other man and a woman who were approximately the same age as Tawi and had witnessed parts of his harsh experience. Apart from minor interjections, they generally concurred with Tawi's version of the sequence of events. For a broader perspective, Tawi's oral evidence of his experiences with the missionaries and government officials is supplemented with both primary and secondary evidence from events in other parts of Papua New Guinea.[1]

In the many villages situated behind the mountains of the Bismarck Range and below the foothills of towering Mount Wilhelm (map 4), the people refer to themselves as Gende and speak the Gendeka language, which appears to have little connection with the languages of the neighboring highlands people. The population at the time of contact was estimated at five thousand (Aufenanger 1976), though this figure appears to be too high. According to the oral traditions of the people, the Gende had lived in the area from long before contact with Europeans. Exactly how long is difficult to determine, as the area remains an archaeological blank. However, from archaeological discoveries made elsewhere about the possible origins of highlands societies, the early ancestors of many Gende people may have originated from the present-day Eastern Highlands and Simbu Provinces, between nine thousand and twenty-six thousand years ago (Griffin, Nelson, and Firth 1979, 1–2). Despite the rough terrain and unfriendly topography of the area, the Gende have adapted themselves well to a hostile environment, eking out a living from the land.

Gende Villages

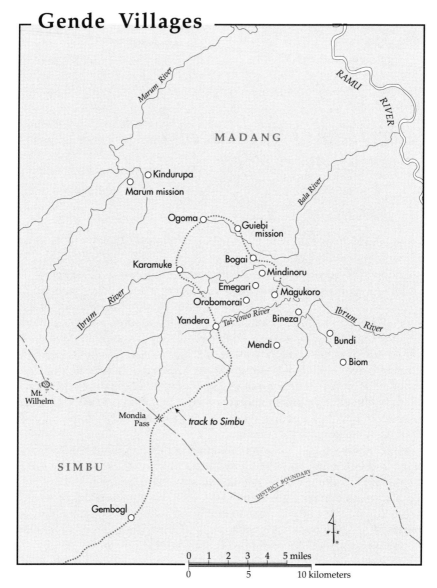

Map 4

Into this Gende society, Tawi, alias "Wizakaiia," the man with the "red eyes," was born to the Nakawa clan of Emegari, before "from over the blue mountain range came the white men" (Muru 1977; photo 42). Divine Word missionaries arrived in Gende on 3 July 1932 and established the first mission station in the Gende area. Later, they started a

Photo 42 "Wizakana" Tawi at home in Orobomarai village, Emegari. He was originally from Magukoro village. (14 July 1985)

wave of missionary activity that spread into Simbu and farther into the Western Highlands. The mission acted as "John the Baptist" or the pathfinder for the government. They regularly told the people that a power much stronger would come to Gende following in their foot-steps. Through daily sermons and fatigue duties, they carried out an effective awareness campaign, perhaps unintentionally, about the com-ing of colonial officials, patrol officers, and the policemen. The path was prepared for the coming of a strong government. In 1932, Tawi was about thirteen years of age.

Tawi, Villagers, and the Policemen

Catholic mission records do not give a date when the first group of policemen arrived in Gende with their patrol officers.[2] In Tawi's view, the Catholic mission had been in Gende for some time before govern-ment officials arrived from the direction of Simbu. The circumstances of their coming to Gende were directly linked to the murder of two missionaries, Father Charles Morschheuser and Brother Eugene Frank, on 16 December 1934 and 7 January 1935 respectively, by the Womkane people.[3] Tawi and the rest of the people of Gende heard about the

Photo 43   Father Charles Morschheuser's grave at Kagrie, Denglagu Mission, Upper Simbu. The grave is located near the road, and I have walked past the site on numerous occasions on my way to my village in Gende. (Courtesy of Bill Gammage)

death of the two missionaries through their Simbu marriage and trading partners.

It was shortly after the missionaries had been to Gende and had begun to expand into Simbu and the rest of the Highlands region when we heard that two of the missionaries were killed by the men from Simbu. One was buried at Kagrie, near Tromabuno [Morschheuser; photo 43], and the other was carried away to the white man's home.[4] As a result of these murders, we heard that the missionaries in Simbu sent a strongly worded letter to the government on the coast for help. The government did send assistance in the form of men with guns, and these men just about wiped out the population of both the Womkane and Inau tribes. Some of the people managed to escape, and they fled to Kouno, Jimmi Valley, Kombo [Eastern Highlands], and our friends took refuge in Gende. Not long after we heard that the government had established a station at Kundiawa to monitor the situation. And, of course, soon after this, the policemen, with two white men, came to Gende.[5] (Tawi 1985)

They first arrived at Bineza (map 6), a popular settlement site of the men and women of Mendi village. They were unable to chop down enough trees to build their temporary rest houses, so they sent word to the nearby villages for able-bodied young men to help. That was when Tawi first saw two officers, carriers, and the policemen. He was impressed by the sight of the policemen, and afraid of their apparent power:

> I thought they were big and strong men. You could see their muscles stretch with every movement. They had splendid physiques, and appeared invincible with their uniforms, guns and stature. They were a picturesque sight when they fell in line to hoist and lower the flag every morning and afternoon. At the beginning, I was rightly scared of them, their guns, and of their strange behaviour, and so were most of the other villagers. After this first patrol, they made regular trips to Gende. The patrol party never stayed for long periods. At the most, they walked around for a week and then returned to Simbu. After the first few patrols, the policemen came without their European officers. One would accompany them if village officials like the *luluais* and *tultuls* were to be appointed, or some trouble had erupted between different clans within the village. Much later the government established a station in Bundi, on a slope overlooking the Catholic Mission establishment. A makeshift prison was built at the side of the station which enabled prisoners to be jailed in Bundi instead of being forced to serve their terms in Simbu as on many previous occasions. We called the policemen's guns *brizivai;*[6] whenever we sighted them coming we would warn people by saying, "the *brizivai* are coming." (Tawi 1985)

In the contact phase the Gende's reception of government officers, policemen, and carriers was peaceful. They had the benefit of having previously met the missionaries and been influenced by their propaganda. The Gende's perception of the police at this time is discussed in the context of three developments: two concerned with the government's operations in Gende, and one specific to Tawi's experience as a prisoner of the government. In Gende, one of the first things the patrol officer, and through his authority the policemen, did was appoint *luluais* and *tultuls* in each of the villages stretching from Biom in the far east to Ogoma in the far west (map 5). Village officials were then left to supply the labor needed for work on government projects and generally ensure that law and order were maintained in the villages. As Gende's difficult terrain did not permit large-scale projects, government officials continued the small ones begun by the Catholic mission. There was nothing sinister about the government's efforts to maintain its influence in the area, but the way its officials conducted their activities was different from that of the mission. Tawi said the government used more force than the mission. In that respect, the missionaries' predictions came true:

> Generally the policemen were good to us. They did not steal from our gardens or shoot any of our pigs without warning. But that was as far as their good nature went. The policemen came and forced us to do a lot of things—build more roads, carry supplies from village to village, maintain the airstrip and the roads, keep the village clean for their visits, build their rest houses to their liking, and a myriad of other small things. The policemen's favourite weapon was the cane, and they used it at every opportunity to punish us at will. If ever we disobeyed or complained about anything we were kicked and caned. If, for instance, I failed to turn up for work on the roads and after a check it was found that I was missing, the kiap or the senior policeman sent out a search party, consisting of other village men and a number of armed policemen to find me, and when they did I would be handcuffed and brought back to the station for punishment; often I would be given a jail term of a few weeks, or even months. Their wrath did not stop with the men only; women also were made to suffer as the men. They were forced to carry large bags of sweet potato and follow their menfolk on road construction, some going as far as Faita and Usino in the Ramu Valley to supply the men with their daily food. (Tawi 1985)

What did the Gende do about the changes in their lifestyle and the pressures put on them by the activities of the policemen? It was a humiliating experience, as Tawi recalled:

> The terrible thing was that we could not do a thing to stop them. We were still frightened of the policemen's guns, and the idea still lurked in our minds that they were just waiting for an opportune moment to massacre all of us. We did not even have the courage to

disobey the *luluai*s and *tultul*s, who were men from our own society. As a result, whenever they came to our village, all our own activities—feasting, gardening, dancing, and so on came to a standstill. We only did whatever they told us to do. Hence, a lot of our own traditional festivities ceased or were performed less frequently. Only among ourselves did we have the courage to grieve about the fact that we had lived an orderly and straightforward existence, but these people had come and disrupted our old way of life. We considered them to be bad people who had come to destroy us. It was always a relief whenever they left for another village or returned to either Bundi or Arava in Simbu. (Tawi 1985)

The second issue raised in the minds of the Gende population was the hypocrisy of the ambassadors of the colonial government. Like the missionaries before them, a succession of patrol officers and policemen told the people to lay down their arms and live with one another in peace. They were instructed to stop fighting, stealing, and anything else likely to disturb the peace that the government was attempting to introduce into the area. Yet to the Gende, the harbingers of peace did not themselves observe the restrictions imposed. If anything, they appeared to have unlimited opportunities, with no apparent penalties attached. Their horrendous activities—the caning of recalcitrant villagers, the shooting of their pigs, the exploitation of their time and labor, the abuse of young Gende women—unsettled the minds of parents, husbands, and potential husbands:

Both the kiaps and the policemen used our young women to gratify their sexual urges. On one occasion, the European officer, whose name I never knew, asked me in gestures that I should bring Kegine to him when we walked down to Bundi with food supplies. She was then the beauty of the village, hardly out of her adolescent years and was not yet ready for courting by potential young admirers.[7] By all accounts, she would have been a virgin then. Amidst protest, and cries, I was forced to bring her to him. The European officer took her by the hand and led her to the top room of the Catholic Mission house, which still stands today in Bundi. There he forcibly had sexual intercourse with the terrified young woman. When the officer had finished with her, he gave Kegine a small mirror as payment. Silent tears streamed down her face when she walked down the stairs, and I comforted her and brought her with me back to the village. We were from the same Nakawa clan. That was one incident that I was involved in personally, but I knew of, and heard stories from other villagers that many of their young girls were prostituted by the European officers. The policemen were involved also. Whenever the women were called upon to bring

food or *kunai* grass to the station at Bundi the policemen selected
the best-looking girls—not married women—to satisfy their lust.
No woman refused because to do so meant punishment through
caning. Often they were dragged, struggling and screaming to the
haus win.[8] Consequently, the women were very scared of the policemen and their kiaps. (Tawi 1985)

A cursory glance at the "Circular Instructions" to the officers of
the Papuan administration during the prewar period does not indicate
whether there were any official regulations regarding European officers'
sexual liaisons with local women. There is a clear division in the officers'
personal views. Downs suggested that officers were "against associations
with women" (1986, 123). Whether this was prompted by official regulation is not certain. The view is shared by Wright: "With most [patrol
officers] there was an accepted taboo on native women. It was self imposed and there was no penalty if it was broken. Its observance was
sometimes an effort, but it paid dividends in gaining respect from the
natives" (1966, 75–76). On the other hand, the roving Kerr had sexual
relations with any woman who came his way; at least that is the impression he gave in his book (1973). It seems that J L Taylor was not prepared to condemn fellow officers who had sexual relations with village
women, if the quotation from a letter to Administrator J K Murray in
December 1947, by the Acting Crown Law Officer is anything to go by:
"There has come to my notice in the file some instructions to Champion. Those instructions relate to the Administration's attitude towards
sexual intercourse with native women or undue familarity and indicate
that Mr Taylor approves or condones such conduct" (Bignold 1947c).

All the ex-policemen I interviewed were unanimous in their claim
that under no circumstances were they allowed to make advances to
women in the areas they were posted, unless they were married to one,
or had received the consent of the parents and relatives of the young
woman concerned.

Gende social convention did not allow unions between men and
women until adequate bride-price had been paid for the young women.[9]
During courting or "singing" sessions between a young woman and a
young man, the mother watched like a hawk over their activities and
did not relax her vigilance until the young man left the house. If he did
not leave after a certain time in the night he was chased out by the
mother, and if he did anything that was considered a breach of the
ethics of courting rituals the mother screamed and the whole village
would come to her assistance. If the young man was from one of the
clans in the young woman's village or from a friendly tribe, a penalty
was incurred, depending on the seriousness of the offense. If, for instance, he had touched the woman's breasts, he was fined a pig. If the

payment was not made, a fight would ensue between the two clans until the matter was settled. If the man was not from the same or an allied village, and was caught, he was killed. The Gende protected their young women from men jealously, because one who was well looked after brought a good bride-price, consisting of well over ten pigs and vast amounts of food and other traditional exchange goods. Most important, however, was the unspoken wisdom of which every Gende was well aware: that promiscuity would make a mockery of their whole system of social organization. Once a man's relatives had paid the determined bride-price, the man and woman received the elders' pronouncements as a married couple. The marriage was for life.[10]

Neither the policemen nor the patrol officers satisfied these requirements when they hurriedly went about procuring young women for their sexual satisfaction.[11] They breached Gende custom, for which they should have been punished. How did the populace of Gende react to such insensitivity?

> My word! We were furious and clenched our teeth in anger and frustration, and discussed amongst ourselves heatedly on how we could stop the onslaught on our girls by the policemen and their officers. But in the end we decided that if we did anything we would all be killed. The guns saved them. So we sat and waited in resignation, as if our hands were fastened to our backs with strong cane ropes. Certainly, when the policemen and their officers abused our girls, our stomachs were heavy with grief, but what could we do against such strong opposition, except to suffer silently? (Tawi 1985)

Tawi as Prisoner

Tawi's traumatic experiences as a prisoner reveal the extent to which people were forced to change their opinions of the police, from awe-inspiring government employees to wicked, mean, unforgiving beings, hiding behind the protective hand of the government. Tawi was jailed five times. The terms of his sentences ranged from one to twelve months. Four of his prison terms, mainly for misdemeanors such as disobeying instructions from both the policemen and village officials, were served in Gende. The sentence for his most serious offense was served consecutively in various highland prisons over a period of twelve months. The narrative that follows is for the last offense, which took place a few years after World War II.

After the establishment of a series of temporary posts, the government set up a permanent base camp in Bundi, but village men from some of the earlier temporary posts were called on for help from time to time, whenever the patrol officer or the senior policeman in charge sought to make arrests or wanted someone to take messages to the more distant villages. During one of these occasions, some men from Bundikara village came to Tawi's original village of Magukoro and demanded that the men and women of Emegari bring their garden produce to the government in Bundi. Tawi was given the responsibility of organizing a group of villagers for a trip to Bundikara. In the midst of it, Tawi noticed that the *bossboi* was paying undue attention to Dinogoi, a young woman whom he was preparing to marry as his second wife. (Tawi had married Aina, a woman from Orobomarai village, in his youth and lived there with his in-laws.) The official's action warned Tawi that his future wife was to be part of the entourage to Bundikara so that she could be used by either the officer, his policemen, or the *bossboi*[12] of the Bundikara men. There was a sickness in his heart. Had not the policemen, patrol officer, and men of already "civilized" villages shamed and degraded enough of the young village women? Tawi was not going to allow another to be humiliated, especially one he fancied marrying. He attacked the government party with the fury of a man possessed. The officials could see, and some felt, Tawi's determination and hastily returned to Bundikara and reported the incident to the district officer. The next day many more Bundikara village men, armed policemen, and one officer marched down to Magukoro determined to give yet another demonstration of the government's power. After a loud and stern instruction from the policeman, the Magukoro villagers lined up, shaking to the marrow of their bones. At the signal of the now swaggering Bundikara men,

> the policemen pulled me unceremoniously from out of the line. They brought me to where the party was standing and handcuffed me. They then handcuffed Ogom, the *tultul*, and then the *luluai*, both of whom were my relatives. During the night both our hands and legs were tied together and we slept in one of the cold government rest houses. In the morning, still handcuffed, we were dragged away forcibly like pigs down to the big Maravizai River. The bridge over the river was in a very bad condition. The kiap asked the *luluai* and *tultul* why the bridge was in that state. They said they had no reason to come that far and therefore had not realised the bridge was in bad shape. The kiap said it was their duty to ensure that bridges and roads were maintained for government patrols. He then ordered them caned for negligence. The struggling men were laid flat on stones and caned mercilessly all over their bodies while they squirmed, screamed, and pleaded for mercy. (Tawi 1985)

The prisoners were then taken to Guiebi (map 6), the site of the arrival of the first missionaries. There they were made to carry thickly made wire coils used by the first missionaries to pull logs for church and other mission buildings. The coils were "so heavy that our blood rushed down to the lower parts of our body and made it hard for us to walk in an orderly fashion" (Tawi 1985). They walked slowly to Yandera village and spent the night there. The following morning they made an early start on their march to the jail at Gembogl. At the foothills of Mount Wilhelm, Ogom, the *tultul,* collapsed from exhaustion. The police shouted in loud voices, "Get up! Do not waste our time!" (Tawi 1985). Ogom lay motionless. The policemen grew impatient:

> One of them pushed the butt of his rifle into Ogom's ear and then shot a bullet into the ground right beside him. Ogom leaped into the air with fright and landed with a thump on the hard, cold Mondia soil. In his weary condition, he leaped into the air two more times to check that he was still alive, and thereafter ran to the front of the party and did not look back until we arrived at Gembogl. (Tawi 1985)

The prison at Gembogl was much bigger than the one in Gende, and was well fortified with barbed wire encircling the perimeter. As was the custom in Gembogl jail, new prisoners were introduced to the rituals of prison life by what was called a "stroll," a euphemism for running around the perimeter of the prison area with a heavy boulder on their shoulders and policemen whipping them at every opportunity. Tawi recalled his own introduction to the "stroll":

> Early in the morning we were forcibly brought out from the prison house and made to stand erect outside. We were then directed to sit on the grass nearby. The handcuffs were taken off. Our hands were swollen. Five men carried five round rocks from the nearby river and dropped them in front of us. I could tell they were heavy from the effects the rocks had on the men who carried them. I was first in line. The sentry selected the biggest of the five rocks and heaved it onto my shoulder. He then ordered me to stand erect, with legs stretched to their limit. The same was done to the rest of the men. The sentries and the policemen of the station stood on either side of the path where we were to conduct the ritual. At the firm order of the policeman in charge, the men near us hit us swiftly across our backs with their canes; the caning continued every inch of the way if one failed to run with the boulder. They told us to rest at midday. We dropped our load, slumped on the ground and lay with our noses buried in the grass, breathing heavily like a pig felled suddenly with a piece of solid wood. After lunch we persevered with our efforts until the late hours of the afternoon. This was our introduction to prison life in Gembogl. (Tawi 1985)

After two months of constant punishment from the sentries and the policemen, coupled with the unfamiliarity of the new and regulated work routine, Tawi jumped the barbed-wire fence to freedom and made his way home to Emegari.

> The main reason for my escape from prison was because I was caned so frequently, in fact, so many times a day by the sentries and the policemen that there was hardly any part of my skin which did not show the marks of a brutal caning. I thought to myself, "If I do not escape now most of my youthful skin will disappear under scars, and even worse, one day they might cane me to death." After all these nauseating thoughts I escaped without even telling my fellow villagers. When I reached home, I escaped into the bush. I lived off nature and hid in caves and abandoned rest shelters to avoid being caught again. (Tawi 1985)

But a government search party arrested him after almost two months of painstaking search. In Tawi's own testimony he gave himself up because he heard that an ultimatum had been pronounced to the effect that if he did not come in freely fellow villagers would be held hostage and caned every day until such time as he did. When he received this message, he gave up trying to hide from the government because

> I thought that if people were caned and imprisoned on my behalf they might die in prison and their relatives would demand compensation from me. I did not wish to jeopardise other people's lives or place my relatives' lives in needless difficulties. For these reasons I walked into the village and the men handcuffed me. After, they stripped off my clothes of woven strings, feathers, cane belt etc, and fastened my feet and arms with strong ropes, and hung me up onto two posts resembling a crucifix, and left me there in the village square for all to see me. I was left in that position all day. (Tawi 1985)

However, Kegeriai, an eyewitness to the proceedings (photo 44), recalled:

> When Tawi escaped from prison, he came to Kuraini, and I heard about his coming at my bush home at Mindinoru. Soon after, he went into hiding. A search party arrived and they forced some of our own men to join in the search. The men were divided into groups and each group was in charge of one of the men from either Bundi, Bundikara, Mendi, or Gembogl. After days of searching one of the groups found him eating raw *kaukau* at Kokowoi. He was forcibly handcuffed and brought to Emegari. There, my husband, Ibrum, bribed the leader of the group with an expensive

traditional necklace made of valuable shells, and betel nuts and said, "Tawi is my son-in-law. Do not cane him. He has suffered enough already." Domande, the leader of the group, was himself a Gende, and he understood the concern of Ibrum by the nature of the bribe he gave him. Domande accepted the bribe and ordered his men not to cane Tawi or cause him any more physical harm. However, he was handcuffed and brought to Magukoro. At Magukoro he was told, "You have suffered so much hardship because of these two women" [Aina his wife, and Dinogoi, the woman he intended marrying as his second wife].

All their "clothes" were then stripped off them—they were stark naked—and their feet and legs were tied with bush ropes to crosses, and the three crosses were placed in the middle of the village square so that the people could have a good look at them. Once the crosses were up, they said, "Have a good look at these misfits and shout when you have seen enough." It rained heavily that day. All the people of Emegari were gathered there for this occasion. The people sat in silence. Many took only one glance and then quickly looked down at the ground in embarrassment. In the middle of the silence Kendi's mother shouted, "I have seen enough. It is a very humiliating experience for the women. I am going to my house." After, everyone slowly stood up and walked back to their houses. They were drenched to the skin by the drizzle that fell all afternoon. The two women were then let loose. Tawi was still handcuffed and in the morning walked back to Gembogl for another term of imprisonment. (Kegeriai 1985)[13]

It is significant that while men were more likely to be subjected to torture and other forms of punishment from patrol officers and policemen, there were instances where women, as in this case, were also made to suffer humiliations, along with their men or individually. Two other examples will suffice. In "The Scientific Aspect of the Pacification of Papua," Hubert Murray wrote that a certain white officer treated a native woman of loose character with utter contempt. The woman was forcibly "stripped naked and compelled to walk up and down before a squad of police who had been fallen in for the purpose" (Murray 1932, 7). The other example comes from Ialibu, in the Southern Highlands, and took place in the 1950s, during the period of sustained contact.[14] During this period Nandie of Nanduka clan (photo 45) watched in horror as a man and woman involved in an adultery case were paraded up and down the now disused Ialibu airstrip (photo 46) for a whole week and forced to perform perverse and sadistic acts never before seen in public, or in the privacy of a home in the Southern Highlands. Nandie described the ordeal:

There was one shocking incident I witnessed at the now abandoned Ialibu airstrip which is not far from where we are now. This incident took place between a man and a woman who had committed adultery. The aggrieved husband informed the authorities—kiap, policemen, and Yamona, the village constable. They were both arrested and then brought to the newly established airstrip. First the man was forced to carry the woman from one end of the strip to the other. And from that end, the woman carried the man to the other end. This continued for a whole week—it started early in the morning and ended late in the afternoon.

But that was not all. Later during the day, Yamona, with the assistance of the kiap and policemen, forced the couple to perform the sexual act during the course of the day before a large crowd. This also continued the whole week.

Photo 44 Kegeriai Veronika, my mother, who observed the hanging at Magukoro and was responsible for feeding Tawi in secret.

Photo 45 As a young man, Nandie Nanduka observed the events described from the side of the small airstrip at Ialibu, which is no longer used. Nandie lived near the Ialibu station. (20 October 1989)

The most unthinkable happened when the man was forced to suck the woman's vagina, and later forced to pick up with his mouth and then eat items of food such as *kaukau* and banana pushed into the woman's vagina.

I do not know what they wanted to achieve from this, but it was a humiliation. The people just stared in disbelief as the couple were forced to do all these things. I was furious with Yamona, and so were the others, but what could we do when the policemen stood poised with their guns and their kiap ready to give the command if our men got aggressive. These officials made no attempt to stop him. They seemed to enjoy watching it because they demanded that the sexual acts take place at their end of the airstrip.

I watched the whole ordeal as a young man. The kiap was also there, and so were the policemen. I saw them with my own two eyes. The kiap's name was *Masta* Ross [phonetic].[15] The man has

oto 46   The abandoned Ialibu airstrip. Here, the people of Ialibu observed for the first
ie the extent of police brutality and perversion. (19 October 1989)

since died, but the woman is still alive and lives at the edge of the now-abandoned airstrip.[16] It was certainly a sad day for the people of Ialibu. The people gathered there were embarrassed for themselves and the unfortunate couple. What could they do except suffer the humiliation. Yamona was the principal instigator, but he had the authority of the government, and the policemen and kiap backed him, and we were afraid. (Nanduka 1989)

Pumuye Nungulu also saw the incident. Parts of his testimony concur in large part with that of Nandie, even though they were interviewed at different locations on two separate days. He said:

The man's name was Rekere Ei of Kebigi clan of Topopul village. The couple were stripped naked and whipped by cane. They were then forced at gunpoint to perform the sexual acts all through the week. Whenever they got tired of performing the sexual acts, they were told to lick each other's sexual organs. The police even pushed ripe banana or cooked *kaukau* into the woman's vagina and forced the man to eat them. Then they were forced to horse-ride each other along the one-kilometer airstrip in Ialibu. This was not the case in the old days. Only the man was killed by the husband and wife's people. In this case the woman was subjected to all manner of humiliation. The people were so ashamed and scared. (Pumuye 1989)[17]

Another example comes from Tari, in Southern Highlands. After his stint in Goilala, Jojoga Yegova, the policeman, was sent to work in the Southern Highlands in 1955. At gunpoint, after learning that a notorious criminal had been arrested and brought to jail, he forced an innocent young man and his mother to have sexual intercourse in prison:

One day a man who had caused some trouble had been arrested and brought to the station. It had been raining that day, and so I was wet and felt very grumpy. But I was jubilant that a wanted criminal had been arrested. I thought I might celebrate the occasion. As I was the NCO of the station, I went into the prison. There were among the prisoners a woman and a young man; it looked as if they were mother and son but I played dumb and asked the young man, "Is she your wife?" to which the man said, "No! She is my mother!" I then ordered in a stentorian voice: "I order you to fuck your mother, now!" The boy naturally objected strongly "No! No! No!" he shouted, "She is my mother!" I interrupted: "If you say she is your mother one more time, I am going to shoot you with this gun." I then brandished the gun in the air and brought it down about an inch from his nose. I slapped him hard around the ears to reinforce my threat. He looked scared. I brought my gun down and pressed it hard against the area of the midriff. I cocked the gun and counted to two, and he jumped up, gave out a furious shout, and before I knew it, he was on top of his mother searching around hastily for the "thing." (Yegova 1985)

These examples suffice to highlight the similarity and the consistency of police practice and behavior on the frontier of contact in both Papua and New Guinea. I return to Tawi's testimony of his experiences as a prisoner. At Gembogl, he was severely reprimanded and caned again by the senior policeman and told that since he had escaped from a barbed-wire fence he would be sent to the "hole" in Kundiawa. The "hole" was a prison cell dug into the heart of the earth.[18] It was a deceptive construction. First, a hole, measuring about fifteen feet deep, or the length of a long ladder, was dug out of the earth. The area of the hole was equivalent to the size of the long church buildings Tawi had seen in Gende. Once a hole of appropriate size had been dug, it was covered by timber—planks nailed together to cover the top of the hole. This timbered floor was covered with grass. A house was then completed with *kunai* roofing. The building was so constructed that any visitor to the area would not have known there was a jail underneath the longhouse. Few people were brave enough to descend to the bottom unless forced to do so by the sentries and the policemen. Tawi was struck with horror and incredulity at what he saw and experienced in the hole—his home for at least three months of his prison sentence:

We entered the longhouse and were made to sit there until the afternoon. At someone's command, a "door" opened in the ground, not far from where we sat. It led to a big dark hole. I was frightened, my legs trembled with fear. On impulse, I thought they were going to kill us all and the hole in the ground was to be the site of a mass burial. All my fears were put to rest when a policeman ordered us to stand and prepare to descend. A long, heavy ladder was dropped to the bottom. All the prisoners were forced into it. When I eventually reached the soil it was cold, filthy, and stank of human faeces and urine and crawled with rats. The soil was moist. The lamps placed at irregular intervals displayed the ugliness and the sordid condition of the prison—cold and repulsively dirty. Drums stood at certain sections of the hole. These had been used as toilets. There were a few beds but these were hardly suitable for human comfort for they also were infested with bed bugs. After everyone had descended, the lamps were collected and sent back to the top. Likewise, the ladder was pulled out and the "door" closed and locked from the outside. The prisoners were left in complete darkness. Men and women, at the other end of the hole, shouted, cried, and invoked their ancestral spirits for help. It was deafening. Hardly anyone slept the whole long, cold night. When the noise got too much for the local sentries, they poured hot water down openings in the timbered floor above, and people below sprang for cover to escape the wrath of the sentries. By early morning the prisoners were like freshwater eels thrown on dry land. In the morning we heard loud footsteps. They were those of the local sentries—big, fierce Simbu men who took no nonsense from anyone. They were all dressed up in their traditional costume, as if for a dance. They carried their weapons of bows and arrows, and awesome-looking long spears.[19] From habit, early every morning they chanted a song, a monotonous and constant reminder of the reasons we were in the dungeon:

> *Aiowe, aiowe, aiowe.* You are imprisoned in that hole as a form of punishment for your stubborn refusal to listen to the advice and obey the rules and regulations of the government. Beware, we are keeping a constant watch on the door. There is no way that you can escape. By the time you have completed your term you will have learned to listen to the policemen, *luluais*, *tultuls*, and the government.

> It was only after the completion of this ritual that the door on top was swung open and we felt a gush of cold, clear air rush inside, after which we were ordered out of the hole for various menial tasks.[20]

Every evening after work for three months, Tawi was forced to spend the night in that hole in Kundiawa, then five months in Mount Hagen prison, and the remaining three months in Mendi, Southern Highlands. Before his release, the patrol officer, through an interpreter, advised Tawi and those to be released with him:

> You are now going to be released from imprisonment because we think that you have suffered enough for what you have done against the government. You must go home now and refrain from committing any more of these crimes. Tell your people to do likewise. If you do not do as I say and you return to prison, your punishment will be even more severe. You are lucky you are alive to return home this time but next time you will not be so lucky, only your corpse will be carried down to your people.[21] If you died no one would be concerned about you because you would have been a bad man. So when you go home now, stay quietly—do not fight, do not kill anyone, man or woman, conduct your daily activities quietly as that of a small child, and listen to what your *luluai* and *tultul* tell you. These were the kiap's parting words to all of us. (Tawi 1985)

Sole Sole of Gorohanota village, Asaro, Eastern Highlands Province, shortly before World War II underwent similar experiences to Tawi, when warriors of his tribe refused to heed the patrol officer's warnings to stop intertribal feuds. Sole Sole told Bob Connolly and Robin Anderson: "If we caused trouble by fighting . . . we would be punished—locked up and whipped. The missionaries warned us about this—that we would be punished by the policemen. One thing they did was to dig a hole and drop us into it. We'd have to urinate, shit, and eat there. And then the policemen would come and urinate on us" (Connolly and Anderson 1987, 263). An Enga big-man, Karapen Kuvin of Aghubum village, told Bill Gammage in 1988 that imprisonment of prisoners in holes was also the method used in Mount Hagen and Wabag. In Mount Hagen during the 1940s and 1950s the practice became useful as a way of stopping laborers from deserting (Strathern 1984, 28). Some men of Wabag underwent similar experiences to Tawi's (see Amean 1973, 23–26). In 1948 or 1949 about a thousand men, women, and children were forced for many days into a hole dug in the earth at Kero village, which is situated about half an hour's driving time from Ialibu station. They probably would have been kept there for many more days if they had not escaped by digging themselves out with the aid of a tiny "stick." There was no apparent reason, except that the policemen and their officer feared revenge attacks for a dead relative (Ongi 1989; photo 47). Ongi was forced into the hole along with the rest of the villagers. He would have

Photo 47 Nivil Ongi was about seven years old when he, along with the "whole" of his clansmen and women, were forced into a dugout hole in the ground. They escaped one night by digging a hole under a carefully constructed house. (20 October 1989)

been about seven years old. His description of the size of the hole (photo 48), the edifice above it, and the sadistic practices of the policemen are similar to those reported for the other three highlands regions.

Certain aspects of prison life taught Tawi about hygiene, comradeship among prisoners, other people and their ways of life, and gave him the courage and determination to adjust to new and strange environments. To this extent, Tawi had no regrets about the time he spent in prison. However, his recollections of his other experiences were not so easily accepted. Of particular importance is the nature of some of the harsh treatment he was forced to undergo. Ideally, prisons should rehabilitate people, so that on satisfactory completion of a given term a person will return to society and live a normal life. Tawi's oral testimony indicates that some of the treatment he received while in prison did not accord with these precepts.

Photo 48   The prison hole is now overgrown with shrubs and pandanus trees and partly filled with soil. No exact measurements were taken, but it must have been a huge hole. Nivil's house is nearby. His description of the hole, the house built on top, and the behavior of the policemen conforms with Tawi's account of the one in Simbu.

For example, at times the sentries and policemen would ask:

> "Do you desire your wives?" If we said no, we were caned merci-
> lessly. In order to avoid punishment we all said yes. The policemen
> and the sentries would then have a good laugh and say, "Oh good!"
> They would then promise to get some of the prison women for us.
> They just tried our patience, of course. On other occasions, they
> thought of something different, "Tomorrow, you will all be released.
> Pack your things and be ready early." But none of these things
> eventuated. They just enjoyed playing tricks on us. (Tawi 1985)

The regular caning, teasing, and the use of scare tactics adopted by
the police to pacify Tawi, his two women, and the two other women mentioned only highlight the sadistic minds of those who were placed in
charge of prisoners and the behavior of the police and their officers generally. The constant beatings left both physical and psychological scars
on Tawi and turned him into a passive, undignified person. It shattered
his hopes of becoming a leader of his clan, a warrior among his peers.
He was forced into submission, becoming like a woman in the eyes of
his people. He was a beaten man physically and in the depths of his
being. He was reformed: his imprisonment in Simbu was the last time
he entered a prison gate or went anywhere near a policeman. His dis-
illusion about the purpose of the policemen and the patrol officers'
coming was all too clear to him now. He had to abide by what they said
or he was going to be in a lot of trouble. Tawi concluded:

> Before the Europeans, both the missionaries and the government
> and their Papua New Guinean assistants came, my people led a dif-
> ferent type of life; there was tribal warfare but it was not as disrup-
> tive, at least we knew how to take care of it. The foreigners came
> and disrupted our culture, our traditions, our very existence. We
> became disoriented. We did not know what we were doing. We
> could not fight them because we were afraid of their guns, they
> humiliated us by sleeping with our women. We lost our self-confi-
> dence as warriors and led a life of submission to the new authority
> that had come in our midst. (Tawi 1985)

Jean-Paul Sartre (quoted in Fanon 1963, 13) described what happens
to such a man, shamed and forced to live in constant fear: this will "split
up his character and make his inmost self fall to pieces."

Chapter 9
Officers' Perceptions of the Police

From primary and secondary source materials, two quite different conclusions are drawn about European officers' views of the policemen and the assessments of their performances. The distinction, however, is arbitrary, and at no stage did the differences of opinion extend to other areas of administration. One represented the views of white officers who had some dealings with the policemen in an official capacity and, in almost all cases, from a great distance. The second represented the views of white officers who had worked with and therefore been in daily contact with the policemen.

Masta Nogut—Bad Master

The first group expressed a negative viewpoint. They questioned the rationale of raising an indigenous police force in a colonial situation. In Papua these sentiments were articulated early: "Doubt was expressed at first by those that knew the Papuan best whether they could be trusted as a constabulary, fear being entertained that they would be too prone to use their weapons, to abuse their position, and perhaps that they might turn on their employers" (NGAR 1897–1898, xxvi). These officers' ideas followed the more traditional and, by the 1930s and 1940s, antiquated, school of thought of hardened colonialists. The people in this category included some planters, miners, some missionaries, anthropologists, and some conservative, paternalistic colonial officers. Most were nervous about the changing world, in which words like *progress, freedom, equality, development, humanity,* and *revolution* had become catchphrases in other colonized countries. They hoped that the events taking shape around the world would change course and revolve back to the days where colonial subjects had been made to show obedience, respect, and loyalty to their colonial masters. For these officers and entrepreneurs the presence of a police force of any great size posed a serious threat to the peace and stability of the colony because there was always the potential for insurrection among the ranks of a highly trained and disciplined force such as the police.

A case in point is the so-called Rabaul Strike of 1929. In this dramatic confrontation, senior members of the Rabaul indigenous police force energetically collaborated with Sumsuma, a boat captain from Tanga Island, and the indentured laborers who staged the demonstration for a pay increase of twelve dollars a month and improvements in living conditions. The subsequent course of events revealed the determination of stalwarts of the colonial regime to silence opposition to their dominance. The protest was quickly suppressed and the leaders, including senior members of the police, were severely punished and dispersed to various regions on the mainland in order to avoid any recurrence (Gammage 1975, 3–29).

There were other poignant reasons why the conservative *masta*s did not relish the idea of raising a police force. They thought it would be humiliating, and a concomitant loss in respect for the white man, if a European were arrested for murder or for any other offense by an indigenous member of the police force. An excellent example comes from the notorious activities of miner Joseph O'Brien, in the Northern Division of British New Guinea between 1903 and 1905. He not only stole a thousand pounds from another white miner, but created havoc among the indigenous community through arson, rape, murder, and destruction of livestock. No one seemed to disagree that O'Brien was a criminal, yet most Europeans in British New Guinea agreed that no criminal act by a white man was bad enough to risk the destruction of white prestige among the local population. The European miners' objection to O'Brien's imprisonment was not so much that he did not deserve it as that he was being supervised by members of the Papuan Armed Constabulary, and that his performance of menial tasks was a bad example to the indigenous population because it threatened to lower prestige and respect for the white man. The incident reveals more about white attitudes than about black police and the indigenous population generally.[1] There have been other times when similar objections to being arrested by a Papuan member of the force were raised. For instance, in 1906 a royal commission was appointed to investigate, among other things, the causes of resentment against the police force:

> The Royal Commission into Papua found resentment at the possibility of being arrested by a member of the Armed Native Constabulary to be so strong among the expatriate population that it seemed advisable to avoid this happening where possible. "There is always this objective," the Commission felt, "that, no matter how little a particular white man may deserve the respect of the native,

it is still necessary in the interests of all white men that the natives
should not be in a position where respect for the ruling race will
be jeopardised." (Wolfers 1975, 18)

The Armed Constabulary may be, though in practice they never
are, employed to arrest Europeans, but the village constables have
nothing to do with any but natives. (H Murray 1912, 243)

The officers who criticized the police included W N Beaver (1920),
an experienced pioneer patrol officer, and, during the 1960s, Martin
Kerr, who in his early years worked in the Sepik. Kerr considered
policemen only "extras" made to do work like the carriers: "No, not my
native police, the sophisticates from the coast, waddling along in white
man's boots. They were cumbersome extras" (1973, 57). In one sense
Sir Hubert Murray and Resident Magistrate Monckton fit into this category, but in an enigmatic way. They both expressed passionate views
about the Papuan constabulary, but there is a qualification in most
things they wrote about them. This ambivalence is constant in their
writings: "The Papuan makes an admirable policeman, his weak point
is that he cannot direct others. Hence, though good policemen are
common enough, good NCOs are very rare indeed" (Murray 1925, 59–
60). Monckton lavishly praised the performance of Sergeant Major
Barigi as a loyal policeman, but always made it clear that he himself was
masta and Barigi the faithful servant (Monckton 1921). Both helped
propagate the white man's myth of the loyal black man always dependent on the white leader.

Europeans who held reservations questioned the intelligence of the
police and were paternalistic and condescending in their praise. They
waited for opportunities for a policeman to overstep his given responsibilities and then without hesitation proclaimed, "We said so." Frequently they recommended severe punishment, which in some cases was not
proportionate to the crime committed. In the case of the "Rabaul Strike"
there is reason to believe that the nature of the decision to punish the
ringleaders was based not on careful consideration but on hysteria.
Many of these people had slight contact with the police and the indigenous people generally, and then only in the course of their duty. Otherwise they lived in seclusion in centers like Port Moresby and Rabaul and
distanced themselves from the people socially, culturally, and sexually.
To gain entry into one of these enclosures, even for a policeman not on
duty, was difficult unless he could memorize and observe the most repressive regulations then in existence—laws that, if not in intent then
in their observance, encouraged complete racial segregation.[2]

Even though these officers and men questioned the effectiveness of
Papua New Guinean policemen, they grudgingly accepted their presence in official circles because they came to the realization that without
the policemen their jobs in Papua New Guinea would be made all the

more difficult. They were also pleased to let the police do the dirty work of colonialism—whether menial or violent.

Gutpela Masta – Good Master

The second group is composed largely of field staff officers. Generally these were young and energetic men who were influenced by the liberal thinking of the time. Many were new recruits who had not spent any length of time in the colonial service or in any other gainful employment. Jack Hides and Ivan Champion, for instance, were born in Papua. In their formative years they spent time with and grew up in the company of Papuan children. Other officers, though not born in the country, developed a liking for the place and the people with whom they lived and worked. Most of them, because of their particular responsibilities, lived on outstations, away from the protected areas of Ela, the Papuan name for Port Moresby, and Rabaul.

These officers wrote about the policemen with warmth, affection, humor, and humanity. They wrote, for example, about the laughing corporal. Lance Corporal Arua was from Ere in the Kumusi Division, which later became the Northern Division. In early 1930 Arua died in the wreck of the *Vaiviri*. He had only recently been promoted and was traveling to his new posting in Kerema. During the late 1920s he had been part of the expedition that crossed New Guinea from the Fly to the Sepik. The *Papuan Villager* printed this account of the journey and of Arua's contribution:

> It was a rough trip and a long one and so little food could be carried that most of the time everybody was hungry. But Arua could use a gun well, and when pigs and pigeons were found he shot many. He was a good man too to find a track and when the party got into swamps, as it often did, it was Arua who always found a way out. And no matter how tired and hungry everyone got Arua was always smiling, so that the white men called him the "ever laughing Arua." Papua lost a fine man when Arua was drowned. (2 [April 1930]: 2)

McCarthy told a story about Constable Nogutman, the "clown" of his police contingent (1963, 35–36). Others wrote of the womanizing sergeant major, or an Orokaiva ready to break into song. In July 1930, while on a patrol to arrest men of a Kukukuku tribe who had raided and stolen property from the veteran prospector Albert C Bethune on the upper Lakekamu, Hides observed of his eight policemen:

> Some police formed an idle group outside their tent and beside a small fire, while from the opposite bank of the creek came the voice of a policeman lifted in song as he chopped wood for the fire

that would blaze that night in the police tent. If you are a man who knows Papua, and who lives in its lowly places, the song of the Oro-kaiva policemen will make your blood surge. On all Papuan patrols, the police tent at night is always a hum of voices until "lights out." This night proved no exception to the rule and as we were on a new venture into new country, our object, and our possible success-ful return, were freely discussed. (1935, 81)

The officers wrote about the policemen's companionship and un-bending devotion to their work and superiors, their strengths, achieve-ments, and failures. "In time they became good companions; some remained lifelong friends. Like you, they came from distant places to join the administration and the people we administered were foreign-ers with a different language" (Downs 1986, 84). The writings revealed that where a policeman overstepped his given responsibility he was rep-rimanded, or discharged from the force if the offense was serious. Where one deserved praise for a feat achieved, praise was given. Such accounts are a rarity in the volumes of official colonial literature and provide some understanding of the origins, character, and behavior of the policemen who would otherwise have been unknown in Papua New Guinea's colonial history.

In a diverse literature, policemen are written about from three per-spectives, two in official reports, and the third in personal reminiscences. First, policemen were reported on regularly, and in an official capacity, in routine reports. Second, errant policemen, depending on the nature of their deviation, often received close official scrutiny. Third, in the officers' writings individual policemen are singled out for criticism or praise for outstanding performance.

Reports and Reminiscences

Routine reports were mandatory and were submitted in a variety of forms. Every field staff officer was by regulation obliged to submit an annual report to the central administration, giving details on every aspect of his activity for the area under his jurisdiction as well as on his personnel. In this type of report the most basic and mundane informa-tion was given. The officers gave assessments of the policemen's perfor-mances since their last submission and made recommendations for promotion, demotion, or termination of contract based on observations of a constable's or noncommissioned officer's work. In these reports, policemen collectively or as individuals received extravagant praises or outright condemnation. In much of the extant literature most police-men received praise from their officers. Some examples of these reports will illustrate the range. The first was written by J K McCarthy after a patrol to make arrests and consolidate government influence over an area that covered the Isimb, Langimar, Vailala, and Tauri Rivers·

> To say that the police carried out their duties would be understating the facts. Every man from corporal Nusa to the rawest recruit, of which we had five, was a credit to the force. They were forbearing and patient with the suspicious and hostile natives met with on the early stages of the patrol, and when suddenly called upon to defend the carriers against an enemy ambush, they behaved really well. Six of the police, my servant Tami, and myself were wounded before we knew there were natives among us. They showed determination and resource in making the stand that drove the attackers off. Constable Anis, a man of long service in the force, was seriously wounded and died later in the Salamaua Hosptial;[3] Suaga suffered severely with body and head wounds and is still an inmate of the hospital. He underwent a serious operation a few days ago and is still an invalid. The remaining wounded are fit after hospital treatment. (J K McCarthy 1933a)

After a patrol in the area "lying between Strickland river and Iaro watershed of the Purari," Hides wrote:

> The courage and discipline of these men of the Papuan constabulary were tested to extreme limits, and their magnificient efforts were worthy of some recognition. Sergeant Orai, Borege, Agoti, Dekadua were outstanding men. Perhaps this NCO could be given an increase in pay? And I would ask that the three constables be given consideration when promotions are next being made. (Hides and O'Malley 1935)

Acting Resident Magistrate H L Griffin in his annual submission wrote of the Papuan Armed Constabulary:

> Yet, when all is said, it must ever remain a marvellous fact that the Papuan who, a few years ago, was looked upon by the scientific world as an interesting relic of almost pre-historic savagery, is now, when led by officers in whom he has confidence, fit to take his place alongside any negro troops in the world. It is, in my opinion, not too much to say that, with officers who know them, and a carefully organized system of training recruits, a force of a thousand disciplined men able to use a rifle could be raised in this country at three months' notice, thoroughly capable of assisting in the defence of their shores. (1907, 100)[4]

Patrol Officer (and later District Commissioner) Jack Reed wrote to Michael Somare, whose father had been a sergeant major in the New Guinea police force, stating that the policeman who escorted a patrol was the real leader of the patrol. Although my own ego may have been loath to realize it at the time, that is what your father was on those early patrols. He was a natural link between our inexperience and the people. In an unobtrusive way he saw to it that we went about things the right way and saved us from making mistakes. In time, I came to realize that during my apprenticeship your father taught me a great deal that came to stand me in good stead throughout my field service. (Somare 1975, 18)

In 1987 some officers who had retired from active service many years earlier still remembered something of the Papua New Guinea policemen.

Pre-war the Police Forces of Papua and New Guinea were among the finest bodies of men I have encountered anywhere. The men were well trained, loyal, determined and proud of their Force and what it achieved. Individually and collectively I have the greatest respect and regard for the police of PNG and could never wish to serve with a more devoted group of men. Their contribution to the administration and advancement of the country was enormous. One of the finest Sgt Major's I ever encountered was Sir John Guise. (Toogood 1987)

Police in the field were in general as good as their officers. When competently led by concerned officers they did fine work in contacting unknown tribes and stopping tribal fighting. Where badly led they could do much harm. There is no doubt that police when allowed to get out of hand could be guilty of rape and plunder, but nearly always you will find that this was because they were not kept under tight control. I can state categorically that I never had any trouble with my police in the bush. I always kept them busy, kept in touch with them, talked with them and treated them as friends. (Sinclair 1985)

It is hard for me to imagine, particularly the period 1947–1969, when I was still patrolling actively, how difficult it would have been to carry out census, listen to disputes and move from village to village without these men.

I can recall many incidents involving courage and resourcefulness in touchy situations.

A lot of the policemen may not have been in urban situations and sadly I know a few who were dismissed after the introduction of drinking to PNG population.

It is difficult for me to decide what area they might have failed. Most were illiterate, in the era I refer to, so responsibility was deliberately limited in respect of individual constables. The old time sergeant, however, was always the right-hand man of the officer in charge, otherwise there were problems. (Ken Brown 1987)

Some reports examined the private lives of policemen. This might include information on a policeman's marital status, sexual preferences, his relationship with other policemen and the villagers, the name of his home district or division, and other details the officer considered necessary. The nature and length of the reports depended on the officers concerned. Some submissions have elaborate introductions, while others stuck to the bare minimum and only reported on the exceptional abilities of the policemen:

> The house is now ready to roof and tile flooring ready to go in. Sergeant Dani did most of the carpentry without nails. Wooden pegs are used. Dani is the quickest worker I have seen among Papuans and the most energetic. He is the best NCO I have had in the Armed Constabulary. (Champion and Adamson 1938)

Errant Policemen

Tawi testified that not all the police were obedient and law abiding. Under the protection of an authoritarian colonial government, many policemen exploited prisoners and villagers whom they were obliged to protect. These men, either through their own volition or peer pressure, or following direct or implied instructions, failed to live up to the expected standards of discipline, loyalty, and obedience and committed crimes. Some officers took action against police for misdemeanors, and, depending on the nature of the offense, the policemen were subsequently fined, demoted, imprisoned, or discharged from the service. In the Papuan annual reports, breaches of regulations by members of the armed constabulary were generally regarded as breaches of discipline. Patrol officers took particular pains to report, either collectively or individually, cases related to breaches of discipline among the policemen.[5] Listed here are examples of the types of offenses committed at the outstations in Papua in 1912–1913, that is, crimes committed by policemen engaged mostly in patrol work among village people, for which some form of punishment was incurred:

> The discipline of the force for the last year leaves much to be desired. There were 70 convictions for minor offences under Section 8 of the armed Constabulary Ordinance; 14 convictions for more serious offences under Section 4 and 5 of the Ordinance; 9 criminal convictions, ie, offences laid under the Criminal Code; and 14 convictions under the Native Regulations. These last are equivalent to charges under Section 8. In all, 107 convictions.
>
> Twenty-six men were dismissed [from] the force during the year for various offences; or, in other words, 10.4 per cent of the force proved unreliable. The following is a summary:

8 were discharged for being concerned in an alleged case of
    rape.
3 were discharged for indecent assault on females.
1 was discharged for assaulting his superior officer.
11 were discharged for continous bad conduct.
2 were discharged for allowing [a] prisoner to escape.
1 was discharged for desertion. (Nicholls 1912, 62)

That is, 107 out of a force of 250 men were formally charged and
convicted of offenses; 26 were dismissed; 133 men, or 53.2 percent of
the total force in the Native Papuan Constabulary received penalties
ranging from fines to dismissal from the force. Minor offenses included
disobedience, absenteeism, voluntary infliction of sores or "feigning
sickness in order to escape duty or failure to report to officer" when a
person had been committed to his charge (Papua 1939, section 11).

These penalties were inflicted on the policemen who were caught
and reported. Some of the policemen I interviewed in 1985 and 1986
did not hesitate to reveal that at times they had been like "snakes," and
able to wiggle their way through the restrictions without ever being
caught.

Some of the most common offenses were minor breaches of a moral
code that the police ignored. One of the many restrictions placed on
the policemen involved gambling, particularly card playing. Section 78
of the Native Regulations proclaimed:

Any native who plays cards for money or money's worth, or who
gambles in any way may be punished. Punishments. The first time
he is caught he may be fined up to two pounds, or may be put in
gaol for four months. . . . If a man is caught gambling a second
time he will get a heavier punishment. He will certainly be fined
one pound or put in gaol for one month; and he may be fined as
much as five pound or put in gaol for six months. (*Papuan Villager*
2 [March 1930]: 2–3)

During training all the policemen were told with monotonous regularity of the existence of this regulation. It was their duty to observe it
and to prosecute people who chose to breach it. Despite their knowledge of its existence, many policemen, at every opportunity, blatantly
overlooked the regulation and gambled for money or anything else
that took their fancy; sometimes a policeman would stop gambling
himself in order to arrest a civilian engaged in the same activity, only to
return to his own game after the villager or indentured laborer had
been fined or locked up. Jojoga Yegova, of Buna, Northern Division,
learned to gamble at his training depot in Sogeri and continued to do
so throughout his police career:

We often gambled for money, tobacco, matches etc. Of course, we gambled in secret because we were forbidden to engage in this activity. I gambled a lot while at training—but those of us who gambled sneaked behind hedges or tall shady trees and gambled there. We could not gamble in the barracks because it was just one big open space. Sometimes we would wait until 9:00 PM for the late and final inspection. When that was over those of us who habitually gambled winked at each other and waited until the lights went out before we stole away to our secret location and gambled away until about 3:00 or 4:00 in the morning. We then returned to our beds and pretended we had been there all night. The reason I became a compulsive gambler was because I never received enough money from my monthly pay. Sometimes I won some money, and lost it at other times. (Yegova 1985)

The Performance of Individual Policemen

The types of offenses the policemen committed that received wide, sometimes sensational coverage in both the patrol and annual reports, and later in the publication of the officers' memoirs, concerned killings and relationships with women. According to the Queensland Criminal Code in force before World War II, the taking of another human life, regardless of the circumstance of the killing, was to be judged in three degrees: "wilful murder," "murder," and "unlawful killing" or manslaughter, and for these the respective penalties were death, life imprisonment, or imprisonment for a shorter term (A Inglis 1982, 28). A number of secondary and primary sources testify to the extent to which policemen were punished if they seriously exceeded the powers given them. Three brief examples will suffice. In 1929, Constable Karo Araua, a Toaripi man from the present-day Gulf Province, received a five-year jail sentence for the murder of Bill, his policeman companion, in the vicinity of Kokoda (A Inglis 1982, 24–30).[6]

The next example, of a relationship grown sour between a policeman and his patrol officer, provides an excellent contrast between the lofty praises of the policemen in the officers' writings and what happened in reality. During the 1930s, Constable Sipi of Vanimo was hanged in Ambunti, Sepik District, at the scene of the murder, after being found guilty of the murder of Assistant District Officer Colin MacDonald on 28 February 1935 (J K McCarthy 1963, 132–134; Simpson 1962, 336). Sipi had been transferred to Ambunti from the Angoram police detachment in early 1935. As MacDonald planned a patrol to Ambunti, Sipi became part of his entourage. While loading supplies onto canoes, MacDonald noticed a bag of rice. When questioned, Sipi told MacDonald that it was rice he had saved from his daily rations for a forthcoming feast. MacDonald was "a stickler for the books." Failing to recognize the social significance of Sipi's action, MacDonald reasoned that if the rice was not eaten then it remained the property of the government. On his orders, Sipi returned the rice to the government storeroom. Sipi was further disappointed when in one of the villages on the way he recognized his dog, stolen from Angoram two weeks earlier by a man working for a trader and recruiter along the river. Despite Sipi's pleadings and the trader's apparent approval, MacDonald remained unconcerned and told Sipi that the dog belonged to the man "on the launch." Sipi turned bitter and felt that he had been wronged by MacDonald. At dawn of their first night at Ambunti, he picked up his rifle, and bullets he had carefully hidden at the bottom of his bag, and

> walked up the hill to the white man's bungalow and on the verandah he released the safety-catch of the .303. He crept into the bedroom, put the muzzle against the mosquito net where MacDonald lay and took the first pressure on the trigger as he had been taught to do. The next moment the roar of the rifle woke Beckett [Reg Beckett—Ambunti station officer] from his sleep in the next room. He stumbled out of bed in time to see Sipi disappear. The policeman seemed to be trying to reload the rifle, but the magazine fell to the floor. They found Sipi sitting on his cot in the barracks. He was mumbling about having lost his rice and his dog. (J K McCarthy 1963, 133)

Finally, according to Amero Bega's oral testimony, Sergeant Awai of Manus was given a life sentence in Salamaua jail in the late 1930s for having damaged government property, for inciting relatives of his Simbu wife to attack a government patrol, and for having shot dead a policeman who pursued him. The details of his arrest were horrifying:

> The *nambawan* kiap [district officer] in Salamaua was [Edward] Taylor. In Simbu a Manus sergeant caused some trouble. He cut the rope off the government flag, and the wireless aerial, and stole six police rifles, three boxes of cartridges, some money from the station, and ran off with his Simbu wife to her village. He deserted from the police force and became a wild man, a bush kanaka, like his wife. Taylor himself brought me up to Kundiawa and placed me second in charge of the police station. It was left to me to command the policemen there, arrest Awai, and retrieve the stolen goods. After a week we found him but he shot dead one of the policemen, and so we retreated to the station. The following day a brother of the sergeant's wife came, and after presenting him with gifts of laplap, salt, tobacco, knife, etc, we asked him to go to the

village and return with news of Awai's movements. He returned
and told me that Awai and his wife had gone to the river to wash. I
told the kiap[7] that we should go and arrest him. The kiap objected,
saying it would be difficult. I did not think so. The kiap agreed
later. On the way we met some people and told them not to say
anything. They knew who we were after. They walked quietly on
because I had a reputation for being harsh. We waited in hiding. A
few minutes later, the kiap remained with two policemen and I
took charge of the policemen and moved in closer. At that instant
Awai walked up. The kiap commanded me to shoot him immediately. I pretended to act as if I had not heard him. He became
angry and commanded me again to shoot him. In the end, and
upon the kiap's insistence, I shot Awai on the knee. Upon impact,
Awai was brought down to the ground. His knee was completely
broken. I rushed over, stood over him, and held him by the beard
and then sat on his stomach. The kiap came, slapped him around
the head in his agony, unbuttoned his shorts and urinated in his
face.[8] He then ordered us to do likewise, saying he was a bush
kanaka, like the rest of the people there. We did not do it, out of
respect for a fallen comrade. He was brought back to the station in
handcuffs. Awai was then sent down to Salamaua hospital. When
his knee healed, he was given a jail sentence of fifteen years. However, he had served only a few years when the war came and, in the
confusion, he escaped and settled down among the people of the
Markham. (Bega 1985)[9]

In a large body of men there will always be a number of murders and
other nefarious acts, and in proportion their numbers were low in
Papua and New Guinea. But, as the three cases suggest, the police were
generally not punished for their actions against villagers; most of the
recorded police offenses were for failure to carry out a specific order
from the patrol officer, losing or damaging equipment, or consistently
being late on parade. Generally, police were punished for delinquencies in their relations with the government, not with villagers (see
Kituai 1988).

Sexual Activity

Police relations with local Papua New Guinean women were sensitive,
and the police treated women with caution. Many reasons were advanced why officers and their policemen were not to interfere with
women in the areas in which they worked. Fundamentally, for the
officers it was a question of maintaining prestige, status, and racial
purity. At least in public, they condemned any association with local

women, recognizing that the need to appear able to treat all village people equally was essential to maintaining their ideal of law and order. However, Tawi's oral evidence of the behavior of the patrol officer and his band of policemen toward the young women in Gende indicates that the actions of at least some officers and their men were not in keeping with public statements. What kinds of evidence reveal something about the policemen's sexual relationships with local women?

The conditions of recruitment and the conditions in the various police ordinances made it highly likely that policemen would be looking for illicit relationships with women. For instance, sections 23 and 25 of the Armed Constabulary Ordinance of 1890 and the Royal Papuan Constabulary Ordinance of 1939 of Papua not only specified the age range of the men to be recruited, but that those recruited were to be primarily unmarried men and were to remain bachelors until a specified period (three years in Papua; five years in New Guinea) had been served. They were energetic, virile, and, most important, removed from traditional restrictions and any customary obligations to intended marriage partners. If they had not already formed associations with women from their own villages, ample opportunities existed wherever they were posted. As the policemen's oral testimonies reveal, they became popular among the women in many areas of Papua New Guinea. They took great delight in passing on European trinkets for the favors of many women.

The policemen's officers seem either to have encouraged marriage among their policemen or condoned such behavior if their men's illicit activities did not disturb public law and order. Downs recalled that "nearly all police and mission helpers interfered with local women. It was not unusual for one policeman to have a girl in more than one tribe and the patrol post at Kundiawa was a fairly promiscuous place. These multiple associations were bound to annoy Chimbu men and were bad for our public relations" (1986, 122). The task of keeping a check on what his policemen did beyond their official responsibilities was almost insurmountable.

> [The police] all [except two] have wives, mostly local women. This has eliminated the old system of each man having about five friends who were all prevented from marrying local men by their association with one constable. There has been no case of venereal disease and medical assistant Burnet said they were the best line that he had ever examined. It is impossible to have the respect of the men if you attempt to enforce restrictions which you are incapable of enforcing and which are illegal. If it is thought that it is possible to prevent police from having any sexual intercourse at Chimbu it will be necessary to employ a special staff of Europeans

to watch every man every night. The groves and the houses lend themselves to evasion. It is far better for them to marry and their wives will watch them. (Downs 1940; 1973, 21)

However, occasionally a case deteriorated to such an extent that the officer concerned had no option but to submit an official report on the policeman to the higher echelons of the administration and leave the matter to them to act on. Such a report was compiled in Kavieng on 8 December 1947 by Sub-Inspector of Police J Palmer, and sent to the Senior Inspector of the New Ireland District:

> Subject: Reg. No. 5225 B Sergeant Sali.
> I beg to report that the recent conduct of the above mentioned member has been such that I am of the opinion that his services should be dispensed with. . . . I am constantly receiving complaints of his attempts to persuade married women to have sexual intercourse with him due, I believe, to the fact, that he is a powerful man with a vicious temper and likely to exact reprisals in his own way.
> In this connection he approached me about two months ago and enquired what would happen to him if he interfered with a married woman. I informed him that the same action would be taken against him as against any other person. His reply to this case was "when I do this don't put me in gaol! Shoot me through the head!" Sali is thoroughly unliked by the detachment here not, I believe, in connection with his duties as a N.C.O. but rather because of his interference in things that are no concern of his. Aware of this attitude towards Sali, I have been most careful to ensure that complaints made against him have been genuine and not actuated by dislike and it is possible that in giving him this benefit of any doubt that may have arisen has led the complainants to believe that I favour him. Not so.
> Excellent record. Jeopardise pension. Disciplinary action against the member in his present mental state would avail nothing, he being of the manic-depressive type, liable to sudden bursts of temper in which state he might do anything.

As far as I have been able to glean from their writings, patrol officers made almost no mention of homosexual practices among the officers themselves, or among their subordinates. The practice is known to have existed among men who were placed in similar situations as the police. Anthropologist S W Reed, who did fieldwork in New Guinea in the 1930s, reported that "few indentured laborers have any normal outlet for their sexual feelings. Some plantations are situated close to native villages, and in such cases the boys may resort to surreptitious prostitutes. Ordinarily, however, homosexual practices are the easiest adjustments; all Europeans agree that they are very common and are increasing" (1943, 220). The 1921 and 1922 annual reports revealed at least two sex-related offenses for which "natives" were charged and brought to trial: sodomy and rape (Reed 1943, 176). In Downs' 1939 patrol report, one of his policeman is said to have developed a strong tendency toward sodomy. Many of the policemen, particularly those from the highlands region, vigorously refuted any claims of having engaged in homosexuality themselves, or hearing of it being practiced among other members of the force. Policemen who worked in the coastal areas had heard of this activity between policemen and other males. Some of the stories they heard were rumors. A number of the men alleged that homosexual acts between males had taken place, but at the time it happened they had been on routine patrols and only became aware of it when they returned to the station. Jojoga Yegova heard of homosexual activities between men during the war in Port Moresby:

> I did not witness any with my own eyes but I heard stories about such activities among the menfolk in the barracks. I first heard about it in Port Moresby during the war. Then, of course, there were men from all over the country and literally thousands of Europeans, Americans, Australians etc, were in Moresby. I did not hear anything about it again in the other areas I worked—Southern Highlands, Sepik, Goilala, and West New Britain. (Yegova 1985)

In 1934 Amero Bega was a new recruit undergoing training at the police training depot in Rabaul. Sometime during that year he first heard about homosexuality between a policeman and a civilian, and between two policemen, and later attended the court case in which two of these policemen were discharged from the force:

> *Yes, i tru, mi save long wanpela stori olsem. Em dispela samdin kamap taim mi stap trenin long Rabaul. Dispela samdin kamap long tupela polisman bilong Manus; wanpela em Sagen Meja "Jimmy," na narapela em Sagen "Bendo." Sagen Jimmy em pakim as bilong wanpela magi man bilong Rabaul na semim gavman, olsem na gavman paitim Jimmy long tripela ten kanda long stik kapiak, na behain kalabusim em long tripela yar. Na narapela ya em Sagen Bendo, em magalim dispela polisman, nem bilong em Kereson [Gershon, who was killed in Wabag in 1938]. Kereson save pilai bugl bilong polis long dopo. Bendo magalim Kereson long longpela taim liklik. Long sarere long wik igo pinis em bin kik soka kros[10] wantaim mi bilong wanem dispela boi em laikim mi. Na wik behain em pakim as bilong Kereson long banis Kalabus, insait long haus bilong Sagen Meja Ulupau bilong Wewak. Meri bilong Ulupau lukim tupela Bendo na Kereson wokim dispela samdin. Meri ya ripot long man bilong*

*en na tokim em, "Mi lukim Sagen Bendo pakim tru as bilong Kereson, kok
igo insait olgeta." Sagen Meja Ulupau igo ripot long kiap bilong mipela,
na kiap ripot long polis masta, Walstab. Walstab tok ino gat rong tru long
dispela samdin tasol Bendo mas pinis long polis. Olsem na ol pinisim
Bendo long polis na em igo planim ol kain kain kaikai long salim igo long
wanpela skul na kisim mani bilong em.*

Yes, it is true. I knew of one such story. The event took place
while I was at police training in Rabaul. The event took place
between two senior policemen from Manus and two other males,
one of whom was also a policeman. The first one involved was Sergeant Major "Jimmy," the other was Sergeant "Bendo." Sergeant
Major Jimmy committed sodomy with a boy from Rabaul. News of
this activity spread fast among the Rabaul community. The government was ashamed of this act by one of its most senior and
respected policemen. In order to appease public condemnation,
and through government endorsement, Jimmy was whipped thirty
times with the branch of a breadfruit tree, after which he was jailed
for three years.

The other case was between two policemen. Sergeant Bendo
liked very much the depot's police bugler, Gershon of Nodup,
Rabaul. Bendo had this feeling for Gershon for some time. The
previous Saturday he had challenged me to a kick cross soccer
game against him because he thought the bugler fancied me instead of him. Only a week after, Bendo committed sodomy with
Gershon inside Sergeant Major Ulupau's house, located within the
precincts of the jail. It would have passed unnoticed had the sergeant's wife not found them in the act. She immediately reported
the incident to her husband, "I saw Sergeant Bendo committing
sodomy with Gershon. There was complete penis penetration."
The sergeant reported it to the kiap of the depot who in turn
reported it to Mr Walstab, the police master. Walstab did not think
it was a grave crime; nevertheless, he consented to Bendo's dismissal from the force. Consequently, Bendo was discharged. He
made his way to Kerevat and became a farmer, and grew all kinds
of vegetables and sold them to the school for money. (Bega 1985)

"Special" Policemen

Two contrasting examples suffice for the third and final point. Most
officers who wrote anything about the policemen gave credence to the
policemen's own statements about what they did. In the eyes of these
officers, the majority of the policemen worked tirelessly for the colonial
government. Their devotion to their officers and sense of duty were

unequaled by any other indigenous groups the officers had worked with. From this collective group, the officers selected certain individual policemen for special praise because, in the officers' opinions, these men were instrumental in effectively spreading the pax Australiana. So convinced were these officers of the policemen's abilities that some of the men were regarded as being indispensable. The officers guarded these men zealously; they could do nothing that would distract them from the responsibilities entrusted to them. Though in the minority, these officers romanticized the capabilities of their policemen. The next story is designed to show the loyalty, good intentions, and essential simplicity of the policeman. It is the stereotype propagated by well-intentioned but paternalistic officers.

Constable Utu was six feet tall, had a splendid physique, and was in perfect health. He was every inch a sought-after man for a police career, and, at the time of this test, he was at Ambunti post. However, the constable was all brawn and little brain, or was so regarded after failing to follow strict orders not to sway under pressure. One evening before night duty, the guards were instructed not to let anyone through the gate unless they gave the password—"Pussycat." A short while later the officer-in-charge took a stroll outside the guarded area and returned to the gate where Constable Utu stood poised for action. He challenged:

> "Whosait, you?" "It's me," said the colonel [Walstab], "I want to go inside." "No can!" snapped Utu. His bayonet point was an inch from the officer's midriff. Impressed, the colonel decided to test the sentry further. "But you know me, Utu. Let me in." Utu was polite but firm. "Me savvy," he said. "Sorry too much. No can!" He still barred the way but the colonel persisted. "But you know me, Utu. Why can't I come in?" All this was beginning to muddle Utu, for he was essentially a man of action. "My orders are to let no man inside until they say the word *Pussycat*," said the obedient Utu. "Say *Pussycat* sah, and you can come in!" (J K McCarthy 1963, 54–55)

The second example illustrates some officers' zeal for achievement against any other consideration. Sergeant Samasam was a member of the New Guinea Native Police Force in the early 1920s. A handsome and powerfully built man, Samasam too epitomized the perfect police-man. He was above average in height, of strong physique, and endowed with a personality demanding respect and obedience from those with whom he lived and worked. Sometime during his early youth he had voluntarily left his home village, Kamikundu, in Bukawa, Morobe District,[11] and allowed himself to be recruited into the police force. Thereafter, he had traveled from one patrol post to another, serving under the guidance of colonial officials and helping to explore and pacify New Guinean communities (J K McCarthy 1963, 27). By 1928, burly

Samasam had been rewarded with promotion to the rank of sergeant of police and was at the time based at Talasea. Samasam's immediate superior on the station was Assistant District Officer George Ellis. In McCarthy's view, Ellis was a tall, strange, and overbearing man, who appeared to have little patience with his superiors and subordinates, both black and white, and much less for New Guinean prisoners and policemen (J K McCarthy 1963, 27). However, Assistant District Officer Ellis had developed a strong and almost neurotic regard for Sergeant Samasam. He therefore had allowed him to work under him from the time he had been recruited into the force. As a result of this neurotic attachment, or because of the trust and respect Ellis had for Samasam's performance, Ellis entrusted him with greater responsibilities than those normally accorded Papua New Guinean policemen of the time. To the distaste of other white officials, Ellis on occasion left him in charge of the Talasea station when he went on patrol. Samasam recognized the special treatment he received from the assistant district officer —extra rations, easier tasks, forgiveness for minor faults, a much-improved status within the ranks of the police—and he was grateful. But Samasam was aware, having served under Ellis since his youth, that his superior officer at times had demonstrated a certain uncouthness toward his fellow policemen, prisoners, and hostile villagers. He also was conscious that Ellis had the power to strip him of his title and deny him the special privileges he received if he did not live up to the expectations Ellis had of him. Samasam was forced by circumstances to be loyal, obedient, and a model sergeant. He performed tasks only to gratify his superior's idiosyncrasies.

Sometime in 1927 Samasam fell in love with a local beauty, Baleki of Kalepia village.[12] As the months passed, he became increasingly infatuated with her and seriously considered marrying her. However, before he could do so he thought it appropriate to ask Ellis for his permission and blessing. Ellis refused permission and continued to maintain this defiant stance whenever Samasam raised the subject. The sergeant stood unperturbed and waited patiently, ever hoping for the elusive bright morning when his officer would finally sanction his marriage. Samasam waited and waited. Slowly and painfully the months of 1927 passed and the months of 1928 appeared and began to slip behind Talasea's blue mountains without Ellis's notice. Samasam continued to wait. One day in 1928, Ellis went on a routine patrol to Bali Island, which fell under his jurisdiction. By a now grudgingly accepted practice, he left Samasam in charge of the station. In his absence, Samasam committed suicide, triggered by months of increasing desperation. He jumped from a nearby breadfruit tree in front of a dismayed crowd of policemen, station hands, and their families. Before he jumped he made a brief but poignant speech to the audience below.

They heard him tell of how he wanted to marry the girl of Waru
[Amero said both the woman and the girl were from Kalepia] but
that Ellis had forbidden him to do so. Ellis was his kiap and so he
had obeyed him, but his obedience had brought him shame because he was no longer a child. The girl and her parents would
laugh at him because he feared to disobey Ellis. "It is better that I
die. . . . Goodbye to you all." (J K McCarthy 1963, 29)

The tragedy revealed that although the officers had developed a
good working relationship with their contingent of policemen, they
sometimes overlooked their basic needs. Police were capable of falling
in love, required decent accommodation, and needed to be fairly rewarded, financially or otherwise, for the services they rendered. While
some officers recognized the disparity in wages and associated rewards
for the contribution the policemen made to the spread of colonialism
and made attempts to rectify the situation, others like George Ellis were
bent on ensuring that the spread of pax Australiana surpassed any
other consideration. Ellis had a neurotic attachment to Samasam, and
given Ellis's status, this placed Samasam in a privileged but vulnerable
position. The same neurotic tendencies in Ellis that helped destroy
Samasam ultimately also destroyed Ellis himself in the Sepik during
World War II.[13]

Summary

The police were enthusiastic carriers of the "civilizing mission": they
rationalized their behavior and took praise for themselves as those who
"brukim bus" [broke bush: early arrivals] and opened a "nupela rot" [new
road, new way] for those who were just "bus kanaka natin" [unpacified
villagers]. Many officers praised the police in their reminiscences, but
there is also much evidence of police misbehaving—in the personnel
records of the police and in lists of offenses committed by police. It is
also in the evidence of the policemen themselves and villagers. How
does one reconcile the two portraits of the police, on the one hand
with their knowledge of the ideal rule and a belief in themselves as the
carriers of the new way, and on the other the evidence of frequent punishments for failures in duty, a few horrendous crimes, and much violence against villagers? A few spectacular and violent crimes can be expected—people, especially men, are sometimes violent, and the police
came from tough societies and were in a tough service. It is not surprising that some of them committed murder. Perhaps another comparable group would have committed more crimes. What must be explained is the contrast between the image of disciplined loyalty and
sense of mission and numerous penalties for neglect of duty and evi-

dence of violence and extortion. Both of these images are valid. The police deserved praise for much that they did, but they were the enforcers of Australian rule and they sometimes exploited this position for their own material and sensual satisfaction. To what extent did Australian officers have an unspoken agreement—You do the dirty work of colonialism, and we will let you take rewards in women, pigs, and a few traditional valuables?

The patrol officer system and the colonial system in general required the police to be tough, dictatorial, and sometimes brutal. The officers may not have known the details of how their police acted, but some of them created a general context in which the police were expected to be tough. The officers shouted at people, occasionally hit someone, and generally behaved as though they expected immediate compliance with orders. Moreover, the system was one of frequent surveillance by an armed party—sometimes with an officer present, and at others with a senior noncommissioned officer and constables. Usually, a brief inspection was carried out by a small group with a much greater status and power than those inspected. It all gave the impression of a small army outpost being inspected by a group of superior officers.

In their methods, the police shifted a long way from the proclaimed ideals of their officers, ideals generally known to the police. But their actions were in conformity with a general toughness practiced by many of their officers and inherent in the system itself. Researchers have been right to see the police as intermediaries, but in doing so they have underestimated the power wielded by the police and the extent to which the colonial state was imposed by violence and intimidation.[14]

Conclusion

On 6 November 1987 the *Papua New Guinea Post Courier* published an eye-catching obituary on Kamuna Hura: "Highlands trail-blazer dies as a . . . forgotten man of Papua New Guinea history!" (Meava 1987). Kamuna, with Jim Taylor, was in the forefront of many significant expeditions into the highlands in the 1930s, and a witness to many subsequent momentous events in Papua New Guinea's history (Radford 1987, 100; Sesiguo 1977, 227ff). His daughter grieved, "My father died a lonely death without anybody knowing. Even I did not know of his death until I was told by some people while I was on my way home to visit him a week after he had died" (Meava 1987). Both the article and Elizabeth Kamuna questioned the government's apathy. Would it not have been appropriate to recognize Kamuna's thirty-one years of dedicated service during an important part of the country's development, to honor him materially by meeting some of the funeral expenses or symbolically by supplying a plaque and relevant inscription?

The majority of the men interviewed for this study expressed deep concern about the lack of interest shown in them since they left active duty. Many felt abandoned and were no longer prepared to recall their evanescent police years with the same degree of pride they once did. The fear was strong among them that they were growing old, a fear not without basis. Between 1986 and 1988 Aladu Iwagu, Petrus Tigavu, and Ben Elipas ToWoworu died of old age and were buried without ceremony in their villages. Some of the survivors, once the beloved sons of colonial governments and of villagers, had become senile and lived destitute in urban squatter settlements or villages. While fellow villagers reaped benefits from cash cropping and other ventures, the old policeman, if he had served his twenty years or more, wandered off to the nearest Bureau of Management Services office to collect his monthly pension check from the government. Goro Sebastin resigned after nineteen years to care for his ailing mother, but was not eligible for pension money, because an inflexible and unsympathetic government regulation is firm on the twenty-year limit. Amero Bega had a permanent back injury sustained on active duty, but received no compensation and no government pension, because he too served fewer than the required number of years; for his daily sustenance Amero depended on the charity of his relatives and fellow villagers.

A significant exception was Sir John Guise. Compared to the majority of ex-policemen, Guise, through his long involvement in politics and statutory bodies, was by no means destitute. Others had been able to supplement their pensions with remittances from their children, but they were in the minority. Peter Daguna, Mohaviea Loholo, Meraveka, James Evara Ori, Lelesi Orovea and Ben Elipas ToWoworu lived permanently in Port Moresby; Kamuna Hura lived for a while in Lae with his daughter, Elizabeth. Petrus Tigavu and Aladu Iwagu, until their deaths in 1986 and 1988, respectively, made regular visits to their children in Madang and Lae.

Some policemen, after a series of de facto relationships, did not marry; the children of others died during the course of their duty. A few wives, either because of official restrictions or voluntarily, remained in their villages. On their retirement or resignation, the returned policemen were either too old or too unpopular or too poor to remarry. Jojoga Yegova said some retired policemen spent their retirement money on beer, as they had done while they were still in the force, and consequently did not have much left to start anything substantial when they eventually returned to their villages. The children of the "foreign" marriages, many already parents, looked on themselves as "half-castes." Although a few returned, or intended to return to their fathers' provinces, the majority opted to remain with their mothers' people, because they had established attachments to them. If—as evidenced by the experiences of Kamuna, Iwagu, Tigavu, and ToWoworu—all else is forgotten about them, at least the interviewed men would like to be remembered as the men who, in their youth and as policemen, helped bring peace, law, and order to many hostile groups and individuals in Papua New Guinea.[1]

A considerable amount has been written about the police, but little of it is based on extensive research. Most of it comes from white officials' memoirs or was written for special occasions. In 1934, for example, Sir Hubert Murray wrote the obituary of Sergeant Major Simoi:

> The Papuan government lost a loyal officer, and I lost a personal friend, by the death of Sergeant-Major Simoi, of the armed constabulary.
>
> Simoi joined the constabulary in 1898 and rose to the rank of sergeant; but in 1905, tempted by a higher rate of pay, he left the police and took service as a "boss boy" on a plantation.
>
> However, the call of the uniform was too strong, and in 1912 he

was back again in the constabulary, and rising rapidly, eventually attained the rank of sergeant-major.

Simoi was a man of proved courage, but personal courage is not a rare quality among Papuans, and certainly it is common enough in the ranks of the armed constabulary. But he was also a strong character and marked personality; and these gifts are not commonly found among natives of this Territory. I myself was under a debt of gratitude to him, for he and corporal Kaubu, of Jokea [Iokea], were chiefly instrumental in saving the lives of the Administrator, Captain Barton, and myself, when we capsized on the Vailala bar in 1905. I remember how extremely difficult it was to persuade these two Papuans that they had done anything worth talking about.

The sergeant-major was on leave at his village at Katatai, near the mouth of the Fly River, and, while he was there a cold which he had brought with him from Port Moresby developed into pneumonia. He was brought into the government station at Daru for treatment, but died on 28th February 1934. He was buried at Katatai with military honours, a compliment which, if he could have foreseen it, would have more than made up for all the pains and inconveniences of sickness. (H Murray 1934, 6)

Often, the writing is full of praise, picturesque, and patronising:

Colonel Mackay refers to him [Sergeant Barigi] as "a non-com beyond price," and he certainly was that. In serving with my regiment in India I had some splendid non-coms, men that Kipling calls "the backbone of the Army," but I never had a better man than the Binandere ex-cannibal, Barigi of the Mambare. Sergeant Barigi could deal faithfully with the roughest and most truculent of savages, even in the mass; he feared neither man, ghost nor devil, nor any peril in Papua. (Monckton 1922, 132)

The police in these writings conform to the ideal of the savage who has become the faithful warrior and servant of the government and empire. There is a simple explanation why men such as Monckton praised the loyalty of the police: they were presenting themselves as worthy of the trust and devotion of "natives." Similarly, it is unlikely that such men would make public the extent to which the police under their nominal control acted illegally or took the initiative. Doing so would reduce the extent to which they themselves were efficient and dominant.

There is no reason to doubt that the police performed acts of valor and exhibited loyalty to fellow policemen and their officers. The most knowledgeable of the field officers are also those who spoke most highly of their police: men such as Champion, Hides, Giddings, Clark, and McCarthy. But even where police bravery is presented in cases other than of naive devotion to the *masta*, the picture of the constabulary that emerges is too simple.

My aim has been to investigate the work of the police and to dispel some of the simplified stereotypes that predominate in the published records. What have the police said about themselves and their work that is different?

Working variously as "civilizing" agents, innovators, and cultural interpreters, policemen knowingly became the vanguard of the *nupela pasin,* the "missionaries of Western culture" (Arnold 1986, 60). They did so for personal as well as humanitarian reasons. The circumstances of their new status, and the interest and enthusiasm generated in carrying out their task, demonstrated a desire to help those they considered less fortunate than themselves. Because they felt they had been advantaged by their position in the colonial administrative structure, they made it their duty to help the disadvantaged, so that "fellow villagers" would not feel left out as the circumstances of their country changed. On the personal level, the vigor with which they attended to the task confirmed the policemen's perceived image of themselves as "civilizing" agents assisting the stereotyped "primitive" villager to rise to an acceptable level—living, on the one hand, a life free of internecine warfare, cannibalism, homicide, head-hunting, sorcery, and witchcraft, and becoming, on the other, law-abiding, tax-paying, road-building, and obedient "citizens" of the colonial government. Joe Naguwean said of his father's work:

> I think one of their best and most noticeable achievements was that their efforts ensured that people lived in peace and no longer lived a life of continual belligerence against their neighbours. Policemen lived close to the community, and through the community's own observation of their actions and behaviour they felt encouraged to follow their examples and become law-abiding citizens. There were no major civil disturbances once the policemen had established a station in the area and brought people under control. (Naguwean 1985)

There is a clear distinction between police who were simply instruments of Australian colonial policy and those who themselves had a vision of a better way and were anxious to convert others.

In their many travels, police, with and without constant supervision and direction from patrol officers, brought with them the ideology of the colonial government and the knowledge they had acquired of its ideals. Police knew, by law and by police ideals, that they were not to shoot people, pillage gardens, kill pigs, or interfere with women. In that respect, whether in training or out on patrol, policemen's activities were supposed to be regulated with military discipline. Nevertheless, most of the men interviewed admitted committing offenses when presented with opportunities, thus offending against what they knew to be the written law and the code of behavior that allowed them to think of themselves as a superior group of men.

How can the policeman who was bound by duty to the protection of personnel and property be reconciled with the one who simultaneously committed crimes? This is one of the many contradictions of police work: *Quis custodiet ipsos custodes?* [Who shall guard the guardians?][2] While they worked variously as the universal and exemplary upholders of western laws and practices, they also were their enthusiastic destroyers. It seems that police behaved as though they were above the law, or understood the intricacies of the system well enough to manipulate it to suit their own purposes.

Three possible reasons are offered for police deviance. First, some of them allowed themselves to be recruited because they wanted to gain prominence for themselves and thereby achieve an improved status in village politics when they returned home. Although it may seem strange to outsiders, a Papua New Guinean policeman who killed many men, or married many women, was regarded by fellow villagers, and by other Papua New Guineans, as a strong and powerful man.

The other two reasons are related. As testified by Avila, Daulei, Girau, and Tawi, the police did not hesitate to use violence to expedite submission. Whereas villagers construed the policemen's actions as hypocritical, the police had a rationalization. The majority of them agreed, in consonance with the official interpretation of the situation, that in order to be successful in dealing with "primitive" Papua New Guineans it was at times necessary to use force to maintain control. Naguwean testified:

> If we go back to the situation then, it was the administration against primitive villagers. And so all available sources were utilised in order to get that basic idea across to the people that the administration was there to enforce law and order. So if one of the villagers did something wrong there were instances where the police kicked, punched, or even used the rifle butt to hit people— just to knock some sense into them. Additional force was applied where it was considered necessary. (Naguwean 1985)

The police had taken over the missionary convictions of their officers, and inevitably they took over the same expedient arguments.

A more fundamental explanation lies not so much with the men as with the system under which they operated. Colonialism created the context for the development of the police force and for police violence, "for there can be no colonialism without coercion, no subjugation of a whole people in its own homeland by foreigners without the explicit use of force" (Guha 1986, 3). Armed with inadequate professional police skills, the .303, and the poorly developed techniques and methods of the colonial police in general, and of the Royal Irish Constabulary in particular, the paramilitary police of Papua New Guinea became the frontline men of the Australian New Guinea Administrative Unit during World War II, and of colonial governments before and after it. Their achievements in both were exemplary, and for those they should be proud and remembered. Previously unknown peace and order, the men said, was realized in the villages from the 1920s to the 1960s. But the policemen's excellent records are tarnished because they were also the violent enforcers of Australian rule—an authoritarian and paternal regime whose early officers had been raised in the Kiplingesque tradition of "God, King, and Empire." Many of them believed in the efficacy of coercion to maintain control at the frontier in pre-1960 Papua New Guinea.

This book offers tribute, criticism, and explanation. The work of the police deserves to be known, remembered, and understood.

Appendix 1
Response of Rick J Giddings to Questionnaire

Because of space limitations, it is not possible to include the responses to my questionnaire from all the patrol officers. Rick Giddings' comments were intelligent, perceptive, and informative. I reproduce them here as an example of what officers experienced as members of field staff. His answers followed leading questions in the questionnaire, which was distributed on 17 June 1987. With the questionnaire, I included an introductory note stating the reasons why I was conducting the investigation. My introductory note, the questions from the questionnaire, and Giddings' verbatim response follow.

QUESTIONNAIRE

Dear Sir,

For the last three years I have been working toward a PhD in history on the "Experiences of Papua New Guinean Policemen from 1920–1960". Although I have completed about two-thirds of my thesis I know that the thesis would be incomplete if I did not include something about the contributions of the European officers under whose directions the policemen worked. For this reason I have devoted the last chapter to discuss the Australian Connection. While secondary sources are available there is, however, an obvious lack of primary material. You made a contribution in Papua New Guinea. I am interested in finding out what you as an individual thought your responsibility was in PNG. I am circulating a short questionnaire among ex-PNG European officials, in anticipation of hearing your side of the story. The questions below should only be guides. If you wish any information that you divulge to be kept confidential, I will ensure that your wish is honoured.

1. AUTOBIOGRAPHY

Background information: nationality of parents and grandparents; early education, marital status at the time of appointment for work in PNG, age on appointment etc.

2. Duration of engagement

When, and for how long, did you work in PNG, and in what capacity? Did you remain in only one job? Did you apply for a job or was one given to you because you wanted to go to PNG, or you were forced to do so because of circumstances (economics, social/political etc.) in your own country? In which areas did you work, and was there any place/people you liked/disliked? Why?

3. Education

Did you have a good general knowledge about the administration of indigenous people in other colonized countries, e.g. Africa? Did you attend ASOPA [Australian School of Pacific Administration]? Was this training/education adequate; did you learn anything, and how did it help you in your work? If you were a subordinate of another officer, was he any better than yourself, e.g. knowledge about administration of people of other cultures?

4. Aim

What did you think you were trying to achieve in PNG? Was this also the official view? Were you satisfied with your achievements? In which areas did you fail? In which areas of administration do you feel you made the biggest contribution? In which areas could there have been improvements?

5. Policemen

What did you think of the performance of the PNGn policemen? Did they perform better than you had expected (examples)? What was their contribution in the overall colonial administration of PNG? Did they show the same determination and zeal as you did? In which areas did they fail the most?

6. European Policemen

Were you a professionally trained policeman from the Australian police forces? If not in what capacity did you work with the PNGn police?

7. Villagers

What was your attitude to the villagers in general, and village officials in particular? What was the general attitude of the times towards the Papua New Guineans?

8. Australia

Given that Australia had no previous experience in colonial administration when she took over the administration of Papua New Guinea, what is your opinion of her performance to 1975? Was she ever a reluctant colonialist? If so, why? As one who assisted in this administration, was there anything that Australia achieved which was outstanding and different from the colonial administrations of other colonial countries during the same period? Could Australia have done better? If so, in what areas?

9. Present

What has been your occupation since you left PNG?

If you have any material on the Papua New Guinean policemen or your own work I would be happy to have them. Please send your responses directly to me at the above address. Thank you for your cooperation.

(signed)
August Kituai
PhD Scholar

GIDDINGS' RESPONSE, 3 JULY 1987

AUTOBIOGRAPHY

I was born into what might best be described as a middle-class country town family. Although both my parents had been born on the land (ie, their parents were farmers in the Wimmera and Mallee districts of north-west Victoria) my father had followed a career as a bank officer, joining in the days when a career in "the bank" was considered a very respectable profession.

My grandparents were, as indicated, farmers. My father's people (from the Wimmera), were descended from British farm labourers who arrived in Australia during the Gold Rush in 1854. My mother's people were a little more interesting. My maternal grandmother was born in 1868, in the Cape Colony, South Africa. Her earliest recollections were of farm life outside Port Elizabeth, and she had pleasant recollections of those native Africans she had contact with as a child. She arrived in Australia in 1876 and, she died as late as 1962, I have vivid memories of her and remember her stories with clarity.

My maternal grandfather's parents were Scottish born, from the Isle of Skye, having arrived in Australia during the early eighteen fifties. Both, as children, had been "cleared" (chased out) from their land during what history calls "The Highlands Clearances." In short, title to the land upon which the Scottish clanspeople lived was legally vested in the chief of each clan. After the Second Jacobite Revolt, which ended in 1746, the chiefs (land owners) found it more economical to chase their clanspeople off the land, to fence it, and to graze sheep upon it. Fortunately, the clearances on the Isle of Skye happened at the time of the Victorian Gold Rush so those displaced persons were able to emigrate to Australia and readily find employment there. Why emphasise this? For reason that my own antecedents indicate that simple people (in terms of their lifestlye) living in clanic societies can advance (or be propelled) into the modern age, and can not only cope with it but contribute towards its development. For that reason, I have always held high hopes for Papua New Guineans to do the same, and do not underestimate their capabilities or, more importantly, their potential.

I received a state school education and, in 1955, completed my examinations for the Victorian Matriculation Certificate (now known as High School Certificate). I received advice of my matriculation pass in January 1956, and joined the Administration of the Territory of Papua New Guinea on 6 February 1956, at the age of 18 years and 6 months. I was, of course, single.

DURATION OF ENGAGEMENT

I joined the Administration as a Cadet Patrol Officer in the Department of Native Affairs. After attending an orientation course at ASOPA [Australian School of Pacific Administration], I arrived in Port Moresby on a DC-4 airliner early in the morning of Monday, 5 March 1956. After completing an induction course at the Public Service Institute at Konedobu for about three weeks I was posted to the Bougainville District, arriving there on 2 April 1956.

I remained employed by the successor departments to DNA [Department of Native Affairs] until early 1978, [when] in recognition of my experience in land dispute settlement work, I was invited to transfer from the then Department of Provincial Affairs to the Magisterial service to become the inaugural Regional Land Magistrate for the Papua New Guinea Highlands Region. At the time, I was stationed at Goroka, having been a kiap in the Eastern Highlands Province since October 1964. In 1982, following the death of the incumbent Senior Provincial Magistrate for the Eastern Highlands, I was given his job to do as well as be RLM. I doubled in both roles until being posted to Chimbu Province at the beginning of 1986. I am currently the senior Provincial Magistrate for the Simbu Province.

I went through school not knowing what I would eventually end up doing as a career. I wanted an adventurous, outdoor life so my first thoughts went towards the Victoria police force and the Army. I do not have perfect eyesight so it was unlikely that I would be accepted into the Victoria police. At the age of 18 years, whilst still attending High School, I joined the Army Reserve, so I gained a little experience of what it would be like to be a soldier, and I decided that I would prefer something other than a full-time career in the regular army.

Fortunately, towards the end of 1955 vacancies for Cadet Patrol Officers were advertised in the Victorian newspapers and I decided to apply. The job suited my interests. It incorporated police work in an out-of-doors situation in an exciting country! I had long been interested in Papua New Guinea, ever since the time my father had returned from the war with stories of enchanting islands, glorious weather, sparkling clear water, verdant jungle and pleasant people to live and work amongst. It sounded good to me! I did not worry at all about the career part of it in terms of salary, conditions, promotions, etc. I was excited at the thought of working in such an exotic place, and my excitement was not misplaced.

My first posting was to the Bougainville District in 1956, and I remained there until being posted to the Eastern Highlands in 1964, apart from 1959, which I spent doing the certificate course at ASOPA. My experience has not been limited entirely to Bougainville (NSP) [North Solomons Province] and Eastern Highlands Province, as I undertook special assignments whilst I was a kiap which took me to most places like Rabaul at the time of the Mataungan troubles (1970) and to Port Moresby after there had been riots between Highlanders and Coastals there, also in 1970. As a land court magistrate, I travelled extensively throughout the Highlands and at times I worked in various parts of the MOMASE Region [Morobe, Madang and Sepik Provinces]. I have not worked much in the Papuan region. I am what used to be called, in those pre-war days when there were two entirely separate administrations for Papua and New Guinea, a "New Guinea man."

As far as likes and dislikes are concerned . . . I have a special feeling for North Solomons people because I grew to maturity, to manhood, amongst them. I learnt much from them about the meaning and practice of life, about inter-personal relationships. In hindsight, I realize that they served me better than I ever managed to serve them. I suppose the fact I have stayed so long in PNG indicates that I enjoy Papua New Guineans as a people. Indeed, I cannot say that I have disliked any group that I have worked with, except that I find Engans very tiresome. I did a lot of land court work amongst them and I found it quite difficult. They are so untrusting and aggressive but, at the same time, they are such intelligent and virile people. You need a lot of patience to work amongst them and I found the tension of working with them barely worth the effort of trying to help them sort out their troubles. It used to be like a gift from heaven to have a land court appeal in, for example, Madang to go to after a couple of weeks work amongst the Engans. How peaceful those coastal people were; how gentle, compared with those wild Engans. Don't get me wrong . . . it is not that I dislike Engans; it is just that their constant state of anxiety and tension wears me out!

I cannot say there is a place in PNG that I have visited that I have not liked. I am attracted to the dense jungle. I love the rugged mountains. I particularly like the Highland weather. Australia is my home, and I will return to it, but Australia cannot compete with PNG when it comes to natural beauty and good weather.

EDUCATION

I attended ASOPA on two occasions; during February 1956 and during 1959. As a result of these courses, I was given a sound grounding in anthropology, government law and the history and practice of colonialism. We learnt much about the British colonial experience in Africa and were grateful that we had more or less come to PNG, at least we're bringing our work to fruition, after the British had learnt the lessons of how and how not to administer dependent people. The great English colonial administrator Lord Lugard was held up to us as a model of what an administrator should be.

The training we received at ASOPA was adequate enough for the purpose it was intended to serve. It aimed, in effect to produce administrators who were attuned to the history and culture of the people they were working amongst and to demonstrate to us both the pitfalls and successes that one human group can have in governing another. The philosophy of ASOPA was progressive in that the faculty saw a not-too-distant future when PNG would govern itself, whereas we kiaps reckoned that self-government in fifty years and independence in 100 years was more likely to be the case. Of course, we sadly over-estimated!

I was particularly assisted in my work, and in my private interests, by the study of anthropology because it provided me with the tools needed to unlock the pattern of Melanesian culture. Before doing the Certificate course in 1959, I had experienced difficulty in finding out about the Bougainville people; about their property inheritance patterns, for instance, because I did not know what questions to ask them. I had little knowledge of the principles governing inheritance in a matrilineal society. Once I was taught those principles it was easy for me to apply them to the people I wished to study, and to find out what I wanted to know about them, because I was able to ask them the appropriate questions. It intrigued me to learn how Melanesian societies operated, particularly to learn the myths and legends which validated it. My work became my hobby after ASOPA, and I was enriched as a human being, not only as an administrator, as a result.

At various times I worked under very conscientious, efficient, and capable senior government officers; at least, they were senior to me in terms of length of service in PNG. Those men were good administrators. The names of Bill Allen, George Wearne, Alex Zweck, come to mind. They applied the Administrator's policy in the field with devotion and efficiency. I stress the word "efficiency." It was the ideal of those times to be "efficient." Efficiency was sometimes a cold-hearted god, to say the least. We don't hear too much about "efficiency" nowadays. Papua New Guineans have other gods of no less stature. My own nature inclined me more towards being understanding and, I hope, compassionate, rather than being efficient, or overly so.

I think that those senior men I worked with were good men. Their hearts were in the right place. They did a conscientious job for Australia and, in doing so, they did a good job for PNG. I speak broadly when I say this. Of course, it was rarely questioned that what was good for Australia was also good for PNG, and vice versa. We Australians knew best, didn't we, because we had learnt from the mistakes of the other great colonial powers? Perhaps our attitude was the same one we despised in Papua New Guinea . . . perhaps we were "bigheads."

I found amongst the kiaps I worked with—both senior to me and, as the years progressed, my juniors—that although at times they displayed certain racist behaviour and appeared to be unfeeling towards Papua New Guineans and their culture, there was always a basis of concern and an overt proudness in respect of them. I recall that whilst at ASOPA we used to compare the attributes of "our" people. I extolled the virtues of the Bougainvilleans to be the best in PNG. But those who had spent their time in the Sepik said that Sepiks were only slightly lower in stature than the Gods; whilst those who worked in the highlands said that you did not know what vigour, energy, and joie de vivre was until you had worked amongst Highlanders! And so it went on. We became immensely proud of "our" people and disappointed when their conduct seemed to let us down . . . as though when Bougainvilleans (Buka people, to be precise), disgraced themselves with Baby Gardens, they also disgraced those of us who had worked amongst them, and who invested the days of our youth in them.

That part of the question "was he any better than yourself?" In terms of having knowledge about administration of people of other cultures . . . kiaps underwent the same training, often with the same lecturers at ASOPA. So we all had a similar grounding in administration and a particular knowledge of Australian aims and aspirations in PNG. If there was to be a conflict between culture and Australian aspirations, culture would have to give way, or at least to bend out of the way.

One of the criticisms I had about the Australian kiap was that he was a fairly godless individual working and living out a secular sort of existence in a naturally religious—well attuned to the spiritual—society. The average kiap gave no thought to religion and their lifestyles were sometimes at variance with the Christian teaching. Much of the bad example of alcohol abuse in PNG today can be traced (I believe) to the example set Papua New Guineans by drunken parties, noisy and loudmouthed, that, alas, were the hallmark of European social life in PNG, and kiap social life in particular.

AIM

Essentially, I believe, we worked in PNG after World War II to develop a modern and free nation mirroring and sharing Australian values and, of course, friendly towards Australia. Papua New Guinea was to be our buffer zone, our bulwark against aggression coming out of Asia towards Australia. If we were to fight an Asian foe for the second time (the Japanese being the first) then we would fight it in PNG, not in Australia, thank-you-very-much! Sure, there was talk of the advancement of dependent people, of our duty to assist in the self-realization and self-actualisation of humankind, but I really doubt that those ideals touched too many Australian souls. But in World War I and World War II we found that our best interests were served in taking the fight to the enemy in PNG, and we believed that those interests would most likely be served in the same way sometime in the future. Those days, the 1950s were the days of the "yellow peril" (the Chinese) who were believed to be waiting [for] the opportunity to sweep down through S-E Asia, the Indonesian Archipelago, PNG, and into northern Australia so as to impose Maoist communism upon us and, probably, to take over our country in which to settle their teeming hordes. Our forefathers had done it to the Aborigines and we didn't want it happening to us in turn.

Sure, we made mistakes. We could have done some things better. But the results so far suggest that we did not blow it completely in PNG. We were wise enough to bow out with dignity and grace when the time came for us to go, and we continue to be astute enough to support PNG financially while she wastes so much of her wealth but grows to political maturity whilst doing so.

Our aims and achievements speak for themselves; a democracy which has lasted past the first ten years of independence is something. Our failures? Our inability to forge one nation in PNG which accepts total responsibility for itself. We certainly left a handout mentality as a legacy for the independent government to contend with. We tried to buy affection in PNG. We paid for everything we took whereas at times we should have taken, gratis, things which were needed for the common good and which were essential for the development of the nation's infrastructure. As an example, of later years every ounce of gravel that ever went on the nation's roads was paid for with Australian money, yet those same roads served the people who held their hands out for gravel royalties!

Particularly in the closing years of our involvement in PNG did we spend money whenever we believed that by doing so we would avert trouble and embarrassment for Australia; like Lady Macbeth—trying to keep our hands clean till the end.

POLICEMEN

I thought that the performance of the native constabulary up until 1960 [was] very good. They carried out the tasks allotted to them with perseverance, loyalty, and, in many instances, great courage—be that courage in the face of warring tribesmen or when confronted by raging rivers which they had to cross on their mail-runs. As in all such forces (the army, for instance) much depended upon the NCOs to maintain standards in discipline amongst the constables. A police detachment without a good NCO soon floundered in petty bickering and dissatisfaction amongst its members, which would have an overall adverse effect on morale. Good NCOs are able to interpret the men to their officers, and vice versa, giving good advice, guidance, and direction to both officers and men. Never underestimate the role good NCOs had in maintaining standards within the Force.... it was not all the officers work ... and keep in mind that prior to 1960 most officers were kiaps, not professional policemen.

A good NCO—one that did his best to keep the detachment operating smoothly, efficiently, and happily—was a man to be reckoned with. I recall being on patrol on Buka Island doing a census in 1956. It was my first time to do census work and I was under direction from a patrol officer. But the man who stopped me from making mistakes, who actually stood behind me and pointed over my shoulder whenever I forgot to make a coded notation in the Village Book—like B/R (birth recorded), D/R (death recorded) etc. was a Sepik policeman, a lance-corporal (First Constable in modern terminology). He was discreet and polite. He would lean across my shoulder and say, "Sir, *yu lusim tingting* [Sir, you have forgotten something]," and point to the place I should have made the notation. It was he, rather than me, who got the Buka Island census for 1956 to balance!

I soon learnt that on all occasions kiaps should listen very carefully to what their senior policemen and NCOs had to tell them. It was wise to weigh what they said very carefully before rejecting it. Indeed, the rule was "reject their advice at your own risk." If a policeman said that a river was too wild (in flood) to cross then you did not cross it. It was as simple as that. If he said it was time to make camp it was time to make camp, and so on and so on. If he said that a particular situation was so intense that to press the point was to risk a showdown and wisdom insisted that we should withdraw and try a different approach on that day, that was invariably the best course of action to follow. I was always very insistent on that point with my juniors—"Listen to the advice your NCO or *Namba Wan polis* [senior ranking constable not having NCO rank] has to give you, and disregard it at your risk."

Fortunately, I was in the NSP in that period (1956–1960), and it was a fairly peaceful place. As a result, much police work was fairly mundane sort of stuff, carrying mail, delivering messages, supervising road building and the planting of cash crops, advertising forthcoming patrols in the villages, arresting a few unlucky souls, but not many! Only once did I have occasion to see my policemen working as a really close-knit team, on guard for any eventuality. That was during the Keriaka cult in mid 1961. It is so close to the end of the period you are interested in and so relevant to your study, that I should make reference to it.

Within a number of incidents which happened during the investigation and suppression of the Keriaka cult was the night I camped with my constables (only four of them) in the rest house complex at Akopai village, Keriaka Census Division (NW Bougainville Island). We had arrested some cult leaders during the day and placed them in the *haus polis* [police house] for guarding overnight. We planned to leave Akopai the following morning and return to Kunua patrol post. Akopai was a small village situated on a knoll cleared out of the tall jungle. On the western edge of the village, astride the walking track which led into it from the coast some miles distant, was the *haus kiap* and the *haus polis*. The Akopai people and their neighbours, the Siwonapatei, were upset because my patrol had arrived the day before the cargo was due to come out of the village cemeteries, and the good times would be ushered in. Our appearance and the arrest of the leading cultists, had put that in jeopardy; so it seemed to most of the villagers who were looking forward to a dramatic improvement in their lifestyles!

We had no option other than to camp the night at Akopai before moving out the following morning. It was tense enough during the day because it was made obvious to us that our presence was not a happy one; however, our little party felt brave enough whilst the sun shone. When darkness fell it became another story! The moon rose high and bathed the village in an errie [*sic*], blue glow. The question paramount in our minds, given the events of the day and the thwarted expectations for the morrow was, would the village people attack us to set free the prisoners—perhaps to kill us whilst doing so and therefore ensure the safe arrival of the cargo. We squatted in the gloomy interior of the *haus polis* and discussed all sorts of scenarios and possibilities until our discussions were brought to a conclusion by Constable Siliven, the *Namba Wan Polis,* a native of the Wewak District. Siliven summed our situation up nicely. He said:

> What we must do throughout the night is listen for the sound of babies crying and of old people coughing. As long as we can hear those sounds we will be safe because that means that the people are in their houses. If the village goes quiet, and we cannot hear those sounds, we could be in for trouble. What that could mean is that the men have evacuated their women and children and the old people out of the village to a safe place before attacking us. Silence, therefore, means danger.

None of us stirred as he continued:

> If they are going to attack us the most likely thing they will do is fire burning arrows at our houses from the safety of the jungle perimeter. Because we are situated on an exposed knoll it will be easier for them to succeed in doing that than for us to shoot at them with any degree of accuracy. If they can set the houses alight we will be forced out of them and they will pick us off one by one in the firelight.

How did he come to this conclusion, I asked? He replied that those were the tactics the Bougainvilleans had used against the Japanese during the War with some considerable degree of success, so we might reasonably expect them to do the same to us because our situation and vulnerability was similar to that which many Japanese had found themselves in.

Fortunately, we survived a very tense and sleepless night and we were able to get back to Kunua Patrol Post without further incident. How grateful we were when, every now and then somebody would be overcome by a bout of coughing, and some baby would cry for its mother's breast. Joyous sounds, I can assure you! The point was that I had no idea what to expect that night; neither did my constables—none but good old Siliven. He had sat down and carefully thought it all out. He had listened to the stories the Bougainvilleans had told him around many a camp fire, and had stored them in the recesses of his mind, awaiting the day when he, and those for whom he felt responsible, would stand in danger from those same people.

Given the stories I had heard about Papua New Guineans—about their obvious limitations ("obvious" that is, to the die-hard colonials who had most to say about Melanesian incapabilities and contrasting them with my own experiences), I can say that the policemen I worked with performed better than I might have been given to expect. Mind you, it was not long before I learnt that Papua New Guineans were "homo sapiens" in the truest sense of the word—just like I was—not "Rock Apes" like some expatriates would have it: that some were worse but some were far better men than I could ever hope to become, and once I came to that realization it was not difficult to say that people (policemen in this instance) performed to a level that one might expect of them as individuals everywhere do, taking into account the cultural differences between society and society.

By the same token, it must be remembered that work was generally so much simpler for the constables to perform in those days compared to now, so the standard required of them was different. They did not need to be literate, but they did need to be strong and healthy. They did not need to have an indepth understanding of the law, but they did need to know what was wrong in Melanesian terms and to be sensible and perceptive when dealing with people. The best policemen were those who learnt and practiced the role of a traditional village or clan leader. He needed to be wise in his handlings with village people, persuasive and patient in his handling of them, and to be trustworthy and unbiased, dealing fairly with all men. The learning and practice of these virtues developed in the pre-1960 policeman the attributes of leadership which not only made good NCOs of them but good leaders in their home communities upon retirement. Not to say that a policeman who had spent his years away from home returned to take over the leadership of his community, but my observations over the years indicate that they did bring with them new insights and approaches towards solving old problems which served their communities better than if they had not been away at all.

As to the contribution the native constabulary made to the overall colonial administration of PNG I would ask—could we have done without them? I wonder! If we could have then it would have cost us a lot more in money and manpower to do what we were able to do with their assistance. They were a cheap (no patrol allowance for policemen and no overtime in those days) and effective means of bringing government to the people—of interpreting one to the other.

Yes. In all they showed the same determination and zeal in extending the authority of government as I did. They certainly had a harder job doing it. The long carrier line on patrol mainly carried bits and pieces of patrol equipment to make my stay in the bush more comfortable and, therefore, more endurable. On the other hand, a policeman would set out for a week's excursion in the bush with nothing more than a haversack over one shoulder and an unloaded rifle slung over the other!

Where did they fail most? Sometimes they showed a lack of discretion in their dealings with people—especially with Europeans who were always quick to criticize Papua New Guineans. I noticed that highland "Simbu" policemen (all Highlanders were "Simbus" to the Bougainville people in the 1950s) were often rude and overbearing to the Bougainville villagers, and some discriminated against them because they did not like the blackness of their skins. Coastal policemen (Sepiks must have made up the bulk of nonhighland policemen in those days) were less capricious and overbearing in their dealings with the people.

EUROPEAN POLICEMEN

I was not a policeman before coming to PNG. My only experience of a disciplined force was the Australian Army Reserve (Citizen Military Forces) in which I served as an infantry private from August 1955 to January 1956. For that reason, I knew a little of what it was to be uniformed and take orders, and to obey them. In PNG I was an ex-officio police officer (Field Constabulary) as a kiap. Indeed, I joined the administration before the RP&NGC (Royal Papua and New Guinea Constabulary) Ordinance came into effect in 1958. For that reason, in October 1956, I was gazetted as an officer of the Royal Papuan Constabulary whilst, at the same time, I was also a cadet officer of the New Guinea Force. I was, and remain, very proud to have held those titles.

VILLAGERS

My attitude to village people in general? I believe I got along well with them. At least I hope I did, and the fact that some remember me with affection indicates that I made good with some of them at least. How was one to treat "the native"? Be "firm and friendly" was drummed into us kiaps during our orientation and induction courses. They were the hallmarks of an officer of the Administration. You must always get the job done, and if you could get it done whilst maintaining a friendly disposition, well and good. You had to be firm if there was slackness or a lessening of effort on the part of the people you were dealing with, and it went without saying that you always had to be fair, having no favourites in whose favour you discriminated . . . and, of course, you never slept with their women!

I always tried to be supportive of the village officials, and they relied on me for support. Unless the kiap and the *luluai* stuck together little was going to happen in the villages. A weak *luluai* could be strengthened (in terms of his power of authority over his people) if the kiap insisted that when it came to matters affecting the Administration they would have to listen to what he had to say, and carry out those orders or instructions which he was obliged to give them.

The general attitude of the times towards Papua New Guineans? It is easy to generalize, and so hard to do justice to men of goodwill and honest intent. For those reasons, you take what I now write "with a grain of salt." Test what I have written against the attitudes and recollections of some of those ex-Territorians you will meet during the course of your studies.

I think that historically, not only in relation to PNG, we Europeans, have a failing in that we tend to judge the collective worth of a people by the extent of their technological development as a culture. I think that history would show that the less advanced in their material culture a people were the more likely they would be considered and rated less. Our forefathers enslaved Africans, but not Indians because Indians were culturally more advanced than Africans. Is that too simplistic? Perhaps, I have confused technology and culture? However, whatever the case might be on a world scale, Europeans certainly saw themselves as superior beings to Papua New Guineans. They showed that superiority in many ways including being inconsiderate of Papua New Guinean sensibilities, or by patronising them, considering them quite incapable of fending for themselves in the modern world, let alone think for themselves.

In 1956 I was propelled from a small, country town in rural Victoria into a European society dominated by planter attitudes (generally discriminatory) and regulated by the influence of a powerful Catholic Mission. The attitudes the planters had towards Papua New Guineans set the tone for expatriate-national relationships in the Bougainville District. It was, in two words, arrogant and racist. However, I cannot say that all expatriate society in Bougainville was that way inclined. The missionaries, as a group, be they Protestant or Catholic, were not. What I write is what I saw and felt in Bougainville. I suspect that race relations in the Highlands was somewhat different; that it never developed along the same lines, being less influenced by an expatriate "coastal" attitude which dated back to (and found its antecedents in) German times.

During the War the soldiers generally referred to Papua New Guineans as "Boongs," a name also given to black Americans. It is not a nice word, but is fair to say that the Aussies held the boongs in quite some affection during the War. In the 1950s "boong" was not used in expatriate society.

Perhaps a more offensive word, also with American origins, was "Coon." It was not used to describe Papua New Guineans. The only time it was used was to describe somebody who was particularly inclined towards Papua New Guineans as "Coon lover." It was more acceptable to be a "Kanaka basher" than a "Coon lover." A "Kanaka basher" was somebody who would use his fists against a native if he needed (?) to. There were a sprinkling of "Kanaka bashers" amongst the plantation overseers.

The use of the words "native" and "Kanaka" were acceptable.

In the early 1950s the then Director of Native Affairs (DDS&NA) either Allan Roberts or Jones (I cannot recall), issued a circular to the kiaps instructing them not to use the terms "PB" or "Police Boy" in their official correspondence and reports. They were police men, not "police boys," he contended. In general expatriate conversation you would often hear native men referred to as "boys." There was a common belief that their behaviour was what one might expect of boys, rather than of men, on some occasions!

Again I run the grave risk of generalising when I say that in those days (pre-1960) there were two broad categories into which all "boys" fitted. They were either "good boys" or "bigheads." The highest honour a European could bestow upon a Papua New Guinean was to refer to him as a "black white-man." This inferred that although his skin was black his attitude, manner, etc was what one might expect of a white man. Such a person was the police clerk at Sohano when I was there in 1956. Constable To Ilot (Toilet!) was an English-speaking Tolai. He was held in high esteem by the Europeans on the Island, and I heard him once referred to as a "black white-man." Mind you if that was an honour—even a somewhat dubious one—I personally felt honoured just a couple of years ago when I learnt that in the police prosecutions section in Goroka I was referred to as "the blackman." It seems that I had something of a reputation for being able to understand criminal behaviour amongst Papua New Guineans, perceptions in some instances that, normally, only Papua New Guineans would be expected to hold.

In summary: expatriates in general saw themselves as superior beings to Papua New Guineans and believed that the more like them Papua New Guineans became the better they would be! Again a generalisation, but it reflects my interpretation of the attitudes I saw around me, and which influenced my development into manhood, remembering that I was only 18 years old when I was put into this situation. Arrogant bastards, weren't we?

AUSTRALIA

Australia's performance as a colonial power can only be judged against the legacy we left behind in PNG, contrasted against the legacy other colonial powers left behind in their ex-colonies. I guess we didn't do too badly. We were smart enough to know when it was time for us to leave, and we left with a considerable degree of good-grace. Indeed, by the early 1970s we were losing control in PNG. We had the Mataungan troubles in Rabaul (1970—I served there for ten days!) and tribal fighting in the Highlands got underway again after a lapse of a quarter of a century following initial contact in the mid 1930s. It is wise to move when you are no longer wanted.

As far as Australia being a reluctant coloniser? That is a bit too academic for me to answer. Australia might plead that she was "forced" into PNG for any number of reasons, geo-political, strategic, humanitarian, etc. I suppose on balance she put more in than she ever got out of it. But that, too, is ultimately a question of economics and I am in no position to determine that. Whatever the attitude of the Australian government at home might have been, and the Australian Administration in PNG was, one thing is for certain. After their husbands, sons, and fathers returned from the Pacifc War, Australians largely forgot about PNG and maintained no great interest in what was going on there, nor how their tax money was spent there.

PRESENT

I remain working in PNG (as a magistrate) after 31 years. My wife returned to Australia last year and is pressuring me to return and join her at the end of my current contract, in December 1987. My moral obligation is to join her. Then, like a fallen angel, I will depart paradise.

AFTERTHOUGHTS

In those days it was very difficult to get a policeman promoted in recognition of the value of his contribution to police work. Particularly was this so with policemen who spent most of their careers on the outstations. It was always simpler for a member to get promoted in recognition of his worth if he served on a District (Provincial) headquarters station, but easier still if he served on one of those few stations where there was a permanent officer of the Field Constabulary (a kiap in other words). It was rare that a young man would be promoted to Lance Corporal. Most Lance Corporals were men in their thirties. It is much better now. Men are promoted as they are worthy, and it is not uncommon to see young sergeants of police. First Constables (L/Cpl) are just as likely to be in their twenties nowadays. The promotion system since Independence is much fairer than it was in colonial times.

Signed: Rick James Giddings. Kundiawa, Papua New Guinea.

Appendix 2
Interview with Sir John Guise

I tape-recorded my interview with Sir John Guise at Port Moresby, on 9 February 1985 at the Tourism Board complex at Waigani. Sir John was knighted in 1975, on being appointed the first governor-general of Papua New Guinea when it gained independence. The interview was conducted in English. I began by sketching the background to my study, including my reasons for interviewing him:

AK Sir John Guise, you were once a policeman. I am researching into the history of the Papua New Guinea police forces from 1920–1960. I believe that the indigenous members of the police from both the Royal Papuan Constabulary and the New Guinea police force made a big contribution to the development of Papua New Guinea, particularly in the early days of exploration and pacification. You were one of these early policemen. I would be interested in recording some of the experiences you had during your days in the force. The information you give me this morning will be used with similar accounts from other ex-policemen to construct a history of the indigenous policemen of the time. I would therefore appreciate it if you could kindly help me with certain information that I seek from you?

What are you doing at the present time? Are you working, and what is the nature of this job?

JG Well, I have been invited by the government to become the chairman of the National Tourist Authority, and this is what I am doing now, as chairman of NTA, a body which operates under the minister for tourism, which gives advice to the minister on policy as directed by the government in relation to tourist development.

AK How old are you?

JG I will be seventy-one on 14 August 1985.

AK Where do you live?

JG   I live at Tokarara, Port Moresby. I have lived here for many years. Yes, I did not live in Port Moresby before the war [World War II]. I lived mostly in the Milne Bay area. It was there that I was born and raised and I spent my young days before the war working for Burns Philp in Samarai. It was only after the war that I moved to Port Moresby.

AK   Do you intend going back to your village?

JG   I am in touch with my family back in Milne Bay. I go down regularly to see them and keep in touch, but I now live mostly in my wife's village at Lalaura, which is in the Cape Rodney area, and because my wife comes from there, I stay with her and my children. Most of my children, in fact, every one of my children are working. You might like to know that I am already a grandfather.

AK   How many wives have you had, and how many children did you have from them?

JG   Two children were born from my first marriage to a Milne Bay woman. One unfortunately has died, and my second-born lives in Australia; he is a citizen of that country. Then I married again to the daughter of the village headman of Lalaura, and from that marriage I have seven children. They are all working now.

AK   How far did your children go in their schooling?

JG   Yes, most of my children started in primary school of the Catholic Mission School at Badili. Then from there they went into higher education; one of them even went to Australia and attended the Warwick High School, but later completed his education at Sogeri High School. All have come up with, you know, passes and things like that, which is required of them, and every one of them is working.

AK   How many other jobs have you had since resigning from the police force?

JG   As I was trained at the Vunadidir Council College, I took up local government council work after I was discharged from the police force after nine years' service. During that employment, I tried to solve the many social problems of the people. I worked in the district office. Some of my duties included (a) making surveys of areas which wanted to have local government councils; (b) my other duty was to attend to other social problems, like marriages, land, custody of children and all these problems that we normally have in the villages. I was appointed to deal with all these problems.

AK   Do you receive a pension now?

JG   I receive a pension now but it is not on account of the fact that I served nine years on the police force; rather it is because I had done twenty-two years' service in the legislative area of parliament.

AK   Why don't you receive a police pension?

JG   I just don't think I am entitled to a pension from the police. Normally a policeman was required to serve a minimum of twenty years' service before a pension was awarded. I had only nine years.

BACKGROUND

AK   What was the name of your district?

JG   It was then known as South-Eastern Division.

AK   What was the name of your tribe, clan, and subclan?

JG   In Milne Bay we follow the mother and not the father [matrilineal society]. In that sense, Ravarata is my clan, because it is my mother's clan. All the children therefore inherit things from the Ravarata clan—sometimes it is known as Uriawa—it is named after the storm bird. When you see a rise in the wind you see these birds come out, you know, in front of the storm. They are our totem birds.

AK   What are or were your father and mother's names?

JG   My father was from Hula. His mother was Alawie, a woman from Hula but her father was a European trader, who then deserted them and left them in their village and later they were cared for by the Anglican Church. My mother was from Poretona village, in the Milne Bay area. I am the firstborn child of that union.

AK   How many were in your father's family?

JG   I would not like to go into this. I must decline to comment because it is a sad history and I do not wish to say anything further.

AK   How many were in your mother's family?

JG   I do not wish to comment on that either. I would not like to probe into my father and mother's past because they are dead now and I will have to respect them.

AK   How many were born into your family (number of males, females)?

JG   There were six boys and three girls.

AK   Are you the eldest or youngest?

JG   I am the eldest.

AK   When were you born?

JG   I was born on 14 August 1914.

AK   When did you first see a white man (Chinese, Polynesian)?

JG   I was born at Wedau beside the Anglican mission. In 1914 there was already a sizable European population in Wedau, and elsewhere in Papua New Guinea. I can't remember the first white man or woman I would have seen; it is, however, most likely that it would have been one of the missionary bodies.

RECRUITMENT AND TRAINING

AK   At what age were you recruited into the police force?

JG   I was recruited into the police force in 1945 or 1946. I was then thirty-two years old.

AK   Who recruited you?

JG   I was recruited by Colonel Elliot Smith.

AK   Did you volunteer?

JG   No, and, yes. When I was first asked to join, I said yes because I wanted to join the police force during the war. However, I was turned down because my brother was killed by the Japanese, leaving four of his children behind. I had to look after his children. My involvement during the war was as a ship hand, transporting cargo from Milne Bay to Polik Harbour, from Polik Harbour to Pongani where they were fighting in the Buna area.

AK   Did any other members of your family join the police force?

JG   No. I was the only one. My other brother was killed in the war. I served in what was then called the Labour Corps, delivering cargo to various places on the front.

AK   To those who may have refused to join the police force, what methods were used to entice these men to join the force?

JG   I think it was not a matter of trying to get people because the majority of the policemen volunteered. Most of the policemen that I knew joined the force on their own initiative. They were not asked. They just came and asked to be recruited. I do not know of any system by which people were asked to join. People volunteered because during the war many people offered their services willingly for the defense of their country. They volunteered to serve their country because there was a war on and therefore they felt that it was their duty to join the police force and fight along with the Australians.

AK   One of the requirements for joining the police force was that you had to have a good physique. Did you have a good physique at that time?

JG   I was thirty-two years old, I was a sportsman. I am damned sure that I had a good physique because I was a very strong sportsman.

AK   It has been reported that prisoners and ex-prisoners were also recruited into the police force. Did you know of these people?

JG   Yes, I knew quite a number of them. One that I knew quite well was an excellent detective. He was Sergeant Major Bagita. And there were quite a number of men who were prisoners and only after or during their imprisonment were they recruited into the force. Some of these men turned out to be very, very good policemen—very loyal, very dedicated to the police constabulary. Some of these men accompanied Jack Hides, O'Malley, Ivan Champion, and others right into the interior of Papua. Some through loyalty and dedication rose to be sergeants and sergeant majors.

AK   How were they treated by the other policemen?

JG   There was no difference. If there was any force here in Papua that had esprit de corps, of brothers in arms, it was the police force, and it made no difference if a prisoner was recruited and he went in, everyone else treated him as a brother policeman, that was all.

AK   Where were you trained?

JG   When I joined the Royal Papuan Constabulary in 1946, I was trained as policeman at Sogeri. I was there for one year.

AK   How did you get to Sogeri?

JG   As new members, we went up in the police truck and went there by motor vehicle because the Sogeri Depot had a couple of trucks—three-ton trucks. I went up in the truck with my wife and stayed there for one year. However, if we wanted to come down every weekend then we had to find our own transport to Port Moresby and back again. It was not provided by the police.

AK   Did not police regulations stipulate that only single men were allowed to join the police force?

JG   I am not too sure about that. However, I think there was a standing order, an understanding that a policeman would be given approval by the commissioner of police to be married after say six or seven years but not in the first three to five years because of accommodation problems.

AK   Who trained you?

JG   The overall training was done by Inspector Sinclair and the nationals who trained me were Sergeant Major Laura, Merire, Christian Arek, Tohian (whose son is now the assistant commissioner of police and now 1988 police commissioner) and many others that I have forgotten already. There were others like Sergeant Major Marga, Fokanau, Sergeant Kari, Kaniugan from Sepik, Sairere from Sepik, Serisis from Gulf, Memafu from Gulf, etc, but I had not been trained by them.

AK What sort of thing did you do at training?

JG We trained in arms drill. Every morning we would go on parade. And then we performed arms drill. First, if you are a recruit you were given an elementary drill, of how to stand to attention by numbers, how to turn about, how to right turn and so forth, that is necessary in an elementary training. And after that when the trainers recommend that you have passed then they issue you with a rifle and then you got to train hard on rifle drill—ie, in fighting, bayonet fighting, in practically everything.

AK How regular was this?

JG For six days a week. We started off at 6:00 in the morning and we finished off at 4:30 PM. But if you disobeyed any sergeant major you knew what you got —a "full pack" on your shoulders and you were made to run for about fifteen or sixteen miles. I underwent such punishments several times.

AK When did you have lunch?

JG We had breakfast, lunch, and supper. The police looked after us very well.

AK How much time was spent on physical exercises, how much on academic subjects, and to what level?

JG For academic subjects, we had a teacher who taught us in law and order and the various other laws that we police had to uphold. We were told about the protection of life and property, we were taught about the protection of the weak, those who were not able to defend themselves; if we saw them in trouble, we were to defend them, we were told to be friends of the people, we were told that we were on duty twenty-four hours a day. Also we were told that even if our families broke the law we were to arrest them. At no time were we to show any partiality.

AK Did you enjoy the sorts of things you did?

JG I enjoyed it very much because I think that my nine years in the force have been the happiest days of my life.

AK How long was your training?

JG It was for one year. I think no one matriculated from the depot until one was able to command a hundred men on parade ground. Failing that you were made to continue until such time that you did.

AK How often did you contact (mail, visits) your relatives at home?

JG I was very busy training etc. Why should I think about my family? I had a duty to do as a policeman.

AK How many successfully completed their courses?

JG I do not have the correct statistics but if my memory has not failed me, I think, a good number did. When I completed mine after twelve months I paraded out with several noncommissioned officers. I have forgotten most of their names but I do remember Igorabae of Ioma, Oro Province.

AK Did any of your *wantoks* complete the course?

JG There is no such thing as *wantok*ism in the police force. Every one is the same—your brothers in arms. You don't favor anyone. You are together as brothers, as esprit de corps, and you work as a team.

AK Did you receive any wages during your training?

JG Yes, I received monthly salaries, but I have now forgotten the amount they paid us—it could have been around £10 a month.

AK How did you spend your money?

JG If you were a policeman you did not gamble because if you did only God would help you escape punishment. I never gambled. I saved my money to feed my wife and children. If there was anything left, I banked it for my family.

AK Do you know of policemen who gambled and were subsequently punished?

JG I do not have any specific examples but I do know that we had very strict sergeant majors. If a policeman breached any of the standing orders such as gambling and he was caught, he was pack-drilled. That means the culprit had to carry a full pack, plus his rifle, and was drilled on the parade ground by very, very hardened sergeant majors. You had to be a man to stand up to it. That was the punishment.

AK What were these standing orders?

JG It was contained in the Royal Papuan Constabulary Act.

AK How large were your rations?

JG Oh, we were given good rations. We received rice, flour, wheat meal, tinned meat and fish, sugar, tea, salt, kerosene, tobacco, and matches. These were issued weekly. Your rations were doubled if you were married.

AK   Were there any monthly and yearly rations?

JG   Yes, the police uniforms, *ramis* were issued on a yearly basis. An inspection was carried out every six months, and fresh items given if anything was found to be missing, lost, or torn in places.

AK   How many meals did you have in a day?

JG   Officially only three.

AK   Where did you live?

JG   All recruits lived in the barracks, which were located at Sogeri, the training depot. It was a barrack you know, and there were both single and married accommodation. All single recruits lived in single barracks and married recruits lived in separate married barracks. Single recruits were not allowed into married accommodation without specific requests from the occupants. This was strictly enforced. The barracks were all built with traditional, or bush material. It was quite comfortable—beds for the single men in the barracks and in the married quarters we had a house with stove (cooking place in ground oven). We had beds, mattresses, blankets, and practically everything else that would normally be supplied to any normal disciplined force.

AK   How many men lived in one barrack?

JG   It all depended on the size of the building. If it was large it could accommodate up to fifty or more men. However, if it was small, it could only accommodate between twenty and thirty men.

AK   At what time were you allowed to return to your house, barrack?

JG   We were told to prepare for bed normally straight after the evening meals, but we could still walk around the perimeter of the barrack. But when the bugles sounded at nine o'clock we would already have been under the blanket. When the bugle sounded at a quarter to nine everyone dived under the blankets and waited for the final inspection. When that was over the lights were turned off by the duty NCO at exactly nine o'clock. By regulation every one was forced to go to bed.

AK   Did everyone go to sleep?

JG   Some stayed awake—talking quietly etc, but you couldn't be shouting at the top of your voice, otherwise you would be paraded the next morning for being disorderly.

AK   While you were at police training, what did the officers tell you about the colonial government, what it was doing, what it was trying to achieve, and what your contribution or role was to be in the process?

JG   I think I will not use the term *colonial* because we are now an independent nation—and I have been in the forefront—when I was in the force,
the police was the mainstay of the government. The police force was the most
important body because it carried out law and order in its bounds on behalf
of the government. Therefore, we were told to be extremely loyal to our
officers whether white or brown, in other words, we had a rank and file—lance
corporal, corporal, sergeant, sergeant major, sergeant major first class. The
white officers occupied the most senior of the ranks irrespective of whether
they were professionally trained or not. We were told to be loyal to our
NCOs, loyal to our officers, and to be friends of the people. When on patrol,
going to restricted areas, we were not to mistreat the people and also not to
steal from their gardens but to ask for any food and not throw our weight
around and be cruel to the people. Those sorts of things were told to us on the
parade.

POSTING

AK   After the completion of your police training you were considered a colonial government employee, if I could use the term again. What did you think of
yourself?

JG   In answer to your question, after training I considered myself to be a policeman serving the country through the Australian government that was then
administering our country. But first and foremost I considered myself to be a
policeman.

AK   Where were you posted?

JG   I was first posted to Abau to investigate a murder charge, and after the
completion of my training program I was posted to police headquarters as the
regimental sergeant major.

AK   Were any of your *wantok*s posted to headquarters?

JG   In the police detachment, we had about forty men, there were about three
men from the Milne Bay area and three from Wedau. Otherwise, there were
men from Rabaul, Sepik, Highlands, Gulf, Western Division, etc.

AK   Did you have a choice in the decision for posting?

JG   No, you don't have any choice whatsoever when you are a policeman. Decisions are made for you by your senior officers. In any case, in any disciplined
force such as the police or the army those in the junior ranks do not participate in the decision-making process. During my time, when you were posted
anywhere we did not question their decision. If we were told to proceed to a
certain area, we just went.

AK   How many were in your group?

JG   The detachment in the police force, which was known as the headquarters detachment, consisted of about thirty constables, two sergeants, one lance corporal, and two full corporals.

AK   Did you feel any apprehension on your first posting?

JG   No, I did not.

AK   How did you get there?

JG   I first came down from Sogeri and went to the headquarters at Konedobu. I was posted as the regimental sergeant major so my duties were mainly those of supervising other policemen.

AK   How long were you at that post?

JG   I was there for nine years, or until I resigned from the force.

AK   Did you have any other postings before your resignation?

JG   No. I finished when I was still regimental sergeant major at headquarters. I was going to sign on for another term after my nine years, but unfortunately there was a change of commissioners and the incoming commissioner was not the type of man that I had much respect for, so I resigned.

AK   What was your substantive rank when you finished training?

JG   Sergeant major first class [regimental sergeant major] for police headquarters.

AK   Was that the highest you ever achieved or were you promoted to any other rank?

JG   By law no indigenous person could be promoted to become an officer. We had to stop at sergeant major first class. That's the end. No further promotion was allowed for Papuans, and I believe the same rule applied to the New Guinean police.

AK   When did you receive that rank?

JG   In 1946 or 1947.

AK   What did you do to receive this promotion or rank?

JG   I do not know. It was up to the commissioner of police. Maybe I had a bit of education or something.

AK   Were you satisfied with the promotion?

JG   Yes, I was satisfied because I liked my police service.

AK   Did the promotion mean extra rations, money, etc?

JG   Yes.

AK   How much money were you paid?

JG   Well, it was about £18 a month. And you had rations like any other constable but you received double rations. If you had a child, your rations increased.

AK   How could people tell you had been awarded a promotion?

JG   People could tell by the badges you wore. For instance, a sergeant major second class had a "coat-of-arms," the English coat-of-arms.

AK   Were any ceremonies held when these promotions were given?

JG   Not necessarily, only in exceptional cases.

Equipment

AK   Were you given rifles to use?

JG   Yes, we were issued with .303s. These were issued to us as soon as we went for training and each person was responsible for its upkeep. But, if something happened to it, it was your responsibility to get a replacement.

AK   Was it loaded at all times? If not, when?

JG   You were only allowed to load your gun while on patrol in restricted areas. The officer gave you a certain number of rounds, and you had to account for every one of those rounds and the object of your target.

AK   How did you feel when you were issued with a rifle?

JG   I did not feel much. I just thought that the gun was part and parcel of being a policeman. In other words, I felt that it was a normal thing for the police in those days to be given a rifle after training. It did not make me feel big and strong and powerful.

AK   Did you ever use the rifle?

JG   Yes, we used the rifle in bayonet training.

AK   Did you ever shoot a man?

JG   No.

AK   Do you know of people who may have shot people?

JG   No, I don't. I think that perhaps you could find it in history books of those big patrols. But I personally do not know of policemen who deliberately set out to shoot people in cold blood. I have heard of people being shot in newly contacted areas, but as I never ventured beyond the precincts of the headquarters I am in no position to make serious comment on your question.

AK   When could policemen shoot to kill?

JG   In self-defense.

SYMBOLS OF AUTHORITY OR POWER

AK   Can you describe the uniforms that you were given: color, special features, shape, size, etc?

JG   It was a *rami,* or laplap, which was dark blue and had a red piping. The same applied to the shirt; it was dark with red piping, and if you were a corporal you had stripes on your shoulders. Then you had a belt with ammunition pouches in it plus a scabbard and bayonet. You would then put the *rami* around you and place a red cover band underneath it. Then you had your belt and your scabbard on it for anchor—the brass chain, that was the anchor, and then you would have the jumper, which is worn inside the *rami.* The cover band had a red pipe in it too, on the sleeve. If you were a corporal, then your marks of insignia would be on both arms.

AK   When could the uniforms be worn?

JG   They could be worn on parades, on duties, etc. During parades we wore the official uniform—shorts and *rami.* At other times we wore the khaki uniforms. Three of each were issued to us. They were supposed to last us for one year. Then the quartermaster would come and inspect them, and if he found any of them to be worn out then he recommended their renewal.

AK   When did you use a bayonet?

JG   Only in training.

AK   What did you feel when you were given all these things?

JG   Well, the first thing I felt was, "I am now a member of a police service." That was the first reaction that came through, that I was now a member of a regular police force which has a very, very proud history in this country.

AK   Did it make you feel strong and powerful?

JG   Well, it gave me a sense of, you know, now I am a policeman. I am now the man responsible to the government, and I am the upholder of the laws that are made by the government and for the protection of life and property.

WORK

AK   What type of work did you do in your position?

JG   In my position as the regimental sergeant major of the police headquarters I was in charge of (a) the police (policemen) responsible to me, (b) all the office staff who worked on records, criminal investigation records, etc, were responsible to me because I was going through the courts (courts of native affairs and court of petty sessions), returns of which were coming in from the districts, and they were all sent to police headquarters. I also had to go through the court returns and try to locate any miscarriage of justice. I managed to pick out a couple, I think, of a magistrate exceeding his powers in jailing a policeman under section 14 of the Police Act. I then pointed this out to the headquarters officer. An appeal was launched to the Supreme Court and the matter was quashed. He had, in fact, exceeded his powers. At half past five I took the parade group and marched them up to the government house with the band and lowered the flag, paid our respects to the administrator, [and] as we returned, I would give the "Eyes left." That was my other duty. Then in the night I was in charge of the night guards in the Konedobu area.

AK   Did you enjoy doing what you did?

JG   Very, very much.

AK   Did you perform any other tasks apart from your regular responsibilities?

JG   Yes, regular police work required guarding government house, guarding Konedobu area, and looking after the parade and so forth. I had to make inspections of the barracks to ensure that they were kept clean and tidy, and all those heavy responsibilities in the office where I was also in charge of secret and confidential matters passing through to the police commissioner, etc. My duties were therefore demanding but very interesting. There was something to be done every minute.

AK   In centers like Port Moresby, what specific jobs did the other policemen do (law and order, prison warders, apprehension of criminals)?

JG   I will say this much—I think that the constabulary of the Royal Papuan Constabulary, when I was a policeman, upheld law and order. They had discipline, very, very strong discipline that ran right through the ranks, and the way they carried out their duties towards the protection of life and property and the way they carried out their patrols every day and every night was something that I look back now and say "I wish it was done again" because it contained the criminal element; it contained it very well. I feel that foot drill, rifle drill, the arms drill on the parade ground which is not being done now, I believe, I don't know, but I hope that that sort of drilling is not discontinued but carried on, because when you are on the parade ground and drilling by firearm it teaches you and trains your mind to be instant. I don't want to see the police force only concentrating on modernizing the force; it should also maintain some of the hard traditions established by the old policemen.

AK   Could you talk to your European officers at any time?

JG   Some, some whom we were used to. I used to speak to several of the ones I knew, especially if they were in charge of any criminal investigation and you were part of the team. I had respect for professional policemen, men who were policemen in Australia and then came up here and became police officers. I had some degree of respect for them. I had a lot of respect for training officers like Sinclair, the commissioner of police, etc, but I had very little respect for say some carpenter in Port Moresby who applied for a police job and was given one in among the senior ranks. He may have been a struggling carpenter and two weeks later he is a full-fledged policeman occupying a senior position with perhaps two or three pips on his shoulders—these were the types that I did not like to communicate with because I felt that I, as a policeman of many years, should have seniority over the new recruit. I used to think, "Why should I start saluting a man who was a carpenter last week and a police officer today?"

AK   What did you do during your spare time?

JG   I played cricket, football, and visited friends.

AK   What was the nature of your relationship with the other policemen?

JG   Very, very well indeed, because we had an esprit de corps right through-out the whole rank.

AK   Did you experience any in-fighting?

JG   No. The only time there was a bit of a squabble was when the army fought some civilians, which we then tried to stop. I cannot recall any incident in which the police fought with the army, at any rate, not in my time.

WAGES AND LEAVE

AK   At what times did you receive your money?

JG   Always at the end of the month; we were paid monthly.

AK   Was any money deducted from your pay at any time?

JG   No.

AK   How often did you *go* on leave?

JG   At the end of every three years we were given recreation leave of three weeks for each year, so at the end of three years we had nine weeks' holiday.

AK   Did you receive your pay in bulk sum?

JG   Yes, we would be given our nine weeks' pay. We were supplied with rations and our fares paid to our home areas.

MARRIAGE AND CROSS-CULTURAL LINKS

AK   Did you say you had married your second wife before you were recruited?

JG   Yes, it was my second marriage. My first wife from Marshall Lagoon died in 1943, and when I joined the police, I was already married to my second wife.

AK   Did you pay bride-price for both your wives?

JG   No, not in the true sense of the word, but I did offer to pay something. The relatives did not propose anything to me but I gave some money anyhow. It was something like £40 cash, plus rice, flour, and things like that. However, the only condition laid by my mother-in-law was that I had to make a promise to see that all her daughter's children remained in her village. My wife is a daughter of a village constable. I gave that undertaking and I have kept it to this day.

AK   Did your second wife speak your language?

JG   My wife understands my language but does not speak it; I understand her language and I can speak only a little of it, but I understand it all. My wife is very conversant in Motu. I can speak Motu.

AK   What was your wife's relatives' reaction to you?

JG   This is a very difficult question. It's yes and no. Let me go through and see if I can get it correct. This happens everywhere in Papua New Guinea today. If you are a man from Madang and you are married to a Milne Bay girl and you try to live in Milne Bay, you will never be accepted. You will always be a man from Madang, a foreigner. That would apply even if you had lived for thirty years in Milne Bay. The society will always consider you as not a part of them. The same principle applied to me. I've spent thirty-three years in my wife's village. I know I am accepted but nevertheless I make it my duty at any public meeting to make it clear to them that I must not pretend to be a Lalaura man. It is better to face up to the fact that I am really a man from Milne Bay, and only my wife and children belong to the Lalaura clan. It is better that you accept the truth of it, but I shall remain at Lalaura and when I die I have asked them to bury me amongst the coconuts that I have planted. That is all I have asked of my in-laws.

AK   Did you introduce anything new to your in-laws?

JG   No. The people of Lalaura are natural carpenters. There is no need to teach them about carpentry, gardening, etc, because they know everything.

They are good gardeners, fishermen, etc. There is little that one can teach them. They make bigger canoes than the Milne Bay people.

Sexual relationships

AK It has been alleged that some policemen were engaged in illicit activities, particularly in matters dealing with sexual relations with both men and women. Is this a fair allegation?

JG If you are saying that only the indigenous policemen were involved, then it is not a true allegation because I have heard that both the indigenous policemen and their European officers were involved in procuring women when on patrol.

AK Do you know of any examples?

JG No. I do not. It is difficult for me to answer that question because most of these incidents took place while officers and their policemen were in the bush on patrol. These things did not take place in Port Moresby. I can understand why they do it. Many of these men were young and single but they did not have girls around for them to let their emotions out in that way. It is only natural for any men or organization to react in that fashion when they have been denied sex for long periods. So the natural thing for men to do is if an opportunity existed they would go for it.

National consciousness

AK Were you then aware of the different identities of the two countries?

JG In those days, because we were two different identities, I considered myself to be a Papuan. So wherever I went, I considered myself to be a Papuan. Many Papuan policemen also felt the same way. I am sure the New Guinean policemen had similar sentiments.

AK Where did you learn of these differences?

JG I was taught in mission schools that we were natives of Papua. The differences were strictly enforced. I do not know whether you realize the hard fact, but even in 1962 when I went over to Lae I was asked by the customs man right in the Lae office whether I had a visa to be over there. And that was as late as 1962. Even today you can see evidence of the differences in the policies by the way people from both sides of the border refer to each other. You only have to scratch a man under the "skin" and ask him where he is from, and he will reply, "I am a New Guinean." It is only natural; it has got nothing to do with a sense of unity at all, but it's a legacy that has been left behind, and such was the extent of the indoctrination that it has remained in people's minds for this length of time. But today, I think, most people prefer to be called Papua New Guineans.

AK Did you have a feeling of nationalism?

JG   There was a feeling. I cannot say whether my nationalistic aspirations included New Guinea but I certainly had a nationalistic fervor for Papua. But within the police force although the Papuans could say "I am a Papuan" and a New Guinean could say "I am a New Guinean," a New Guinean constable did not refuse to obey instructions given by a Papuan noncommissioned officer. There was complete obedience to the senior officer, complete obedience. In my own experience, there was never at any stage a refusal to follow orders, no one ever said, "You do not do this to me because I am a Papuan." No. That was one of the many reasons why I stated earlier that the nine years that I spent in the police force were some of the best years of my life, because it showed me the spirit of comradeship which no other organization has been able to teach me before or since.

GOVERNMENT

AK   What did you think of the government?

JG   Frankly, I never liked the government, perhaps because I spent a long time working for private enterprise, Burns Philp & Company, from 1926 to 1942. It was only when I joined the police force in 1946 that I had a glimpse of the government. But I was always suspicious of the government and what its intentions were in the country. Always at the back of my mind I believed, even when I was a policeman, that the day would come when these foreigners would leave the reins of control in our hands and they would go back home. I did not trust them either. I will give you an example. In 1960 I applied for a job which fell vacant. One of the conditions was that the applicant would need to have some police training. I applied, thinking that my police background as well as my reponsibilities in the prosecutor's office would make me the best candidate for the job. It was a magisterial position for the Central District. However, I was told by the former secretary of the Department of Territories that I could not be given the job because I was just a dropout from grade 4. I told the Department of Territories that from that time onwards, you will be sorry because I am entering politics, and by the time I am finished you will be cut away from this country. I entered politics in 1960 and was there until I retired. And I lived to see the day when not only self-goverment but independence was achieved. And I became the country's first governor-general. My words to the secretary came true. I had said this to the secretary because I felt I had been discriminated against.

AK   Were you impressed with European wealth?

JG   Well, all governments are powerful. If the Australian government paid in proportion to the amount of work we did, we would have had the same amount of wealth as the Europeans. They received much more money for doing very little.

AK   Did you fear the government?

JG   Yes, only when I worked for Burns Philp. It was the strength of the government over private enterprise that made me fear it. I was thrown in jail twice. I hated the government.

AK   Why were you thrown into prison?

JG   One was for riotous behavior, and the other was for drinking liquor when I was a native. I received one month for the first offense, and six months for the second.

AK   Why did you want to work for the government?

JG   I wanted to learn, because after spending twenty-odd years with private enterprise, I thought that by coming into the government I could learn the inner structure and the inner powers of the government.

AK   Did you have any idea of the purpose of the colonial government and what it was trying to achieve in Papua New Guinea?

JG   I do not really know how to answer this question, but let me put it this way. While employed in the police force I, in my own way, looked into the structure of the government and the power of the colonial government upon the people. It was from there that I had this urge to try and do something to diminish that power and to transfer that power into the country. I observed, as I sometimes worked in the summons office, during my police career, that some of the senior government men went down to Australia and did things which were against the laws of both countries, Australia and Papua New Guinea. Naturally, summonses were sent up from Australia to prosecute these men. The commissioner would often call me into his office and say, "Serve this notice to so and so." And I began to think after a while that even a white man, a government officer, had his Achilles' heel somewhere. At the same time I had many good friends in the government, because one had to be human, to accept the fact that in spite of disagreements you are bound to have some very good friends. Dr John Gunther was a very good friend of mine—oh, he was very close to my heart.

AK   Were you loyal? Were you ever disobedient?

JG   Well, since we were policemen, I could say we could not be disobedient. In private I would grumble about something that I did not agree with but I could not do it in public. We carried out orders without question. The same applied to my colleagues. I will give you an example. During the colonial time Ela Beach had a notice—"No dogs allowed." My son, with other Papuans, had come up from Australia (I was the sergeant of police). They went to swim at Ela Beach but they were told to get out. So my son then came to me and said, "Daddy, you are the sergeant major of police. Can you help us, because we have been chased off Ela Beach with no reasonable excuse? Can you take the matter up to those in authority?" I replied, "Sorry son. I can't. I am a policeman working within the system which rules us now, but you can complain, and I as a father will operate from the back but never will I do it in public."

AK   Did you operate from the back?

JG   I did. It was one of the reasons why I was determined to go into politics, to break this stronghold that Europeans had in the country.

AK   How could anyone gain entry through the fence at Ela Beach?

JG   You could gain entry through the gate but there were policemen posted there twenty-four hours. Being a policeman serving the system you could hardly kick against it because you were bound by an oath of loyalty. If I were to have kicked against it and consequently dismissed, what would happen to my wife and children? My very security would have gone. Only Europeans were allowed entry. Natives entered at their own risk.

AK   What happened to those found there illegally?

JG   We had a section in the Act called petty breach of discipline. I think, if my memory is correct, it was section 14. Now petty breach of discipline is every-thing—if you had a dirty belt, if you had not shaved, if you did not salute your superior officer, if you were lazy, if you were sitting down and a sergeant walked in and you did not stand, if you entered the gate without lawful authority, all these were considered petty breaches of discipline; it covered any little thing you did. You could be fined 10 shillings, £1, or even £2. Worse, you could end up confined in the barrack—but if it was a serious thing like punishing some-body, then you would get a jail sentence for a month.

AK   Can you tell me again about your involvement in the war?

JG   I worked as a civilian when my application to engage as a policeman fell through. I assisted in running supplies on a boat from Milne Bay to Polokana in the Cape Nelson area. From there we brought it to the front lines in Pongani in Sanananda when the battle of Buna was raging. But we were not considered as a fighting unit because (a) we were civilians; (b) we were working for the Aus-tralian government at 17 shillings and 6 pence a month, with rations; (c) we did not take any oath of allegiance like the police or the soldiers. Those in the dis-ciplined forces such as the navy, army, AIB [Australian Infantry Battalion], the secret service, PIB [Papuan Infantry Battalion], NGIB [New Guinea Infantry Bat-talion], etc, all these men took oaths of allegiance. They became part of the disciplined forces which actually took part in the war. They were entitled to rib-bons, gratuity payment, and so forth, which most of them have not yet received from the Australian government. That was the difference between them and my-self. We, on the other hand, were civilian laborers attached to the army. Though many of our men died (I lost a brother and a cousin during the landing in Milne Bay) we were still not part of the fighting men. To this day, I have not received any compensation for the death of my brother and cousin.

ADDITIONAL QUESTIONS
AK   Were you ever a businessman?

JG   No. I was never a businessman.

AK   Was your time as a policeman exciting?

JG   I think the most exciting time in my life as a policeman was attending the Queen's coronation in London in 1953. We went as a contingent of the Royal Papua and New Guinea Constabulary. We stayed at the guards' depot. We were in London for six weeks. I remember the occasion well.

AK   Was there any stage that you felt you wanted to leave the police force, that you could not stand it any longer?

JG   The worst thing being a policemen is that you must always know that you are serving the public who will always say "help me, help me," but will not turn around to say "thank you" to you. But these same people would not hesitate to report you to your seniors if they saw you winking at a girl, or criticize you and blow it out of all proportions to make you look like the ugly policeman. That's the hard part of a policeman's life. When you join the police you must always remember that you are serving a public who are mostly ungrateful. They will never reward you for the good that you do but judge you on the little faults that you make.

AK   How would you describe your relationship with government officers?

JG   Yes, they varied. There were some who were very good men, but, you know, being a policeman I had to respect all my superior officers irrespective of their idiosyncrasies. In an official capacity I respected all my officers. In private, I got along with only a few. I never could get myself to really respect those men who joined the police force who had no professional training. Part of the reason being that I had long years of service in the force but a new European recruit saw fit to boss me around. In the bush, I think, the kiaps had a lot of time for their police because the police were the "eyes and ears" of the kiap, assistant kiap, or district officer. But in the urban situations where I worked the situations were quite different. Officers were not in constant fear of attacks from hostile tribes, did not need shelters to be put up for them for the night, did not require as much guidance for getting through thick bush, finding tracks, etc, so they kept their distance and only on official duties made any contact with us. I had genuine respect for professionally trained policemen who were recruited and brought up from Australia.

AK   Can you give me any examples of the former recruits?

JG   Yes, there were many, but I will only give you one example. There was this man who was self-employed, and worked in his shop in Port Moresby. A police officer's position became vacant and he applied. Naturally enough he was given the job. Within the week he was made a police officer signified by his two pips. He came in to the police headquarters where I normally worked in the morning. The time was about 9:30 AM. He walked past me and I stood up and said, "Good morning, Sir." He not only said not a word, he did not acknowledge my greeting. He returned and looked down at me, and I stood up and said, "Good morning, Sir." He gave no response. He returned a third time and I remained seated and he said, "Do you know that I am an officer?" I got up and said, "Yes, I do know." I said that I had stood up each time he passed and paid my respects. He replied sternly, "No, you did not." He then asked me to go through the whole process and repeated his actions. I had to salute him each time he did it. After that time, I had no time for that officer.

AK   Did you ever receive invitations to their houses?

JG   Only sometimes. It was because I knew them and they knew me, some from way back when I used to be employed with Burns Philp in Samarai and during the war.

AK   Who were your favorite government officers you worked with?

JG   There were a number of them. In fact, it would be quite impossible for me to name all of them since so many officers won my respect. One I can still remember with some affection was Kemrich. He is dead now, poor bugger, but he was a brilliant officer. He worked hard and he played hard. He was one man, out of many, who principally taught me about public administration, about police work, court procedures, and elementary law. He was a brilliant man. He was born in Milne Bay, spoke Suau, Dobuan, Trobriand Islands, Goodenough Islands, Motu, Pidgin, and English languages fluently. He spoke Suau before he learnt English. He was a Cambridge graduate. He was the most multilingual person around at that time. He died in 1984, in his wife's village, Patawe [phonetic], Fergusson Island.

AK   Did part of your job on the station involve magisterial duties?

JG   Yes, that was part of my duty. I continued with it when I eventually left the police force. I think I was still doing that job until about 1958 or 1959. It entailed advising people with social problems before they went to court. I can say with some certainty that it was, for a while, my principal job. In fact, I think, I held two jobs, both as a social worker and as a local government officer. Some of the problems that I dealt with were related to marriage break-ups, custody of children, land ownership of property, etc. I always tried to the best of my ability on behalf of the government to solve them before they came to court. On two occasions, I actually attended court on my clients' behalf: (a) to defend in the court of native affairs a man charged by the police for stealing. I won that case. (b) I also defended a man in the district court, a man who had committed incest with his daughter and his daughter became pregnant. So I was called in by the then district commissioner to defend his case, and I did. The case was moved to the Supreme Court, but I was not allowed to defend the man there because the judge said I had no qualification.

AK   The use of force—did the police hit and kick people?

JG   That is natural in any police force, whether it be in Australia, England, America, or Papua New Guinea. It's natural for any policeman to do, especially when you know that that man is telling you lies. And I will admit that, when in cross-examination, when I was a policeman, when I knew that the facts had been revealed, when I had witnesses to prove that this man did something but kept on denying, I had on occasion struck a few, and kicked a few on the arse. I make no bones about it.

AK   Did a sergeant or kiap ever order them to punish people?

JG   No. I think most of them were spur-of-the-moment reactions, it was never a premeditated action. For instance, if a policeman was sent out to investigate a murder and all the evidence pointed to one guilty person but he insisted on his innocence and continued to glare at you and said, "Oh, *lau diba lasi, lau diba lasi*" [I do not know], I would smack that man on the face.

AK   Were you officially instructed to exact punishment?

JG   No. We were not allowed to lay a hand on anyone without legal authority from our superior officers.

AK   What happened to you if you were caught?

JG   Oh, yes, we could be sent to jail if the matter was serious and we were caught. I punished a few stubborn men and women but was never reprimanded because we policemen stuck together. We corroborated our evidences when we went to court to defend each other.

AK   Can you give me an account of a single day's activity?

JG   On a single day, the bugle sounded at 6:00 AM. We got up immediately and made our way to the parade ground and went through rifle drill between 6:00 and 7:00 AM. After this we returned to the barracks for breakfast. During this time the night duty men's reports were collected and submitted to the commissioner of police or to the headquarters officer. When this was over and breakfast had been eaten the police were lined up (only the headquarters detachment) and their day's duties were assigned to them. Most of this was fatigue, or manual work. Those who had night reponsibilities had the day off. At about 8:00 AM, I had to report to the office and attend to all the correspondence (kept them in their respective files). For some days that was all I did until twelve o'clock. Work commenced again at 1:00 PM and continued until 4:30 PM. At 4:30 PM we performed physical drill again for one hour and thirty minutes. At 5:00 PM the bugle sounded again for parade. At about 5:30 PM we prepared ourselves on the parade ground and marched up to Government House. At exactly 5:45 PM the flag was lowered to the accompaniment of the bugle and then [we] returned—[we] gave our general salute to the administrator as the commandant of police and then we came down, and some were marked out for guard duties, where the police, you know, would be on foot patrol—protecting life and property. That would be the average daily activity of those who worked on the station.

SUMMARY—PRESENT AND FUTURE

AK   Did you enjoy life as a policeman?

JG   Very much indeed. I think that my nine years in the police force were the happiest times of my life because I learnt to be brothers and team mates with people from all parts of the Territory of Papua New Guinea; it also taught me to look at other people as people of this country and not as people coming from Milne Bay, Sepik, or Madang. No, in the police it taught me that you were a man working with an esprit de corps, with a high degree of discipline. Loyalty to your officers, and loyal to whichever government is in power for the benefit of your society. This is what I learnt in the police, and I still carry with me today the hardened discipline that I had been taught in the police. I will say again that the nine years in the police force have been the happiest years of my life because I learnt about work, learnt esprit de corps, learnt to be brothers with other people—the police force taught me all that. I think that ideas about nationalism first started off with the police force.

AK   Did you encourage any of your children into the police force?

JG   I wanted some of my sons to become policemen, but it was one of my ambitions that never got fulfilled, as none of my sons showed any interest in becoming one. I was sad about this prospect because a lot of my police friends, men who instructed and drilled me in the depot, now have sons occupying important positions in the police service.

AK   Have you noticed any changes in the force?

JG   Yes. The Royal Papua New Guinea Constabulary is an armed constabulary, that means that in times of war, the force is there to defend and assist the military towards the security and safety of this nation. It started off as an armed constabulary. It had the ranks of lance corporal, corporal, etc, right up to sergeant major first class. The changes that I have observed have taken place in the following areas:
      (a)   They have dismantled the ranks of corporal and lance corporal and have called the constables first and second class. In my view, that has no meaning within the proud history of the force.
      (b)   I am very sad indeed to see the lack of and breakdown of discipline among the policemen of today. For example, during my days in the police service you couldn't chew betelnut during working time. If a corporal called you and you were a constable, you would not just go up to him and say, "Hullo," but you stood to attention. All these small things I valued very much, but these things have almost disappeared. I don't know but I have this feeling that the changes today are helping to make the once-very-proud history of the Royal Papua and New Guinea Constabulary as an armed constabulary into disrepute. They want to make it resemble the New South Wales police. And that is a sad moment in my life. If ever that change takes its full course, I will be the saddest man in Port Moresby, because why should we imitate other police forces when

we have our own proud and very historic disciplined force. I see these changes as being detrimental to the force in Papua New Guinea.

(c)   Another change I have seen is that the academic standards of the recruits have been raised. Today they want young men and women who have completed grade 9 or 10, or those who have reached a high level of education. They seem to disregard the great potential that is in a grade 6 dropout. I can't see that that should be the case now, when in the past prisoners were recruited and some of the most outstanding men in the service were convicted criminals —they had been the men who had reached high standards of efficiency and loyalty. In that sense they should continue to recruit young men who show potential in practical things rather than high academic achievements. At any rate, the world is not made up of high-grade people only, it is also made up of people who might fail in some pursuits but excel in others.

(d)   The most disturbing thing I have observed today is, if a police officer gives an order it is never obeyed immediately. The constable sort of looks at the order and then questions whether it's right for him to carry out his instructions. Now I have seen them, and speaking to one very senior officer (who knows me very well), I pointed out the development of this new phenomena within the force and he replied, "My dear uncle, you have been a policeman, and you are right." He said when they issued orders to these highly educated people they questioned their officers before actions were taken. They talked about their rights first and then decided to carry out a certain instruction. I think that once a police force starts doing these sorts of things, then it is heading downhill. The maintenance of discipline now is well below the discipline that we experienced with men like Sairere, Laura, Bapi, Pokanau, Maga, Sevese, Memafu, etc. All these old men, you know, were the best in the force during my time. That type of discipline is no longer there now. I am very sad indeed.

AK   Have you got any further comments to make?

JG   No, no. I think I have mentioned all the relevant things. But I will end up on this note. Once you are a policeman, you will always have that attitude of being a policeman. In other words, once you are a policeman, you will always be one.

AK   Thank you very much Sir John Guise. Could you give me permission to use some of this material in my thesis?

JG   I would give you my permission on the condition that I see your first drafts.

Appendix 3
Interview with Petrus Tigavu

The interview, which was conducted in *Tok Pisin,* took place at Yomba, within the township of Madang, on 16 April 1985. Tigavu was visiting his son, John Tigavu. John was then employed by Jant, a Japanese timber company operating out of Gogol. At the time of the interview, Tigavu was in good health. He died the following year, 1986, from illness. By the time of his death, Tigavu had not returned home to his village in Yandera, Gende [Bundi]. The title of this work, *My Gun, My Brother,* was inspired by Tigavu's recollections of his affection for and belief in the inherent strength of his gun.

PRESENT

AK What is your name?

PT My name is Tigavu Petrus.

AK How old are you?

PT I do not know.

AK Have you been in Madang long?

PT No. I have been in Madang town for fourteen weeks. I will return to my village in either June or July.

AK Are you married?

PT Yes. I have two wives, the first wife lives in Banz, and the second lives in my village in Yandera. I had three children, two sons and one daughter. The first-born son was from the first wife. He is dead. The second wife has a son and a daughter. Her daughter received very little education. She is now married. My son completed form 4, became a policeman but was discharged, and is now working for Jant, the Japanese timber company. His name is John and he shares my surname. I am happy that he has been educated because I was never educated myself, and he often helps me with money, etc.

AK   When did you retire from the police force?

PT   I retired in 1977, then I was earning K50.00 a fortnight. I am now receiving K108.00 a month, which is slightly more than what I earned as a policemen in 1977.

AK   What was the name of your district?

PT   We have always been under the Madang District.

AK   What is the name of your clan?

PT   My clan is called Yadima. My subclan is Kaubaginarawa.

AK   What was your father's name?

PT   My father's name was Dimiri. He had three brothers. My father was a warrior. Six children were born into my family, four died, there are two of us left. I was born in the middle somewhere.

AK   Can you give me an estimate of your age?

PT   I do not know the exact date but I was quite a big boy when the first missionaries came and settled at Guiebi. [He may have been about ten years old. Tigavu heard about the missionary's arrival while he was still in his village in Yandera. Tribal wars in Gende were still on. His father therefore brought him, with the rest of his family, to a place of refuge near where the missionaries had come to settle.] The people called the European missionaries *poroi krunaga* when they first arrived at Guiebi. [In Gende cosmology *poroi krunaga* were one of the dreaded spirits who lived in caves on the lower altitudes. They were predatory spirits who, for their daily sustenance, drank human blood.] Some spoke of them as returned dead ancestral spirits. They searched around the excreta to see if they had dropped any valuable beads, kina shells, etc. At first only three of them arrived. I learnt later that two of them were priests and the other a Catholic brother. They brought interpreters from Ramu, with whom we had trading connections in feathers, women, salt, cassowary birds, etc. I was scared when I first saw them. I would not even go near them. When I went there they had disposed of their tents and lived in a thatch-roofed house. Two houses were still under construction. Later I worked for them as a domestic servant. When the war came, the missionaries left me in charge of the station at Guiebi and Bundi and they left—I do not know whether it was for Madang or for some other place.
     I did not know the war had come to an end until one morning the soldiers were in a very jovial mood. They threw each other into the water, let off gunshots, and jumped about in merriment. I found out later that the war had come to an end. I was then in North Goroka. Consequently, the soldiers left. I wondered whether to return home to Yandera or remain in Goroka. I was afraid to return home to Yandera because the area through which I would be

traveling was inhabited by some people of the Goroka region. I'd heard long ago from my elders that these people were cannibals, so I did not fancy walking through the area alone. I had been reflecting on this when police master *Masta* Kramer asked me to join the police force. I accepted because of my fear of the alleged cannibals on the way to Gende. Otherwise, I was already sick and tired from eating improperly cooked rice, poor accommodation, etc, during the war and I was definitely not in the mood for performing a similar job again. Had it not been for my fear of the Goroka, I would not have joined the force. *Masta* Kramer brought me down to the training depot near the Kefamo River. This was in January 1944. I knew it was 1944 because when I enlisted that was the date mentioned to me. There was no other Gende with me. I was the only one from my area. At the depot my army uniform was taken off me and I was issued with khaki, or police uniforms.

TRAINING

AK   Was your police training done in Goroka?

PT   Yes. You know that Goroka is a very cold place, but during training we were made to get up between 5:00 and 6:00 in the morning. If anyone continued to sleep, a bucket of cold water was poured over his head. We then cleaned up the barracks, folded our two blankets, made our bed, and ensured that our sleeping place was neat and tidy. We then went and had a "shower" despite the mountain cold. After, the bell rang and one of the officers shouted "Cups!" for our morning breakfast. We drank black tea, flour, and biscuits. After breakfast, we returned to the barracks and changed and waited for the call for us to fall into line. New recruits wore laplaps only for drill. We did all manner of exercises until 12 o'clock for rest and lunch and resumed at 1:00 PM until about 4:00 in the afternoon. After 4:00 PM, recruits from the Goroka area wandered off to their villages. I normally stayed behind at the depot. We ate our dinner at about 6:00 PM. The food consisted of *kaukau,* tinned meat, and local vegetables. As I remember it now, we were not given a lot of food while at training, so much so that our intestines grew very small. [Surely they must have had flat stomachs from constant physical exercise.] We also ate plenty of brown rice and vegetables. I used to trade with the locals for extra food with my tobacco, matches, etc.

The barracks were made of traditional bush material; beds were woven bamboos; there was a lock on the door; no pillows were issued and no boxes. But they gave us rucksacks. There was nothing on the floor [dirt floor]. The bugle sounded between 8:30 and 9:30 PM and we all went to sleep. The NCO called "Lights out!" and the lights, in all the barracks, were turned out. If lights were seen in any barrack after the call the occupants of that barrack were punished en masse in the morning with pack-drills.

Even after training I did not know much about what the colonial government was trying to achieve in Papua New Guinea. At training we were instructed to look upon the rifle as *our brother* and *cousin* and to take good care of it at all times, because without it we may not live to see our villages again.

I finished training the same year I was recruited in 1944. After the completion of my training, I was posted to Banz with another policeman. I remained in

Banz for eight years. During those eight years, I supervised men working on the highlands highway. Other policemen were stationed in other areas of the highlands doing basically similar jobs to myself. I still remember a few of their names—Buase, Mindwao, Wadow, and Kuagle of Simbu. At that point in time, many of the policemen were involved in the construction of the road from Lae to the highlands.

SEXUAL RELATIONSHIPS

AK   What was your relationship with women?

PT   Officially there was a regulation that all policemen had to follow. At no time were we allowed to interfere with women. We would only make a move if a girl showed an interest in us. If I was interested in a girl, I was allowed to make friends with her parents and they would allow me to see their daughter if they so wished. If a policeman or trainee had been seeing a girl or married woman in secret, and it was found out by the husband or parents and reported to the officer in charge, the punishment for it was severe—one was pack-drilled for a week, fined, given a prison sentence, received a demotion, or expelled from the force.

While I was at training, I did not do any of those things, because I was new and did not wish to get into trouble. But later on I did fool around with women, but somehow I always escaped punishment. Much, I think, had to do with the fact that I was trustworthy and was a reliable worker. So maybe a policeman's work was more important than random affairs with women.

For instance, when I was in Minj my officer begged me to get married to one of the local girls because if I didn't it would put my police career in jeopardy, suggesting that I should settle down with one. I would not have a bit of it and refused to heed his advice. Part of the reason was that I had become a Christian while still in Gende. If I were to get married, I was going to do so in church and preferably to a girl from my own village. The stronger reason, however, was that most of my peers in the village were not yet married and if I were to marry first they would react adversely to me. So for a time, I refrained from getting serious with any of the girls that I courted. But my kiap insisted. In the end, in about 1950, I gave in to the kiap's wishes and got married to a local girl. After this I was transferred to Kundiawa. The reason for my transfer was that at Minj I shot dead a man who tried to escape from police custody. He was one of two men I shot dead from the area. A short time later, a Simbu policeman accused me of sorcery and we had a fight. Consequently, after my leave I was brought back to Goroka for further training. While there I had an affair with the wife of a Manus sergeant, Angai. I was caught by him and he charged me and his wife [a Simbu woman] with adultery. As punishment, I was transferred to Wabag. After a while I was transferred to Koroba in Southern Highlands. I think therefore that because I was a hard and reliable worker my officers turned a blind eye to my affairs with women. Of course, I was reprimanded and transferred to stations which I did not fancy working in, but these alternative forms of punishment were better than expulsion.

NATIONAL CONSCIOUSNESS

AK   When you joined the police force, did you consider yourself a Papua New Guinea national?

PT   When I joined the police force, I did not consider myself as a man working for Papua New Guinea or as a New Guinean working for New Guinea. These are new concepts. At the time, I considered myself to be a policeman from my own area, Gende.

AK   What were your views on the colonial government?

PT   Before the war and my enrollment in the police, I was naturally scared of the representatives of the government, kiaps, policemen, etc. But after my experiences in the war and police my fears disappeared. I then looked upon the government as a protector, and us policemen were its agents. We were told that we were the Queen's men, and that it was for her sake that we should work hard, be loyal, and show respect. Myself and most of the other policemen did not see the Queen in person. However, the majority of the policemen were very loyal. The older policemen set good examples, and this was carried on by those that came after us. They carried on the good tradition established by the earlier recruits. I enjoyed my years in the force. The force has been good to me. It even pays me a pension now that I am retired. However, I do not think I would join it again if I were to become young again because I think I had enough. I was happy I was in the force, but I would not want to repeat it. I am sad to say though that the policemen nowadays are slack. They do not work as hard as we did. They do as little work as possible and yet receive a lot more money than we ever did.

PROMOTIONS

AK   What was your rank after training, and what did you have to do to be awarded a promotion?

PT   After training I was what they called *Nambawan polis,* a policeman without a rank. After some time with that status, I was made a constable, and soon after I was made a senior constable. That was when I was stationed in Minj. I was promoted to such a status because I retrieved three guns that had been stolen by the people of one of the villages in the area. On another occasion I went and brought back medicine for a dying kiap. As I had walked through hostile territory, they rewarded me with the rank of corporal. In 1971 I was made a sergeant due to my seniority.

AK   Were you given rations?

PT   At that time we had big rations. On some of these stations I was in charge so I made sure I had a lot for myself and family. But generally speaking we were not paid enough money, but this was compensated for with big rations.

AK   When were you issued with a rifle?

PT   All policemen were issued with a .303 during and after training. When it was issued to me I was told that symbolically the gun was to be like my father, my brother, and other people I loved most. If I took good care of it and never left it out of sight, I would be saved and would be able to return home to see those that I loved. When I was armed with the rifle, people got scared of me, not because I threatened them with it but because they had seen how dangerous the rifle could be when used. Naturally they held the holder with awe. So much so that in the areas I worked, people held me in such esteem that my reputation and popularity as a policeman grew from strength to strength. In the end, I had the same reputation as some of our very best traditional fight leaders back home.

AK   Did you kill anyone with the gun?

PT   Besides the two men I killed in Minj, I also killed another in Kundiawa. One day I was supervising some prisoners carrying a slaughtered cow from the vicinity of the present Kundiawa airport to the hospital. In between the airport and the hospital word came to me that a *wantok* patient from Nombri, Gende, had only minutes ago died in hospital. I quickly told the prisoners to sit and have a rest while I raced over to the hospital to check on the information. Sure enough my *wantok* had not a breath left in him. Before his death, I had heard that he had been a victim of sorcery. The sorcery had been performed on him by some Simbu men. I said little and returned to the prisoners. Upon my arrival, they got up and lifted their load onto their shoulders. I hurried them along. On the way to the hospital there was a slope. As we descended, two prisoners slipped due to the weight they were carrying, and for minutes were literally buried under portions of the cow. Immediately I had flashes or images of my dead *wantok* covered in blankets waiting to be buried. I could visualize the Simbu sorcerers hard at work mixing their deadly poison. I became very angry. Simultaneously, I picked up the nearest object in sight, which was a banana stock, and placed it heavily on one of the fallen men's head. He did not move from where he had fallen. He was dead after a few minutes. I did not kill this man with a rifle, but then I was a policeman. I was not charged with murder, because everyone thought he had died from the fall. However, I was transferred back to Minj. While there, I shot a prisoner trying to escape from police custody. Later, we discovered that he had dug a hole through the pit. The prisoners of that time slept in big holes dug in the ground. Policemen's houses were built on top of these holes. As we had no pit latrines away from where we lived, we relieved ourselves into this hole where the prisoners slept. [Confirms Tawi and Niyil Angi's testimony of imprisonment in Kundiawa and Ialibu, Southern Highlands.] I was not charged.

   I should perhaps make myself clear. I did not harm people needlessly. Often people attacked me first and I only got into action afterwards. I was often bothered by my conscience for I was a Catholic. For this very reason I went and spoke to the Catholic priest at Mingende. During this conversation I asked Father Anton what I should do when people attacked me, and he replied, "You are working for the government. If people attack you and you do not retaliate, people will not listen to you. In order to win respect from the people, you must retaliate because only then will people around here pay heed to what you tell them. If that means shooting people, you will have no alternative but to carry out that action." After that I shot dead many people, especially men who were belligerent, men who attacked my patrol or disobeyed our orders. My kiap's instructions were to shoot to kill if people became troublesome. With *Masta* Jim Taylor and Kiap Costelloe we killed about a thousand people at Gumine. It was like this. The people of Gumine threatened to cut the bridge there. The people's threat was conveyed to *Masta* Taylor and Kiap Costelloe. They arrived and overnighted at Gumine within the vicinity of the bridge. Policemen were assigned to guard them. I, with other policemen, kept a vigil at both ends of the bridge. During the night, the men of Gumine attacked from the other side. We attacked with such ferocity that when it was all over, I estimated that around a thousand men had been shot. Bodies were sprawled all over the place. Some could not be buried due to the exhaustion of the men left to bury them. The birds had a feast for weeks. This incident took place at the site of the present Catholic mission station. At no stage was I brought before the court to testify for those killings.

EQUIPMENT AND SYMBOLS OF AUTHORITY AND POWER

AK What type of uniforms did you wear?

PT First, I was given khaki uniforms. Later I was issued with uniforms which we called *zulu,* [sulu] or laplap. We wore those uniforms every day. Much, much later we were given shoes [after the 1960s]. I think we were given sets.

AK What did the uniforms make you feel?

PT First, because the police forces of both territories were combined I thought that we should try and establish a good relationship with the Papuan police and work hand in hand. Second, I considered myself (because I was older) to be the father of other policemen who were much younger than myself.

WORK

AK What types of work did you perform?

PT In the beginning I worked on the station. I did foot patrols around the station, sometimes at night and sometimes during the day. I also worked on shifts. Our noncommissioned officers were very strict. If they caught you sleeping, or talking with *wantoks* you were punished with a pack-drill, etc. Sometimes I supervised prisoners at work, saw to it that they did as they were told and got fed in the afternoon. During the course of the week, I also had a day off. When I was promoted to more senior positions, I was given supervisory jobs, supervised other policemen, etc. Later I did a lot of work. Patrolling was very important during those early days. I was very good at it and consequently I was credited with promotions to lance corporal, corporal, sergeant, and sergeant major. I worked in places like Jimmi Valley (with Jim Taylor & Kiap Costelloe), Porgera, Lake Kopiago, and Mendi. These were places where I carried out the bulk of my patrol work.

During our patrols we often had twelve policemen, quite a big group. Every new territory we traversed was considered to be enemy territory. I did anyway. I can still recall the many sleepless nights I had then because as the most senior policeman in both rank and age, it was my responsibility to ensure the safety of the rest of the policemen, the carriers, and the patrol officer(s). During the old days when I patrolled with Jim Taylor and Kiap Costelloe we shot dead a lot of men, but later when peace had been brought amongst the communities there was no more shooting. We used the .303 carbine Enfield.

AK What were your views on the people that you contacted?

PT I considered them to be like men and women from my own village. Many were, of course, wild. I knew, for instance, that when only men appeared from the bushes, an attack was imminent. If women accompanied their menfolk, I knew that everything would be all right. I did not consider myself to be better than them because only a short while before I had been like them myself. Just because my fortunes had changed did not make me feel any different from them. If, however, they attacked, we retaliated with stronger force than they used, but mostly in self-defense. After all, we were only human.

AK What were your views on prisoners?

PT I treated them humanely. If they made attempts to escape, we gave them more severe punishments. On every patrol we had carriers. They carried all our stuff. People from one area would carry cargo to one spot near their enemy tribe and leave and we would then recruit new carriers from there to carry our stuff to or near another tribal area. We paid them with salt, beads, knives, axes, etc. We treated them humanely because the success of our patrols depended on their assistance and guidance.

AK How would you describe your relationship with the kiap and other European officers?

PT Before, the relationship was very distant. Any contact was in the line of duty. Later, the relationship was cordial. My kiap would sometimes offer me a cup of tea but he never gave me any drinks [beer, whisky, etc].

AK What did you do on your off-duty days?

PT I stayed mostly at home and did my laundry, etc.

AK Did you play any sport?

PT   On Saturdays we played soccer. We called it "pilai horse." The games played now-a-days are clean and orderly. During my time games were chaotic. Often a player would leave the ball and physically attack an opponent, even punch and kick players.

AK   How would you describe your relationship with the other policemen?

AK   I got on well with the other policemen. I never did get on well with the highlands police, especially those from Simbu.

AK   How long were you in the police force?

PT   I was in the force for thirty years.

AK   How did you spend your money?

PT   I spent most of it on clothes and extra food. At other times we used the money to pay off my family's debts. Later, when I had children, I saved up my money for my children's school fees.

AK   How often did you have leave?

PT   After every three years, I was given three months leave. I was given extra rations, etc.

AK   Were you satisfied with your pay?

PT   Looking back upon it now I think it was quite adequate. The policemen now-a-days are earning more money for doing less and inefficient work. The work I did then was hard and dangerous but I, with my colleagues, did good work.

AK   Did you pay bride-price for your wives?

PT   Yes. My relatives assisted me to pay. My wife from Banz could speak *Tok Pisin,* and I taught her Gendeka, my language. Her relatives did not object to our marriage. I learnt her language and could speak it very well. A final word on policemen's relationships with women. Many a policeman's term in the force ended abruptly because of his involvement with females. The government's law was explicit: Unless the girl or woman showed interest a policeman should never initiate advances.

WAR

AK   Did you involve yourself in the war?

PT   Yes, I did. But it was before I joined the police force. I did not have the faintest idea what the war was all about and when it had arrived in Papua New

Guinea. I only knew that something was afoot when the missionaries in both Guiebi and Bundi left and asked me to "hold the station's keys" for them until they returned after the war ended. So for a short while I traveled back and forth from Guiebi to Bundi in order to keep a vigil on the mission properties on both stations. A short while after the missionaries had left a patrol officer came and advised me, "If you see people with uniforms coming from the Ramu River side, run away into the bushes. If, however, they approach from the opposite direction they will be friends, you must do all you can to guide them to safety." One day while I was in Guiebi I saw a long line of people coming. It was obvious that they were not village folk, so I climbed a big tree and watched their advance closely. They arrived, passed my tree, and walked down to the station. Some, I could guess, were mission workers from the coast. I could tell this from their clothes, hair, and physical build. Some Simbu people also accompanied them. This I could tell from their songs, dress, and language. Among them were some policemen, three of whom I could tell were Papuans. They had very big hair. I had seen policemen before this meeting. The Papuan policemen also had different uniforms. I descended from my hiding place, walked down to where they were, and exchanged greetings with them. I then told them that I was left in charge of the station during the missionaries' absence. I then opened the door to the missionaries' supply house. The party spent a day there and left on the following day. During their short stay they slaughtered two cows, three pigs, and helped themselves to food and vegetables from the mission garden. Before they left, the policemen told me that another group would be coming down in a matter of days. Sure enough, another party arrived from the direction the first group had arrived. There was one white man, a white female (who I later learnt was a Catholic nun). At that time, I had thought her to be a very strange person, clad in that funny looking outfit. There were also two Simbu females, dressed in traditional costume, *kina* shells, etc. The white man's name was Jim Graham, I think. He asked me where I was from and I told him that I was from one of the villages nearby. He shook my hand and told me that he was a district commissioner or assistant district commissioner in Madang, but had run away from the Japanese. Before he and his party left, he gave me some money as well as a letter to give to the next white man who came that way.

Three days later literally hundreds of men—soldiers, both black and white, descended on me and caught me by surprise. The European officer was a *Masta* Ken. I handed over the district officer's letter to him and he read through the contents. When he had finished he looked me up and down for what appeared to be an intensely long moment and then signaled to me that I should join the group. From there on I was appointed a guide for the soldiers and men. That was my main contribution in the war: I was a guide. Since I was familiar with the geography, language, and tracks of the people of the immediate area and even beyond, I carried out this task without fail. I was given army uniform. The main area we walked in was the area between Bundi, Ramu, and Morobe, particularly around the present township of Lae and Nadzab airport. All this happened in 1942. In 1943 I was flown up to Goroka and was stationed there until the war ended in 1945. And I was recruited into the police force after that, that is, after the end of the war.

The relationship established between the various groups in the army was warm and cordial. There was no animosity between the whites and blacks. We ate together, shared smokes, watched films, etc. We all behaved as if we were all born and brought up by one mother. At that time, I did not think I was fighting to defend Papua New Guinea. I was not paid for my services. We were only given rations and lots of it. As compensation payment, I was given K1,000 last year, 1984. Our officers did not promise us anything. Besides, at that time we were all like pigs, it did not occur to us to ask for payment. We had no education.

I did not kill any man during World War II. We all underwent a lot of humiliation, slept in very poor conditions, ate little food (sometimes we ate raw rice).

I could tell the war had come to an end from the actions of our officers in Goroka. One morning they got up and there was much exaltation, rejoicing, etc. They threw each other into the pond. They were generally in a spirited mood. It was obvious that something nice had happened. Soon after the officers were airlifted to Port Moresby. I was not scared to "fight" in the war. I won four war medals, three stars. They all got burnt in my village at Yandera.

I was recruited into the police force, and I trained in the Police Training Depot at Kefamo. We called it Highland Bush.

I give you my permission to use whatever information in this interview for your work.

Appendix 4
Interview with Sasa Goreg

Following is a transcript of my interview with Sasa Goreg at Gabsongekeg Village, Markham, on 12 August 1986. The interview was conducted in *Tok Pisin*.

PRESENT

AK What is your name?

SG My name is Sasa Goreg. Goreg is my Christian name and was given to me when I was baptized by a representative of the Lutheran missionary in this very village. At that time all the older people were baptized first, leaving the children and babies till last.

AK Do you know how old you are?

SG No. I do not know my age. When I was recruited in 1939, I was already a young man. It is possible that I was born in the early 1920s.

AK Have you always lived in this village?

SG Yes, my mother gave birth to me here, and apart from the time I spent in the police, I have lived here for most of my life.

AK Are you married?

SG Yes, I am married. I have been married only once and to one woman. She is still alive and is still married to me. From this marriage we had eight children. The first two girls and two boys died in early childhood. Later we had another three girls and one boy. Two of the girls have married. The elder one is not married and lives with me in the village. My son is married. My second daughter is married to a Papuan.

AK Have all your children been educated?

SG Yes, they all received some education. They, however, did not achieve high qualifications, and most returned to live in the village.

AK Do your children help you with money, clothes, etc?

SG I am proud of my children. They assist me wherever they can with work in the gardens, clothes, etc.

320

AK   When did you leave the police force?

SG   I left the force when World War II ended in 1945. I then returned home and have been here since. I do not receive a pension.

BACKGROUND

AK   What was the name of your district, and clan?

SG   It was Morobe. My clan's name is Moswara.

AK   What was your father's name?

SG   My father's name was Lola.

AK   What was his status in the village?

SG   I do not know much about my father. He died when I was a little boy. My mother's name was Onoun. She was big physically. She came from Givesi village. There were five in my family. The first two girls died at an early age. Two others died of old age, and I am the only one left in the family.

AK   Were there many Europeans here when you were born?

SG   Yes, when I was born white men had already established themselves here, in particular, the Lutheran missionaries.

AK   Were you earning any money before your recruitment?

SG   I was not engaged in the cash economy but I did earn some cash through selling garden produce—coconuts, bananas, betelnut, etc.

AK   Where did the Lutherans establish themselves?

SG   Over there, at Gavmaju.

AK   Did you have any form of education before you joined the police force?

SG   The mission started up a catechist school and we received instructions in Yabim. We were in school for about six years.

RECRUITMENT

AK   Can you describe your physical features at the time of your recruitment?

SG   I did not know my age then. But I was a young man. I had not grown a beard yet, but there was hair under my armpits. Recruiting officers came and asked for young men to join the police force. They came to my village and requested likewise. The recruiting team consisted of a kiap and one policeman. I do not remember the name of the kiap but the policeman was from Kaiapit. His name was Tatawa. All the young men recruited were sent to Rabaul. They made camp at the kiap's house. Then they asked for volunteers from among the young men. I stood at a distance from the scene of the activity because I did not think I was old enough to enlist. So I just stood and looked on with great interest.

Later the Kaiapit policeman approached me and asked, "Young man, what's up?" I replied, "No, I am just observing the recruiting procedures of the kiap." He then asked me if I were a little bit interested in enlisting. I answered that I was keen but that I did not think I would be able to do a good job. As soon as I made that statement he encouraged me by saying, "Go up to the kiap and tell him that you are interested." I went up as he had suggested and approached cautiously. He took my measurements on a nearby tree [post] brought for the occasion. I was accepted.

AK   Did you volunteer?

SG   At that time I did not wish to join, but it was the encouragement of the policeman that gave me the incentive.

AK   What year were you recruited?

SG   I was recruited in 1939. Three of us from this village were recruited. There was an older man who had been a policeman on an earlier occasion but had left temporarily due to some sickness. During this occasion he made attempts to re-enroll but was refused on account of his age.

AK   Was any kind of force used to entice reluctant young men?

SG   Some of the young men refused to enroll because they were scared of losing sight of their village, family, and people. With these young men, cajolery was used, but even this did not provide the incentive for them to enroll. They could not be pushed either way.

AK   Did you have a good physique?

SG   At that time every effort was made to recruit only the best young men—healthy, agile, wise, and nearly all were above average height. Any young man who showed any sign of defect was rejected. I am big physically and at the time of my recruitment, I had an excellent physique. Generally the policemen of the period were tall and broad shouldered.

AK   Do you know if any ex-prisoners or prisoners were recruited on account of their good conduct?

SG   Yes, I knew of a few of these men. They had been jailed for murder, rape, theft, etc, but proved to be good men and possessed good physique, were intelligent, and hence their terms were either reduced or acquitted outright on condition that they enrolled in the police force. There were one or two from Sepik, Morobe, and Madang. They were very loyal and worked with great diligence. Many were exemplary policemen and served with distinction.

TRAINING

AK Where did they bring you for training?

SG From Gabsongekeg we walked down to the Markham River, made a raft, and floated down to Lae. We stayed in Lae for a few days until the government trawler came from Salamaua. [At that time the headquarters or main administrative center was in Salamaua.] That ship picked us up from Lae in August and brought us to Salamaua. We waited in Salamaua for a ship for four months to take us to Rabaul. During the four months in Salamaua we helped the older policemen build houses, chop down trees, bamboo, cut grass, etc. We finally left for Rabaul in January 1940.

AK Where was the training depot located?

SG It was located in Rabaul itself—near the hospital in Raipidik, near the volcano, Mount Kabiu.

AK Who were your instructors?

SG There was a corporal from Waria. His name was Sepila. He was from Garaina. He was my main instructor at the depot. There was a Manus policeman. His name was Selep. Both these NCOs instructed us.

AK When you got off the ship, who came and greeted you and brought you to your sleeping quarters?

SG When we jumped off the ship two constables came and welcomed us on shore. One was from Kaiapit. His name was Awaru [phonetic] and another from Morobe. His name was Kiwere [phonetic]. These two constables worked on the ship and helped recruits on and off board. They brought us to the depot and issued us with blankets, trousers, knapsack (khaki trousers). New recruits were not issued with shirts until sometime later. The same applied to the issue of rifles. We were given three trousers each. After a period of initial training we were issued with rifles, shirts and other relevant items. When we finished training we were issued with a new rifle, water bottle, shirts, caps, shirt numbers, etc.

AK At the depot, what did you do on an average day?

SG When the signal went I got up, washed my face, then returned to the barrack and tidied up my things, cleaned the rifle, and got ready for exercises on the parade ground. We drank tea, with flour [pancakes], etc, before we proceeded onto the field.

AK   What types of exercises did you do?

SG   We started off with elementary training, drills, marching left, right, left, etc. After we excelled in this we were given rifle training. For target training we dug a big hole on the side of the mountain and across it were placed numbers: one, two, three, four, etc. During target shooting practice we had to lie down on the ground before we took aim to shoot any of the numbers. If your aim was good and you shot any of the numbers, then you were considered a good shot. You were thought highly of because that was some indication that you would be a good policeman. Precise and accurate shooting was emphasized for an individual's own protection when on patrol. If during a bush patrol you were attacked and you were slow in taking aim, then you would probably end up being killed by spears, arrows, clubs, etc.
       We rested after each exercise. After lunch we started again at about one o'clock and did not finish until about four thirty. We then returned to the barrack, cleaned the rifle, our clothes, washed, and attended to general cleanup of the area. We would then play sports, etc. Later we walked around the premises of the depot, Chinatown, visited friends if they were laboring on plantations close to the barracks area. But we had to be back at a certain time—before it got too dark—or risk punishment. We were not issued passes for these short walks, but if we thought we would be late for any reason we asked for one.

AK   Did you enjoy the kinds of things you did at training?

SG   Yes, very much. I really enjoyed it because I knew that at the end of it all I would become a policeman.

AK   Did you have any rest days?

SG   Yes, we had rest days—we would work on shifts—only one day.

AK   What did you do on your off days?

SG   I did my laundry or walked around Chinatown. During that time many women from Kavieng or Namatanai were employed by Chinese people in Rabaul as domestic servants. Many police trainees befriended (mama long ol) them. These women sometimes did laundry for us.

AK   Did you ever think about your family back in the village?

SG   No. I never did. Well, because my parents died while I was a child, I did not really think there was anything for me back in the village. I had a brother and sister back in the village but they were taken care of by a lapun tumbuna [grandmother] and a cousin sister.

AK   Did they pay you any money during training?

SG Yes, but not good money (not enough). At the end of every month we received five shillings. Rations for the bachelors were sent to the mess. Married men received their own rations—for their families and friends. These applied only to NCOs. No new recruits were in this category. We ate in the mess.

MARRIAGE

AK Were there any married men in your group?

SG No. Only young men without wives were recruited. Later, after serving for some years, they were allowed to get married if they found a suitable partner.

ACCOMMODATION

AK Can you describe the barrack you lived in?

SG When I went there, there was one big barrack. It was a two-story barrack with corrugated iron roofing. It had a timbered floor and beds placed on top. There were two doors at either end of the building. All the new recruits undergoing training slept in the house. Let me qualify this statement. All the new recruits slept underneath, and those in the advance stages slept on the second story with the NCOs, etc.

AK What did your instructors tell you about what you would be doing as a policeman?

SG Apart from the physical exercises, we were taught how to tell the time because it was going to be important in our job. We also were told about the laws of the government, the types of work that we as policemen would be doing after we completed our training. When we became "real policemen" we would work for the government, protect the "kanaka" and refrain from making unnecessary trouble. They briefed us on these things. If I was posted to some outstation I would go and remain there and conduct bush patrols, and generally maintain law and order. During this time tribal fighting was still raging throughout much of the land. These were trying and difficult times. It was your responsibility to ensure that peace was maintained among the communities. That meant that if there were any fights, policemen had to go in and stop them, often at great risk to themselves. These were some of the things we were taught at the depot. Of course we did not take notes but we memorized those things in our heads.

AK Where was your first posting?

SG I was at the depot for six months. I was not sent anywhere after. I remained at the depot because they wanted me to instruct incoming recruits. They said I had a good record and that I would make a good instructor. I was happy they had confidence in me. I spent the whole of 1941 in the depot at Rabaul, then World War II came in 1942.

AK What was your rank after training?

SG I was a constable when I finished training.

EXPERIENCES DURING THE WAR

SG In 1942 the war came to Rabaul. At this time Michael Somare's father [Samara] was there. He was one of the first sergeant majors in Rabaul, and was put in charge of the depot. That was when I was there in 1939. When news of the war came in early 1942, soldiers from Australia came to Rabaul and they stayed with us at the depot. The war years were taxing times for the police. We were given the task of protecting the villagers, properties (government or villagers'), lives, etc. It really was a mammoth task. We had to keep an eye out for the bridge, oil station, etc. We kept vigil day and night. We hardly ever slept. We worked very hard. When the Australian soldiers came they brought with them machine guns. They constructed barbed-wire fences along the beach to prevent the Japanese from making a quick entry from the shore. After these preparations we waited for a little while before the war came.

   Then the Japanese attacked Rabaul. Many planes came and dropped bombs on Rabaul. Their ships shelled the shores. But the ships did not come quickly to the shore or wharf because of the machine guns. It therefore kept them at bay for awhile. There was a heavy exchange of artillery fire between the Japanese planes, ships, and the Australians on shore. It did not last long. The sheer force of the Japanese drive defeated the small Australian defensive quite overwhelmingly. The onslaught lasted for only two days—Thursday and Friday. The Japanese took over on Saturday morning. Their ships then moved to the shore. The small Australian force knew they had no chance of success, so instead of waiting around to be slaughtered, they abandoned their camp and ran away at night. Our police master said we should leave Rabaul too. So we left Rabaul and went to Toma—near the airport [probably Vunakanau]. The idea was that we would go and guard the airport so that if any Japanese parachuted down at the airport we would shoot them down. There were two of them—the police master himself and another from the police band—the former was Sinclair, and the latter was Crawley [David]. During the time when the Japanese were about to come we went to the ammunition store and were issued with bullets, etc, so that we were armed.

   From Rabaul we started at six in the evening. As I remember, it was difficult on the policemen, especially those who were married and had children. The distance was long. We walked and walked. Sometime around twelve o'clock, the two officers asked us to sit down and rest. Everyone was rested. I do not have the exact numbers, but there were definitely hundreds of policemen. We all sat down and ate hard biscuits and tinned food. Japanese planes were still flying around in the dark sky above. Supplies were carried by the new recruits. This consisted of rice, tinned meat, biscuits, etc. Recruits therefore were used as *kago bois*. The policemen carried only their rifle, cartridges, etc. We arrived at Toma at about midnight. We rested for about an hour. It was there that tinned meat and biscuits were distributed among the policemen, families, and others in the party. As Rabaul was the training depot, there was always a great number of both senior policemen and new recruits undergoing training. In 1942 it was no exception. Therefore the number of men, women, and children that walked to Toma was quite big. The food supplies that we brought with us were not enough to feed us for long. So we were put on rations. For instance, the first evening four men had to share one tin of biscuits—one whole and a half of biscuit for one man. After the meal we slept until about three in the morning, when our two European officers and New Guinean NCOs woke us— we brushed our sleepy eyes and started again on the march.

To our surprise we discovered that there were literally thousands of Australian soldiers hiding in the bush there. Like us, they escaped from the coast from another direction and were scouting around in the hope of catching Japanese soldiers who might dare to land at Toma airport. We left them there and walked some distance to a little village in the mountains—and rested again. I have forgotten the name of the village. When we arrived, our officers asked us if everyone had arrived safely. The answer was in the affirmative. After a cursory investigation of the area, our officers told us to sit down and rest. Though it had been raining in the area and thick clouds hovered above us, they wanted us not to congregate near big trees, stumps, etc, just in case the Japanese discovered our presence and started shooting at us.

After this the officers instructed the new recruits to boil rice for lunch. Because it had been raining, the rice had to be boiled in a small hut. In the midst of this activity, the Japanese warplanes spotted the smoke and attacked us. We took cover in the nick of time and escaped serious injury. Unfortunately one of the large pots of rice was hit so badly that the pot, rice, and water were spread all over the hut. After a short while the Japanese pilots, realizing that they were hitting at an ordinary village, left as quickly as they had come. When they left, we rebuilt the fire and boiled more rice. After the meal we walked farther up the mountain. At about three in the afternoon, we came upon a school area, still in the vicinity of Toma—there were teachers, pupils, a *luluai* and a *tultul*. They were more than happy to see us. We stayed at the teachers' quarters. Our European officers asked the teacher why the schoolchildren were still there when a war was raging. The children were all sent home. We used the school facilities as our sleeping quarters.

It was on a Friday. We walked about the school yard and from this vantage point looked down at Rabaul. From there we could see vividly Japanese warships. Most were berthed along the Rabaul Harbour, and we knew immediately that the small resistance there had been overcome by the sheer force of the Japanese military might. Our officers called us together and told us to dig a big hole in the ground. It was a big, deep, long hole. It looked somewhat like a trench. Into this hole we buried our rifles, uniforms, and any other material that belonged to the government. We followed a set procedure. When it was completed the officers stood at each end of the hole. NCOs from each squad directed their men to the edge of the hole and to hand over anything they had which belonged to the government. The officers then passed the items down to two sergeants inside the hole, who were responsible for their arrangement. When everything was buried, it was covered over with corrugated iron and timber, after which soil was used to cover the whole of the hole.

When this was over, we fell into line, and our two officers instructed us on what steps we should take next—most of which consisted of how we should escape from the Japanese and make our way back home. They said, "You must not follow us." They then appointed a sergeant from Talasea who was familiar with the surrounding area to guide us to Talasea and later to assist us to travel to the Siassi Islands, after which we were to make our way to Finschhafen. The European officers were either airlifted or shipped to either Finschhafen or Lae to be evacuated to Australia.

The indigenous members were given no such treatment. We had to find our own way home, even those of us who not only had to cross a group of islands but even an ocean. Ships were not readily available. Our travels to West New Britain were full of hardships. Some tribes on the way were not very friendly. Some even sought to attack us. We heard rumors that some villagers had deliberately planned to attack us. They obviously thought we were traitors, that we had run away and not helped fight the war. As you know, we had buried our guns and uniforms at Toma. So we walked through the jungles without the aid of arms. If these rumors had been true, we would have become easy victims. Only a few of the men had weapons such as rifles. These had been picked up on the way from other policemen or from fleeing Europeans who had thrown everything into the bushes in order to lighten their travel.

When we arrived at Gasmata, there was a man there from Sio, Finschhafen. He had been a policeman, a sergeant for that matter. He got married to a local woman during his term in the force. He had two sons. There was something peculiar about his sons. They could not talk, and only used sign language to communicate. Both were deaf and dumb. When we arrived at Gasmata, he said, *"Ol rait ol pikinini mi tink yupela kam na ino inap long igo, yupela mas istap wantaim mi pastaim behain rot klia bai yupela ken igo"* [All right children, you have come to my adopted home. You cannot go now so you must stay with us. Later when the road is safe for travel you may continue on your journey]. After his retirement from the force, the community there had trusted him as a leader and accepted his appointment as a *luluai* of the area.

We accepted his kind hospitality, considering the number of men in our group. We thought it would be a heavy drain on his resources, but we knew that the forests nearby were not lacking in food supplies.

Besides we needed to rest our bodies from the long journey. This respite also afforded us the necessary time to prepare for any attack that might be made on us by neighboring tribesmen. We prepared some spears, and the men from Vanimo made bows and arrows. On Saturday of that week all the men from Markham left the others (Sepik, Madang, Vanimo) and paddled out to an island of Gasmata. In our absence, warriors of Kaulong (mountain men) attacked and killed the Sio *luluai*.

On the following day, Sunday, we got into another canoe and paddled to another village. The men of that village informed us of the death of the *luluai* of Sio. They said the warriors of Kaulong had conspired to kill the *luluai* for some time, but an opportunity had not availed itself until now. It is possible that the hospitality he extended to us inflamed their long-awaited intentions and found an excuse for his murder, because rumor had it that the men did not like our presence. In fact, when we went to this other village the men there followed us everywhere, but at a discreet distance, armed with their weapons.

Anyway, the Kaulong men descended on the *luluai* while he was in his garden with his daughter and a male in-law. The other man and the daughter escaped the wrath of the warriors and warned the other village men, but by the time they arrived the Kaulong had fled to the safety of the mountains. The men then brought the *luluai*'s body and buried him in the village cemetery.

The other members of our party assembled in this village. We then decided to split, with one group following another route. Members from the other group walked to Talasea. We walked and walked and by nightfall came upon a village. We spent the night there. Earlier in the day a messenger went ahead and told the *luluai* and *tultul* of our coming. A feast was prepared for us. We were more than pleased with the people's generosity. The *luluai* and *tultul* asked us to spend the night there and we did. In the morning men and women of the village accompanied us in their canoes down the Kapioru River. Most of the women came to collect bush hens' eggs farther down the river. When we arrived, we got off the canoes and helped the women collect these eggs. We learnt that the men and women of the coast often came there to collect eggs. After the collection, we accompanied the coastal people down to the coast. The *luluai* from there asked us, as others had done on earlier occasions, to spend the night in his village. We did. During the course of the evening the *luluai* said, "It is a long road for you to travel on and if you continue on your journey many dangers lie ahead. Why don't you settle down among us until it is safe for you to return home?" We accepted his invitation and stayed among his people.

In the meantime the Japanese had taken full control of Rabaul and rumor was rife that they were in hot pursuit of European police officers from Australia who had left Rabaul and fled into the bush. It was rumored also that they were looking for New Guinean policemen who had also fled and were now living with the local villagers. The Japanese wanted these men to return and work for them.

Not long after a Sepik and an Aitape man, both Japanese police recruits, came to Talasea and enquired about New Guinean policemen who had fled to some of the villages. The people of some villages told them of our presence. We were assembled and told to return and work for the Japanese army. Much to our objections we were issued with police uniforms—the same ones we used under the Australians—a red patch sewn on the khaki, shorts, and caps signified Japanese "control." The Japanese did not seem to have any police uniforms of their own. We were then brought to a Japanese camp in Talasea. It was on a mission station. We found out later that there were many Australian soldiers, civilians, and New Guineans working behind enemy lines in the mountains of Talasea, Nakanai, etc. For that reason the Japanese soldiers went on daily patrols into the bush. On one of these patrols a Kaiapit policeman was killed. By whom no one knew—it could easily have been one of the Australian men [coastwatchers].

I was selected from the rest to accompany the Japanese clerk back to Rabaul. Through an intepreter the Japanese man said, "Only you Sasa Goreg will accompany me to Rabaul." He wanted us to bring back some uniforms, food, clothing, etc, for the employees. We first went by canoe to Cape Hoskins. We remained there for awhile, and I was given the responsibility of supervising the construction of the Hoskins airport for Japanese planes.

During that time a cargo cult was in full swing among the Nakanai people. They killed off most of their livestock of pigs, chickens, etc, swept their cemeteries clean, and did nothing but wait for some mysterious cargo that was to arrive from across the sea in a huge ship. When the ship arrived, a bridge or wharf would appear from nowhere, and the ship would offload the goods to the waiting people. The people of the area believed all this nonsense and wasted the day feasting and dancing. Some of us did not know what to make of it. The Japanese became aware of this movement. They arrested the instigators, two men with their wives, and kept them in jail. Their followers were also given jail terms. They were not issued with knives, spades, rakes, or any other equipment. Their punishment was to pull out everything with their bare hands.

I and the Japanese clerk then left for Rabaul in a warship. It had very great speed. We arrived in Rabaul at about six in the morning. Rabaul wharf was packed with Japanese ships. So much so that the warship we traveled in was anchored far out at sea, and we walked over ships until we were just about near shore, when a barge brought us to the shore through a small open passage.

Perhaps I should mention that I was in Talasea for the rest of 1942 and the whole of 1943. We left Hoskins sometime towards the end of December 1943, and arrived in Rabaul in early January. In point of fact when we arrived in Rabaul the Japanese soldiers were celebrating an occasion which could have been an important Japanese day or simply the festivities of the new year. Whatever it was, the soldiers had a great time marching, firing guns, eating, etc. I was surprised that the Japanese did not seem concerned about the war. Unlike them, I was scared, so I went ashore with my Japanese companion and remained there just in case the Allied forces attacked us. However, the Japanese must have been aware of an impending attack because they kept sending up balloons of different colors to indicate each phase. The colors were white, blue, and finally red. They were used to signal impending attacks. Just then the Australians and Americans attacked. We were told they had flown over from Nadzab, which is located about half an hour's walk from my own village.

The sky was blackened with planes and machine-gun fire. Hundreds of bombs dropped—they fell like coconuts from the sky. Their impact was horrifying—trees, houses, etc, were blasted out in all directions. The machine guns attacked with such fury that some of the Allied bomber planes were made ineffective and crashed in the mountains of Baining. I took cover after about an hour. The bombers disappeared after this, save for one single-engined plane, which kept circling the sky and attacked for a long while longer, before it too disappeared over the mountains. The Japanese fought bravely. When the situation got hot, I crawled into a hole dug by the Japanese to escape bomb attacks. The holes were camouflaged by coconut fronds so they could not be easily identified.

That day was hot and steaming, with one of these tropical heat waves. So much was going up in the blue sky. Its effects could be seen all over Rabaul— dead men, dismantled planes, destroyed houses, gardens, coconuts, shells, holes as big as mountain craters, etc. At about twelve o'clock there appeared to be a truce. I and my Japanese friend jumped into a vehicle, and it took us to one of the barracks used by the New Guinean police recruited to work for the Japanese. I was happy to be reunited with some of the men who had been with me at the training depot. We were recruited by the Japanese not to fight. Our task was mainly to supervise Japanese prisoners, in particular New Guinean prisoners. It was also our duty to patrol the surrounding villages and bush with a Japanese officer and make the people contribute food from their gardens. We made gardens too. Down at Kerevat, men previously employed on plantations were engaged in planting *kaukau* and tapioca for us.

I returned to the barracks when the war ended in 1945. For the whole of 1944 we stayed in tunnels constructed by the soldiers. I have vivid memories of the conditions then. We all slept in tunnels in the side of the mountains. The holes were fenced off by corrugated iron. Inside were two doors. In the event that one got destroyed during the bombing, the other was used as an escape. The beds were like bunks in a dormitory or ship—one slept on top and another slept below. Most of the amenities were there—electricity (lights, toilets, showers—hot and cold—etc). All the policemen slept in one section. It wasn't very safe to walk around. In 1945 we were moved to the barracks. Then we were told the war had ended.

The Australians then arrived and took over Rabaul. The captured Japanese were made prisoners of war. Those of the New Guinean policemen who had worked for the Japanese were charged by the villagers and brought to court. The court was set up by the Australians. New Guineans employed by the Japanese as laborers suffered badly at their hands. It was worst if you were a prisoner. You were handcuffed every day of the week and tied to a pole for most of the time. You were also starved for days, without food and drink. If you committed a serious crime (according to the Japanese classification of offenses—disobedience, fighting, theft, suspicion of cooperating with the enemy, etc) you were given more severe punishments, for instance, whipping as well as starvation.

Prisoners were kept in other sections of the holes in the mountains. New Guinean policemen were given the task of supervising the prisoners at work. I, of course, was one of the main supervisors because I was singled out as "Boss" of the other police. I was their NCO. I would not personally inflict wounds or hit the prisoners, but if I was ordered to do so by the Japanese, I would do whatever they ordered me to do. Most of the time I was forced to cane people on their bare buttocks. The Japanese thought highly of me and gave me greater responsibilities than other policemen. I also was given a position similar to that of a prosecutor. That is to say, that if a New Guinean prisoner was going to court I would be asked to assist him or her in court. The Japanese on many occasions asked me to tell them how Australians had dealt with offenses of similar nature, and punished the individual according to the severity of the crime. In other words, as Australians would have done for the same or similar offense. I therefore was used as an adviser by the Japanese. Sometimes men were fined. At other times they were given jail terms of three or more months. Sometimes I would hear cases and try and settle them myself. However, if the Japanese considered it too serious they sat in court themselves and passed their own punishments, and I only sat as an observer. On these occasions I was allowed to say whatever I wanted to say.

Many times I saved men from death—through either hanging or throats slit by swords. Had I not intervened, many men would have been killed, because the Japanese were brutal and did not seem to place a high value on human life. I was successful in persuading the Japanese to give alternative punishments. I was most surprised that the Japanese would listen to what I had to say. They could speak *Tok Pisin*. Therefore men who would otherwise have been killed had their sentences commuted to either short or long jail terms. They thought I was a great humanitarian, hence I was promoted to a senior rank with the Japanese *Kempitai* [police]. So during my term with the Japanese, I was given responsibilities for supervising prisoners, and either attended or actively participated in court proceedings. My first responsibility was for the prisoners. Later, with the trust the Japanese had in me, I stopped working with the prisoners and instead acted as a prosecutor or clerk of court. I personally dealt with minor matters. Serious matters were brought before the attention of the residing Japanese soldiers for punishment.

In my observation at these court proceedings, the Japanese were a very different people. They were thorough in their investigation of even minor crimes and demanded complete silence during the whole proceedings. If at any stage you made any sort of noise, or started up a fight, they said, "Oh, you want to help the Australians." In their anger, if they did not bring that person to us, he would be killed immediately. I only dealt with the ones who escaped the Japanese sword—*samurai*—for jail terms of one, two, or three months. I worked in that capacity until the war ended.

AK   Did you enjoy working for the Japanese?

SG   It was alright considering the situation, but I was not happy being with them. In the very beginning I tried to run away and join up with the Australian and American soldiers. I tried very hard, but I did not succeed. It was quite impossible to run away from Rabaul. Many of us considered running away from the Japanese but we knew it was futile for us to do so. Of course when the war ended, the Americans and Australians came to Rabaul and rounded up all the Japanese and left them in one camp as prisoners of war. All the policemen and civilians who had assisted the Japanese were placed in another camp. We waited for impending court cases brought against us by the local community—they made allegations of brutality, killings, etc. We were not kept in jail as prisoners. Actual prisoners wore the prison uniforms. However, while we waited for trial, we were made to build houses for the soldiers in Rabaul. As there were too many policemen, only representatives were chosen to stand trial. For instance, a spokesman was appointed from among the various districts—Morobe, Manus, Madang, Kavieng, etc—to represent the other men from these areas. Though in many cases we had not been party to the Japanese atrocities, policemen nonetheless were implicated in these charges because we had worked closely with them during the war. I argued successfully that the other men selected to stand trial with me should be acquitted because I knew more about the charges than they did. Therefore, I alone should stand trial with the Japanese even though I knew I could be hanged if I was found guilty, because I knew of a man from Butibam who had been hanged for either sedition, treason, or some other offense against the Australian administration. After eight months of court case, I was acquitted. They found, through interrogation from the Japanese, and I told them myself, that I had only acted upon Japanese directions, that on no occasion had I acted on my own impulse. The villagers seemed to concur with these statements, so I was not convicted. After the court case, I was given the opportunity to remain and reengage in the New Guinea police force. I returned to the barracks and the police master persuaded me, so I agreed to sign on again. However, a Manus sergeant got mad with me and said, "Why do you wish to sign on again when you could easily have been hanged or given a long prison sentence for helping the Japanese police? You have just been through eight months of court. If people [Australians and villagers] have not appreciated your effort as a policeman before the war, I do not think they will give it to you now. You would be better off in your village."

The Manus man's words made a lot of sense and made me all the more determined to go home. I left my uniforms in the barracks and wandered off to Rabaul, deep in thought. A ship was berthed on the wharf that day which had arrived from Morobe, and the men that manned it were men from Salamaua, Bukaua, and Markham. One of them was my cousin. He recognized me and asked me what I was doing there. I told him I was looking for transport to go home to Markham. Through his and the other men's assistance I eventually returned to my village in Markham in 1946. I did not sign on again or engage in any other European-established business from that day.

After resigning from the New Guinea Police Force, I became a subsistence farmer. I grew some coconuts and made copra from which I earned some cash. I also started up a cattle farm, but they were attacked by disease, and officers from the DPI [Department of Primary Industry] came in 1970 and destroyed them. I only have coconuts left now. [Buffalo flies destroyed his cattle.]

AK   Did you kill any man or woman during the war?

SG   During the whole of the war period I killed or shot men under orders. It was like this. A man from Sepik had a serious argument with a Japanese warden over food. This Sepik man had been a laborer on one of the plantations in Rabaul before the war. When the war came the Japanese used the laborers to grow *kaukau,* taro, and to carry supplies from one locality to another. They were housed in compounds built by the Japanese. This Sepik man was the overseer of the laborers. Acting as their spokesman, he spoke up against the amount of food the workers were given one day. He and the laborers felt they should be given more nutritious food, which would give them the extra energy to do a hard day's work. However, the argument got out of hand, and the Japanese soldier in his anger punched the man from Sepik. The Sepik man *sakim han bilong em na faitim em long pes bilong em* [brushed aside the punch and threw one in return in the face]. It made impact. The soldier reported the incident to his superiors. His senior officers decided that the matter should be settled by me. The two men were driven to my barrack. They left the Sepik man in my care, with specific instructions that he should be imprisoned in the hole and should not be fed any food or water for days. You know, you could feel sorry for your *wantok* but, under the circumstances, what could you do to help him without taking the risk of ending up in the same situation as your friend? If you disobeyed orders, or helped your *wantok*, you were imprisoned or killed if they considered your crime warranted it.

After some weeks of imprisonment, it was decided by the Japanese that the Sepik man should die. I tried to prevent it, but all my powers of persuasion did not convince the Japanese that day. They were convinced that he was a trouble-maker and that he was surely trying to assist the Allied forces. Therefore, he should die. The Japanese then picked me and the Manus sergeant to do the dirty job. They got some rifles and ammunition and loaded them onto the truck. They often gave us the uniforms that were normally worn before a hang-ing or before rifle fire—with bayonets, swords, and all. Later we drove to Matu-pit. In the car were three prisoners, the Sepik as well as two Tolai men.

First the Sepik man was blindfolded with a red piece of cloth. I made one last attempt to save his life, but it proved futile. I told the Japanese soldier that I did not wish to participate in it. He was furious and said that if that was the case I would die with him, and he attempted to blindfold me too. I said that it was all right, that I would like to die with him. He was obviously bluffing, for he quickly placed the red cloth back in his pocket. After that he forced me and the Manus man to pull the trigger of the rifle. The Sepik man died instantly.

For this and other deaths and atrocities the local villagers brought us to court when the Australians arrived. As I said before, I successfully argued for the other policemen to be let off, because for one thing they were saying things which were, I thought at the time, going to make us look guilty. When they were acquitted, I then argued strongly that we did not kill those men because we felt like having a bit of fun. We had to do it under orders from the superior Japanese soldiers, otherwise we would have been killed ourselves. On the strength of this argument, I and the rest were set free from blame.

AK   Were you paid any money?

SG   Yes, I was paid some money. They were in Japanese currency [yen]. They became useless after the war, but during it I could buy things from the Japa-nese stores.

AK   Did you win any awards or medals?

SG   Yes, I won some medals [Japanese] but I did not think they were of any use. Besides, I never did like the Japanese, so I threw those medals away after the war on my way back to Markham, because I did not wish to be reminded of them. They were not a very nice people. They were very bad, very strict and severe, and did not seem to have any compassion or feeling for human life.

I give you permission to use the material in this interview in any way you please. Thank you.

Appendix 5
Interview with "Wizakana" Tawi

I interviewed "Wizakana" Tawi at Orobomarai Village, Gende, Madang, on 14 July 1985. The interview was conducted in Gendeka, my first language, and transcribed by me.

BACKGROUND

AK   What is your name?

WT   My name is Tawi. Sometimes people call me by my nickname, Wizakana.

AK   How many children have you got?

WT   I have had a total of eleven children. Unfortunately, four sons and three daughters died. Of my eleven children only two sons and two daughters are alive. One son and the two daughters are married, one youngest son is still in school in Goroka.

AK   What is the name of your village?

WT   Generally it is known as Emegari. I consider myself to be a part of the "lines" of Kuraini, Bedum, and Bogonogoi. These were the sites where our fathers gathered to plan attacks on enemy tribes.

AK   How many languages can you speak?

WT   I can speak Kuman [Simbu language], Kuman Nagaka [a dialect of the Simbu language], and the language of the people of Kouno [Jimmi Valley], and my own Gende language, Gendeka.

AK   In which province is Gende located?

WT   It is in the Madang Province.

AK   What was your father's name?

WT My father's name was Kaiago.

AK What was his status in the village?

WT Physically he was a very big man, he was above average height. He was somewhat of a rogue, a troublemaker. He was a fight leader and was held in esteem by those around him. I am a bit like my father in physique.

AK What was your mother's name?

WT Her name was Dunduwa Kindari [Elder Dunduwa].

AK What was her status?

WT She played a lesser role but was more outgoing than a good number of the other women. She helped her husband raise pigs, rear children, made feasts, and on the whole involved herself in the daily and important occasions of the village.

AK How many children were born into your family?

WT There were only three in my family, one sister and two boys. The sister and my elder brother are dead. I was the last born. My mother married again and she had a daughter. My stepsister is alive. She is married to a man from Karisoko.

BEGINNINGS OF ALIEN CONTACT

AK When did you first see a white man?

WT When I was quite a big boy, about twelve years of age. At that time, the white men who came into Gende were missionaries from Madang [see Mennis 1982]. They first arrived in Guiebi and then made their way around the villages in Gende. I first saw them when they arrived at Yenemi, the land of the Duwakai Narawa Clan, Emegari. The missionary entourage left Guiebi, passed Bogae village, and made their way to our territory. At Yenemi, they bought land from the people. Payments for the land were made only to adults, and I was in tears because I knew I owned some of the land there. The "fathers" had two dogs named Meri and Kemizemi. When I, as a young man, objected to the payments for the land, they untied the leash on the dogs and they chased me and others from the scene of the land transaction.

AK When did you first see a policeman?

WT It was well after the missionaries had arrived in Gende. The missionaries had begun their expansion into the highlands, particularly in the area of Simbu; first at Toromabuno, then in succession Mingende, Gogme, and Kunabau. After that, we heard in Gende that government officials from Madang had established themselves at Kundiawa, the main administrative center for the Simbu

region. The government had only been there for a short while when two missionaries were killed by the men from Simbu. One was buried at Kagrie, near
Toromabuno. [Here Tawi is talking about the murders of Brother Eugene
Frank and Father Carl Morschheuser in Simbu in December 1934 and January
1935.] As a result of this murder, we heard that the missionaries in Simbu sent
a strongly worded letter to the government in Madang [Salamaua] and consequently government officials from both Madang and Lae [Salamaua] came to
the area of the murder and just about wiped out the population. Those of the
people who escaped the government's vengeance fled to Kouno [Jimmi Valley],
Kombo [Eastern Highlands], and Gende. Later, the refugees were brought back
to their villages and peace was restored. In those areas, government officials
were appointed from among the population and given the government's responsibilities. Later, government officials from Madang arrived at Bineza, Gende.
The party came and chopped down some very hard *yar* trees [a hardwood used
for fences and house construction], but they were unable to complete the task
so they asked the assistance of the menfolk of the nearby villages. Some of the
Emegari men were called on to do it, but you must remember that the Mendi,
in whose territory the trees were logged, were our traditional enemies; they
conjured up all manner of tricks to attack us, but in the end one of our cousins
warned us of their cunning plot and we escaped a massacre. The man's name
was Uva Kindari [Elder Uva]. In the party of arrivals were two Europeans and
many policemen.

AK Why did you think they had decided to come to Gende?

WT We thought it had something to do with the arrival of the missionaries.
Sometimes the people refused to work on the roads, etc, for the missionaries,
and they warned us they were soft and easy on us. But they warned of a stronger
force [government] that would come and force us to do things. The prediction
turned out to be true; the government came and forced us to do many things
—build more roads, carry cargo, maintain the airstrip that we helped build for
the missionaries, and a myriad of other jobs. Incidentally, whenever the people
refused to help build roads or churches, or make gardens, the missionaries
looked in the direction of Madang and said, "Oh, we wish the government
could come soon and drive some sense into these people."
    At first we thought the European missionaries were *poroi krunaga,* spirits of
the bush and rivers.
    When the government officials came to Gende they appointed village offi-
cials, *luluai, tultul,* and medical *tultul* from among the leaders of the various villages. The names of some of the village officials as I remember them were Uva
[Mendi village], Aziue [Bundi], Yananda [Magukoro], Gere [Bogae], Yaunde
[Tigina], Keni [Guiebi], Tuegi [Geguru], and Woi Kanakagi (red-skinned man)
[Dikini and Maiyabana]. Just as the missionaries had predicted, when the government men came they forced us to do much more than what the missionaries had done. We were forced to carry cargo, build roads in all directions, dig
pit latrines, live in villages, refrain from fighting among ourselves, build the airstrip, etc, etc. The big difference was that they used force, they caned us and
hurried us along at every occasion with or without loads. I think the mission-

aries had been with us for about four years before government officials came to Gende. [Missionaries arrived in Gende in 1932; the murders of the two missionaries took place in 1934 and 1935. Missionaries would therefore have been in Gende for just over three years.]

AK Who else came in the first government party?

WT There were two Europeans and many policemen and carriers. On subsequent occasions one European officer came. I think it depended on the occasion. If there was trouble the numbers would increase. Otherwise there was one European officer. At other times only the policemen came. There was always a good number of policemen. We called the policemen *brizivai*. If we saw them at a distance, we called out "The *brizivai* are coming!"

AK In the beginning, how did you communicate with them?

WT It was very difficult. They spoke in what turned out to be *Tok Pisin*. We did not understand a word of it. There was only one man who could understand a smattering of *Tok Pisin*. He was a member of the Koruku clan. His name was Mui Kiagi. He learnt a bit of *Tok Pisin* from some very early Lutheran missionaries in the Ramu Valley. Kiagi lived with his relatives from his mother's side, who was from Ramu, and when the Lutheran missionaries came he carried their supplies and went with them to Madang on their return trip. In Madang he picked up *Tok Pisin*. Before the missionaries came to Gende, Kiagi told us a lot about the white man's town he had seen in Madang. He told us he had seen lots of white men, cars, big wide roads, large houses, etc, and said that one of these days the whites would come to Gende. They did, years later. So he was the only one among us who could conduct some sort of conversation with the visitors.

AK Did you provide them with food?

WT We gave them the best from our gardens, sugarcane, bananas, taro, *kaukau* [sweet potato], *marita* [a fruit], etc. We also gave them pigs. Our being nice to them was a mixture of apprehension and uncertainty about the reasons for their coming. Oftentimes we were trembling with fear. In return for our generosity the visitors gave us *kina* shells, *girigiri* [shells], salt, and other valuables. We exchanged our pig for their *kina* shells. The shells were given to the girls to decorate themselves. We do not think much about them nowadays, but, at that time, they were valuable to us both for decoration for girls and as brideprice exchanges. The girls wore them around their necks.

AK Did you do the same thing when the missionaries came?

WT Most certainly. Their items of exchange were much the same as those of the missionaries. Many times we gave them plenty of food and fully grown pigs, but they gave us very little in return. However, we did not complain of this unequal exchange for they had already demonstrated to us the power of the rifle. If anyone tried to complain, pigs were shot in front of them. We therefore were so scared that we accepted their goods without question. At the sound of the rifle we ran into the bush. They also had savage dogs and they unleashed them on us. Their dogs were huge: most of the time they were used for attacking both wild and tamed pigs. Most of our transactions were done in silence. We talked among ourselves and said that these were very strange men, the likes of whom we had not seen before. We said if we complained or objected to whatever they did they would kill us all. So we conducted ourselves very passively, out of fear.

AK   How long did they stay?

WT   They never stayed for any length of time. At the most they stayed for a week and then continued to another village or went back to Simbu or Madang. However, the policemen, carriers, and kiap came quite regularly.

AK   What did you say among yourselves when the patrol had left?

WT   It was a relief whenever they left. When they came, all our own activities, feasts, gardening, trade, etc, stood at a standstill. We only did whatever they told us to do. Whatever they requested we attended to promptly. We were still fearful of them. We still thought they were *poroi krunaga,* the most dreaded spirits of the bush.

AK   Did you see the policemen yourself?

WT   Of course, I was a big boy then. I saw them with my own two eyes.

AK   What did you think of them?

WT   I thought they were big and strong men. You could see the muscles stretch with every movement. Physically they were big. They also had good physique. They appeared invincible, with uniforms, physique, and guns. They were a picturesque sight when they fell in line to hoist and lower the flag every morning and every evening. In the beginning I was rightly scared of them and of their strange behavior. Patrols to our area were made after the end of every month, sometimes from Kundiawa or Gembogl, and sometimes from Madang.

AK   Did the policemen always carry guns with them?

WT   Yes. They never failed to carry their guns with them. At the arrival of most patrols, we saw first the kiap and then we saw the policemen with their guns on their shoulders. We called the guns *brizivai.* At the approach of the policemen, we metaphorically called out, "Here come the *brizivai!*"

AK   What did you think of the gun?

WT Well, I had never seen, and never in my wildest dreams, thought that a thing as powerful and destructive as that existed anywhere. At first I thought, "Now I have seen the source of what makes thunder and lightning." The noise of the rifle sounded like thunder itself.

AK What type of clothes did they have on?

WT The policemen wore short trousers, faint white [khaki], and black in color. They wore khaki shirts.

AK What did you have on?

WT My normal clothing at the time. Clothes made of woven strings, hats made of possum fur, and belts woven together from certain plants and decorated myself with feathers. It was an occasion when they came into our village, so we wore our best traditional clothing. Unlike nowadays, the men and women of that time decorated themselves for every occasion, and sometimes when there was no occasion to celebrate.

AK What did you think of their clothing and that of the kiap?

WT I thought I had never seen anything like it before, and I thought they hid their weapons in their clothes to kill us all. If ever we disobeyed or complained we were kicked, caned, and jailed at Bundi station for weeks or even months. We did not know where they came from, but now we have been told that the early policemen may have come from Sepik, Madang, or Morobe. I remember the names of two of them, Aigal and Nogrombu. They were like giants. Often these men came from the direction of Simbu, but I could tell that they were not all from the highlands. Their facial features were different.

AK Did you notice anything about their hair?

WT They kept it short and sharp, somewhat like the policemen of today.

AK What was the general feeling of the people about these strangers' constant comings and goings?

WT We said to ourselves that we had lived an orderly and straightforward existence, but these people had disrupted this orderly existence of ours. We considered them to be people who had come to destroy us, and we were grief stricken. We feared them greatly. We did not have the courage to disobey the *luluai* and *tultul,* who were men from our own village. From the time of their coming, most of our time was spent on building roads in all directions [Aufenanger 1976], keeping the villages clear, building the klap and policemen's rest houses, etc. Hence, a lot of our own traditional customs ceased to function or were performed less frequently.

AK Did the policemen ever punish the people for disobeying orders?

WT Yes. We were caned, handcuffed, etc. The women did not escape their wrath either. They were made to carry bags of sweet potatoes and accompany their husbands on the construction of roads, or the airstrip at Bundi. Some were forced to go as far as Faita [Ramu] and Usino [Ramu] with food for their men.

AK Did you ever rebel against this treatment?

WT How could we? We were very scared.

AK How did they treat the women?

WT Very badly. Quite regularly, the women were used to satisfy the sexual urges of the policemen. This also went for the kiap. On one occasion the kiap asked me in gestures to bring Kegine to him. I never knew the kiap's name. However, the kiap fucked Kegine in the old missionaries' house at Bundi, the house with the red roof. He brought her to the room upstairs and fucked her there. When he had finished with her, the kiap gave Kegine a small mirror as payment. She was still in tears when she came down the stairs, and I brought her home. We are from the same Nakawa clan in Emegari. She was a virgin, because she was not yet married, and boys had not yet begun courting her. [She died in 1985.] Traditional laws regarding premarital sex were strict, on pain of death. That was one incident that I was personally involved in, but I heard from other villagers that many of their young girls were prostituted by the kiap and his men. The policemen were just as bad. Whenever they were called on to bring food or *kunai* to the station at Bundi, the police often selected the best-looking girls, not married women, to satisfy their sexual lust. No woman refused because to do so meant punishment, which frequently involved kicking, caning, or outright force. The women were very scared of the police.

AK This went against your customs. Did you feel bad?

WT My word! We were furious and clenched our teeth with anger and discussed amongst ourselves how we would stop the onslaught on our girls. But in the end we decided that if we did anything we would all be killed. So we sat and waited as if our hands were tied to our backs. In the past, of course, anyone who dared touch a girl without paying the necessary bride-price was killed instantly. Tradition has it that in the beginning there was no tribal fighting and everyone in Gende lived in peace. However, tribal wars began when a Mendi man was seen to be fooling around with a woman from Karisoko. Alliances changed, but the tribal wars continued until the missionaries arrived [in July 1932]. Certainly when the policemen and the kiap disfigured our girls, our stomachs were heavy with grief but what could we do but keep a straight face.

AK How did the policemen treat the people?

WT Generally they were good to us, but only if we did as we were told. For example, we carried cargo, built roads or airstrip, and provided food and women. If we disobeyed or failed to carry out any order we were punished. If, for instance, I failed to turn up for work on the roads and it was found out from their own checks that I was missing, they sent out a search party and if I was found I was handcuffed and brought to the station for punishment. I would either have been caned or sent to prison in Bundi. The punishments were also meted out for those who ran away after enlistment.

AK   Did you notice anything about the relationships between the kiap and the policemen?

WT   They seem to have got on very well. The only time I saw the kiap speaking harshly to his men was when the people brought complaints against the activities of his men. This may have involved sexual harrassment or the shooting of a pig. Otherwise they had cordial relations.

AK   Did the policemen steal from your gardens, shoot your pigs without sufficient cause, etc?

WT   No. They did not do any of those things. They demanded pigs but they never actually shot them without our approval. There was the occasional shooting of pigs through misunderstanding.

AK   Were you ever punished or imprisoned for any offense?

WT   Yes, I was jailed five times. I will tell you about the biggest and cruelest of the lot. One day I was in Magukoro. Some men from Bundikara [they had already been pacified] came to Waitara and yodeled to Magukoro and shouted, "The kiap at Bundikara demands that the people of Emegari supply food to both the kiap and his policemen. We have come to ensure that you go to your gardens now and collect whatever food you can for the kiap." When the men arrived, I had completed a house that day and was digging a small drain. Some of the women had already returned from their gardens with bags of food, one of whom was Dinogoi. Dinogoi was my girlfriend. I had sung *kago* with her for many months. The men immediately forced her to carry one of the string bags of food. Then the men asked me to yodel for the rest of the women to return quickly. I replied that I would. I then proceeded to yodel but then stopped. They shouted at me to yodel some more and to stop wasting their time. I yodeled only once and looked into Dinogoi's eyes. She winked at me. This was a sign that I should start up some trouble because she did not wish to go to Bundikara. I told her, by signs, that she should move into my new house. She quickly left her string bag of food and moved inside. I yodeled again and pretended to move to a better spot but instead moved behind the house where I had left my bow and arrows. I picked them up and attacked the men with a flurry of arrows. The men were taken completely by surprise. They knew how fierce the men from there were because they were our tribal enemies. They did not stop to ask questions because the policemen were not there to help them. They hurried back to Bundikara and reported the incident to the kiap.
    The following morning, the kiap and policemen armed themselves and, with

the numbers of the village men reinforced, arrived at Magukoro. They told the people to line up. They arrested me and handcuffed me. They then handcuffed Ogom, the *tultul*, and then the *luluai*. The village officials were also my immediate relations. Our hands and legs were still tied during the course of the night, and we slept in the cold rest house. In the morning, with our hands still handcuffed, we were dragged away like pigs down to the river, Maravizai. It is a big river. The condition of the bridge was not good. The kiap asked the *luluai* and *tultul* why it was in a dilapidated state. They said they had no reason to come that far and therefore had not realized the bridge's poor condition. The kiap said it was their responsibility to ensure that roads and bridges were maintained for government patrols. He then ordered them caned. The two officials were forced to lie flat on some flat stones and caned all over their bodies while they squirmed and pleaded for mercy. The kiap said I should not be given the same treatment because I was only a villager and therefore ignorant of the government. I only heard the word *boi*, but the rest was told me by the interpreter. In the morning we started on the first leg of our journey to Gembogl-Kundiawa, Simbu, via Guiebi and Yanderra. At Guiebi, the site of the early missionary settlement, we were made to carry thick coils of wire used in a sawmill by the missionaries to pull logs for the church and other buildings. They were thick and very heavy. We were told to carry them all the way to Gembogl as punishment. They were so heavy that our blood rushed down to the lower parts of our body and made it hard for us to walk in an orderly fashion. We walked slowly and arrived at Yanderra in the late afternoon, weary and starved. We were so tired that we lost our appetite for food and slept soon after we arrived. On the following morning we walked to Mondia Pass for Gembogl. At Mondia, Ogom collapsed or fainted from exhaustion. The policemen would not have any of this. They shouted, "Get up! Do not waste our time!" Ogom did not move from his fallen position. One policeman pushed the butt of his rifle into his ear and then shot a bullet on the ground right beside him. Ogom leaped into the air with fright. He then leaped two other times to ensure that he was still alive. He then ran to the front of the party and never looked back until we arrived at Gembogl.

At Gembogl, the Simbu people commented on how strong we were to have carried the heavy wire for such a long distance. We slept soundly that night, in the prison cell. The prison covered quite a big area. It was enclosed by barbed wires. The prison building was long and covered almost the whole length of the prison grounds. Early the following morning the sentries, who were local men, called out, "Where are the criminals from Gende?" We were then forcibly brought out from the prison house and made to stand erect outside. We were directed to sit on the grass nearby. The handcuffs were removed from our hands. Both our hands were swollen. Five men carried five round rocks from the nearby river and dropped them in front of us. I could tell they were heavy because of the effect the rocks had on the five men who carried them there. When they dropped them at our feet they sighed with relief and quickly sat down near us. Incidentally, the interpreter was a man from Gende. He was one of the few Gende men who could speak a smattering of *Tok Pisin*. His name was John. John warned us in Gendeka, "They are now going to ask you to carry the rocks back and forth. You must show them how strong you are by carrying these rocks like men. Even if their weights are unbearable don't show them that you are weak. Bear the pain and torture until you are finished." I was the first in line. They selected the biggest of the five rocks and heaved it onto my shoulder. They ordered me to stand erect, with legs stretched to their limits. The same was done to the other two men. In the meantime, the police and other government employees stood about a yard apart along the path that we were to run on. Each held firmly onto a cane. At the firm order of the policeman in charge, the policemen near us hit us swiftly with the canes. We had to run. If we walked we were caned. This continued until the end of the prison walls. It went on and off from early morning until lunchtime. At midday we had lunch. We dropped our load, slumped on the ground, and lay on it with our noses buried in the grass, breathing heavily like a pig killed suddenly with a solid piece of wood. It continued the whole day. At the end of the day John, the interpreter, told us that what we had just completed was our introduction to prison life and that the following day we would be given ordinary fatigue duties. For a month we cleared bush. At the beginning of the second month, I escaped from prison. It was nighttime, with clear moonlight, when I climbed the barbed-wire fence, jumped to the ground to freedom, and ran all the way home to Emegari.

When it was discovered in the morning that I had escaped during the night, the policemen in charge, at the orders of the kiap, organized a search party. The party, including policemen and carriers, walked to Bundi for reinforcements and later came to Emegari and demanded that I be handed in for punishment. My people all stood by me and refused to betray me. They said that for all they knew, I was a prisoner in Gembogl. After some more futile attempts, the people, including mostly women and children, were taken "hostage" at Magukoro until I was found. The men of the village were forcibly enlisted to search for me with the rest of the government agents. In the meantime, I lived in caves and abandoned bush shelters or hamlets. But then hunger forced me to visit garden sites and make the occasional fire. I lived that kind of lifestyle for about two months. However, Emegari is a small place, and about thirty men were looking for me, many of whom were also Gende men who knew how I would behave in situations of that nature. They frequented garden sites, bush shelters, and any other place where I was most likely to be. I was immediately left at a disadvantage when the people were moved to Magukoro. When they were in the vicinity, they knew the whereabouts of the searchers and warned me about them, but when they left I was on my own, and the risk of apprehension grew enormously.

In the end, I thought that if I did not give myself up other people would be punished, so I gave myself up to the authorities—policemen and appointed villagers from Bundikara at Magukoro. I was then handcuffed and stripped of my clothes in the village square. It rained all day. I was left in that state until the late afternoon. My relations, including both men and women, were caned, kicked, and punched for refusing to tell them of my whereabouts. In the morning, the policemen, with the assistance of their men, handcuffed me and, with some of my relatives with their pigs, brought us to Gembogl. When we arrived there, the kiap was furious with the policemen for bringing my relatives. They were sent back immediately. I, of course, remained there, a prisoner for one whole year.

I was told that since I had escaped from Gembogl I would be sent to Kundi-awa to be sent to the "hole." From there I would be sent to Hagen. Not long after, I was escorted by police to Kundiawa. At Kundiawa I was brought inside a very long house which looked something like the school buildings we had in Gende. I was made to sit inside that long building, with other prisoners from the area, until the afternoon. Then, at someone's command, a "door" was opened in the ground not far from where we sat. It led to a big, dark hole. I was frightened. My legs trembled with fear. I thought they were going to kill us all, and the hole in the ground was to be the site of our burial ground. It turned out to be quite the opposite. The policemen in charge gave orders that we should all stand up and prepare to make our way into the hole. I thought I was hearing things. Were they going to bury us alive? Before our eyes a very long ladder, of which there were two (one at either end), was dropped into the hole. All the prisoners descended into it. When I eventually reached the soil it was cold, filthy, and stank of human feces and urine and crawled with rats. The soil was moist. I could just see the other end in the distance with the assistance of dim lights. Lamps placed at irregular intervals displayed the ugliness and sor-did condition of the prison, in the heart of the earth, cold and revolting. Drums also stood at regular intervals. These had been used as toilets. The stench, quite nauseating and poisoning our minds, was coming from these open-ended drums. There were a few "beds" but they were hardly suitable for human comfort for they also were infested with bedbugs. When the prisoners had descended, the lamps were collected and sent back to the top. Likewise, the ladder was pulled up and the door closed and locked from the outside. We were left there in complete darkness. Men and women shouted, cried, and invoked their ancestral spirits for help. It was deafening. Hardly anyone slept the whole long night. When the noise got too much for the local sentries, they poured hot water down openings in the timbered floor above. Prisoners sprang for cover to escape the wrath of the sentries. In the morning, we looked like eels thrown upon dry land.

There was some deception about the longhouse. First, the hole in the ground was about the length of a long ladder and the width of two longhouses [not round highlands houses but the new variety introduced from the coast]. It was then covered over with timber, planks nailed together and placed over the hole. Then a house was built on top to provide shelter for the hole and sleep-ing quarters for the policemen. The prison hole was deceptive in the sense that if you were a visitor and entered the longhouse you would not have been able to tell there was a hole underneath it.

In the morning we heard loud footsteps. They were those of the local sen-tries. They were big, fierce Simbu men who took no nonsense from anyone, either prisoners or villagers. They were all dressed up in their traditional cos-tumes as if for a dance. They carried their weapons of bows and arrows and spears. Early every morning they chanted a song, a constant reminder of the reasons we were in that dungeon.

The words rang:

> You are imprisoned in that hole as a form of punishment for your refusal to obey the rules and regulations of the government. Beware, we are keeping a constant watch on the door. There is no way you can escape.

By the time you have completed your term you will have learned to listen to the policemen, *luluai,* and *tutuls* of the government.

After the chant, the door on top was swung open and a gush of clear, fresh cold wind rushed inside. They ordered us to have a morning wash in the crystal-clear, fast-flowing river. We had to move quickly. Laggers were caned swiftly. If you were a victim of their anger and caned, it felt like the sting of a disturbed bee. We had no time to take our "clothes" off, mostly made from bark of trees. Those who tried to were pushed in. Once these string woven clothes we had on got wet they were virtually like a sponge that not only soaked up water but also shrank. Some shrank so much that by the time our term of imprisonment was up, we were just about naked because our meagre "clothing" had turned into knots. The policemen did not give us clothing to wear. Anyway, in the highlands not many people washed because the mornings were cold and bitter and the evenings chilly. We were forced. When we finished our teeth were clenched tight and muscles taut in our bodies in order to withstand the biting cold.

From Kundiawa they transferred me to Mount Hagen. They said I was a bad and ignorant man who acted like a stupid person, so I had to be brought farther and farther away from my home area. I spent four months in Hagen, Mendi [Southern Highlands] another four months, returned to Hagen for another month, and was finally brought back to Kundiawa for the last three months before I was released from police custody. It was a total of twelve months.

I cannot emphasize strongly enough that during those twelve months I was made to work very, very hard under conditions that I have not experienced since. I was told at the beginning of my term that if I died during my term no one would be too concerned about it because I had brought it on myself. They said I had disobeyed the government, I was a bad man, and one less man of my attributes would save them a lot of needless effort. In the end, it would have been my own stupidity that would have led me to my death.

AK   How many times did you end up in jail?

WT   What I have just told you was my biggest and longest jail term. On the whole, I served five other shorter terms, ranging from two to six months. One of these involved a fight over a pig, and another over a woman.

AK   Do you have any idea about the number of prisoners who served with you?

WT   There were literally hundreds of them, most of them were from the area. If I had been able to count I would have the exact figure but at that time and even now I am unable to say how many there really were.

AK   What types of crimes had they committed?

WT   All sorts. They had stolen pigs, disobeyed government orders, engaged in fights, wife bashing, etc. Some were only minor offenses. Others were of a more serious nature, such as murders.

AK Were you given any European clothes to wear?

WT None whatsoever. I wore my traditional *konabi* [strings woven together from the bark of a tree] until the end of my term. That was why I stated earlier that when I washed in the mornings the sentries kicked us in and mine was always wet. In the end my *konabi* shrank so badly that there was hardly any left. I then used leaves to cover myself. My wife and people were miles away, and so I persevered with the little I had on.

AK What type of food did they give you?

WT Mostly traditional Simbu food, sweet potatoes being the main one. They never gave us rice. We were always envious of the police and others issued with rice. We did not have breakfast. We had *kaukau* for lunch.

AK How would you describe the longhouse?

WT As I have already mentioned, it was a longhouse. It had *kunai* roofing, and the posts and *blain* [blinds—cane or *ticktick* woven together as a wall or screen] were from local materials. Underneath that was the hole in which the prisoners were made to sleep. The hole was dug first. It was the length of a long ladder [fifteen feet?]. Placed over the hole were planks nailed together to form the floor of the longhouse. It was then covered over with grass, which effectively cut off any form of light reaching inside the hole. It was like living in a pigpen. It was unhealthy, inhuman, and the sheer force of the stench would have killed men. They did not give us any blankets. As you know, the nights in the highlands are very cold. They told us they would not issue us with blankets as a form of punishment for our mistakes. It was terrible there. I am lucky I came out alive. Women prisoners also slept there, but at the other end. Like the menfolk, we heard them screaming and wailing every night.

AK What kinds of work did you do?

WT We performed a variety of jobs. We pulled logs with big wires. Because of the sheer prison numbers, the logs were pulled quite easily. We also built houses, roads, fences, pulled *kunai,* etc. These were all fatigue duties.

AK When did you start of a morning?

WT Very early when the willy wagtail sang, at about six o'clock. In the afternoon we had our dinner cooked by ten men in large *mondono,* a Simbu method of cooking, using a hollowed log in which food was roasted with hot stones.

AK Did you have any days off?

WT We had Sundays off and only half a day off on Saturday.

AK How many policemen supervised prisoners at any one time?

WT This depended on the number of prisoners. On average, there were two
for a big group and one for a smaller one.

AK What happened to you if you were lazy or disobedient?

WT We were caned like lightning. Supervisors never stopped saying; *"Ariap,
ariap, ariap"* [Hurry up, hurry up, hurry up]. We were too frightened to do anything. I would never want to repeat this ugly experience again because the treatment we received from both the sentries, who were not policemen, and the
policemen, was one of the most frightful events of my life. I do not know where
they got their orders from, or from whom, perhaps from the kiap, but the manner in which they carried out those orders was atrocious. Those of us who were
in jail, once proud warriors, were humiliated to such an extent that we acted
like embarrassed dogs, crawling on our faces with our tails protecting our hides.
We, or rather I, was reduced to almost a person of no consequence because I
feared the gun which, in my estimation, was the only weapon that saved the
government from the angry people around it. I knew the men from my own
village, once feared throughout the Gende land, swallowed their pride and became like scared children.

AK How did you get along with the other prisoners?

WT Splendidly. We got along very well. I could speak the Kuman language
quite fluently. During traditional times, we traded with the Simbu people for
bird of paradise plumes, pots of salt, and, much later, axes, when the Europeans
came. They told me why they were in prison, and I volunteered similar information to them. In a short time we became friends.

AK What did you think of your experience?

WT As I stated before, I felt very bad. I would rather have been dead than
alive. All my thoughts were centered on the fact that I would be a dead man
before I finished jail.

AK What happened to the women prisoners?

WT They were the *abus* [food, meat; metaphor meaning the women were used
for sexual gratification] for the policemen and the sentries. The women worked
elsewhere during the day, but at night there was a buzz of activity where they
were kept. They were dragged out of the cell at all hours of the night by both
the sentries and the policemen. I could tell from the languages used, *Tok Pisin*
and Kuman. Male prisoners were mocked by the sentries and policemen. They
would ask us, "Do you desire your wives?" If we said no, we were caned merci-
lessly. So whether we liked it or not we felt compelled to say yes. The policemen
and the sentries had a good laugh and said, "Oh, good." Then they would say
that they would get some prison women for us. On other occasions they said,
"Tomorrow, seven named men will be released." But the truth was that none of
those things happened. They just enjoyed playing tricks on us. I was then a

young man, fit, strong, and courageous. As you can see now, I am above average height, and I was a man of some position in my village. I was groomed to become a warrior when the Europeans came to my place. I did not take too kindly to these insults but what could I do?

AK Were you paid any money?

WT No. I did not know what it even looked like. Prisoners were not paid money at this time. The missionaries told us something about it as a means of exchange. But, at the time of my arrest, I do not recall the missionaries using money either. However, the missionaries did say at one stage that when the *owo* [Gende word for money, meaning "stone"] arrived we would then be able to buy European clothes with it. It would also change our lives. Their prophecy turned out to be true. The people here now wear European clothes. The *konabi* and *izo tarawa priki* [dried bark used as a belt] have become things of the past. Mission assistants told us about some of these things.

AK Just before you were released, what did the kiap and senior policeman say to you?

WT They said, "You are being released from *kalabus* [jail] because we think you have suffered enough for what you have done against the government. You must go home now and refrain from disobeying the government. Tell your people to do likewise. If you do not do as we say and we see you back in prison, your punishment will be even more severe. You are lucky that you are alive to go home this time, but you might not be so lucky next time. Only your corpse might be carried down to your people. If you died no one would be concerned about you because you would have been a bad man. So when you go home now, conduct yourself quietly like a child." These were the kiap's parting words to all of us who were to be released. The kiap spoke in *Tok Pisin,* and the interpreter translated the message to us.

AK When you were imprisoned you were sent to places your forefathers had never been to, or even heard of. What were your impressions of the places, people, customs, environment, etc?

WT I held a fatalistic view. I thought to myself, "No one asked me to do what I did. I did it of my own volition, so if I died it did not really matter." It was a combination of the strange places I was brought to and the different lifestyles of the people I saw and the rough treatment I endured in jail that contributed to my formulation of this train of thought. I was quite frightened by it all. All these activities led me to lead a somewhat dazed life—unfamiliarity with the lands, people, and prison, etc. I was flabbergasted by it all. I would have died of despair, had it not been for Tigavu, who was then a policeman serving in Hagen [a Gende policeman whom I interviewed in Madang. He died in 1986]. Corporal Tigavu came and spoke to me in the Kuman language, "Son, where are you from?" I replied in Kuman, "I come from a place near Gembogl. I was imprisoned for attacking a government party and I have been transferred here."

AK Did you know him before?

WT I thought I had seen someone like him working for the missionaries in Guiebi (Gende), but I did not think that he would have become a policeman, and I certainly did not expect to find a Gende man in Hagen. But I remembered a scar on his nose. The scar was still there, but I did not say anything at first. He then spoke in Gendeka and said, "Are you really from near Gembogl?" I almost fainted. These were the most precious Gendeka words I had ever heard. I shouted in tears, "Are you really Tigavu?" He said he was, and we had a long, long embrace, as if we were long lost brothers. He asked me again how I came to be there, and I told him everything. He said he was very sorry for me and gave me directions to his house in the police quarters. He then said he would return on Saturday with some pork, etc. We went to his house and he killed a chicken and gave it to me. He also boiled me some eggs. I was most grateful for his concern and kindness and ate most of the chicken and some of the eggs. It was a real treat, almost a feast. In prison the food was quite boring, consisting mostly of sweet potatoes and vegetables. We would have loved a tin of corned beef, but no luck was ever bestowed on us, at least not while I was there. After the meal Tigavu walked me over to the prison and repeated his promise to bring me pork on Saturday. His presence there gave me the courage and determination to survive and return home to my people. Without him, I think I would have died of despair, or my mental state would have allowed me to commit other crimes which would have led to an extension of my term, or if I had escaped the people of these places would have killed me. In retrospect therefore, I think, the fact that Tigavu was there gave me the energy to live because before this time I had thought only of the fact that I would die without the knowledge of my people and family because I was so far away.

AK Why did other Gende people [men of Mendikara, Nombri, Bundi, etc] behave badly towards you and other Emegari in general when government influence spread to the region?

WT The explanation for their hostility was quite simple. Before either the missionaries or the government officers came, Gende people waged tribal wars on each other, for reasons that I am not sure of, even though it is generally believed that the wars began over disputes about women. These tribal wars had been going on for a long, long time. My father was born during the wars. He remembered his father telling him the same when he was a boy. All the tribes in Gende fought against only two other tribes, Emegari, my village, and the Karisoko warriors. The Emegari and Karisoko were allies. They had been allies for a long time. That meant that warriors of all the major villages—Biom, Bundi, Aranam, Bundikara, Mendi, and even our neighboring villages such as Yandera, Geguru, etc—were our enemies. Our warriors were fearless, courageous, and strong and killed many of the warriors from the other villages, stole their pigs and their women, and generally brought about destruction to their property. For years, the warriors of these villages tried to defeat us, but until the time of the foreigners' arrival, their attempts were never successful. After so many battles and so many casualties they could never defeat us with the resources they had at hand. However, the arrival of the policemen and the kiap gave them new hope. It provided them with the opportunity they had been waiting for. It happened like this. The policemen with their kiap came from the direction of Simbu. I learnt later that their headquarters were situated on the present site of Kundiawa [1941]. When they first came to Gende their influence spread to a few people living nearest to Simbu. These villages were Mendi, Bundikara, and those around the Bundi mission station. So their influence first followed a northwesterly direction. Therefore, men from these villages learnt to speak *Tok Pisin* and heard about the intentions of the government. The people who lived to the southeast of Gende were mostly unaware of the presence of government influence. They heard about its intermittent presence when a patrol party visited the villages. For a while the policemen and kiap made patrols for only short periods, and returned to Gembogl and Kundiawa. However, later, when the station at Gembogl was well established, they constructed a semipermanent station at Bundi, where it still is today. During this time the men from these villages "raided" our village, initially to get men and women to build roads, the airstrip at Bundi, kiap houses, etc. Later, either the same men or others "raided" our village if any of our men had committed an offense, however small it may have been. They said to us, "Before your men were strong and killed many of our men, both young and old. No matter how hard we tried we were never able to defeat you in tribal wars. But now we have the upper hand over you because the policemen and kiap are our friends. Anyone who refuses to do as we command will be shot by the policeman. You are still *bus kanaka* and the government will not be worried about you. Now we will see how strong you really are." We were scared because the men were not speaking empty words. They did it with deeds. They came with a vengeance. Whenever they came to our village they humiliated us by sleeping with our women, wives and daughters, while we stood aside gritting our teeth with anger. They whipped our men with canes, and forced them to work like slaves. They destroyed our properties, trees, *marita* [a fruit], sugarcane, etc. I would not be surprised if some of the children born after their coming were fathered by them. Whenever they came to our area with the policemen, they made all kinds of accusations against us, some of which were true and others false. How were the policemen to know, because we could not speak to them in *Tok Pisin*? These men were very bad. Many years of frustration and anger surfaced with a vengeance. For the first time in our lives, we did not know how to combat an enemy.

AK Did your people take their revenge when they understood what was going on (eg, when some of their men understood *Tok Pisin,* etc)?

WT My word, yes. I will only tell you of two important occasions. The first incident took place indirectly. Like these men, we had relatives in Simbu. One of them was Maina. Maina was a *luluai* of one of the tribes in Simbu, near Gembogl. When he heard that our people were being mistreated through the activities of our tribal enemies, he came in his capacity as a government *luluai* and ordered the men and women to be caned at Bineza, in front of the villages of the Mendi people. The men were made to look silly because this time it was our men who had the canes. They were shocked but they could not lift a finger. The other incident took place in our village at Magukoro. I think the kiap was trying to promote promiscuity among the Gende populace because they thought the population was declining. The kiap said that from now on instead of the young men and women sitting side by side when singing *kago* the woman should sit on the man's thighs. [There was concern during the middle part of the colonial period that there was depopulation. To encourage population growth colonial officers were told to encourage people in the Gende region to have more children.]

Anyway, one evening some men from Mendi came and, as was the custom, held a *konandi* session in the village. Kobonarawa, one of the men, picked a very young girl and sang with her sitting on his thighs. Dawa, a fearless warrior of Emegari, found this hard to swallow and fought this man from Mendi. The other warriors helped him, and four of the Mendi men were beaten severely. Their meager clothing was stripped off them and in their nakedness, they ran into the darkness, all the way to Mendi. From then on these men did not cane us or commit other atrocities on our women. They said we were fearless people, that no matter what tactics they employed to get their revenge we always ended up on top of them. So they stopped seeking revenge through direct and physical means, and reverted to using sorcery and poison against us. But this had no effect on us either.

AK Why did you run away from your first imprisonment?

WT The main reason was that I was caned so frequently, in fact, many times a day by the sentries and policemen, that there was not a part of my skin that did not show the marks of a brutal caning. I thought to myself, "If I do not escape, most of my youthful skin will disappear in scars and one day they will cane me to death." For this reason, I escaped without even telling my fellow villagers. When I returned to my home, I escaped into the bush. I slept under big trees, caves, abandoned garden shelters, etc. The search party failed to find me immediately. Eventually they did, but only after a long and tiring search. Also the people were held hostage. An ultimatum was sent out that if I did not give myself up to the authorities the people would be caned en masse, and they would continue to be caned until such time as I gave myself up. When I heard about the ultimatum, I decided to give myself up, and I did. I thought that if people were caned and imprisoned on my behalf they might die in prison and demand compensation from me. I did not wish to place my relatives in needless difficulties. I walked into the village and I was handcuffed and brought to Gembogl-Kundiawa.

TAWI'S CONCLUDING STATEMENT

Before the Europeans—both the missionaries and the government—came, my people led a good life; there was tribal warfare but it was not as destructive. At least we knew how to take care of it. The foreigners came and disrupted our culture, our traditions, our very existence. We became disoriented. We did not know what we were doing. We could not fight them because we were scared of the *brizivai*. They humiliated us by sleeping with our women. I do not know from whom the Mendi, Nombri, and Bundi men and the police received their orders, but the manner in which they carried out those orders was frightening. They treated us so badly that memories of their activities still haunt us today. The European officer demanded women on two occasions, but the police and village men abused their powers many times over. The Emegari men, once proud and fearless fighters, were brought down on their knees and made to plead for mercy. It was a black period for us all. The policemen were from the coast. The men that mistreated us were from Simbu, Mendi, Nombri, and Bundi.

This is my story of my experience with the government. As you have shown a keen interest in what I have been through in my life, and since you are working on a project, you may use whatever I have stated that is of relevance to your work. Thank you.

Appendix 6

Kegeriai's Eyewitness Account of Tawi's Ordeal

The following is a transcript of my interview with Kegeriai at Orobomarai village, Gende, Madang, on 14 July 1985. The interview was conducted in the Gendeka language and transcribed by me. Kegeriai, my mother, was a young married woman when the activities that Tawi described took place. She died in 1992 after a short illness; she would have been about eighty-four years old. Kegeriai's husband, my father Ibrum, offered a bribe to the leader of the search party not to cane Tawi when he was eventually found. Tawi left members of his own clan and, at the time of the incident, lived with the people of Kegeriai's clan because his first wife, Aina, was a close relative of the clan. Aina's mother had married into Simbu but had since returned to Emegari. Kegeriai only narrated those parts of the incident that she observed herself.

AK   What connections did you have with Tawi?

KV   Tawi is from the Nakawa clan in Emegari. But he got married to a girl whose mother was from my husband's subclan. Her name is Aina. They are still married today. After his marriage to Aina, Tawi left his lands and relatives and came and settled among my husband's people. My husband is the oldest in his subclan since most of the others died at an early age. Tawi and his wife, Aina, with the rest of her brothers and sisters, moved from Simbu and settled with us. I and my husband, who died in 1985, have lived with Tawi, his wife, and children before and after that incident. It is with authority that I can now comment on the events that followed as I saw it.

When Tawi escaped from prison, he came to Kuraini, and I heard about his coming at my bush home at Mindinoru. Soon after, he went into hiding. The menfolk of the village discussed among themselves and decided not to reveal Tawi's whereabouts under any circumstances. A search party from Simbu, Bundi, and Mendi came to Emegari. There was no policeman among them.

After some weeks of searching, the leader of the search party sent orders for everyone to assemble in the main village at Magukoro. So the men, women, and children of Kuraini moved en masse down to Magukoro. This order included old men. The younger men were forced to assist in the search. The men were divided into groups and each group was in charge of one of the men from Bundi, Bundikara, Mendi, or Gembogl. After days of searching, one of the groups found him eating raw *kaukau* at Kokowoi. He was forcibly handcuffed and brought to Emegari. At Kuraini, my husband, Ibrum, offered the leader of the party a valuable and expensive traditional necklace made of valuable shells, and betel nuts as bribe. The leader of the search party was Domande. When Domande accepted the necklace Ibrum told him that Tawi was his "son-in-law," that Tawi had been through enough, and that he should not be caned further. Domande was from Gende and he understood Ibrum's concern by the nature of the bribe he gave him. He accepted the necklace and the betel nuts and ordered his men not to cane Tawi anymore or cause him any further physical discomfort. However, he was handcuffed and brought to Magukoro.

Upon arrival Tawi was told, "You have suffered so much hardship because of these two women" [Aina, his wife and Dinogoi, his boyhood sweetheart]. So they stripped off the clothing of the two women as well as that of Tawi and tied their hands and feet with strong bush ropes on crosses and stood the crosses in the village square so that the people could have a good look at them. In the meantime the Mendi men were playing around with the women and young girls of the village. It took place sometime in the afternoon. Once the crosses were erected they said, "Have a good look at these deviants and shout when you have seen enough." It rained heavily that day. All the people of Emegari were gathered there for this occasion. The people sat in silence. Many had only one peep at the unfortunate three and quickly looked down at the ground in embarrassment. In the middle of the silence, Kendi's mother [Kendi died in 1987] shouted in Kuman language [Simbu], "I have seen enough. It is a very humiliating experience. I am retiring to my house." After that everyone slowly stood up and walked back to their houses. They were drenched to the skin with the rain. The two women were then let loose. Tawi was still handcuffed and in the morning walked back to Simbu for another term of imprisonment. Tawi did not marry Dinogoi; she married another man. He is still married to Aina. Three of his remaining children, one male and two females, are married. His youngest son attends high school in Goroka.

This is all I can say of that episode in Tawi's early life. It was quite tragic, but then it was not unusual. Many other men went through similar or worse experiences. Admittedly not many from my village, but there were a few from Karisoko [a neighboring village].

If you think this information is useful for your work, you may use it.

Notes

INTRODUCTION

1. It is not my intention to add to the plethora of discussions on the who and why of European expansion during the eighteenth and nineteenth centuries, or to discuss the subsequent events that brought colonialism, at least in most parts, to its end in the latter part of the twentieth century. The process, complex as it was, has been dealt with from various points of view by many scholars. Only five books out of many are mentioned here. For the early Dutch period, which was probably responsible, or at least set an example for later European expansion, Masselman (1963) serves as good introductory reading. For the later periods, Wallerstein (1966) and Fieldhouse (1986) provide broad surveys of the whole process from the beginning until its end, when colonialism was no longer considered fashionable, although some countries have persistently denied that it has become decadent. Mason (1971) has excellent discussions on race relations between the colonizers and the subjugated, after the euphoria of conquest ended, and European settlement began in many of the territories. A related, albeit revolutionary, work written for subordinated peoples, is Fanon's *The Wretched of the Earth* (1963).

2. "European" is used here because it is relevant for Papua New Guinea. It could apply to other people who had similar inclinations.

3. These examples are used because of their geographical proximity to Papua New Guinea; other examples, particularly from Africa, could have been cited.

4. There are numerous extracts from primary and secondary sources on the extent of government control in both Papua and German New Guinea during the period in Jinks, Biskup & Nelson (1973). See, for instance, the editors' comments regarding the area under effective German control by 1914, and an excerpt from Burridge (1960, 193), of areas that were under nominal control. Even in 1951 Sir Paul Hasluck expressed his disappointment at the slow rate of progress: "Yet even in some places close to these well-established districts there were small pockets of uncontrolled country, for example, in the mountains behind Finschhafen, in parts of New Britain and in the country behind Wau" (Hasluck 1976, 77). That says nothing of the highlands region. Murray ex-

pressed similar sentiments for Papua in 1912, "Papua has been British for nearly thirty years, but half of it is still totally unexplored [including the whole of the Southern Highlands] and of the other half there is but a comparatively small proportion that is really well known" (Murray 1912, 247).

5. The opposite style of colonial administration was indirect rule. While there is some confusion about the exact definitions of both these terms (see, for instance, Mair 1948, 65–66), "Indirect Rule" simply meant that there was in existence in native societies a political structure that was in some ways compatible with western notions of exercising "state" authority, which was used to expand colonial administration. In other words, "there were chiefs and courts and a native administration already in existence, and all that was necessary was to stiffen the administration, to strengthen the courts, and to rule through the chiefs" (Murray 1935, 1). The method was used extensively throughout most British or British-influenced colonies, particularly in Africa. Some useful books, articles, and discussion papers have been written on the subject of indirect rule. Lugard (1922) was probably the first authoritive account ever published on this system of administration, even if he was not the first colonial official to have used the method in Northern and Southern Nigeria. Scarr (1984, ix) stated that the system was first applied in Fiji and not Nigeria, although the principles of indirect rule had been around since the time of the Romans (Barnes, in Wallerstein 1966, 222). Fieldhouse (1986) discussed it in the context of the administration of subordinated peoples. According to Nayacakalou (1975, 92), indirect rule, as practised in Fiji, failed. Murray (1921, 104–106), wrote favorably of the method as practiced elsewhere, but complained in a subsequent report that it was inapplicable in the Papuan administration: "We cannot fulfill the letter of Indirect Rule; but we are true to its spirit" (1928, 82–85).

6. My impression, from Murray's writing, is that Europeans were generally baffled by the seeming lack of efficient organization in traditional society. Common sense told them that this was highly unlikely as some form of organization, however crude it might be, was essential for ensuring the society's continued existence. But because the average European of the time did not understand clearly what made Papua New Guinean societies conform to rules, it was explained away by the phrase "collective unconscious," which can be interpreted to mean that they knew there was a system there in operation but it was unintelligible to a westerner's mind. In other words, it was a convenient phrase to cover for ignorance (see Murray 1935, 3).

7. Sir William MacGregor wrote this in his introduction to Sir Hubert Murray's book, *Papua or British New Guinea* (1912, 27). Similar sentiments were expressed in British New Guinea *Annual Report, 1897–98*, 45.

8. For accounts of the village constables, see Joyce (1971); Healy (1962); Murray (1912, 243–245). For the *luluai* and *tultul* system in New Guinea see Hahl (1980); Biskup, Jinks & Nelson (1968, 3); and for both systems, see the relevant sections in Jinks, Biskup & Nelson (1973); Mair (1948); Wolfers (1975).

9. In 1925 Sir Hubert Murray introduced the village council system in Papua. Murray perhaps realized that the village constables were government agents whose sole responsibility was for and on behalf of the government. The appointment of village councillors was therefore intended to get views from the

other side, the villagers. In other words, "these men were intended to be the representative of native opinion" (Mair 1948, 70).

10. The regulations were allegedly translated into *Tok Pisin,* but I wonder who would have understood the following regulation prohibiting gambling: *"107. Boy he no can play paper long catch im money."* (New Guinean *Tok Pisin* speakers would have much preferred the following directive: *"Lo namba 107. I tambu tru long man na meri i pilai kas/laki long winim mani.*) Considering that a total of ninety-three (some may have been repeated) such incomprehensible regulations were in force in Papua New Guinea in 1924, there was adequate room for much confusion.

11. In general "New Guinea's Native Administration Regulations imposed harsher penalties than their Papuan counterparts—and, from 1923, all prison sentences for offences against the Native Administration Regulations, were deemed to 'be with hard labour unless it [was] expressly enacted' that the reverse was true" (Wolfers 1975, 92).

12. Imposed "peace" was one of the great achievements of colonial rule in Papua New Guinea. But it came later, and its nature requires a complete study in itself. In large part, this book examines the first phase, that of "conquest."

13. For Papuan examples, see, for instance, Joyce (1971, 129ff); in this incident MacGregor's determination to use heavy-handed tactics to punish the perpetrators of Captain Ansell's murder formed the basic framework for his future dealings with Papuans. For other Papuan examples, see Waiko (1972, 76–88); and, for New Guinea, see Connelly and Anderson (1987, on the highlands); Townsend (1968, about hangings in the Sepik as a way of establishing government control); and the film, *First Contact* (Connolly & Anderson 1983, for activities in the highlands area, in particular, the Southern Highlands).

14. A total of twenty-one Finintugu died at the hands of the three officers—cadets Tommy Aitchison and John Black, and District Officer Edward Taylor.

15. Munster (1981, 2); NGAR (1933–1934, 28).

16. One theory pursued persistently by African and Pacific historians is the claim that colonial subjects generally collaborated or resisted, or did both depending on the circumstances. An analysis of the African situation appears in a collection of papers in (Collins 1970, 41–68); for the Pacific scene the most comprehensive work is that by Hempenstall (1978). Although this theory has much support, the weight of evidence here affirms the theory advanced by Indian historian David Arnold (1986), who suggested convincingly that the growth of police power in India kept Indians under subordination for almost two hundred years.

17. For German New Guinea, see Firth (1982); Hahl (1980). For Germany's activities in other Pacific colonies, see Hempenstall (1978); Hezel (1995).

18. See Keesing and Corris (1980) for the British Solomon Islands example.

CHAPTER 1: THE ROLE OF THE PATROL OFFICER IN PAPUA NEW GUINEA

1. Useful books, articles, and discussion papers have been written about, and by some of the patrol officers of both territories. Although informative, many of the books written by participants are basically reminiscences and do

not present broad perspectives. Among the few who have written excellent accounts of their work are Downs (1986), who presents the picture fairly and with much insight, Sinclair is the most prolific: he alone has written half a dozen or more books and articles on former patrol officers, and on Papua New Guinea generally—some are relevant. Although they are autobiographies, Sinclair's books (1969; 1981) are also informed accounts of the kiap system in Papua New Guinea. J K McCarthy (1963) and Townsend (1968) wrote of their experiences as patrol officers. Lett (1935) wrote about the officers who worked in Papua in *Knights Errant of Papua*. Hides wrote three useful books on his experiences in Papua; *Savages in Serge* (1938) is his version of the Papuan Armed Constabulary. It deals specifically with the work of the Papuan police. Two chapters in Murray (1925) are exclusively devoted to "recent exploration" involving the patrol officer and policemen in Papua. While it was not incumbent upon Murray to explore Papua, he made yearly "tours of inspection." Nelson (1982, 33–56) has three good chapters.

2. Summary of discussion with Dr Hank Nelson, Port Moresby, 1992.

3. For further details on personal experiences, see Downs (1986); J K McCarthy (1963); Townsend (1968).

4. Rowley was of the view that "Paul Hasluck preferred school leavers and insisted on reducing the academic content of ASOPA" or those parts of the course that dealt with "kiap programmes" (comment from Donald Denoon, June 1988).

5. See appendix 1. Many of those who lectured at ASOPA were, or became, significant scholars: Charles Rowley, Kenneth Read, Peter Lawrence, and James McAuley.

6. Calculated from 1921, when the Australian civil administration of New Guinea began under the terms of a class c mandate of the League of Nations.

7. Accounts of the patrol officers' daily official engagements are dealt with by Downs (1986); Nelson (1982); and Sinclair (1981). In this section I examine only that aspect of their work that controlled the policemen and the villagers, including the policemen's views on how they felt they were subordinated to the patrol officer, and how a combination of both their efforts kept the villagers subordinated to them. The patrol officers' perceptions of the policemen's work are discussed in chapter 9.

8. Before this the huge highlands region variously fell within the jurisdiction of both the Madang and Morobe Districts. However, by the late 1950s the highlands area was divided into Eastern, Western, and Southern Highlands (Ward and Lea 1970, map 2c).

9. A handbook for cadets stated: "A cadet patrol officer is regarded as a patrol officer in training. [A] cadet is essentially a newcomer. [He is a] junior officer and commences at the lowest rung of field staff ladder; but develops to become the principal medium of direct contact between the administration and the indigenous peoples of the Territory" (J C Williams 1959).

10. Except for the medical officer, the term *kiap* included all members of the field staff—patrol officers, district officers, and district commissioners (Sinclair 1981, 7).

11. Only the regular police officers supervised the town police. They performed "orthodox" or "normal" police duties as known in developed countries

within the town's precincts. Of the policemen interviewed between 1985 and 1989 eight served, at various times, in the townships of Lae, Port Moresby, and Rabaul. Of these, Sir John Guise and Panau served their entire terms in the township of Port Moresby.

12. Generally, policemen developed a love-hate relationship with their patrol officers.

13. The scale of wealth is obvious in the highlands, but similar things have happened in small communities elsewhere.

14. See the conclusion for an alternate view.

15. In Downs' view this is the nature of the power that was acquired by patrol officers who worked in the highlands region before World War II (1986, 108). In other words, Downs agreed with Bertrand Russell that "as the beliefs and habits which have upheld tradition decay, it gradually gives way either to power based on some new belief, or to 'naked' power . . . the kind that involves no acquiescence on the part of the subject [the] subjects respect it solely because it is power [and] it results merely from the power-loving impulses of individuals or groups, and wins from the subjects only submission through fear, not active co-operation" (Russell 1938, 84, 99, 41). Chapter 9 provides examples of the impact on the people of this style of colonial administration.

16. Implied in Downs (1986, 77). The point is elaborated in chapter 9.

Chapter 2: Recruitment of Police

1. Some of the reasons are given in chapters 1 and 6.

2. After this date the noncommissioned officers are included in the total numbers at the depot, making it impossible to identify recruits separately.

3. In other words, some men are being counted many times. For instance, if a Papuan volunteered at the age of seventeen, and remained in the constabulary at the end of his forty-first year, having reengaged for three years each time uninterrupted, then he would have reengaged an additional seven times after the expiry of his first three-year term. At forty-one, he would therefore have been counted a total of twenty-four times, representing the total number of years he had been in the constabulary. Each year for twenty-four years he would have been enumerated along with new enlistments to get the total establishment figures for the year. (The total number of police in any given year equals continuing plus reengaged plus new recruits.)

4. This was noticed early in Papua. A summary of the commandant's report for 1897–1898 indicated that in the beginning Papuan men were naturally suspicious of the armed constabulary and refused to be recruited, but, by the middle of the 1890s, it became a purely Papuan force, and contained "a considerable number of the strongest men in the country, and the Commandant is able to select the best men out of many applicants" (*PAR* 1897–98, xxv).

5. For clarification on the position and role of a chief in Papua New Guinea, see Hogbin (1951, 118).

6. In terms of place of employment, the man from Ambunti should come under the category of "Papuan" recruit because most of his police years were spent in the Southern Highlands. Were this to be the case, then the Papuan tally would equal that of New Guinea at 14.

7. Kambian (the perfect example), although from Ambunti (Sepik) spent 90 percent of his working life in Mendi. Rewari and Yegova worked for part of their time in the Western Highlands and Enga. None of them changed their work habits after being transferred, nor were they instructed to do so by their superiors.

8. A few refused to be interviewed unless I paid them money. Their rationalization: the process of interviewing was hard and tedious work. If they were willing to sit down and tell a story, they said, it was no different from office work. They should therefore be paid by the hour. Others were simply not interested. Although I gave money and made gifts to my interviewees, out of principle, I deliberately chose not to interview the men who requested payment. Had I interviewed these men, my total sample would have been about forty.

9. Before 1949 Papua New Guinea was known as Papua–New Guinea. After this date the country was referred to as Papua and New Guinea, in accordance with the provisions of the Papua New Guinea Act, 1949 (NGAR 1948–49, 12). Papua and New Guinea became Papua New Guinea in July 1971.

10. With the assistance of a guide, I walked the track to Ioma from Tave village in 1989. It took me two days to cover the distance, and three days to recover from the muscle aches, and so on. After that experience, I concluded that in comparison walking down from Gembogl (Simbu) to my village in Gende (Bundi) was a lazy man's Sunday stroll.

11. In 1932 the name of Gende was changed to Bundi by members of the Divine Word Mission. Although linked culturally to the people of the highlands, administratively Gende falls under the jurisdiction of present-day Madang Province.

12. Ross (1968, 319). The mission stations at Bundi and Guiebi were established in 1932 by Fathers Alfons Schaefer and Brother Anthony Baas.

13. Sono claimed that he received four shillings in cash each month; what was left of his salary was kept in some sort of an account at Wau. He did not know the exact total he was paid a month.

14. Perhaps Bill Kyle, later killed in World War II.

15. As described by Kamuna, this was a ceremonial house in which young males were initiated. No female of any age or description was allowed into this building, which was the preserve of only men of sound knowledge of the people's traditional wisdom, the old and wise men of the village.

16. Sir John Guise did not feel inclined to disclose information about his parents and grandparents out of respect. The three other men claimed their fathers to have been ordinary villagers without any outstanding qualities.

17. Sir Hubert Murray first used this phrase as an expression of praise for the Papuan Armed Constabulary in 1931 (1931, 571).

18. The most likely Robinson is the Yorkshireman Eric (Wobbie) Robinson, who served most of his time in the Sepik area. Robinson is mentioned a number of times in McCarthy (1963).

19. Lutheran missionaries had penetrated the Kainantu region before 1920, but had not yet gone into Goroka (Munster 1984, 1; see also Radford 1987, 76). See Radford's meticulous work on the activities of both European and New Guinean evangelists in the area for further details.

20. A string bag woven from the bark of a special type of tree.

21. These were none other than police uniforms. They were wrapped around the waist like a thick towel.

22. Goroka Teacher's College is now a college of the University of Papua New Guinea.

23. Similar views were expressed of colonial officials—kiaps and policemen —when they arrived in Gende later. I am from Gende and am familiar with my people's customs and beliefs. See also Ross (1968, 319).

24. Most of the annual reports for both Papua and New Guinea during this period list this as being an important condition.

25. Originally, the height requirement was placed at 5 feet 6 inches, but when many of the potential recruits were found to be shorter, the requirement was reduced to 5 feet 5 inches, and in New Guinea in 1932 reduced further to 5 feet 4 inches (NGAR 1932–33, 113).

26. Though not spelled out in the annual reports, it is implied in them that men, especially ex-prisoners, should at least be well versed in the daily operations of the government. For obvious reasons no great emphasis was laid on educational qualifications until much later.

27. There are several omissions, and errors in the arithmetic. On the whole, the reports on the police force are good.

28. In other words, Papuan men who, because of a shortage, had been compelled to enroll under the authority of paragraph 23 of the ordinance could not be forced to reengage for a second term. However, volunteers could reengage any number of times if they were so inclined.

29. Wriford (1891, 85); see also Beaver (1920, 34).

30. See, for example, Alatas (1977). In this book Professor Alatas, from a wide range of sources, discusses convincingly the stereotyping by Europeans of the Malays, Javanese, and the people of the Philippines during the nineteenth and twentieth centuries.

31. The Papuan Armed Constabulary and the New Guinea Native Police "were legislatively combined as a single force in 1955" (Hayes 1978, 141).

32. Waria was an extension of the Orokaiva-Binandere area, which straddled the border, and so both the Papuan and the New Guinean administrations were recruiting out of the same area.

33. Amero, my analysis from information expressed during 1985 interview.

34. This was the version of the story I was given by Kamuna and his daughter, Elizabeth, in Lae in 1985. But see Sesiguo (1977, 221–222) for a slightly different version of the same story.

CHAPTER 3: TRAINING

1. I have not seen the German annual reports, and Hayes did not indicate where he saw them. I have quoted him because his is the only summary available to me. The same source may have been used by Firth, who provides details on pacification of the area (1982, 96–98).

2. This was the overwhelming viewpoint of the ex-policemen I interviewed between 1985 and 1989. See chapters 4, 7, and 8.

3. There is simply not enough information available for the period before 1890 (phase one) to make a considered judgment.

4. Australian Commonwealth 1926–27, 89; also 1932–33, 113. While exploration and pacification remained the policemen's important responsibility during this period, some worked in the growing urban centers of Samarai, Port Moresby, Wau-Bulolo, Lae, Madang, and Rabaul. Most of those temporarily employed in towns were taking a breather from patrol work.

5. Lance Corporal Osborne Garuwa, a member of the Papuan Armed Constabulary composed this song between 1928, when he joined the force, and his death in 1932. He was a man of many talents: he could read and write English as a boy and quickly rose through the ranks. He was from the Ari district, North-Eastern Division. The song was apparently well received among the police and villagers in Papua (*Papuan Villager* 5[10]: 75 [1933]).

6. The song is from the American Civil War.

7. Amero 1985. In 1936 Amero had no knowledge of English, and, except for some vulgar English expressions, he could not speak it at the time of the interview. Despite this impediment, he remembered, and sang for me, at least part of the words of the English tune he, and others with him, learned to sing every weekday morning at the training depot.

Sometimes villagers found aspects of police training fascinating, to the point of being ridiculous. Folk singer ToUna of Rabaul composed a song years later to record one of the first, and earliest, things policemen were expected to perform after recruitment: the marching drill and other strenuous physical exercises. From the song's content, ToUna revealed not so much a lack of ability on the part of the policemen as an apparent inability to come to terms with new alien concepts that prevented them from achieving early success. The song is an excellent example of the way in which languages and material cultures were used to master complex alien concepts (ToUna nd).

8. Whether this was the same, or a modified version of the manual of "Infantry Training 1911" is not clear.

9. Moru Moag of Gabsongekeg village, Markham Valley, said he tried very hard during training at Sogeri because his noncommissioned officer, a Tolai, kept saying any recruit was capable of being promoted to a noncommissioned officer if he persisted. Unfortunately he did not make it to that rank.

10. This discussion can only be brief because policemen were not being taught a great deal at this time.

11. Of the six men I interviewed who had passed through the training depot in Rabaul during the 1930s, none could recollect what they had learned.

12. *Papuan Villager* 4(10): 74 (October 1932). The policemen I interviewed did not recall receiving any instruction in English. Apart from Beu, the Papuan ex-policemen interviewed were recruited during or after World War II.

13. The other ten Papuan men were interviewed in 1986 and 1989.

14. According to Sarepamo the police established a station at Kefamo long before it became an officially recognized training depot in the 1950s. The Allied Forces used the facilities there to enlist and train young men for police work during the war.

15. Of the twenty-eight men interviewed, only Sono had fresh information about what was expected of him at the training depot. Before his recruitment, Sergeant Siria, a close acquaintance from a neighboring village, informed him of the lifestyle he would experience there. The other twenty-seven men did not have this advantage.

16. About a yard of specially tailored cloth, distributed among the Papua New Guinean soldiers and policemen to be worn when they were not engaged in official duties.

17. Yegova did not often understand what was being said, especially if the instructor spoke in English. But he understood instructions given in Police Motu.

18. Only Sasa Goreg did not offer any views because he felt that he did not spend enough time in the police force.

19. Murray's paternalism was shared by most whites in Papua.

20. Townsend (1968, 152–153) offers a Sepik example of such a tradition; see also Hides (1938, 5) for a similar cultural practice among the Koiari of Papua.

Chapter 4: Policemen at Work

1. Interestingly, *plantation* was the term used by Amero, Kasse, Sono, and the others trained in Rabaul to designate both subdistrict headquarters and the remote stations built on the frontier of government influence. When asked, the three men concurred that this was the term the young men used while they were at the training depot. They felt that working in the bush and on government stations was like working on a coconut plantation. This could be used as a synonym for bush work (Amero 1985; Kasse 1985; Sono 1985).

2. A number of the men interviewed worked as the headquarters detachments at some stage of their police career.

3. NGAR (1914–1926, 26). Most annual reports for Papua and New Guinea give details of patrols carried out during the relevant years. Murray described the approach used by his officers in Papua (1932, 1–18).

4. An example of how Samara (Michael Somare's father) introduced Patrol Officer Jack Reed to the rituals of patrol work is given in chapter 9.

5. In *The Outside Man*, published in 1969, James Sinclair referred to Jack Hides as the "outside man," an affectionate term for the patrol officers of the Papuan service.

6. E L Schieffelin and Robert Crittenden (1991) followed Hides' tracks and chronicled the degree of violence. At least thirty–two villagers were shot dead by rifle fire (Sinclair 1981, 111).

7. It is also possible that Guise knew that he had no way of succeeding if he were to try to assist his son.

8. For Binandere [Oro Province] examples see Waiko (1972), in particular chapters 4 and 5, pages 76–88 and 89–101.

9. Different varieties were used at different times (Giddings 1967, 9–11).

Chapter 5: The Use of Force

1. A cadet was an "apprentice" who worked with a patrol officer for a number of years until he familiarized himself with the responsibilities. When he was promoted to the position of patrol officer, he was entitled to work independently (Reed 1943, 165).

2. Hides and O'Malley (1935); see also Schieffelin and Crittenden (1991);

Sinclair (1981, 111). In Sinclair's account, the seven months' exploratory patrol that went through the Southern Highlands was responsible for thirty-two deaths from police rifle fire. This figure, he wrote, was a conservative estimate.

3. See Downs (1986, 60), who said a good report was one that did not cause questions to be asked.

4. Costelloe did not return until 23 July (Costelloe 1947).

5. Forty-four were returned "leaving eleven rounds to be accounted for by Symons' party" (Costelloe 1947).

6. See Mek's recorded testimony during the inquiry held in November–December 1947 (McDonald 1947).

7. Not much was said of this inquiry. It appears to have been abandoned prematurely in favor of McDonald's officially approved inquiry. Bernard's inquiry is mentioned almost in passing in Taylor's letter of 10 October to the acting director of the Department of District Services and Native Affairs, Mr J H Jones. It is also referred to by Jones in a "secret" memorandum to the government secretary on 28 October 1947. Both documents are in the Australian Archives, Canberra, CRS A518, item W841/1.

8. "Belated Report of Fatal Papuan Clash Last July." *Canberra Times,* 21 January 1948; "Hush-Hush on N.G. Killings Alleged." *Sydney Morning Herald,* 20 January 1948.

9. The government secretary's report was attached to the administrator's report to the minister for External Territories, Mr Eddie Ward, as "Portion of Memorandum prepared by Government Secretary," dated 8 November 1947. Australian Archives Canberra, CRS A518, item W841/1.

10. The three letters by Taylor referred to state both explicitly and implicitly that Symons was a young and inexperienced officer who was still learning the tricks of the trade, that in this instance he was too honest, perhaps in an attempt to please his superior.

11. Amero (1985). Amero said most of the killings took place during the course of patrols into unpacified territories, or on raids after attacks on other tribes or patrol parties. There is a possibility that sections of Amero's testimony are tough talk, as indicated by the shot through the vagina, but at the time of the interview he said he had nothing to gain by exaggerating his accounts. They were as they had happened.

CHAPTER 6: POLICE INVOLVEMENT IN THE WORLD WARS

1. The pacification of Papua New Guinea was uneven. Most coastal regions were pacified by either Australian or German colonial forces before the 1940s, but the entire highlands area was not brought under control until the 1960s. Most recent ethnographic materials on warfare deal with the highlands. A selected few are mentioned here. For theoretical discussions, see Turney-High (1971), Koch (1974), and Meggitt (1977). For regional or local types of warfare preliminary readings include P Brown (1982), Reay (1982), Podolefsky (1984), Strathern (1977), and Wedgewood (1930).

2. The parents of the twenty-eighth man, Empere, died when he was a child.

3. For details on the 1914–1918 war in Rabaul, see the official account in Mackenzie (1987), particularly the introduction by Nelson; see also Hart (1972).

4. For World War I in Papua New Guinea and subsequent developments, see the annual reports for the relevant years and Mackenzie (1987) and Lyng (1919).

5. Robinson (1981, 1); Griffin, Nelson & Firth (1979, 73).

6. *par* (1945–46, 1). For detail on World War II see Long (1973; 1963); Dexter (1961); D McCarthy (1959). For the causes of the war, see Snell (1966).

7. Robinson (1981, 11). Chapter 2 provides further details on the working of ANGAU during the war.

8. More work needs to be done on the Papua New Guineans' involvement in the war. See Nelson (1980b, 1) for the part Papua New Guineans played; Robinson (1981) for the experiences of villagers in Toaripi, Hanuabada, and Butibam; and Dutton (1985, 108ff) for the formation of ANGAU in Papua and the Papuans' active involvement in the military's administrative structure.

9. The material for this discussion comes from the Australian War Memorial Archives, secondary written material, and oral testimonies. Every attempt has been made to check oral evidence against secondary sources where they are available.

10. Griffin, Nelson & Firth (1979, 98). Long estimated that about 4,700 Papua New Guinean men would have enrolled for the Pacific Islands Regiment, which included 700 Australian officers (1963, 83).

11. Nelson (1980a, 19). Two other battalions were recruiting and training and one was planned (Long 1963, 82).

12. Nelson (1980a, 19, 23); Barrett (1968, 493). The date of formation is given by Nelson as 1 June 1940, by Barrett as 19 June 1940.

13. Beu was the only prewar Papuan policeman interviewed; a few were sons of prewar policemen.

14. He was right. The Japanese fleet was first visible in the harbor on Friday, 23 January 1942.

15. AWM (1939–1945b). If, in practice, it was a new police force, did ANGAU have the authority of King George VI to retain the prefix "Royal" that he had bestowed on the former Papuan Constabulary in 1939 for the force's meritorious service in Papua?

16. AWM (1944). This view is contrary to those expressed by White (1965).

17. For example, Ben Elipas ToWoworu of Rabaul Police Depot said that while the rest of the policemen were told to find their own way home, even those from the New Guinea mainland, he and four others were retained and persuaded to guide their European officers first to Jacquinot Bay and later to the Baining Mountains (ToWoworu 1985).

18. Dutton (1985, 114). The totals that follow were taken from Dutton's book.

19. According to Long, at the end of 1944, there were a total of 2,560 men serving in the Royal Papuan Constabulary (1963, 83).

20. Townsend (1968). On pages 257–263 Townsend provided details on how the Far Eastern Liaison Office achieved its objectives. The office resulted from the initiative of Commander J C R Proud. Its headquarters were in Melbourne. "Its purpose was to lower the morale of Japanese forces and impair their fighting efficiency; to mislead them regarding our military intentions; and to influence native populations in enemy-occupied areas so they would impair the Japanese effort and assist the Allies" (257).

21. Evidence of such behavior is in Nelson (1980, 202–216) and in the various documents and appendixes filed in AWM (1939–1945a). For Murray's ambivalent view of a Papuan's potential as a soldier and his weakness, see Griffin, Nelson & Firth (1979, 72).

22. *Bik lain* is a *Tok Pisin* expression that means where the majority of people are employed. In this instance, they worked with carriers, laborers, and so on. Figuratively, and in the sense used here, it means a demotion, someone who is not really good enough to perform special jobs so is kept with the rest.

23. AWM (1939–1945c [SP 223]). I have seen the text; only a reference to its existence is made in this document.

24. AWM (1946). For further details on Japanese activities in Rabaul, see Leadley (1976).

25. K S Inglis (1968, 504). In the article, Inglis gives a detailed and comprehensive summary of the views expressed in various forms by participants, observers, anthropologists, and academics in general over a period of the performance of Papua New Guineans during World War II.

26. Peter Ryan (1986). For the total see Dexter (1961, 599).

27. For further information on Paliau see Mead (1956); Paliau (1970, 144–161); on Peter Simogun see Wright (1965); Maher (1961); on Tommy Kabu see Oram (1967); and for Yali see Lawrence (1964).

28. Three useful references are Barrett (1969, 493–502); Nelson (1980a, 19–27; 1980b).

29. Appointed to that rank on 4 April 1942 (Feldt 1946).

30. Details of coastwatchers' activities on Bougainville are in Feldt (1946, 116–146).

31. "George Medal—Sergeant Iwagu, Royal Papuan Constabulary No. 1879" in ADET.

32. The George Medal is sometimes given to servicemen for actions of distinguished bravery when not under immediate enemy fire, for example, when dealing with an unexploded bomb. Volcanologist George Taylor was awarded the George Medal for his work in 1951 when he frequently made close inspections of Mt Lamington immediately after its first eruption.

33. "BEM Corporal Arwesor, RPC, no 2577," in ADET. Warrant Officer Lumb was killed in a surprise attack earlier on that day.

34. "BEM Corporal Merire, RPC, no 9876," in ADET.

35. See Sinclair (1991, appendixes A and G) for more details on awards.

CHAPTER 7: PERCEPTIONS OF THE POLICE BY GOILALA VILLAGERS, PAPUA

1. This statement was made on the basis of the information provided by the relatives of the deceased. Siwoi's testimony indicates that the story may have been fabricated.

2. It is said that during Edwards' tenure "frightening stories began to [emerge] of atrocities alleged to have been committed by members and followers of the Edwards patrol[s]: assault, rape, arson, perhaps worse." Edwards was relieved of his duty as officer-in-charge of Goilala in late 1949 as a result of alleged atrocities committed by members and followers of his patrol (Sinclair 1981, 35).

3. Bariza must be a neighboring village. It is not clear whether the trip was made on the same day.

4. Girau was not told whether Anderson had accompanied his policemen to Ilopo village for the arrest of the two men.

5. I have not come across any evidence in New Guinea. Pumuye's son, Hilary Pumuye, director of the University Centre in Mendi, had heard the story before and confirmed his father's testimony (Pumuye 1989).

6. Girau believed strongly that Siwoi and Matai had told the truth. How did he know? He claimed a Goilala cannot keep a secret for too long. If Siwoi and Matai had killed the old woman, the truth would have surfaced somewhere along the line. The fact that the woman's death is still a mystery, long after the deaths of both Siwoi and Matai, is testimony to their innocence.

7. Sinclair did not mention whether a magistrate or a Supreme Court judge made the decision to acquit Siwoi (1981, 155).

8. Girau was told Siwoi had been given some money for the trouble he had been through, but did not know the exact figure. As stated earlier, it was £200.

9. The facts of this case bear some resemblance to that of Patrol Officer Symons in chapter 4.

10. *Boi haus.* These were mostly one-bedroom low covenant houses built at the back of larger houses for the use of domestic servants of people living in the large houses, who, during the colonial period, were usually whites.

11. This action has a strong resemblance to the ordeals of Tawi in Gende (Bundi), described in the next chapter.

12. If more than one man was implicated, all of them were forced to undergo this painful ordeal.

13. There were reasons why that particular story was not told. In 1985 while I was interviewing Yegova at Buna, Goro, my other informant, walked over from Sanananda village in response to my previous day's message that he should come to Buna village for an interview. At the time of Goro's arrival, Yegova had narrated up to the killing of the Goilala girl in her garden in revenge for policeman Hareho's death. The massacre occurred a few weeks after that incident. I did not interview Yegova again until the following day, and because we had used two cassettes for his experiences in Goilala he thought he would begin his narrations on his police work in Mendi on the unused cassette. This combination of factors—the interruption, the arrival of a visitor, the postponement of the interview, fear of the Goilala experience taking precedence, and lapses in Yegova's memory—all contributed to the story not being told the first time around.

14. *Boi haus.* It was the single men's quarters. There was one in each Goilala village. Often visitors were accommodated in them.

15. An edible plant. It is usually harvested before it turns into a flower.

16. Appears as Lauavai in the patrol report.

Chapter 8: Perceptions of the Police by Gende Villagers, New Guinea

1. For additional information on villagers' perceptions, see Hides (1938, 9); H Murray (1932, 10–11; 1925, 63); Sinclair (1966, 9); and Mann (nd), which

contains a parody that is a comment about the people preparing to receive Taylor and his policemen during a tax-collecting patrol.

2. The government records are missing. Many New Guinea records did not survive the war.

3. Simpson (1962, 166–168). Simpson gives a comprehensive account of the events that led to the attack on the missionaries and the subsequent retaliatory actions taken by the colonial government. Some warriors were shot dead and 89 men were arrested to serve prison terms in Salamaua, the main administrative center. However, after closer examination, it was decided that 22 of the prisoners were in no physical condition to walk the long distance to the prison in Salamaua, which would take a week or more, so they were made to return to their village under police escort. The remaining 67 men walked down to Salamaua with Assistant District Officer Jim Taylor and his band of policemen. In an unusual turn of events in a colonial situation, no formal charge was brought against them. The men were virtually free, except for a six-month period when they were made to build houses as contributions for their stay in Salamaua, which was then responsible for Simbu right through to Mount Hagen. On their return, they instigated peace movements in the Simbu Valley (Simpson 1962, 164–172).

4. Brother Frank was flown to Salamaua hospital, where he died a week later (Simpson 1964, 169).

5. A permanent government presence was established in Simbu by Acting Assistant District Officer Alan Roberts in March 1935. I could not find any mention of it in the government records (Simpson 1962, 173). Most likely, government patrols came to Gende during 1935 or shortly after. The second European officer could have been either Assistant District Officer Alan (Bill) Kyle or Patrol Officer Leigh Vial. Both of them, and Roberts, had served in Simbu before Patrol Officer Ian F G Downs arrived in September 1939 (Simpson 1962, 173–174n).

6. Tawi was unable to provide an immediate definition of this term. However, on reflection he conceded that it could be a combination of two words: *briki* = bad, and *ivai* = come; that is, "the bad one comes."

7. Kegine was from Emegari village. She later married Mumro of Koinarawa (my own) clan and they raised four children, two sons and two daughters. She died in 1979 after a long illness.

8. Rest house. Its figurative usage, and in the context used here, refers to any safe place where sexual intercourse was to take place.

9. This is not to suggest that no premarital sex took place in Gende. It is only to affirm that the society's rules on social behavior did not tolerate promiscuity, and that if indivduals were found engaged in such activity they were punished for a breach of traditional law.

10. I was born in Emegari village. The discussion is based on my personal knowledge of Gende society, and the information passed to me by my father and elders in the village.

11. It is not possible to correlate oral testimony with documentary evidence for the Gende area. However, on two separate occasions I interviewed Kegeriai, my mother, and Akuai, an old man who died in 1992, both of whom had witnessed such arrogant behavior among the policemen, their officers, and other

villagers. Both strongly agreed with Tawi. They said it had been a sad day for
Gende, and they were not proud that they witnessed such degradation of their
young women. In chapter 9 the revelation of the patrol officers about the
weaknesses of the policemen with regard to their sexual habits is, to some
extent, an official confirmation of Tawi's allegations that many policemen used
their position to obtain women without paying due consideration to their
host's traditional laws.

12. *Bossboi,* usually village leaders appointed to supervise men and women
on mission or government activities: road construction, carrying patrol equipment from one village to another, constructing a rest house or airstrip.

13. At the time of my interview, several eyewitnesses were living in the village, and they all concurred with Kegeriai's version. These people claimed that,
out of respect for his wife and the public humiliations that she courageously
endured, Tawi has never told the story in front of her. The day I interviewed
Tawi, his wife was within earshot of our conversation.

14. The Southern Highlands became a District on 4 September 1951, and
was the only highlands district in Papua. The area was first penetrated by the
Strickland-Purari patrol of 1935, led by Jack Hides and Jim O'Malley. It was
visited again the following year by a patrol led by Ivan Champion and Bill
Adamson. Michael Leahy might have been among the first white men to have
gone to Ialibu when he went there from Mount Hagen in 1934 (Mike Bourke,
personal communication). Generally, "the highlands part of Southern Highlands Province was partially explored by Europeans during the 1930s. However,
sustained contact with outsiders for most Southern Highlanders dates from the
1950s; and for some . . . it dates only from about 1960 onwards" (Bourke 1988,
34). For the contact history of the Southern Highlands see Kurita (1985, 55–
66); Schieffelin and Crittenden (1991); Simpson (1962, 381–400); Sinclair
(1969, 1981, 1988); Souter (1963).

15. So far I have not been able to establish his true identity.

16. At my request, I was driven to her village in 1989 in the hope that I could
snap a photo of her, but she had risen early and gone to her garden. I have not
been able to return to Ialibu since.

17. Pumuye's son, Hilary Pumuye, director of the University Centre of
Southern Highlands, interpreted for me.

18. I did not get close enough to see the "hole" at the old Kundiawa prison,
but from a distance I could see the broad outline, which is now overgrown with
shrubs.

19. Tawi's description agrees with Downs's testimony on the selection of
prison warders in Simbu before World War II: "The prison warders we
employed were selected sons of fighting leaders who were paid in steel axes.
They stood over prisoners at work dressed in their full regalia and with
their long fighting spears to discourage anyone thinking of escape" (Downs
1986, 125).

20. Tawi (1985). Tawi had no difficulty in understanding the Kuman,
Simbu, language. He had learned to speak it from an early age.

21. Perhaps the patrol officer just wanted to imply that next time he would
serve a much longer term, which would naturally take him longer to return
home.

372 Notes to Pages 245–261

CHAPTER 9: OFFICERS' PERCEPTIONS OF THE POLICE

1. O'Brien's story is told by Nelson (1976, 164–170); also Monckton (1922, 107–111).

2. A detailed analysis of the race relations in the 1920s and 1930s is given by Wolfers (1975); those specifically related to prohibitions on sexual relations are discussed by Amirah Inglis (1974).

3. In his book, *Patrol into Yesterday,* McCarthy wrote of Anis's death: "In the meantime I was despondent at two pieces of bad news. In fact, I wept when I was told that, first, Lance-Corporal Anis had died, and then Ian Mack" (1963, 112).

4. Griffin's statement was made more than thirty years before the Australian administration in New Guinea decided they could not arm New Guineans in the face of imminent Japanese attack. His paternalism was symptomatic of European views of the time.

5. In chapter 4 some indication is given of the attitude of the patrol officers toward the lack of discipline within the force. Evidence given by Rowley, Downs, and the policemen suggest that many officers did not know what their policemen did. When they were aware of their policemen's illicit activities, with few exceptions, they chose to ignore them.

6. Karo was hanged in 1938 for the murder of a Papuan prison warder, his wife, and their daughter.

7. Amero recalled that the officer's name was Bais (phonetic). Checks in written documents for the identity of this man, who would have worked in Simbu in the late 1930s, were unsuccessful. The closest I could get to an officer whose name resembled "Bais," was Charles Dowson Bates, but he seemed to have worked only in the area between the Ramu police post and the Kainantu region (Radford 1987, 10–11). However, there was a policeman called Awai. In late 1930 he was a corporal in charge of five other policemen working between Ramu and Kainantu. It is possible that he was promoted and sent to Simbu in the late 1930s, when Amero was waiting to be posted to a "plantation" in Salamaua (Radford 1987, 70).

8. In comparison, this is perhaps not as bad as the Papuan officer who chopped off the heads of the villagers that he and his policemen had killed and stuck them onto poles for all to see (H Murray 1932, 7).

9. I am unable to confirm Bega's evidence from documents or other informants. Even if what he says here is of uncertain validity, his statement is important evidence about police attitudes to violence and police beliefs about their own powers.

10. Wolfers (1971) described this game.

11. Though it is not mentioned in McCarthy's narrative, Amero Bega knew Samasam while Samasam was stationed at Talasea station. Through this acquaintance, Amero knew which village Samasam originally came from.

12. The girl's name and that of her village are missing from McCarthy's testimony. These were provided by Amero Bega (1985). In Amero's oral evidence, Samasam had fancied two women, one a young girl and the other a married woman. However, he preferred the younger woman for a permanent relationship. Contrary to McCarthy's account about the destination of Ellis's trip, Amero

maintained that Ellis had gone on a boat to Bali Island when the tragedy occurred (Amero 1985).

13. McCarthy (1963, 215–217). When the Japanese captured Rabaul in early 1942, Europeans living in the Sepik District were instructed by J H Jones, the district officer at Wewak, to move to Angoram for possible evacuation farther inland. Ellis, then assistant district officer at Angoram, opposed such a move, branding those already gathered at the station as cowards. Ellis stated that he would not abandon the station and expressed confidence in the ability of his policemen to fight the Japanese to the last man. A concerned Jones instructed Assistant District Officer Jim Taylor to take charge of the station. When Taylor and a party of officers arrived, Ellis ordered everyone off the station, after which an exchange of gunfire took place between Taylor's party and Ellis and his policemen. Taylor's party retreated after he was wounded. When the party returned two days later, Ellis was found dead with a bullet through his head. His police detachment dispersed, but a small group "reverted to savagery" and hunted down unsuspecting Europeans still operating along the river. Had it not been for the gallant efforts of officer John Milligan in arresting the trigger-happy policemen, many more traders and colonial officers would have been killed. "And so George Ellis died, a man whose illusions of greatness resulted only in grief and death for so many others" (J K McCarthy 1963, 216).

14. Some of the material in this conclusion appeared in Kituai 1988.

CONCLUSION

1. Some of the material here appears in Kituai 1986, 28.

2. This very old Latin tag was provided by Professor Donald Denoon of the Australian National University in 1985.

Glossary of Tok Pisin *Words*

bilum	a string bag woven from the bark of a special type of tree
boi haus	boy house. In town, mostly one-bedroom low covenant houses built at the back of larger houses for the use of domestic servants. In villages, single men's quarters, often used to accommodate visitors.
bossboi	boss boy; village leader, supervisor
brizivai	no exact translation is available; perhaps, "the bad one comes"
bus kanaka	villagers, backward people
gutpela	good
gutpela masta	good master
haus tambaran	ceremonial house where young males were initiated
haus win	rest house
kaukau	sweet potato
kiap	patrol officer, government agent; also used for district officers, district commissioners, and resident magistrates. See Sinclair (1981, 7); Nelson (1982, 33); Read (1943, 174n40). The term was not used in Papua before World War II.
kunai	long grass
lo bilong tumbuna	traditional laws; laws passed down from the earliest ancestors
luluai	government-appointed village official
man natin	ordinary man, without status; unimportant person
masta	European, white man (New Guinea)
misis	white woman
nait klab	entertainment center, disco

375

nambawan	best, first
nambawan polis	senior ranking constable not having noncommissioned officer rank
natin	nothing, unimportant
nogut	no good, bad
nupela lo bilong gavman	the new laws of the government
nupela pasin	new fashion; new ways of doing things; an innovation, a change from the old, such as a shift in the frontier as areas were pacified and brought under government control
nupela rot	new road, new way
pitpit	an edible plant, usually harvested before it flowers
poroi	spirits, abstractions
poroi briki	bad spirits
poroi krunaga	most dreaded spirits
poroi uva	untamed spirits
taubada	European, white man (Papua)
tultul	village official appointed by the government

References

Adams, Ron
1984 *In the Land of the Strangers: A Century of European Contact with Tanna, 1714–1874.* Canberra: Australian National University Press.

Adamson, C T J
1936 Prospecting Report. Copy with Ivan Champion.

ADET, Australian Department of External Territories
var Correspondence file multinumber series, classes relating to External Territories. "Films to Record Australian Administration in Papua & New Guinea 1945–1957." Australian Archives, Canberra. CRS A518, item U 141/3/1. Part 1.

AGS, Allied Geographical Section, Southwest Pacific Area
1943 *You and the Native: Notes for the Guidance of Members of the Forces in Their Relations with the New Guinea Natives.* 12 February, 1.

Ainsworth, John, Colonel
1924 *Administrative Arrangements and Matters Affecting the Interests of Natives in the Territory of New Guinea.* Report. Melbourne: Government printer.

Aitchison, T G
1987 Response to questionnaire, 19 June.

Alatas, H A
1977 *The Myth of the Lazy Native.* London: Frank Cass.

Allen, Bryant J
1976 Information Flow and Innovation Diffusion in the East Sepik, Papua New Guinea. PhD thesis, Research School of Pacific Studies, Australian National University, Canberra.
1983 A Bomb or a Bullet or the Bloody Flux? Population Change in the Aitape, Inland Papua New Guinea 1941–1945. *The Journal of Pacific History* 18:219–235.

Amean, A
1973 Early Methods of Punishment in the Highlands 1936 to 1960. *Oral History,* no 7:23–26.

Amero, Bega
  1985   Interviewed at Nukakau village, Talasea subdistrict, West New Britain
         Province, 2 March.

Anderson, F D, Assistant District Officer
  1956   Patrol Report, District of Central, Report No 10/55–56. Area
         Patrolled: Upper Kunimaipa Valley. Central District Patrol Reports
         1955–1956, Tapini.

Anderson, George
  1987   Response to questionnaire, 12 July.

ANGAU, Australian New Guinea Administrative Unit
  1943   "Patrol Reports, Monthly Reports, etc, by District Personnel." Issued
         by Australian Military Forces, ANGAU HQ, Ramu District, 22 March.
         In Fulton Papers. Copy provided by Dr Bryant Allen, Department of
         Human Geography, Australian National University.

Anka, Sakarias
  1986   Interviewed at Okiufa village, Goroka township, Eastern Highlands
         Province, 19 August.

Arnold, David
  1986   *Police Power and Colonial Rule: Madras 1859–1947*. Delhi: Oxford Uni-
         versity Press.

Aufenanger, Henry, Father
  1976   Report on the Early Days when the Catholic Mission Started Its Activ-
         ities in the Unexplored Areas of the Bismarck Mountains. Typescript.

Australia, Commonwealth
  1927   Report to the Council of the League of Nations on the Administra-
         tion of the Territory of New Guinea, from 1 July 1926 to 30 June 1927.
  Var   Police Forces of the External Territories of the Commonwealth of
         Australia. Australian Archives, Canberra. CRS A518, item AQ 112.

Australia. Parliament
  1920   Interim and Final Reports of Royal Commission on Late German
         New Guinea. 15.

Avila
  1989   Interviewed at Tapini station, Tapini subdistrict, Central Province, 23
         November. Kemigara, a community leader at the station, helped
         with the interview.

AWM, Australian War Memorial
  1939–1945a War of 1939–1945 document 419–5–6. Received from first Aus-
         tralian Army. Indexed 80–6–546–1. AWM SP 676.
  1939–1945b Police and Prison Policy. Royal Papuan Constabulary General
         1045, received from 8MD. AWM: War of 1939–1945, No, 506–8–3.
         Indexed 447–1–783–1. AWM SP 1108.
  1939–1945c "European and Native Constabulary—Use of as an Armed
         Force. Papua and the Mandated Territory of New Guinea," by Lieu-
         tenant Colonel, GSN Command. Received from 8MD. Classification
         no 506–5–15. Indexed 576–1. AWM SP 223.

1944 "Papuan Infantry Battalion. Raising, History and Purpose. Administration and Control of Native Battalions in New Guinea 1943–44. Australian Military Forces." Received from MIIS. Classification no 721–8–9. Indexed 419–3506–8. AWM file 422–7–8.
1945 "Statistics and Employment of New Guinea Natives 1942–1945. . . ." AWM 54, 506/5/19.
1946 Statement by Native Police Boys re the Treatment of the Inhabitant Natives. Received from 8MD, Rabaul. AWM: War of 1939–1945. No 1010–4–161. Indexed 506–2. AWM 422–7–8.

Balandier, G
1966 The Colonial Situation: A Theoretical Approach. In *Social Change: The Colonial Situation,* edited by Immanuel Wallerstein, 34–61. New York: John Wiley & Sons.

Ballard, John J
1976 Wantok and Administration. Public lecture, University of Papua New Guinea.

Barnes, J A
1966 Indigenous Politics and Colonial Administration with Special Reference to Australia. In *Social Change: The Colonial Situation,* edited by Immanuel Wallerstein, 214–231. New York: John Wiley & Sons.

Barrett, Don
1969 The Pacific Islands Regiment. In *The History of Melanesia,* edited by K S Inglis, 493–502. Port Moresby: Second Waigani Seminar.

Bateson, Gregory
1932 Social Structure of the Iatmul People of the Sepik River. *Oceania* 11 (March): 245–291.

Bayley, David H
1969 *The Police and Political Development in India.* Princeton, NJ: Princeton University Press.

Beaver, W N
1920 *Unexplored New Guinea.* London: Seeley, Service.

Belshaw, Cyril S
1950 *Island Administration in the South Pacific: Government and Reconstruction in New Caledonia, the New Hebrides, and the British Solomon Islands.* London: Royal Institute of International Affairs.

Berkley, George E
1969 *The Democratic Policemen.* Boston: Beacon Press.

Beu, Iworo
1989 Interviewed at Tave village, Eia, Oro Province, 6 December.

Bignold, E B, Acting Crown Law Officer
1947a Letter of 28 October to J K Murray on "Shooting of Five Natives by an Administration Patrol near Kouno, Central Highlands, 21st July 1947." Australian Archives, Canberra. Territory of Papua New Guinea. CRS A518, item W 841/1.

1947b Letter of 8 November on "Shooting of Five Natives by an Administration Patrol near Kouno, Central Highlands, 21st July 1947." Australian Archives, Canberra Territory of Papua New Guinea. CRS A518, item W 841/1.

1947c Letter of 23 December to J K Murray on "Shooting of Natives at Kouna." Australian Archives, Canberra. Territory of Papua New Guinea. CRS A518, item W 841/1.

Biskup, Peter
1968   Dr Albert Hahl: Sketch of a German Colonial Official. *Australian Journal of Politics and History,* (December): 349–350.

Biskup, Peter, Brian Jinks, and Hank Nelson
1968   *A Short History of New Guinea.* Sydney: Angus & Robertson.

Black, Algernon D
1968   *The People and the Police.* New York: McGraw-Hill.

Boino, John
1989   Interviewed at Laloki squatter settlement, Central Province, 20 September.

Bordua, David J
1967   *The Police: Six Sociological Essays.* New York: John Wiley & Sons.

Bourke, R M
1988   *Taim Hangre:* Variation in Subsistence Food Supply in the Papua New Guinea Highlands. PhD thesis, Research School of Pacific Studies, Australian National University.

Bowber, W
1912   Copy of Official Journal of Assistant Resident Magistrate, Rigo, Central Division. October. Australian Archives, Canberra. CRS G91, item 608B, 11.

Bramell, J B C
1987   Response to questionnaire, 7 July.

Braudel, Fernand
1982   *Civilization and Capitalism 15th–18th Century,* volume 2: *The Wheels of Commerce.* Translated from French by Siân Reynolds. London: William Collins & Sons.

Bridge, K W J, Patrol Officer
1933a   Notes on Natives Encountered during Patrol in Upper Watut Area, June 1933, Morobe District. Report on Patrols. Australian Archives, Canberra. CRS AS 13/26.

1933b   Report of a Patrol through the Area Inhabited by the Manki Tribe of Natives, Upper Watut, Morobe District, May 1933. Australian Archives, Canberra. CRS AS 13/26, item 32.

British New Guinea. *See* Papua.

Brown, Ken
1987   Response to questionnaire and enclosed article, 1 July.

Brown, Michael K
    1984   *Working the Street: Police Discretion and the Dilemmas of Reform.* New York: Russel Sage Foundation.

Brown, Paula
    1973   *The Chimbu: A Study of Change in the New Guinea Highlands.* London: Routledge & Kegan Paul.
    1982   Chimbu Disorder: Tribal Fighting in Newly Independent Papua New Guinea. *Pacific Viewpoint* 22:1–21.

Buna: Station Journals 1920–1921
    1921   Microfilm. Commonwealth Archives, Canberra. CRS G91, item 105.

Burnell, F S
    1915   *Australia versus Germany: The Story of the Taking of German New Guinea.* London: George Allen & Unwin.

Burridge, Kenelm
    1960   *Mambu: A Study of Melanesian Cargo Movements and Their Ideological Background.* New York: Harper Torch Books.

Carr, E H
    1961   *What Is History?* Harmondsworth: Penguin Books.

Carrington, Charles
    1970   *Rudyard Kipling: His Life and Work.* Harmondsworth: Penguin Books.

Champion, Ivan F
    1936a *Annual Report 1936,* 47.
    1936b Bamu-Purari Patrol. Patrol report. Copy with Mirin Jani Champion, Canberra.
    1966   *Across New Guinea from the Fly to the Sepik.* London: Lansdowne.
    1987   Interviewed at Curtin, Canberra, 2 January.

Champion, Ivan F, and C T J Adamson
    1938   Establishment of First Camp at Lake Kutubu. Patrol report. 11 January. Item 11.

Chappell, D, and P R Wilson
    1969   *The Police and the Public in Australia and New Zealand.* Brisbane: University of Queensland Press.

Chester, K I
    1949   Murder of No. 4102 Constable Hareho. Patrol Report. Goilala 1948–1950. Report No 6 of 1948–1949. Area: Lauavai [Ravavai], Ilai, Goilala Police Post. Purpose: 1. To investigate murder of No 4102 Constable Hareho, and to make arrests of those responsible.

Chinnery, E W
    1920   The Opening of New Territories in Papua. *The Geographical Journal* 55 (1): 439–459.

Claridge, R M
    1956   Patrol Report No 7 of 1955–1956, Mendi, Southern Highlands District. Territory of Papua and New Guinea.

Clark, Herbert E (Lynn), Patrol Officer
1951 Attack on Upper Purari Patrol Delta Division. Report on Patrols. Department of Territories. February. Australian Archives, Canberra, CRS AS 13/26.
1985 Letter in response to request in *Una Voce* newsletter seeking information on police.
1987 Response to questionnaire, 25 June.

CLO, Crown Law Officer
1939–1945 Police as Combatants. Memo from the Crown Law Officer to His Honour the Administrator. Received from 8MD. AWM: War of 1939–1945, no 506–5–15. Indexed 576–1. AWM SP223.

Coatman, John
1959 *Police.* London: Oxford University Press.

Cole, Robert R
1955 Patrol Report 7–[Mendi]–1955/56, Mr R M Claridge. Letter to Director, Department of Native Affairs, Port Moresby, 10 November.
1985 Letter in response to request in *Una Voce* newsletter seeking information on police, 29 March.
1987 Response to questionnaire, 17 June.

Collins, Robert O, ed
1970 *Problems in the History of Colonial Africa 1860–1960.* Englewood Cliffs, NJ: Prentice-Hall.

Connelly, Ken
1987 Response to questionnaire, 23 July.

Connolly, Bob, and Robin Anderson
1983 *First Contact.* 16 mm video. 54 minutes. Arundel, Sydney.
1987 *First Contact: New Guinea's Highlanders Encounter the Outside World.* New York: Viking.

Conrad, Joseph
1984 Heart of Darkness. In *Youth, Heart of Darkness: The End of the Tether,* edited by Robert Kimbrough. London: Oxford University Press.

Costelloe, John A, Assistant District Officer
1947a Letter of 11 August, from Kundiawa, addressed "Dear Jim [Taylor]" and signed "JAC." Australian Archives, Canberra. CRS A518, item W841/1.
1947b Statement to Inspector J H McDonald at Kerowagi, 2 December. Enclosed in McDonald 1947.

Cramer, James
1964 *The World's Police.* London: Cassell.

CT, *Canberra Times.* Daily.

Danns, George K
1982 *Domination and Power in Guyana: A Study of the Police in a Third World Context.* New Brunswick, NJ: Transaction Books.

Daulei, Enau
1989   Interviewed at Two Mile Hill, Port Moresby, 10 September.

Davidson, J W
1971   The Decolonization of Oceania. *The Journal of Pacific History* 6:133–150.

Denoon, Donald
1983   *Settler Capitalism: The Dynamics of Dependent Development in the Southern Hemisphere.* London: Oxford University Press.

Dexter, David
1961   *The New Guinea Offensives.* Canberra: Australian War Memorial.

Donaldson, Mike
1984   Articulation at the Level of the Political: Colonial Intrusion in the Highlands of Papua New Guinea. In *Social Stratification in Papua New Guinea,* edited by R J May, 193–218. Working paper 5. Canberra: Department of Social and Political Change, Australian National University.

Downs, Ian F G, Patrol Officer
1973   Annual Report, Chimbu Sub-District 1930–40. New Guinea Patrol and Other Reports 1936–1949. Pacific Manuscripts Bureau 607: 21.
1986   *The Last Mountain: A Life in Papua New Guinea.* Brisbane: University of Queensland Press. Excellent, fair account of his work as a patrol officer, with much insight.

Dutton, Tom
1985   *Police Motu: Iena Sivarai (Its Story).* Port Moresby: University of Papua New Guinea Press.
1987   "Successful Intercourse Was Had with the Natives": Aspects of European Contact Methods in the Pacific. In *A World of Language: Papers Presented to Professor S A Wurm on His 65th Birthday,* edited by Donald C Laycock and Werner Winter, 153–171. Pacific Linguistics C-100. Canberra: Department of Linguistics, Research School of Pacific Studies, Australian National University.

Eggleston, F W, H L Murray, and H O Townsend
1939   Report of Committee Appointed to Survey the Possibility of Establishing a Combined Administration of the Territories of Papua and New Guinea. Commonwealth Parliamentary Papers, 24. Canberra.

Emery, John
1984   *The Sky People.* Adelaide: Rigby.

Empere, Piaka
1986   Interviewed at Gabsongekeg village, Markham, Morobe Province, 13 August.

Eri, Vincent
1976   *The Crocodile.* Brisbane: Jacaranda Press.

Evara, James Ori
1986   Interviewed at Erima squatter settlement, Port Moresby, National Capital District, 5 August.

Extract from Report to League of Nations
  1930   Extract from Report to the Council of the League of Nations on the
         Administration of the Territory of New Guinea from 1st July 1929 to
         30th June 1930. CRS A518, item AA 840/1/4 P2, page 143. Australian
         Archives, Canberra.

Fanon, Franz
  1963   *The Wretched of the Earth,* translated by Constance Farrington. London:
         Penguin Books.

Feldt, Eric
  1946   *The Coast Watchers.* Melbourne: Oxford University Press.

Fieldhouse, D K
  1986   *The Colonial Empires: A Comparative Survey from the Eighteenth Century.*
         London: Macmillan.

Firth, Stewart
  1982   *New Guinea under the Germans.* Melbourne: Melbourne University
         Press.

Fitzpatrick, Peter
  1980   *Law and State in Papua New Guinea.* London: Academic Press.

Foran, Robert W
  1962   *The Kenya Police.* London: Robert Hale.

Fulton Papers
  1943   Patrol Reports, Monthly Reports, etc., by District Personnel. 22
         March. Issued by Australian Military Forces, ANGAU headquarters,
         Ramu District. Pacific Manuscripts Bureau 610.

Fusitu'a, 'Eseta, and Noel Rutherford
  1977   George Tupou II and the British Protectorate. In *Friendly Islands: A
         History of Tonga,* edited by Noel Rutherford, 173–189. Melbourne:
         Oxford University Press.

Gammage, Bill
  1975   The Rabaul Strike. *The Journal of Pacific History* 10 (3–4): 3–29.

Garuwa, Osborne
  1932   Corporal Garuwa's Examination Paper. *The Papuan Villager* 4 (10): 75.
  1933   Garuwa's Marching Song. *The Papuan Villager* 5 (10): 75.

Giddings, Rick J
  1967   Constabulary Arms: A Short History. *Kumul* 1 (4): 9–11.
  1987   Response to questionnaire, 6 September.

Gore, R T
  1966   *Justice versus Sorcery.* Brisbane: Jacaranda.

Goro, Sebastin
  1985   Interviewed at Sanananda village, Oro Province, 26 June.

Griffin, Andrew
  1980   Story of a Brave Soldier: Warrant Officer Yauwiga. *Times of Papua New
         Guinea,* 7.

Griffin, H L
   1907   Report on Armed Constabulary 1906–1907: Papua Report year ended
            30 June 1907. Canberra: Parliament of Australia, 100.

Griffin, James, Hank Nelson, and Stewart Firth
   1979   *Papua New Guinea: A Political History*. Melbourne: Heinemann Educa-
            tional Australia.
   1988   The Men Who Saved the South-West Pacific. *Times of Papua New
            Guinea*.

Grimshaw, J S
   1947   Investigation by Mr J H McDonald, Inspector of Police, in the Alleged
            Unlawful Killing of 5 Natives in the Kouno Area, Central Highlands
            District. Memorandum to Government Secretary dated 18 December.
            Australian Archives, Canberra. CRS A518, item W841/1.

Grimshaw, Peter
   1972   Police after World War II. In *Encyclopaedia of Papua and New Guinea*,
            edited by Peter Ryan, 2:916–919. Melbourne: Melbourne University
            Press in association with the University of Papua New Guinea.

Guha, Ranajit
   1986   Idioms of Dominance and Subordination in Colonial India. Written
            for Second Subaltern Studies Conference, Calcutta, January. Austra-
            lian National University, Canberra.

Guise, Sir John
   1953   *I Gazed in Wonder*. Port Moresby.
   1985   Interviewed at Waigani, Port Moresby, National Capital District, 9
            February.

Hahl, Albert
   1980   *Governor in New Guinea*, translated by Peter G Sack and Dymphna
            Clark. Canberra: Australian National University Press.

Haldane, Robert
   1986   *The People's Force: A History of the Victoria Police*. Melbourne: Melbourne
            University Press.

Halligan, J R
   1938   Administration of Native Races. *Oceania* 9 (September): 266–285.

Hallpike, C R
   1977   *Bloodshed and Vengeance in the Papuan Mountains: The Generations of
            Conflict in Tauade Society*. Oxford: Oxford University Press. Especially
            the introduction: 1–25.

Hart, J M
   1951   *The British Police*. London: George Allen & Unwin.

Hart, Liddell B H
   1972   *History of the First World War*. London: Pan Books.

Hasluck, Sir Paul
   1976   *A Time for Building: Australian Administration in Papua New Guinea
            1951–1963*. Melbourne: Melbourne University Press.

Hau'ofa, Epeli
   1971   Mekeo Chieftainship. *The Journal of the Polynesian Society* 80 (2): 152–
          169.

Haydon, A L
   1911   *The Trooper Police of Australia.* London: Andrew Melrose.

Hayes, Maxwell
   1967   The Royal Papua New Guinea Constabulary: Some Notes on Its Ori-
          gin. January. Typescript. Quoting *Report of the* Neu Guinea Kompagnie
          of 1887.
   1978   Papua New Guinea. *The Australian Stamp Monthly* 141 (September).
   1986   Response to request in *Una Voce* newsletter seeking information on
          police, 7 January.

Healy, A M
   1962   Native Administration and Local Government in Papua 1880–1960.
          PhD thesis, Research School of Pacific Studies, Australian National
          University, Canberra.

Hempenstall, Peter J
   1975   Resistance in the German Pacific Empire: Towards a Theory of Early
          Colonial Response. *The Journal of the Polynesian Society* 84 (1): 5–24.
   1978   *Pacific Islanders under German Rule: A Study in the Meaning of Colonial
          Resistance.* Canberra: Australian National University Press.

Hezel, Francis X
   1995   *Strangers in Their Own Land: A Century of Colonial Rule in the Caroline
          and Marshall Islands.* Pacific Islands Monograph Series 13. Honolulu:
          University of Hawai'i Press.

Hicks, E G, Acting Assistant District Officer
   1951   Special Investigation Report: Attack by Porei Natives on Government
          Patrol. 31 July. Australian Archives, Canberra. CRS AS 13/26, item 60.

Hides, Jack G
   1935   *Through Wildest Papua.* Glasgow: Blackie.
   1936   *Papuan Wonderland.* London: Blackie.
   1938   *Savages in Serge: The Story of the Papuan Constabulary.* Sydney. Angus &
          Robertson. Deals with work of the Papuan police and describes
          author's experiences in Papua.

Hides, Jack G, and James L O'Malley
   1933   Seven Extracts of Report on Patrol North and West of Mt Yule and
          along the Kunimaipa Valley. Australian Archives, Canberra. CRS AS
          13/26.
   1935   Report on Strickland-Purari Patrol, 1934–1935. Central Division. Re-
          port of Patrols. Papua New Guinea 1922–1935. Department of Exter-
          nal Territories. Australian Archives, Canberra. CRS AS 13/126, item 5.
   nd   Extracts of Patrols to Tauri and Tiver River Headquarters Including
          Notes on the People of the Kaipou. Australian Archives, Canberra.
          CRS 13/26, item 3.

Higginson, G H, Resident Magistrate, Eastern Division
1921   Conflict with the Inland People, Kwabikwabi, Fergusson Island. 7 January. Addressed to Government Secretary. Commonwealth Archives, Canberra. CRS G118, item A173.

Hogbin, Ian H
1951   *Transformation Scene: The Changing Culture of a New Guinea Village.* London: Routledge & Kegan Paul.

Howe, K R
1984   *Where the Waves Fall: A New South Sea Islands History from First Settlement to Colonial Rule.* Sydney: George Allen & Unwin; Pacific Islands Monograph Series, 2. Honolulu: University of Hawai'i Press.

Hudson, W J, ed
1971   *Australia and Papua New Guinea.* Sydney: Sydney University Press.

Hughes, Ian
1978   Good Money and Bad: Inflation and Devaluation in the Colonial Process. *Mankind,* no 11, 308–318.

Humphries, W R, Major
1923   *Patrolling in Papua.* With an introduction by J H Murray. London: Fisher Unwin.
1945   Comments by Experienced Administration Officers: First Papuan Infantry Battalion. Appendix D. Australian Military Forces HQ ANGAU, 15 September. Reference AQ 204.

Igarobae, Athanasius
1986   Interviewed at Tokarara, Port Moresby, National Capital District, 4 August.
1989   Interviewed at Ioma, Oro Province, 10 December.

Inglis, Amirah
1974   *Not a White Woman Safe: Sexual Anxiety and Politics in Port Moresby 1920–1934.* Canberra: Australian National University Press.
1982   *Karo: The Life and Fate of a Papuan.* Port Moresby and Canberra: Institute of Papua New Guinea Studies in association with Australian National University.

Inglis, K S
1968   War, Race and Loyalty in New Guinea 1939–1945. In *The History of Melanesia,* edited by K S Inglis, 503–529. Port Moresby: Second Waigani Seminar.

Iwagu Aladu, Sergeant
1986   Interviewed at Taemi village, Finschhafen, Morobe Province, 22 November, by Klaus Neumann.

Jeffries, Sir Charles
1952   *The Colonial Police.* London: Max Parrish.

Jinks, Brian, Peter Biskup, and Hank Nelson
1973   *Readings in New Guinea History.* Sydney: Angus & Robertson.

Johnston, George H
    1943   *New Guinea Diary.* Sydney: Angus & Robertson.

Jones, J H
    1947   Central Highlands. Death of Five Natives in Chimbu Area. Secret memorandum to government secretary's office, dated 28 October. Australian Archives, Canberra. CRS A518, item W841/1.

Joyce, R B
    1971   *Sir William MacGregor.* Melbourne: Oxford University Press.

Kambian
    1989   Interviewed at Mendi station, Southern Highlands Province, 18 October.

Kamuna, Hura
    1985   Interviewed near Bumbu River, Lae township, Morobe Province, 17 May.

Kasse, Aibuki
    1985   Interviewed at Nukakau village, Talasea subdistrict, West New Britain Province, 25 March.

Kegeriai, Veronika
    1985   Interviewed at Orobomarai village, Gende, Madang Province, 14 July.

Keesing, Roger, and Peter Corris
    1980   *Lightning Meets the West Wind: The Malaita Massacre.* Melbourne: Melbourne University Press.

Keogh, Gerard, Acting Assistant District Officer, and A Coomber, Medical Assistant
    1934   Special investigation—Korosomeri River Area, Sepik District. Object: Investigation of reported killings. Patrol Report SD 5/1933–34. Australian Archives. Canberra. CRS AS 13/26, item 18.

Keogh, Jim
    1987   Response to questionnaire, 30 June. He was not a patrol officer.

Kerr, Martin
    1973   *New Guinea Patrol.* London: Hale.

Kituai, August
    1977   Patrol Officers: Beasts of Burden of the Administration. *Yagl-Ambu* 4 (4): 239–217.
    1986   Papua New Guinean Policemen of the Colonial Period. In *Law and Order in a Changing Society,* edited by Louise Morauta, 20–29. Political and Social Change Monograph 6. Canberra: Department of Political and Social Change, Research School of Pacific Studies, Australian National University.
    1988   Innovation and Intrusion: Villagers and Policemen in PNG. *The Journal of Pacific History* 23 (2): 156–166.

Koch, Klaus-Friedrich
    1974   *The Anthropology of Warfare.* Addison-Wesley Module in Anthropology 52. Reading, MA: Addison-Wesley.

Kurita, Hiroyuki
    1985   Who Came First? The Contact History of the Fasu-Speaking People, Papua New Guinea. *Man and Culture in Oceania* 1:55–66.

Kyle, Alan F (Bill), Assistant District Officer
    1934   Upper Ramu to Biakira and Kambadidan, Morobe District, 21.7.33–4.8.33. Patrol Report B3/33–34. Australian Archives, Canberra. CRS AS 13/26, item 38.

Lacey, Roderic
    1979   Where Have All the Young Men Gone? Village Economies in Transition in Colonial Papua New Guinea. Paper presented at congress of Australia New Zealand Association for the Advancement of Science, November–December, New Zealand.

Lawrence, Peter
    1964   *Road Belong Cargo.* Manchester: Manchester University Press.

Leadley, A J
    1976   A History of the Japanese Occupation of the New Guinea Islands, and the Effects, with Special Reference to the Tolai People of the Gazelle Peninsula. Master's thesis, History Department, University of Papua New Guinea, Port Moresby.

Leahy, Michael
    1935   Reports of Patrols: The Central Highlands of New Guinea. Australian Archives, Canberra. CRS AS 13/26.

Legge, J D
    1956   *Australian Colonial Policy.* Sydney: Angus & Robertson.

Lett, Lewis
    1935   *Knights Errant of Papua.* London: William Blackwood. About officers who worked in Papua.
    1944   *The Papuan Achievement.* Melbourne: Melbourne University Press.

Long, Gavin
    1963   *Australia in the War of 1939–1945* (Series 1). Volume 7: *The Final Campaigns.* Canberra: Australian War Memorial.
    1973   *The Six Years War: A Concise History of Australia in the 1939–1945 War.* Canberra: Australian War Memorial.

Low, D A
    1973   *Lion Rampant: Essays in the Study of Imperialism.* London: Frank Cass. A comprehensive study of British imperialism in Africa.

Lugard, F D
    1922   *The Dual Mandate in Tropical Africa.* London.

Lutton, Nancy
    1978   C A W Monckton: Reprobate Magistrate. In *Papua New Guinea Portraits: The Expatriate Experience,* edited by James Griffin, 48–74. Canberra: Australian National University Press.

Lyng, J
    1919   *Our New Possession.* Melbourne: Melbourne Publishing Company.

MacGregor, Sir William
  1912   Introduction. In *Papua and New Guinea,* by Sir Hubert Murray. London. T Fisher Unwin.

Mackenzie, S S
  1987   *The Australians at Rabaul: The Capture and Administration of German Possessions in the Southern Pacific.* Volume 10 of *The Official History of Australia in the War of 1914–1918.* Brisbane: University of Queensland Press.

Maher, Robert
  1961   *New Men of Papua: A Study in Culture Change.* Madison: University of Wisconsin Press.

Mair, Lucy Philip
  1948   *Australia in New Guinea.* Melbourne University Press. Reprinted 1970 (London: Christophers).

Malaguna Commission
  1929   Report of Commission Appointed to Inquire into and Report upon Matters Relating to the Mass Meetings of Natives that Occurred at the Roman Catholic and Methodist Mission Stations at Malaguna on the Second and Third Days of January, One Thousand Nine Hundred and Twenty-nine, Including the Origin and Causes of the Meetings. Australian Archives, Canberra. CRS A518, item AA 840/1/4 P2.

Mann, Ira J, Reverend
  nd   "Lieut Taylor." In Mann Diary and Papers, 1914–1941. PMB 630.

Mannoni, O
  1956   *Prospero and Caliban: The Psychology of Colonization.* London: Methuen.

Mason, Philip
  1971   *Patterns of Dominance.* London: Oxford University Press.

Masselman, George
  1963   *The Cradle of Colonialism.* New Haven: Yale University Press. Good introduction to early Dutch period.

Maude, H E
  1968   *Of Islands and Men.* Melbourne: Oxford University Press.

May, R J, ed
  1977   *Change and Movement: Readings on Internal Migration in Papua New Guinea.* Canberra: Papua New Guinea Institute of Applied Social & Economic Research in association with Australian National University.

McCarthy, Dudley
  1959   *South-West Pacific Area—First Year: Kokoda to Wau.* Canberra: Australian War Memorial.
  1980   *The Fate of O'Loughlin.* London. Macdonald General Books.

McCarthy, J K, Patrol Officer
  1932   Investigation of the Leahy Brothers Incident, Tauri River, Morobe District. Department of External Territories. Report on Patrols. Australian Archives, Canberra.

1933a Isimb, Langimar, Vailala, and Tauri Rivers. Object: Consolidation—
       Covering of Some New Country. Patrol Report B19/32–33, 12–3–
       1933 to 26–4–1933. Australian Archives, Canberra. CRS AS 13/26,
       item 34a.

1933b Tauri Langimar Patrol: Progress Report from 7.8.33–2.9.33. Austra-
       lian Archives, Canberra, CRS AS 13/26, item 43.

1933c Being the Report of an Armed Patrol that Proceeded from the Oti-
       banda Post to the Tauri Rivers, District of Morobe, Salamaua, Terri-
       tory of New Guinea. 13 December. Australian Archives, Canberra,
       CRS 13/26, item 44.

1963   *Patrol into Yesterday: My New Guinea Years.* Melbourne: F W Cheshire.
       Describes author's experiences as a patrol officer.

McDonald, J H, Inspector of Police
1947   Kouno Area, Central Highlands: Death of Five Natives. Report to
       Director of District Services and Native Affairs, Port Moresby. 11
       December. Australian Archives, Canberra. CRS A518, item W841/1.

McNicoll, W Ramsay
nd   "Defence Scheme." Letter to Secretary, Prime Minister's Department,
       Canberra. Australian Archives, Brighton. MP729/6, file 16/401/272.

Mead, Margaret
1956   *New Lives for Old: Cultural Transformation, Manus 1928–1953.* New York:
       Mentor.

Meava
1987   Highlands Trail-Blazer Dies as a . . . Forgotten Man of Papua New
       Guinea History! *Papua New Guinea Post-Courier,* 6 November.

Meggitt, Mervyn
1977   *Blood Is Their Argument: Warfare among the Mae Enga Tribesmen of the
       New Guinea Highlands,* Palo Alto, CA: Mayfield.

Melbourne Age
1986   Saturday Extra. 20 September. Sent to me by Peter Ryan, 22 June
       1987.

Melrose, Robert
1941   Letter addressed to "General," dated 29 August. Australian Archives,
       Brighton. MP729/6, file 16/401/456.

Mennis, Mary
1982   *Hagen Saga: The Story of Father William Ross, Pioneer American Missionary
       to Papua New Guinea.* Boroko: Institute of Papua New Guinea Studies.

Meraveka
1986   Interviewed at Ten Mile squatter settlement, Port Moresby, National
       Capital District, 31 July.

Mercer, P M
1979   Oral Tradition in the Pacific: Problems of Interpretation. *The Journal
       of Pacific History* 14 (3–4): 130–153.

Milligan, J S
  1937 Report of Attacks on Patrol Party and on Kobakini Base Camp by Natives of Towedo and Hogenciwa. 22 November. Australian Archives, Canberra. CRS AS 13/26, item 54.
  1937 Report on Native Constabulary. In Patrols Conducted from Kobakini Base Camp during the Months of September, October and November 1937. Report. Australian Archives, Canberra. CRS AS 13/26, item 53.

Milte, Kerry L
  1977 *Police in Australia: Development Functions and Procedures.* Sydney: Butterworths.

Moag, Moru
  1986 Interviewed at Gabsongekeg village, Markham No. 1, Morobe Province, 11 August.

Mohaviea, Loholo
  1986 Interviewed at Erima squatter settlement, Port Moresby, 6 August.

Monckton, C A W
  1921 *Some Experiences of a New Guinea Resident Magistrate.* London: John Lane.
  1922 *Last Days in New Guinea: Being Further Experiences of a New Guinea Magistrate.* London: John Lane.

Monk, Lieutenant F D
  1944 Report on Native Affairs during Enemy Occupation, Madang Area 1944. Australian War Memorial document received from HQ Morotai Force. No 419–5–9. Indexed 599–7. AWM file 417–1–4.

Morrah, Patrick
  1963 The History of the Malayan Police. *Journal of the Malayan Branch, Royal Asiatic Society* 36 (202): 1–172.

Morris, Basil, Brigadier Commander
  1940 European and Native Constabulary: Use of as an Armed Force in Papua and the Mandated Territory of New Guinea. Australian War Memorial document received from 8MD. No 506–5–15. Indexed 576–1. AWM SP 223.

Morris, James
  1968 *Pax Britannica: The Climax of an Empire.* London: Penguin Books.

Munster, Peter
  1981 That Desperate Finintugu Affray: A Tragic Chapter in the Story of Contact between New Guineans and Europeans in the Central Highlands of New Guinea. Copy in the New Guinea Collection, University of Papua New Guinea.
  1984 A History of Contact in the Goroka Valley 1930–1952. PhD thesis, University of Papua New Guinea, Port Moresby.

Murray, Sir Hubert
  1908 Armed Constabulary. In *Papua Annual Report 1907–1908,* 23–24.
  1909 Official instructions on how officers of the armed constabulary and . . . policemen should conduct themselves. Quoted in Bignold 1947a.

1912   *Papua or British New Guinea.* London: T Fisher Unwin.

1918   Report on the Shooting of a Villager by Police and Subsequent Investigation. Report addressed to Minister for State, Home and Territories Department, Melbourne. 22 January. Australian Archives, Canberra. CRS A1, item 18/15 47.

1920   Review of the Australian Administration in Papua from 1907 to 1920. Port Moresby: Government Printer. Published with the assistance of the Commonwealth Government.

1921   Anthropology and the Government of Subject Races. Appendix 1 in *Papua Annual Report, 1919–1920,* 104–111.

1923   Introduction. In *Patrolling in Papua* by W R Humphries. London: Fisher Unwin.

1925   *Papua of Today or an Australian Colony in the Making.* London: P S King & Son. Has two chapters on "recent exploration" involving police and patrol officers.

1928   Indirect Rule in Papua. *Papua Annual Report, 1927–1928.* Appendix A, 82–85.

1929   The Response of the Natives of Papua to Western Civilization. In *Proceedings* of Pan-Pacific Science Congress, 1–15. Port Moresby: Government Printer.

1931   The Armed Constabulary of Papua. *The Police Journal* 4 (1): 571–582.

1932   The Scientific Aspect of the Pacification of Papua. Sydney: Australia New Zealand Association for the Advancement of Science.

1934   Death of Sergeant-Major Simoi. In *Papua Annual Report 1933–1934,* 6.

1935   *The Machinery of Indirect Rule in Papua.* Port Moresby: Government Printer.

Murray, J K
    1947a   The Honourable Minister, through the Secretary, Department of External Territories, Canberra, ACT. Memorandum of 8 November. Australian Archives, Canberra. CRS A518, item W841/1.

    1947b   Death of Five Natives—Highlands Area. Letter to Minister, Department of External Territories, 24 December. Australian Archives, Canberra. CRS A518, item W841/1.

Muru, Fridolin
    1977   Interviewed at Yandera village, Gende, Madang Province, January.

Naguwean, Joseph
    1985   Interviewed at New Guinea Collection, University Library, University of Papua New Guinea, Port Moresby, 12 February.

Nanduka, Nandie
    1989   Interviewed at Ialibu station, Southern Highlands Province, 20 October.

Nayacakalou, R R
    1975   *Leadership in Fiji.* Melbourne: Melbourne University Press.

Nelson, Hank
    1974   *Papua New Guinea: Black Unity or Black Chaos?* Melbourne: Penguin Books.

1976   *Black, White and Gold: Goldmining in Papua New Guinea 1878–1930.*
        Canberra: Australian National University Press.

1978   The Swinging Index. *The Journal of Pacific History* 13:130–152.

1980a   As Bilong Soldia: The Raising of the Papuan Infantry Battalion in
        1940. *Yagl-Ambu* 7 (1): 19–27.

1980b   Hold the Good Name of the Soldier. *The Journal of Pacific History* 15:
        202–216.

1982   *Taim Bilong Masta: Australian Involvement with Papua New Guinea.*
        Sydney: Australian Broadcasting Commission. Three good chapters
        on patrol officers.

1987a   Sergeant-Major Yauwiga. Typescript, 1–5.

1987b   *Taim Bilong Pait na Taim Bilong Hatwok Tru:* Papua New Guinea
        Labourers during the War, 1942–1945. Department of Pacific and
        Southeast Asian History, Australian National University. Typescript.

Neumann, Klaus
1992   *Not the Way It Really Was: Constructing the Tolai Past.* Pacific Islands
        Monograph Series, 10. Honolulu: University of Hawai'i Press.

New Guinea, Territory of
1922   New Guinea Police Force Ordinance, No. 12 of 1922. *Laws of the Terri-
        tory of New Guinea.* In *Commonwealth of Australia Gazette,* no 28 (24
        March): 122–126.

1925   *District Standing Instructions, 1925.* Copy in my possession courtesy of
        Dudley McCarthy, Canberra.

NGAR, New Guinea Annual Reports
1914–1962 Canberra: Australian Department of External Territories.

Niall, N R
1933   Reports of Patrols—Western Half of the Talasea Sub-Division. De-
        partment of Territories, MY1/1932–33. Australian Archives, Canberra,
        CRS AS 13/26, item 24.

Nicholls, G H
1913   Armed Native Constabulary. In *Papua Annual Report 1912–1913,* 62.

Normoyle, Chris
1987   Response to questionnaire, 13 September.

NRB, Native Regulation Board
1892   Village Constables. Native Regulation Number 1, 1892. Supplement
        to *British New Guinea Government Gazette* 5, Saturday, 31 December.

Nurton, Allert
1934   Unexplored Country South of the Ramu Police Post, 22-6-1933 to
        13-7-1934. Object: Prospecting and Mapping. Patrol Report B2/33–
        34. Australian Archives, Canberra, CRS AS 13/26, item 37.

nd   Patrol to Long Island for Purposes of Collecting Head Tax and Cen-
        sus, Madang District, Rai Coast. Australian Archives, Canberra. 1920s?

O'Donnell, Gus
1967   Sergeant Adisa: "There Is No Way to the White Man's Things." *New
        Guinea and Australia, the Pacific, and South-East Asia* 2 (2): 10–16.

Ogaia, Girau
    1989   Interviewed on the grounds of the Tapini Hospital, 11 November.

O'Malley, J T
    1908   Report on the Armed Constabulary. In *Papua Annual Report 1907–1908,* Appendix G, 84–45.

Ongi, Nivil
    1989   Interviewed at Kero village, Ialibu, Southern Highlands Province, 20 October.

Oram, Nigel D
    1967   Rabia Camp and the Tommy Kabu Movement. *New Guinea Research Bulletin,* no 14: 3–43. Canberra.
    1976   *Colonial Town to Melanesian City, Port Moresby 1884–1974.* Canberra: Australian National University Press.

Orovea, Lelesi
    1986   Interviewed at Erima squatter settlement, Port Moresby, 5 August.

Orwell, George
    1967   *Burmese Days.* London: Heinemann.

Paliau Maloat
    1970   *Histori Bilong Mi Taim Mi Bin na i Kamap Tede:* The Story of My Life from the Day I was Born until the Present Day. In *The Politics of Melanesia,* edited by Marion Ward, 144–161. Fourth Waigani Seminar (May). Canberra and Port Moresby: Research School of Pacific Studies, Australian National University, and University of Papua New Guinea.

Panoff, Michel
    1969a   An Experiment in Inter-Tribal Contacts: The Maenge Labourers on European Plantations 1915–42. *The Journal of Pacific History* 4:111–125.
    1969b   The Notion of Time among the Maenge of New Britain. *Ethnology* 8 (1): 153–166.

Panau, Peter Daguna
    1986   Interviewed at Gerehu, Port Moresby, 2 August.

Papua (British New Guinea)
    1888–1908 Minute papers. Annual single number series 1888–1908 [1888–1907] British New Guinea, and Papua Government Secretary, etc. Commonwealth Archives Office, Canberra.
    1890   Armed Constabulary Ordinance No 1 of 1890. In *British New Guinea Government Gazette,* volume 3.
    1890–1941 Files of Correspondence, Journals and Patrol Reports from Outstations, 1890–1941. British New Guinea and Papua Government Secretary. Commonwealth Archives Office, Canberra. CRS G91.
    1892   Village Constables [of the Native Regulations Board]. Regulation 1 of 1892. Supplement to the *British New Guinea Gazette* 5, Saturday, 31 December.
    1914–1930 Papua: Correspondence Files, A Series C. Government Secretary, CRS G118. Commonwealth Archives Office, Canberra.

1939   Papua: An Ordinance Relating to the Royal Papuan Constabulary.
        No 11, 1939, paragraph 7(1). Australian Archives, Canberra. CRS
        A432, item 39/947.

Papua New Guinea, Territory of
1948   Death of Five Natives—Central Highlands Area. 3 January. Austra-
        lian Archives Canberra. Department of External Territories. CRS
        A518, item W 841/1. This document contains most of the correspon-
        dence pertaining to the shooting of five unarmed men from Kouno
        in 1947.

Papuan Villager
1930–1935; 1939–1941. Monthly newspaper.

PAR, *Papua Annual Report*
1891–1961 Canberra: Australian Department of External Territories.
1907   Report on the Armed Native Constabulary. In PAR *1906–1907,* 16, 100.
1911   Armed Constabulary: Report by Acting Headquarters Officer. PAR
        1910–1911, 57.

PIB, Papuan Infantry Battalion
1944   Papuan Infantry Battalion: Raising, History and Purpose. Administra-
        tion and Control of Native Battalions in New Guinea 1943–1944: Aus-
        tralian Military Forces. Received from MHS. AWM: War of 1939–
        1945. No 721–8–3. Indexed 419–3506–8. AWM File 422–7–8.

Piggott, Michael
1984   The Coconut Lancers: A Study of the Men of the Australian Naval and
        Military Expeditionary Force in New Guinea, 1914–1921. BL thesis,
        Australian National University, Canberra.

Pike, Andrew, Hank Nelson, and Gavan Daws
1982   *Angels of War.* Film. 16mm. 54 minutes. Canberra.

PIM, *Pacific Islands Monthly.* Suva.

PNGPC, *Papua New Guinea Post Courier.* Daily. Port Moresby.

Podolefsky, Aaron
1984   Contemporary Warfare in the New Guinea Highlands. *Ethnology* 23
        (2): 73–87.

Pumuye, Nungulu
1989   Interviewed at Yakena village, Ialibu, Southern Highlands Province,
        19 October.

Radford, Robin
1977   Burning the Spears: A Peace Movement in the Eastern Highlands of
        New Guinea 1936–1937. *The Journal of Pacific History* 12 (1–2): 40–54.
1987   *Highlanders and Foreigners in the Upper Ramu: The Kainantu Area 1919–
        1942.* Melbourne: Melbourne University Press.

Radi, Heather
1971   New Guinea under Mandate, 1921–41. In *Australia and Papua New
        Guinea,* edited by W J Hudson, 74–137. Sydney: Sydney University
        Press.

Ranger, T O
 1970   African Reaction to the Imposition of Colonial Rule in East and Cen-
        tral Africa. In *Problems in the History of Colonial Africa 1860–1960,* edited
        by Robert O Collins, 68–82. Englewood Cliffs, NJ: Prentice-Hall.

Reay, Marie
 1982   Lawlessness in the Papua New Guinea Highlands. In *Melanesia: Be-
        yond Diversity,* edited by R J May and Hank Nelson, 2:623–637. Can-
        berra: Research School of Pacific Studies, Australian National Uni-
        versity.

Reed, S W
 1943   *The Making of Modern New Guinea.* Philadelphia: American Philosoph-
        ical Society.

Reith, Charles
 1938   *The Police Idea: Its History and Evolution in England in the Eighteenth Cen-
        tury and After.* London: Oxford University Press.
 1956   *A New Study of Police History.* London: Oliver & Boyd.

Rewari
 1989   Interviewed at Laloki squatter settlement, Central Province, 27 Sep-
        tember.

Roberts, Alan A, Acting Assistant District Officer
 1935   A Report on the Native Inhabitants of the Chimbu Valley: Being a
        Broader Outline of Observations Made in Patrol Report No. B.40/
        1934–1935. Australian Archives, Canberra. CRS AS 13/26, item 51.

Robinson, Neville K
 1979   *Villagers at War: Some Papua New Guinea Experiences in World War II.*
        Pacific Research Monograph 2. Canberra: Australian National Uni-
        versity.

Roe, Margriet
 1971   Papua New Guinea and War 1941–5. In *Australia and Papua New
        Guinea,* edited by W J Hudson, 138–150. Sydney: Sydney University
        Press.

Ross, W A
 1968   The Catholic Mission in the Western Highlands. In *The History of
        Melanesia,* edited by K S Inglis, 319–327. Second Waigani Seminar.
        Port Moresby: Australian National University in association with the
        University of Papua New Guinea.

Rowley, C D
 1958   *The Australians in German New Guinea 1914–1920.* Melbourne: Mel-
        bourne University Press.
 1972   *The New Guinea Villager: A Retrospect from 1964.* Melbourne: Cheshire.

RT, *Rabaul Times*
 1925–1942; 1957–1959. Weekly.

Russell, Bertrand
 1938   *Power: A New Social Analysis.* London: George Allen & Unwin.

Ryan, John
  1969   *The Hot Land: Focus on New Guinea.* Melbourne: Macmillan.

Ryan, Peter A
  1939–1945 Report and Map Showing Patrol Route of Captain L Howlett,
          FELO and Warrant Officer Class 2. AWM 741–5–14. Indexed 587–2.
          AWM File 422–7–8.
  1968   The Australian New Guinea Administrative Unit (ANGAU). In *The
          History of Melanesia,* edited by K S Inglis, 531–548. Second Waigani
          Seminar. Port Moresby: Australian National University in Association
          with the University of Papua New Guinea.
  1985   *Fear Drive My Feet.* Melbourne: Melbourne University Press. Reprint of
          1960 edition.
  1986   Debt of Friendship Must Be Honoured. *The Melbourne Age.* Saturday
          extra, 20 September.

Sack, Peter G
  1974   The Range of Traditional Tolai Remedies. In *Contention and Dispute:
          Aspects of Law and Social Control in Melanesia,* edited by A L Epstein,
          67–92. Canberra: Australian National University Press.

Salisbury, R F
  1962   *From Stone to Steel: Economic Consequences of a Technological Change on
          New Guinea.* Melbourne: Melbourne University Press.

Sarepamo, Tate
  1985   Interviewed at Okiufa village, Goroka township, Eastern Highlands
          Province, 25 July.

Sasa Goreg
  1986   Interviewed at Gabsongekeg village, Markham, Morobe Province, 12
          August.

Scaglion, Richard
  1985   Kiaps as Kings: Abelam Legal Change in Historical Perspective. In
          History and Ethnohistory in Papua New Guinea, edited by Deborah
          Gewertz and Edward Schieffelin, 77–99. Oceania Monograph 28.
          Sydney: University of Sydney.

Scarr, Deryck
  1984   *Fiji: A Short History.* Sydney: George Allen & Unwin.

Schieffelin, E L, and R Crittenden
  1991   *Like People You See in a Dream: First Contact in Six Papuan Societies.* Stan-
          ford: Stanford University Press.

Schwartz, Theodore
  1962   *The Paliau Movement in the Admiralty Islands, 1946–1954.* Anthropo-
          logical Papers of the American Museum of Natural History, volume
          49, part 2. New York: American Museum of Natural History.

Sesetta
  1985   Interviewed at Garasa airstrip, Au village, Garaina, Morobe Province,
          10 May.

Sesiguo, Arenao K
  1977   Life Story of Kamuna Hura as a Policeman. *Yagl-Ambu* 4 (4): 221–237.

Shane, Paul G
  1980   *People and Police: A Comparison of Five Countries.* Toronto: C V Mosby Company.

Simpson, Colin
  1962   *Plumes and Arrows: Inside New Guinea.* Sydney: Angus & Robertson.

Sinclair, James
  1966   *Behind the Ranges: Patrolling in New Guinea.* Melbourne: Melbourne University Press.
  1969   *The Outside Man: Jack Hides of Papua.* Melbourne: Lansdowne. Informed autobiographical account of patrol officer system.
  1972   Police. In *Encylopedia of Papua New Guinea,* edited by Peter Ryan, 2: 916–919. Melbourne: Melbourne University Press in association with the University of Papua New Guinea.
  1981   *Kiap: Australia's Patrol Officers in Papua New Guinea.* Sydney: Pacific Publications. Informed autobiographical account.
  1985   Reponse to request in *Una Voce* newsletter seeking information on police, 9 March.
  1988   *Last Frontiers: The Explorations of Ivan Champion of Papua. A Record of Geographical Exploration in Australia's Territory of Papua between 1926 and 1940.* Gold Coast: Pacific Press.
  1990   *To Find a Path: The Life and Times of the Royal Pacific Islands Regiment,* volume 1: *Yesterday's Heroes 1885–1950.* Gold Coast: Boolarong Publications.

Snell, John L, ed
  1966   *The Outbreak of the Second World War: Design or Blunder? Problems in European Civilization.* Boston: D C Heath & Company.

Somare, Michael
  1975   *Sana: An Autobiography of Michael Somare.* Port Moresby: Niugini.

Sono
  1985   Interviewed at Garaina subdistrict, Morobe Province, 8 May.

Souter, Gavin
  1963   *New Guinea: The Last Unknown.* Sydney: Angus & Robertson.

Strathern, Andrew
  1977   Contemporary Warfare in the New Guinea Highlands: Revival or Breakdown? *Yagl-Ambu* 4 (August): 135–146.
  1979   *Ongka: A Self-Account by a New Guinea Big-Man.* London: Duckworth.
  1984   *A Line of Power.* London: Tavistock Publications.

Strong, W M
  1911   Armed Constabulary: Report by Acting Head-quarters Officer. In *Papua Annual Report 1910–1911,* 61.

Symons, C A J
1947a   Patrol [of] Kouno Area Chimbu Sub-District, District of Central High-
        lands. Confidential report to assistant district officer, 7 September.
        Australian Archives, Canberra, CRS A518, item W841/1.
1947b   Statement to Inspector McDonald at Paramok village, 24 November.
        Enclosed in McDonald 1947.

Tamutai, Naguna
1989   Interviewed at Mendi station, Southern Highlands Province, 18
        October.

Tawi, "Wizakana"
1985   Interviewed at Orobomarai village, Gende, Madang Province, 14 July.

Taylor, Edward
1934   Salamaua: Report. March. Australian Archives, Canberra. File L8/
        41/1.

Taylor, J L
1933   Reports of Patrols. Report on Ramu, Purari Areas, March 1933.
        Morobe District, 1932–1933. Department of External Territories. Aus-
        tralian Archives, Canberra. CRS AS 13/26, item 30.
1947a   Kouno Area—Fracas. Letter to Assistant or District Officer, 13 August.
        Australian Archives, Canberra. CRS A518, item W841/1.
1947b   Kouno Area, Chimbu—Deaths of Five Natives of Names Unknown.
        Confidential letter to Director [J H Jones], Department of District
        Services and Native Affairs, Port Moresby, 10 October. Australian
        Archives, Canberra. CRS A516, item 841/1.
1947c   Letter to J K Murray. 12 December. Australian Archives, Canberra.
        CRS A516, item 841/1.

Thomas, H K, Patrol Officer
1933   Patrol Report to the Hinterland of Sissano, no. A8, Sepik District,
        1932–1933. Australian Archives, Canberra. CRS AS 13/26.

Tigavu, Petrus
1985   Interviewed at New Town, Madang township, Madang Province, 16
        April.

Todd, J A
1935   Native Offences and European Law in South-West New-Britain.
        Oceania 5: 437–460.

Tomasetti, W E
1987   Response to questionnaire, 13 July.

Toogood, C W
1987   Response to questionnaire, 3 July.

ToPagur, Raphael
1982   A History of the Police Association of Papua New Guinea. BA
        Honours thesis (History), University of Papua New Guinea, Port
        Moresby.

ToUna, Blasius
    nd   *Kunai Dumdum.* Recorded by the Institute of Papua New Guinea
          Studies in association with Larrikin Records, Paddington, Australia.

Townsend, G W L
    1933 The Administration of the Mandated Territory of New Guinea. *Geo-
          graphical Journal* 82:424–434.
    1968 *District Officer: From Untamed New Guinea to Lake Success 1921–46.* Syd-
          ney: Pacific Publications. Describes author's experiences as a patrol
          officer.

ToWoworu, Ben Elipas
    1985 Interviewed at Konedobu, Port Moresby, 20 February.

TPNG, Times of Papua New Guinea. Weekly. Port Moresby.

Turney-High, Harry H
    1971 *Primitive War: Its Practice and Concepts.* Second edition. Columbia:
          University of South Carolina Press.

Vial, Leigh G, Patrol Officer
    1938 Some Statistical Aspects of Population in the Morobe District, New
          Guinea. *Oceania* 8 (June): 385–397.

Visit of Native Police
    1942 Visit of New Guinea Native Police to Australia for Propaganda Pur-
          poses. Received from Boris Bane, H A. AWM: War of 1939–1945. No
          431–8–3. Index 50–10–95–2. AWM file 411–3–12.

Waiko, John
    1970 A Payback Murder: The Green Bloodbath. *The Journal of Papua New
          Guinea Society* 4 (2): 96–108.
    1972 *Oro, Oro:* A History of Binandere People. BA Honours thesis, Univer-
          sity of Papua New Guinea.
    1982 *Be Jijimo:* A History According to the Tradition of the Binandere
          People of Papua New Guinea. PhD thesis, Department of Pacific and
          South East Asian History, Australian National University, Canberra.

Wallerstein, Immanuel, ed
    1966 *Social Change: The Colonial Situation.* New York: John Wiley & Sons.

Ward, E J
    1948 Death of Five Natives—Central Highlands Area. Letter to Minister,
          Territory of Papua and New Guinea, 2 January. Australian Archives,
          Canberra. CRS A518, item W841/1.

Ward, R Gerard, and David A M Lea, eds
    1970 *An Atlas of Papua New Guinea.* Port Moresby: University of Papua New
          Guinea and Collins & Longman Atlases.

Wedgwood, Camilla H
    1930 Some Aspects of Warfare in Melanesia. *Oceania* 1 (1): 5–33.

West, Francis J
    1958 Indigenous Labour in Papua New Guinea. *International Labour
          Review* 77 (2): 89–111.

1961   *Political Advancement in the South Pacific: A Comparative Study of Colonial Practice in Fiji, Tahiti and American Samoa.* Melbourne: Oxford University Press.

1968   *Hubert Murray: The Australian Pro-Consul.* Melbourne: Oxford University Press.

West, H
1985   Letter in response to request in *Una Voce* newsletter seeking information on police, 2 April.

White, Osmar
1965   *Parliament of a Thousand Tribes: A Study of New Guinea.* London: Heinemann.

Whittaker, Ben
1964   *The Police.* London: Eyre & Spottiswoode.

Whittaker, J L
1968   New Guinea: The Ethnohistory of First Culture Contact. In *The History of Melanesia,* edited by K S Inglis, 625–643. Second Waigani Seminar. Port Moresby: Australian National University in association with the University of Papua New Guinea.

Wickes, Merry
1975   The Khaki Connection: Of Coups, the Military and Australia. Papua New Guinea Issue of *Meanjin Quarterly* 34 (September): 251–259.

Williams, F E
1928   *Orokaiva Magic.* London: Oxford University Press.
1942   Relations with Natives of New Guinea in War Time. 1 December.

Williams, J C
1959   Training Document Number One. July. Department of Native Affairs, Port Moresby.

Willis, Ian
1974   *Lae Village and City.* Melbourne: Melbourne University Press.

Winston, A W
1922   Patrol Report. Detailed Account of Punitive Expedition to Nakanai/Bainings—Talasea District, New Britain. August 1922. Department of External Territories. Australian Archives, Canberra. CRS AS 13/26, item 22.

Wolfers, Edward P
1971   Games People Play: Whose Ethnohistory? *New Guinea,* (March–April): 43–55.
1975   *Race Relations and Colonial Rule in Papua New Guinea.* Sydney: Australia & New Zealand Book Company.

Wriford, George
1891   Report of the Commandant of the Armed Native Constabulary. In *Papua Annual Report 1890–1891,* 85.

Wright, Malcolm
    1965   *If I Die: Coastwatching and Guerrilla Warfare behind Japanese Lines.* Melbourne: Lansdowne Press.
    1966   *The Gentle Savage.* Melbourne: Lansdowne Press.
    1987   Response to questionnaire, 2 July.

Yegova, Jojoga
    1985   Interviewed at Buna village, Oro Province, 21 June.
    1989   Interviewed at Buna village, Oro Province, 13 December.

Zimmer, Laura
    1985   The Losing Game: Exchange, Migration, and Inequality among the Gende People of Papua New Guinea. PhD dissertation, Bryn Mawr College, Bryn Mawr, Pennsylvania.

Index

Page numbers in **boldface** refer to maps, figures, photos, and tables.

activities, daily, 93, 94, 116–117, 306. *See also* work

Adamson, C T J (Bill), 251, 371n 14

administrative districts, 1, 32–34, **33,** 161, 181; District Standing Instructions, 140–141, 161, 162. *See also* Australia New Guinea Administrative Unit

Administrative Order Number 4, 176

administrative patrols, 117

adultery, 235, 257, 312

age: of patrol officers, 26; of policemen, 70

Agoti, 249

Aina, 232, 235

Aitape, 79

Aitchison, T G, **24–25,** 26

Akopai, 278–279

Akuai, 370n 11

Akuru, 158–159

alcohol abuse, 276–277

Allied Forces, 169, 171, 172, 182–185, 367n 20

Amele, 183

Amero Bega, 36, 38, **51, 59;** arrest of Awai, 254–255; background and recruitment, 58, **177;** killings by, 161, 366n 11; knowledge of homosexual activity, 258–259; reasons for joining police, 82–83; relationship with patrol officer, 36, 38; service injury, 265; training, 101

Anderson, Francis William, 21–22, **24–25**

Anderson, Frederic David, 206–212, 215, 217–218

Anderson, Robin, 39, 241

Angels of War, 195–196

Anis, 249

Anka, Sakarias, **51,** 62, **64,** 124–126, 129, **177,** 188–189

Ansell case, 11

anthropologists, 244–246

Anton, 199

Arms Acts, 9

arrest: resisting, 139, 140–141; of white men by black police, 245–246

Arua, 247

Arwesor, 200–201

Ashton, Lea, 23

Ashton, Sid, 23

assault: indecent, 252; on a superior officer, 252

Ataimbo, 208, 217

atrocities, 142, 212, 218, 222, 368n 2

Australia, 2, 166–167, 283

Australian army, 172, 188

Australia New Guinea Administrative Unit (ANGAU), 52–53, 87, 167–168, 169, 171, 176, 181

Australian Naval and Military Expeditionary Force (ANMEF), 80, 166

Australian School of Pacific Administration (ASOPA), 29–32, 275

Avila, **214,** 215–218

Awai, 254–255

awards and medals, 197, 199–201, 334

Baas, Brother Anthony, 362n 12

background, policemen, 49–52, 68–70, 70–75, 165–166, 287, 321

bad conduct, 252
Bagita Aromau, 115
Baleki, 261 262
Barigi, 246, 266
barracks life, 91–94, 292–293, 311, 325
Barton, Captain, 14
Barton, Sir Francis, 14
Basiana, 11
Bateson, Gregory, 69
Baubau, 184
Beaver, W N, 246
Bell, William, 11
Bendo, 259
Bernard Inquiry, 147, 366n 7
Beu Iworo, 49, **51, 54,** 54–55, 60–61, **177,**
    367n 13
big-men, 20, 68–70
Bignold, E B, 142, 149, 150, 156, 230
biklain, 186, 368n 22
bilum, 73
Biskup, Peter, 4
Black, John, 10, 26, 176
Boe Vagi, 10
boi haus, 213, 369nn 10, 14
Boino, John, **51,** 52–54, **53,** 61, 82, 165,
    177
Borege, 249
Bosanquet, Hort Day, 13
bossbois, 181, 232, 371n 12
Bougainville, 81, 169
Bourke, R M, 371n 14
Bramell, J B C, 23, **24–25**
bride-price, 230, 317
brizivai, 227, 370n 6
brotherhood of police. *See* esprit de
    corps
Brown, Ken, **24–25,** 250
Brown, Michael K, 135, 138
Buna, 169
Bundi. *See* Gende
Bundikara, 232
burning: houses, 141, 144, 167; as punish-
    ment, 210–212, 213–215
Bus, 151, 153, 154
bushcraft, 121, 123–124, 126, 191–192,
    201–202
bush-kanaka (Kanaka), 130, 262, 282
bush work. *See* patrols

cadets, patrol officer, 29–32, 32–33, 360 n 9,
    365n 1 (Chap 5)
camps, 119–120, **120**

Canberra Times, 366n 8
caning, 213, 228, 229, 233, 234, 242, 352
cannibalism, 71, 118, 130, 311
cargo cults, 278–279, 330
census taking, 117, 278
Central Division, 78, 79
Central Highlands, 37–38; case, 144–157
Champion, Alan, 23
Champion, Claude, 23
Champion, Ivan F, 22–23, **24–25,** 29, 194,
    247–248, 251, 371n 14
Chester, H M, 22
Chester, K I, 218–222
children, 165, 265, 286, 320, 352
Chimbu. *See* Simbu
Chin Him, 190–191
civilizing missions, 129–131
Clark, H E (Lynn), **24–25,** 26
coastwatching, 196
coercion, 138–139, 269
Cole, Robert R, **24–25,** 159–160
colonial government (colonialism), 2–8,
    204, 357 n 1; administrative districts,
    1, 32–34, 161, 181; changing course
    of, 244–245; direct rule, 3–5; extend-
    ing influence of, 118–121, 119, 122;
    indirect rule, 3, 5, 358 n 5; objections
    to native police force, 244–246; pater-
    nalistic nature of, 6–8; police as
    agents of, 12–14, 164, 247, 267, 280–
    281; policemen's perceptions of, 301–
    302, 311, 313; resistance to, 8–12; role
    of village officials, 4–8
Colonial Police, The (Jeffries), 97
Commonwealth of Australia Gazette, 80
Congong, 197
Connolly, Bob, 39, 241
Connolly, K E, **24–25**
constables, village, 2, 4–8, 55
contact patrols (first patrols), 119–120,
    204, 205–206, 336–339. *See also* first
    contact
coronation, 88, 304
Corris, Peter, 11
Costelloe, John Amery, 144–157, 315
Court for Native Affairs, 112
Crawley, David, 60, 174
crimes, 118, 268, 346. *See also* offenses;
    specific crimes
criminals, 70, 213–215
cults, 5, 278–279, 330
customs. *See* traditional society

daily activities, 93, 94, 116–117, 306. *See also* work
Dani, 251
Daru Island, 73
Daulei, Enau, 213–215, **214**
deaths, 10–11, 39, 142–144, 167, 365n 2 (Chap 5); Central Highlands case, 144–157; Korna village massacre, 218–222; Southern Highlands incident, 157–163. *See also* killing
Debbedowa, 184
"Debt of Friendship Must Be Honored" (Ryan), 192
dedication of policemen, 131–132
Defense Scheme for the Territory, 187
Dekadua, 249
Department of District Services and Native Affairs, 144, 148–149
desertion, 252
detective skills, 115–116
Dika, 144–157
Dinogoi, 232, 235
disbandment of police forces, 172–173, 174, 175–176, 188
discipline, breaches of, 251–253, 303
dismissal, 251–252
disputes, settling, 117
district officers, 1, 32, 161
districts. *See* administrative districts
District Standing Instructions, 140–141, 161, 162
dogs, 339
Domande, 235
Donaldson, Mike, 38, 131
Doriri, 14
Downs, Ian F G, 31, 34, 39, 230, 248, 256–257, 361n 15; camp, **120**
drinking. *See* alcohol abuse
Dugan, Bob, 10
Dutton, Tom, 78, 86
Dwyer, Mick, 73

Eastern Division, 78, 143
East New Britain, 81
Edwards, E R (Roy), 207, 368n 2
Ellis, George, 20, 261–262, 373n 13
Emegari, 350
Empere, Piaka, **51**, 62, 63, **65**, 124–126, 366n 2
enrollment form, 76, **76**
escort service, 112, 370n 3

esprit de corps, 106, 107, 112, 134–136, 163, 289, 291. *See also* loyalty
evacuation, 168, 169
evaluation of policemen, 110–111, 246, 247–253, 277–281
Evara, James Ori, **51, 60,** 61, 114–115
examination paper, 99, **100**
exploration, 118–119, 122

Fanon, Franz, 10
Far Eastern Liaison Office, 367n 20
Fasu, 12–13
fatigue duties, 92, 113–114
Fear Drive My Feet (Ryan), 192
Fifth Independent Company, 193
Fiji, 3, 77–78, 358n 5
fines, 252
Finintugu massacre, 9–10, 40
first contact, 12, 73–74, 204, 224–227, 235, 336–337. *See also* contact patrols
First Contact, 17, 204
Firth, Stewart, 175
food, 92, 106, 127, 291–292, 311, 313
force, use of: Central Highlands case, 144–157; examples of, 8–12; in Gende, 228–229, 337; lawful and unlawful, 138–144; legal authority for, 144; rationale for, 268–269; rationalization for, 10, 14–17, 163; Southern Highlands incident, 157–163; unnecessary condemned, 139; viewed as necessary by policemen, 161, 305–306
Fox brothers, 16
Frank, Brother Eugene, 225–227, 370nn 3–4

gambling, 252, 291
Gammage, Bill, 241
Gande, 151
Garuwa, Osborne, 92, 99, 364 n 5
"Garuwa's Marching Song," 92
Gembogl prison, 233–234, 239–240, 343–344
Gende (Bundi), 74, 164, **224;** cosmology, 310; first contact, 227; interview with Tawi, 335–353; marriage in, 230–231; perception of police, 227–231; response to police, 228–229, 231. *See also* Tigavu, Petrus
George Medal, 368n 32

German New Guinea, 5, 166; police, 79–80, 86
Gershon, 259
Geru, 144–157
Giddings, Rick J, **24–25**, 26, 30–31, 41, 110–111, 123; response to questionnaire, 273–284
Goilala, 83, 204–227
Gona, 169
Gore, R T, 186–187
Goro, Sebastin, **51**, 63–64, **66**, 165, **177**, 264–265
Goroka, 65, 88
government. *See* colonial government
Grahamslaw, Tom, 23
Griffin, Andrew, 196, 197, 199
Griffin, H L, 175, 249
Grimshaw, J S, 152
guard duty, 111–112, 297
Guha, Ranajit, 269
guides, 192, 318
Guiebi, 232, 310
Guise, Sir John, **51, 57**, 192, 250, 265; background and recruitment, 42, 55–56, 60–61, 99; duties, 115; interview with, 285–308; loyalty, 131–132; opinion of training, 103
Gulf Division, 79
Gumine, 315
guns, 10–11, 102–103, 132–134, 227, 231, 243, 295–296, 311, 314, 338–340. *See also* weapons

Hahl, Albert, 4–5
Hailey, Lord, 14
Hallpike, C R, 205, 206, 210, 218, 222
hanging, 167, 234–235
Hanuabada people, 10, 168, 179
Hareho, 219, 222
Hasluck, Sir Paul, 357 n 4, 368n 2
haus tambaran, 65, 362n 15
haus win, 370n 8
Hayes, Maxwell, 86
head-hunting, 118, 130
headquarters detachments, 111–113, 114
height requirement, 75
Hides, Horace, 1–2
Hides, Jack G, 23, 29, 71–72, 127–128, 143, 247–248, 249, 371n 14
highlands area (region), 17, 37–38, 172, 360n 8, 366n 1

"hole," 239–240, 241–242, **242,** 345–346, 347
homicide, 118, 139–142. *See also* force; killing; murder
homosexual practices, 257–259
hostages, taking, 141
Hughes, Ian, 37
humiliation, 235–239, 242
Humphries, W R, 173
Huon, John, 207
hypocrisy, 229

Ialibu, 210, 235–238, 371n 14; airstrip, **237**
Iatmul people, 69
Ibrum, 234–235
Igarobae, Athanasius Mandembo, **51,** 61, **62, 177**
Imita Ridge, 169
Inau tribe, 227
Infantry Training 1911, 90–91, 93
Inglis, K S, 368n 25
instructors, 289–290, 323, 325
insurrection, 245
integrity, 131–132
intellectual (academic) training, 98–99, 290, 325
intelligence gathering, 191, 192, 193
internecine warfare, 82. *See also* tribal warfare
interviews: Kegeriai, 354–355; Petrus Tigavu, 309–319; policemen, 49; Sasa Goreg, 320–334; Sir John Guise, 285–308; "Wizakana" Tawi, 335–353
Irish Peace Preservation Act constabulary, 97
Ivairime, 215–217
Iwagu Iaking Aladu, **51,** 62, **63, 177,** 264

Japanese army: brutality of, 189–191; decorations awarded by, 201, 334; invasion, 169, 174, 326–334, 367n 14; New Guinea policemen working for, 189–191, 329–334; prisoners, 331; propaganda, 182–185
Jeffries, Sir Charles, 97
Jinks, Brian, 4
Johnston, George H, 194, 195
Jones, J H, 148–149
Joyce, R B, 11

Kabu, Tommy, 192, 199
Kainantu, 73

Kaintiba, 126–127
Kambian, **51,** 66, **68,** 82, 362n 7
Kamuna, Elizabeth, 264
Kamuna Hura, **51,** 65–66, **68,** 83, 101, 165, **177,** 202–203, 264
Kanga Force, 193
Kara, 158–159
Karap, 144–157
Karapen Kuvin, 241
Karatok, 55
Kari, 192–193
Karisoko, 351
Karo Arau, 253
Kasse Aibuki, **51,** 64, **67,** 75, 101, 105, **177**
Katue, 192, 194–195
Kaubu, 266
kaulong, 130
Kavieng, 79, 169
Keesing, Roger, 11
Kegeriai Veronika, 234–235, **236;** interview with, 354–355
Kegine, 229, 370n 7
Keogh, Jim, 21, **24–25**
Keriaka cult, 278–279
Kero village, 241
Kerr, Martin, 230, 246
Kerri, 184
kiaps, 360n 10. *See also* patrol officer
killing, 139–142, 295–296; degrees of, 253; payback, 83, 84; by policemen, 253–255, 314–315. *See also* force; murder; taking of life
kinika, 130
Kivivia, 184
Koito, 218
Kokopo, 79
Kolta, Mokei Korua, 38
Kominiwan, 200–201
Korna village massacre, 218–222
Kouno, 144–157
Koupa, 215–218
Kukukuku, 126–127
Kundiawa, 256, 345–349, 371n 18
Kurita, Hiroyuke, 12–13
Kwaio, 11
Kyle, Alan (Bill), 370n 5

labor, 167; contracted, 171, 172; forced, 227, 229, 336–342; police as, 113–114; recruiters of, 16; strike of 1929, 245
Lae, 168–169
Lalor, Peter, 207

languages, 75, 99, 102, 107, 365n 17. *See also* Police Motu; *Tok Pisin*
laplaps, 73, 296, 315, 363n 21, 365n 16
la tache d'huile, 120–121
law and order, maintaining, 111, 116, 118, 138, 181–182, 293, 297–298
laws, new *(nupela pasin),* 40, 118, 130
League of Nations, 166, 186, 188
Leahy, Danny, 17
Leahy, Michael (Mick), 16–17, 73, 143, 204, 371n 14
leave (recreational), 298–299, 317, 324
Le Hunte, Sir George, 14
Lett, Lewis, 5
Lion Rampant (Low), 3
lo bilong tumbuna, 118. *See also* traditional society
Logan, Leonard, 186
Loholo, Mohaviea, **51,** 61, **61**
London Missionary Society, 61
Long, Gavin, 191–192
Long Island, 81
longlong, 209
Low, D A, 3, 9
loyalty, 6, 131–132, 293, 302. *See also* esprit de corps
*luluai*s, 2, 4–8, 228, 281, 337, 351

MacDonald, Colin, 253–254
MacGregor, Sir William, 4, 5, 6–7, 11–12, 13–14, 17, 40
Mackenzie, S S, 167
Madang, 79, 81, 168
magisterial duties, 117, 305
Mai, 157
mail delivery, 112, 114
Maina, 351
Mair, Lucy, 169
Mamadeni, 93
Manus, 79
marksmanship, 133–134. *See also* guns; weapons
marriage, 128, 256–257, 265, 286, 299–300, 309, 312, 320, 325. *See also* bride-price
Masep, 189–190
massacres, 9–10, 17, 40, 218–220. *See also* atrocities; force; violence
masta, 8, 37
Matai, 208–210, 212, 215, 369n 6
McCarthy, J K, 81, 176, 186, 247, 249, 254, 260, 262

McDonald, J H, 150–156
McGrath, Bernard Lawrence, 9–10
McNicoll, Ramsey, 187
Meava, 264
medals, 197, 199–201, 334
Mek, 144–157
Melrose, Robert, 187–188
Menyamya, 126–127
Meraveka, **51, 60,** 61, **177**
Merire, 201
military use of police, 79–80, 176, 185–189, 307
Milligan, John, 373n 13
miners, 193, 244–246
misdemeanors. *See* offenses
missionaries, 37, 38, 232, 244, 310, 362n 12, 370n 3; in Gende, 224–228, 336–338; Lutheran, 321, 338, 362n 19; murder of, 225–227; perceived as spirits, 74; trade with, 338; use of force by, 16; during World War II, 318
Moag, Moru, **51,** 62, 63, **65,** 126–127, 165, 364 n 9
Monckton, C A W, 14, 246, 266
Monk, F D, 183
Morobe, 79, 81
Morris, B M, 169
Morschheuser, Father Charles, 143, 225–227, 370n 3; grave, **226**
Motu, Police, 10, 130, 179
Mount Hagen, 241
Mumro, 370n 7
Munster, Peter, 9, 10, 17, 40, 143
murder: of missionaries, 225–227; in Papua New Guinea society, 70–72, 118; punishment for, 210, 213–215. *See also* killing
Murray, Sir Hubert, 23, 167, 176, 235, 246; government control, 2, 3, 357n 4; meeting of black and white races, 8; murder in Papua New Guinea society, 70–71; obituary of Simoi, 265–266; police training, 94, 97, 105–106; staff selection criteria, 28–29; use of force, 14–16, 138–139; village council system, 358 n 9
Murray, J K, 149, 150, 153–154, 155, 156–157, 230
Murray, Leonard, 179
Muru, Fridolin, 224
myths, 246. *See also* prejudices; stereotypes

Naguwean, **51,** 56, **57,** 60–61, 81–82, **177,** 199–200
Naguwean, Joseph, 82, 267
Nakanai, 10–11
naked power, 39, 361n 15
Namatanai, 79
namba wan polis, 123
Nanai, 184
Nanduka, Nandie, 235–238, **236**
national consciousness, 300–301, 313
Native Administration Regulations/Native Regulations, 7–8, 252, 358n. 10
"Native Offences and European Law in South-West New Britain" (Todd), 118
Nelson, Hank, 4, 29–30, 175
New Britain, 118. *See also* East New Britain; West New Britain
New Guinea: administrative districts, 32, **33;** Japanese invasion and occupation, 326–334; *luluai* or *tultul* system, 4–8; nationalism, 300–301; Native Administration Regulations, 7–8, 359n 11; patrol officer backgrounds, 23; World War II population, 171. *See also* Gende
New Guinea Annual Reports (NGAR), 43, **48,** 80, 88, 98, 118
New Guinea Company, 85
New Guinea Diary (Johnston), 195
New Guinea Infantry Battalion (NGIB), 172, 185–186
New Guinea Police Force: combined with Royal Papuan Constabulary, 176; disbandment, 172–173, 174, 175–176, 188; district recruitment, 79–81; numbers of, 42–43, **44–45,** 173; ordinances, 80, 114; policemen working for Japanese, 329–334; regulations, 114; use of force, 140–141, 140–142. *See also* Royal Papua and New Guinea Constabulary; training
New Guinea Volunteer Rifles, 192–193
Niall, N R, 130–131
Nicholls, G H, 110
Nogutman, 247
Normoyle, W E, 24–25, 26
Norris, Kingsley, 191
North-Eastern Division, 79
Northern Division, 79
North Simbu, 164
numbers of police, 42–43, **44–45,** 173
Numibi, 151, 153

nupela pasin, 40, 130
Nurton, Allert, 81, 127
Nusa, 249

obedience, 6, 79, 94
obituaries, 264, 265–266
O'Brien, Joseph, 245
offenses, **47**, 118, 251–253, 303. *See also*
    crimes
Ogaia Girau, 208–210, **209**
Ogom, 232, 233, 343
O'Malley, James L (Jim), 143, 371n 14
O'Malley, J T, 114
Ongi, Nivil, **241**, 241–242
Opeba, Wellington Jojoga, 218
Orai, 249
Oropai, 73
Orovea, Lelesi, **51**, 61, **61**

pacification, 118–119, 164, 218, 222,
    366n 1
Pacific Island Regiment (PIR), 172
Pacific theater, 169
Palawan Island, 174
Paliau, 192, 199
Palmer, J, 257
Pamoi, 189–190
Panau Daguna, Peter, **51**, 56, **57**, 60–61,
    115, 165
Papua: administrative districts, 32, **33**;
    contracted laborers to the Allied
    Forces, 171–172; locally recruited
    officers, 23; nationalism, 300–301;
    Native Regulations, 7–8; pacification
    of, 14, 40, 173–174; village govern-
    ment, 4–8, 358n 9; World War II
    population, 171
Papua Annual Reports (PAR), 43, **45–47**,
    71, 77; police work, 112, 113, 123–
    124, 143–144; training, 91, 93, 107,
    133
Papuan Armed Constabulary: divisions,
    78–79; Infantry Training 1911, 90–91,
    93; lawful taking of life, 139–140,
    141–142; Ordinance, 42, 77–78;
    recruitment, 42, **44–45**, 77–79; train-
    ing, 14, 42, **95–96**, 97–98. *See also*
    Royal Papua and New Guinea
    Constabulary
Papua New Guinea, 169, **170**, 172. *See also*
    German New Guinea; Papua; tradi-
    tional society; villagers

Papua New Guinea Administration Order
    No 4, 181
Papua New Guinea Post Courier, 264
Papuan Infantry Battalion (PIB), 172, 176,
    177, 178–180, 185–186, 194, 195
Papuan Villager, The, **100**, 168, 247, 252
paramilitary duties, 185–189
patrol officers (kiaps), 19–41, 23; age of,
    26; Australian School of Pacific
    Administration (ASOPA), 29–32, 275;
    background and experience, 1, 20–
    28, 26–27; cadets, 29–32, 365n 1
    (Chap 5); evaluation of policemen,
    110–111, 246, 247, 253, 277–281;
    numbers of, 20–21; power, 19, 34–39;
    questionnaire, 21, 271–273; relation-
    ship to policemen, 35–36, 40, 123,
    162; responsibilities of, 2, 19, 277;
    selection criteria, 27–29; sexual
    liaisons, 230–231; use of force, 140–
    141; written accounts about and by,
    358 n 1. *See also* police officers
patrol reports, 143–144, 146–147, 158–
    159, 366n 3 (Chap 5)
patrols, 117–137, 315–316; administrative,
    117; camps, 119–120, **120, 122**;
    contact, 119–120, 204, 336–339;
    description of typical, 124–126; enjoy-
    ment of, 121–123, 126; hardships,
    127; villagers responses to, 126–127;
    wartime, 181. *See also* patrol reports
pensions, 264–265, 286–287, 313
Piggott, Michael, 167
pigs, 39, 164, 167, 229, 230–231
pitpit, 220, 369n 15
plantations: agricultural, 166, 167, 171;
    police stations, 113, 365 n 1 (Chap 4)
planters, 16, 193, 244–246
police camps, 119–120, **120, 122**
Police Force Regulations, 173
police forces. *See* New Guinea Police Force;
    Papuan Armed Constabulary; Royal
    Papua and New Guinea Constabulary;
    Royal Papuan Constabulary
policemen. *See specific topics such as* evalua-
    tion; marriage; recruits; training;
    work, etc.
Police Motu, 10, 179
police officers, 1, 180
police regulations, 114, 116–117, 173, 246,
    267–268
poroi, 74

poroi krunaga, 310
Port Moresby, 88, 168
power, 39, 83–84, 361 n 15
prejudices, 105–106. *See also* myths; stereotypes
prestige, 83–84
prisoners, 124, 252, 316, 331, 348, 352; police recruitment of, 71–72, 289, 322–323
prisons, 181–182, 227, 231, 233–234, 239–240, 241–242, 342–349
prison warders, 113, 181–182
promotions, 283–284, 294–295, 313
propaganda, 182–185, 367n 20
prospectors, 9–10, 16, 37, 38, 39, 73, 143
Proud, J C R, 367n 20
psychological force, 8–9, 12
Pumuye, Nungulu, 210–212, **211,** 238
punishment: fire used as, 210–212, 213–215; of policemen, 233, 246, 252, 253, 291, 312; of prisoners, 352; of villagers, 167, 228, 232–233, 235–238, 351. *See also* prisons
punitive expeditions, 10–11, 143

questionnaire, 271–273
Quinlivan, Peter J, 207

Rabaul, 79, 80, 88; Japanese occupation, 181–182; strike of 1929, 89, 245; during World War II, 326, 330–331, 366n 3 (Chap 6)
racial segregation, 246
racism, 276, 282–283
rami, 296. *See also* laplaps
ranks, 293, 294, 313, 326
rape, 210, 252
Read, W (Jack), 196
recognition, lack of, 264–265, 283–284
recruitment, 42–84, **50,** 77–78, 288–289, 321–322; of prisoners and ex-prisoners, 71–72, 289, 322–323
recruits: age, 70; background, 49–52, 70–75, 165–166; reasons for joining, 81–84, 268–269; selection criteria, 75–76. *See also* training
Reed, Jack, 249–250
Reed, S W, 68–69, 257–258
refugees, 164
regulations: "Native Administration Regulations" and "Native Regulations," 7–8; police, 114, 116–117, 173, 246,

267–268. *See also* District Standing Instructions
Rekere Ei, 238
relationships of policemen: to government officers, 304–305; to patrol officers, 123, 162, 260–262, 298, 316; to villagers, 128–136. *See also* esprit de corp; marriage
requirements: for patrol officer recruits, 27–29; for police recruits, 5, 75–76
revenge, 83, 84
Rewari, **51,** 61, **62,** 165, **177,** 362 n 7
road construction, 113, 117, 312
Roberts, Alan, 370n 5
Robinson, Eric (Wobbie), 72, 362n 18
Robinson, Neville K, 168
Ross, Father William, 16
Rowley, C D, 19–20, 135–136
Royal Papua and New Guinea Constabulary, 87, 88, 101, 304, 307–308
Royal Papuan Constabulary: combined with New Guinea police force, 176; disbandment, 172–173, 174, 175–176, 188; as emergency military force, 188; enrollment form, 76; numbers prior to World War II, 173; reconstituted, 176; recruitment 1942–1945, 177–178; training, 178–180; wartime visit to Australia, 184. *See also* Papuan Armed Constabulary
Russell, Bertrand, 361 n 15
Ryan, Peter, 192–193

Salamaua, 168, 169
Sali, 257
salt, 127, 164
Samasam, 260–262
Sarepamo Tate, **51,** 64–65, **68,** 73–74, 82, 99–101, 165, **177**
Sartre, Jean-Paul, 243
Sasa Goreg, **51,** 62, 63, **64,** 174–175, **177,** 182, 201, 320–334
"savages in serge," 195
Savages in Serge (Hides), 71–72
scare tactics, 242
Schaefer, Father Alfons, 74, 362n 12
self-defense, 139, 140, 162, 296
Sepik, 69
Sesetta, **51,** 64, **67,** 70, 101, 104, 174, **177,** 199
Sesiguo, Arenao K, 165, 202

sexual relationships, 230–231, 255–259, 300, 312, 341
shells, 37–38, 338
Siliven, 279–280
Simbu (Chimbu), 38–39, 143, 144–148, 225, 336–337, 370n 5; warriors, 240, 371n 19. *See also* North Simbu
Simogun, Pita, 192
Simoi, 78–79, 93, 115, 265–266
Simpson, Colin, 16, 370n 3
Sinclair, Alex, 174
Sinclair, James, 176; Anderson case, 206–207, 208, 212; deaths of villagers, 364n 2; Goilala, 205, 206; performance of policemen, 250; use of police as combatants, 176
Sipi, 253–254
Siwoi, 207–210, 212, 213, 215, 369n 6, 369n 8
skills: police, 97–98, 114–116; traditional, 201–212
social workers, policemen as, 121, 128–131, 305
sodomy, 258
Sole Sole, 241–242
Solomon Islands, 11, 77–78
Somare, Michael, 199, 249–250
songs, 92, 125, 247–248, 364n 5–7
Sono, **51, 57;** background and recruitment, 56, 60–61, 72–73, **177;** description of patrol, 124–126; training, 101; war experiences, 174
sorcery, 130, 314
Southern Highlands, 12–13, 17, 157–163, 235, 371n 14
Special Branch Section, 99
Speedie, Ronald, 23
spirits *(poroi),* white men perceived as, 74
station work, 111–117, 306, 315
statistics. *See* numbers
stereotypes, 116, 195, 260, 267. *See also* myths; prejudices
strike of 1929, 89, 245
"stroll," 233
Strong, W M, 123–124
Suaga, 249
suicide, 261–262
Sumsuma, 245
Sydney Morning Herald, 366n 8
Symons, Andrew John, 144–157, 366n 10

taking of life, 139–142. *See also* killing
Talasea, 75, 130
Tami, 249
Tamutai, Naguna, **51,** 66, 68, **69,** 73, **177**
Tari massacre, 17
Taro Cult, 5
taubada, 37
Tawi ("Wizakana"), 223–243, **225,** 231–235, 239–240, 242–243, 354–355; interview with, 335–353
taxation, 167
tax collection, 117
Taylor, Edward, 10, 254–255
Taylor, George, 368n 32
Taylor, James Lindsay (Jim), 38, 73, 143, 155–156, 230, 315, 370n 3, 373n 13; Central Highlands case, 144–157
Thompson, Halford W, 42
Tigavu, Petrus, **51,** 58, **59,** 74, 134, 165, **177,** 264, 348–350; interview with, 309–319
Todd, J A, 118
Tok Pisin, 107, 145–146, 179, 338, 351
Tomasetti, W E (Bill), **24–25** (chart), 26, 29
Toogood, G W, 250; background, **24–25** (chart), 26
torture, 208, 215, 218, 235; of Chinese, 190–191. *See also* "hole"; violence
town guards, 111–112
Townsend, G W L, 119, 182–183
ToWoworu, Ben Elipas, **51, 59,** 165, 264, 367n 17; background and recruitment, 60, 61, **177;** police band, 101, 103; training, 101; war experiences, 199, 202–203
trade, 37–38, 124, 164, 310, 338, 346
traditional skills, 201–202
traditional society (practices), 130, 275; disruption of, 108, 229, 242, 243, 340; lack of organization in, 358n 6; marriage in Gende, 230–231, 352, 370n 9; murder, 71, 118; payback killing, 83–84. *See also* tribal warfare
training, 85–109, 289–293, 311, 323–325; barracks life, 91–94, 292–293, 311, 325; centers for new recruits, 88–89; daily schedule, 93–94; history of, 85–88; Infantry Training 1911, 90–91, 93; instructors, 289–290, 323, 325; intellectual (academic), 98–99, 290, 325; languages, 99, 102, 107, 354 n 12;

physical, 89–98, 106, 290, 324;
recruits opinion of, 102–105; results
of, 105–108; songs, 92, 364 nn 5–7;
Special Branch Section, 99. *See also*
weapons, training
tribal warfare, 71, 118, 130, 164–166, 202,
243, 325, 350–352, 366n 1
Trobriand Islands, 5
tultuls, 2, 4–8, 228, 337
tunnels, 181–182, 331
Tutama, 158

uniforms, 296, 315. *See also* laplaps
University of Sydney, 29
Utu, 260

Vaiviri, 247
Vetigan, D H, 174
Vial, Leigh, 370n 5
village council system, 358n 9
village officials, 281, 337. See also *luluais*;
    tultuls
villagers: impact of contact with each
    other, 204–205; perceptions of
    police, 34, 227–231, 336–342; police
    attitudes toward, 281–283, 316; pun-
    ishment of, 340, 341–342, 351; reac-
    tions to show of power by patrol
    officers, 34–35. *See also* deaths
violence, 39, 163, 167, 268–269. *See also*
    force

Wabag, 241
wages (pay), 291, 298–299, 317, 324–325
Waim, 151, 153
Wanigela, 14
war. *See* tribal warfare; World War I; World
    War II
Ward, E J (Eddie), 149, 150, 154
Waria, 81
Watkins, Wally, 207
weapons, 9, 10–11, 123, 202; training, 90,
    91, 93, 97, 102, 133–134, 289, 290.
    See also guns

Western Division, 78–79
West New Britain, 10, 143
White, Osmar, 185
"Who Came First" (Kurita), 12–13
Williams, F E, 171
Willis, Ian, 169
Wolfers, Edward P, 245–246
women, 228, 229–230, 232, 235, 341, 348,
    370n 11. *See also* marriage
Womkane people, 225, 227
Woria, 158
work: police, 110–137, 297, 315–316;
    magisterial duties, 305; station, 111–
    117, 306, 315; during wartime, 180–
    191. *See also* patrols
World War I, 166–168
World War II, 168–203; *Angels of War*, 195–
    196; compensation, 319; decorations
    awarded to policemen, 199–201, 319;
    experiences of policemen, 192–201,
    303, 317–319, 326–334; individual
    police achievements, 192–201; lack
    of recognition to policemen, 199–
    200; military use of police, 79–80,
    185–189; numbers of Papua New
    Guineans serving, 172; policemen as
    agents of propaganda, 182–185;
    policemen's desire to fight, 186;
    police work during, 180–191
Wriford, George, 77–78
Wright, Malcom, **24–25**, 27–28, 230

Yali, 192, 199
Yamona, 236
Yauwiga, 192, 195–199, **197, 198**
Yegova, Jojoga, **51, 59;** background and
    recruitment, 61, 70, 82, **177,** 362n 7;
    gambling, 252–253; Korna village
    massacre, 218–222; training, 102,
    104–105, 179; treatment of villagers,
    162–163, 238–239
Yongamugl tribe, 39

zulu, 315

OTHER VOLUMES IN THE
PACIFIC ISLANDS MONOGRAPH SERIES

1 *The First Taint of Civilization: A History of the Caroline and Marshall Islands in Pre-Colonial Days, 1521–1885,* by Francis X Hezel, SJ, 1983

2 *Where the Waves Fall: A New South Sea Islands History from First Settlement to Colonial Rule,* by K R Howe, 1984

3 *Wealth of the Solomons: A History of a Pacific Archipelago, 1800–1978,* by Judith A Bennett, 1987

4 *Nan'yō: The Rise and Fall of the Japanese in Micronesia, 1885–1945,* by Mark R Peattie, 1988

5 *Upon a Stone Altar: A History of the Island of Pohnpei to 1890,* by David Hanlon, 1988

6 *Missionary Lives: Papua, 1874–1914,* by Diane Langmore, 1989

7 *Tungaru Traditions: Writings on the Atoll Culture of the Gilbert Islands,* by Arthur F Grimble, edited by H E Maude, 1989

8 *The Pacific Theater: Island Representations of World War II,* edited by Geoffrey M White and Lamont Lindstrom, 1989

9 *Bellona Island Beliefs and Rituals,* by Torben Monberg, 1991

10 *Not the Way It Really Was: Constructing the Tolai Past,* by Klaus Neumann, 1992

11 *Broken Waves: A History of the Fiji Islands in the Twentieth Century,* by Brij V Lal, 1992

12 *Woven Gods: Female Clowns and Power in Rotuma,* by Vilsoni Hereniko, 1995

13 *Strangers in Their Own Land: A Century of Colonial Rule in the Caroline and Marshall Islands,* by Francis X Hezel, 1995

14 *Guardians of Marovo Lagoon: Practice, Place, and Politics in Maritime Melanesia,* by Edvard Hviding, 1996

About the Author

August Ibrum K Kituai, a Papua New Guinean, was educated at the University of Papua New Guinea, Flinders University of South Australia, and Australian National University, where he received his PhD in 1994. He is presently senior lecturer in history at the University of Papua New Guinea. This is his first book.

PAPUA NEW GUINEA

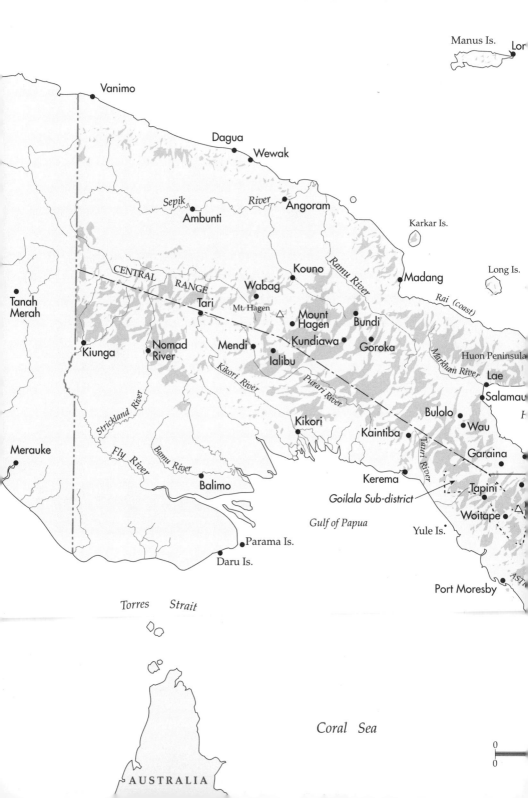

Manus Is.
Lor

Vanimo

Dagua
Wewak

Sepik · River · Angoram
Ambunti

Karkar Is.

Kouno
Ramu River
Madang
Wabag
CENTRAL RANGE
Tari
Mt. Hagen △ Mount Hagen
Bundi
Long Is.
Rai (coast)

Tanah Merah

Kiunga
Nomad River
Mendi
Ialibu
Kundiawa
Goroka
Markham River
Huon Peninsula
Lae
Salamau

Kikori River
Strickland River
Purari River
Bulolo
Wau

Kaintiba
Tauri River
Garaina

Merauke
Fly River
Bamu River
Balimo
Kikori
Kerema
Goilala Sub-district
Tapini

Gulf of Papua
Woitape △
Yule Is.
AST

Parama Is.
Daru Is.

Port Moresby

Torres Strait

Coral Sea

AUSTRALIA

0
0